ARAB-ISRAELI CONFLICT AND CONCILIATION

ARAB-ISRAELI CONFLICT AND CONCILIATION

A Documentary History

Edited by

BERNARD REICH

PRAEGER

Westport, Connecticut
London

The Library of Congress has cataloged the hardcover edition as follows:

Arab-Israeli conflict and conciliation : a documentary history /
  edited by Bernard Reich.
    p. cm.
    Includes bibliographical references and index.
    ISBN 0–313–29856–4 (alk. paper)
    1. Israel–Arab conflicts—Sources. 2. Jewish–Arab
  relations—1917– —Sources. 3. Zionism—History—Sources.
  I. Reich, Bernard.
  DS119.7.A67233   1995
  956.04—dc20   95–31620

British Library Cataloguing in Publication Data is available.

A hardcover edition of *Arab-Israeli Conflict and Conciliation* is available
from Greenwood Press, an imprint of Greenwood Publishing Group, Inc.
(ISBN 0–313–29856–4).

Library of Congress Catalog Card Number: 95–31620
ISBN: 0–275–95430–7 (pbk.)

First published in 1995

Praeger Publishers, 88 Post Road West, Westport, CT 06881
An imprint of Greenwood Publishing Group, Inc.

Printed in the United States of America

The paper used in this book complies with the
Permanent Paper Standard issued by the National
Information Standards Organization (Z39.48–1984).

10 9 8 7 6 5 4 3 2 1

CONTENTS

PREFACE

The Arab-Israeli conflict has been a notable element of the international relations of the Middle East for more than a century. Its evolution has been the subject of substantial attention and has generated numerous official and semi-official documents and a voluminous descriptive and analytical literature, both popular and academic. Many of the documents central to an understanding of the conflict have been published in collections that have appeared over the years, but these often have been focused on a particular theme or have been designed to substantiate a particular case or to present the arguments for a special perspective. Also, there have been official collections produced by parties to the conflict (or their advocates). Some volumes have contained the essays, articles or viewpoints of observers and analysts, again often seeking to provide a "perspective." In all instances these collections are useful for background but are not up-to-date and do not reflect the substantial movement and progress on this conflict of recent years.

This volume seeks to avoid the presentation of one perspective or another but includes those documents deemed essential to understand the evolution of the conflict and the progress toward its resolution. It is also up-to-date -- while it includes the central documents of the past 100 years, it focuses on those of the past few years that bring the story to the present, including the Israel-Jordan Peace Treaty of 1994. It concentrates on the diplomatic-political history and evolution of the Arab-Israeli conflict. It presents the texts (in whole or in excerpt) central to the evolution of the conflict and to the efforts to resolve the competing claims to Palestine as well as to the broader Arab-Israeli conflict.

Documents were selected based on their significance to the ongoing conflict and to the peace process. Thus, they provide both a historical record and elements involved in a resolution of the problem. References in the bibliography and the text will point the reader to other materials that may be of further interest.

The format of the volume is straightforward. A brief introductory essay is followed by a chronology of the major events and developments in the conflict over the century since the establishment of modern political Zionism and the development of Arab nationalism. The documents are presented in chronological order and, thus, provide a documentary history of the Arab-Israeli conflict. The selection of documents is based on several criteria -- a document is included if it has been central to the evolution of the conflict and continues to be important in the ongoing peace processes or in the content of the conflict. The documents are drawn from official English language sources, when available, or from reliable translations when original official English sources are lacking. The documents are all official -- of international organizations, governments or major organizations such as the World Zionist Organization and the Palestine Liberation Organization. Some have been translated from their original languages, in which case official translations have been utilized where they exist or, in their absence, the best available translation has been utilized. In all cases the original flavor has been retained, to the point of retaining variations in spelling (i.e., British as opposed to American English) or transliteration. Each document is preceded by a discussion of its place in the history and in the evolution of the conflict. In most cases it is brief, as the document itself needs little introduction; in other instances it seeks to clarify the content of the document (and discuss segments that have been omitted here). A selected bibliography provides more details on the documents and on the conflict and will allow the reader to pursue these themes further. The index permits appropriate cross-referencing and the tracking of themes over an extended period.

The interested reader should note a companion volume -- *An Historical Encyclopedia of the Arab-Israeli Conflict* -- that provides a reference to the events, personalities and elements of the Arab-Israeli conflict.

ACKNOWLEDGMENTS

This book results from a substantial effort over a long period during which a number of individuals make valuable contributions. This book has benefitted from the editor's long-time interest in, and research and teaching on, the Arab-Israeli conflict. Over the years variations of this collection were required reading for students in my courses on the Arab-Israeli conflict at The George Washington University and the Defense Intelligence College, and the selection has been guided by their observations and suggestions. Three individuals were particularly helpful in reading and commenting on the manuscript and finding the errors that often seemed to appear from nowhere -- Gershon R. Kieval, Mark Erickson and Anamika Krishna -- and their assistance is greatly appreciated. Mim Vasan was, as always, instrumental in ensuring that the project moved from concept to reality. Jane Lerner served ably as production editor. Nevertheless, the book would have been impossible without the constant help and support of my wife and the special technical skills of my son Norman who was responsible for the design of the book.

ARAB-ISRAELI CONFLICT AND CONCILIATION

INTRODUCTION

The Arab-Israeli conflict, the central issue of which is the status of a territory known as Palestine, has existed for more than a century. Arab nationalism began to take form in the 19th century. Zionism also had its origins as a political ideology in the 19th century, but its antecedents are in the Biblical period. The competition between Jews and Arabs can be traced to Abraham and his two sons, Ishmael and Isaac, who founded their respective lines of descent.

Zionism's historical/political significance is a 20th-century phenomenon. World War I and the consequent dismemberment of the Ottoman Empire made the disposition of Palestine (and other Ottoman territories) a practical political question that required attention and decision and advanced the "Palestine problem" to the center of international attention.

Since World War I the issue has been joined in terms of the future of the territory called Palestine. Theodor Herzl, as the founder and ideologue of modern political Zionism, proposed a Jewish state, preferably in Palestine, as a solution to the Jewish problem (anti-Semitism). Arab nationalist leaders saw Palestine as a component of a restored Arab world stretching from the Atlantic Ocean to the Persian Gulf.

During World War I the Arab perspective was enhanced by the Hussein-McMahon Correspondence while the Zionist claims were reinforced by the Balfour Declaration. The peace treaties and other agreements and arrangements that followed the hostilities did not resolve the issues, rather they effectively postponed them. The Mandate System, and especially the Mandate for Palestine, put off the question of Palestine's ultimate status. For the moment the Mandate gave control over the area to Great Britain which was enjoined, by the preamble in which it was quoted, to implement the Balfour Declaration.

During the mandatory period a number of attempts were made by the British government to resolve the issues as they arose. Riots and demonstrations, and violence, led to British policy reassessments and White Papers that sought solutions to the issues at hand. Various ideas emerged. These included measures to restrict Jewish immigration to, and land purchases in, Palestine. A solution was propounded that included the concept of partitioning Palestine. Despite these and other efforts, by World War II, the problem was not resolved. The Holocaust compounded the problem -- the need for a refuge for displaced Jews added urgency to the question of Palestine's future. World War II also led to a reassessment of Britain's world-wide position and especially that east of Suez. By the spring of 1947, Britain had reached a decision to relinquish the Palestine Mandate and to turn the matter over to the United Nations. The United Nations Special Committee on Palestine (UNSCOP) examined the issue and produced two alternative plans. The majority proposal was adopted by the United Nations General Assembly in November 1947 as Resolution 181 (II), the Partition Plan. The plan sought to separate two antagonistic groups in Palestine by creating two independent states -- one Jewish and one Arab -- that would be linked economically. Jerusalem and its environs, deemed too important to be awarded to either side or to be divided between them, primarily because of the religious significance of the city, was to be a *corpus separatum*, under an international regime. Although the Zionists and the Jewish leadership in Palestine accepted, reluctantly, the partition as what was feasible, the Arab League and the Palestinian spokesmen rejected the resolution and suggested they would take action in response. The failure of the Partition Plan to adequately address and resolve the issues to the satisfaction of the parties led to the first of the Arab-Israeli wars.

The termination of the British Mandate on May 14, 1948 was followed by Israel's declaration of independence and an Arab declaration that it would seek to restore the rights of the Palestinian Arabs in Palestine. After the end of the resulting war -- known in Israel as the War of Independence and in the Arab world as *al-Nakba* (the Disaster) -- four armistice agreements were signed in early 1949 between Israel and each of the states on its borders (Egypt, Syria, Jordan and Lebanon). This formally ended the hostilities and established the frontiers between Israel and its neighbors until the Six Day War of 1967.

Although the armistice regime was to be followed by peace negotiations, these did not occur. Extra regional powers, especially the United States and the United Nations, made efforts to achieve peace but most of these, particularly in the early 1950s, were designed to deal with specific and limited issues such as water allocation, border demarcation, or the plight of refugees, and no significant progress was made. Cross-border exchanges (raids and retaliations) between Israel and its Arab neighbors ultimately fueled an arms race and led Israel, in collusion with Britain and France, to invade Egypt and advance across the Sinai Peninsula to the Suez Canal in late October 1956. As planned, Britain and France soon intervened and landed troops in the Suez Canal Zone. Eventually Britain, France and Israel withdrew under United Nations and United States pressure. At the same time a United Nations Emergency Force (UNEF) was interposed between Egypt and Israel. In addition to the pressures to withdraw, and the monitoring function of UNEF, the United States provided a pledge to Israel concerning the freedom of navigation through the Strait of Tiran.

After the Suez War the Egypt-Israel frontier remained calm until 1967, while the frontiers between Israel and its eastern neighbors became more problematic. Efforts to resolve aspects of the Arab-Israeli conflict were limited both in scope and intensity and no significant breakthroughs were achieved.

The Six Day War of June 1967 dramatically altered the military, political and geographic, as well as the economic and social, aspects of the Arab-Israeli conflict, but it also spurred serious efforts to achieve a comprehensive peace. Each of the major actors, and the superpowers, articulated positions concerning the elements of the new situation that provided the bases for subsequent negotiations and peace proposals.

President Lyndon Johnson's five principles of peace delimited in June, soon after the end of hostilities, became the centerpiece not only of subsequent United States policy but also of United Nations Security Council Resolution 242 of November 22, 1967 that has remained at the center of all subsequent peace efforts. For its part, the Arab world's position, constructed and pronounced at the Arab Summit in Khartoum, Sudan, at the end of the summer focused on the three no's -- there would be no negotiations with Israel, no recognition of Israel, and no peace with it. This remained the Arab position even after Egyptian President Anwar Sadat's journey to Israel in 1977 and the Egypt-Israel peace treaty of 1979 and has continued to reflect policy for some even after the momentous events of 1993 and 1994 involving Israel, the Palestine Liberation Organization (PLO), and Jordan.

Despite the altered circumstances and the increased tempo of peace proposals and efforts, no dramatic breakthroughs prevented either the Egypt-Israel War of Attrition in the Canal Zone in 1969-70 or the Yom Kippur (or Ramadan) War of 1973. Diplomacy by Gunnar Jarring, acting on behalf of the United Nations, and by the four powers (the United States, the Soviet Union, the United Kingdom and France) brought no substantial achievements. Nevertheless, Jarring did achieve a prisoner of war exchange between Israel and Egypt and United States Secretary of State William Rogers secured a cease-fire along the Suez Canal in August 1970.

The Yom Kippur War marked the beginning of a series of negotiations that led to five agreements over the next years. The results of the 1973 war were less clear than those of the 1967 conflict, providing an opportunity for initial negotiations to achieve the disengagement and separation of Israeli and Arab forces in the Sinai Peninsula and in the Golan Heights. Agreements between Israel and Egypt and Israel and Syria were achieved with the active involvement of United States Secretary of State Henry Kissinger in January and May 1974 utilizing a technique called "shuttle diplomacy."

Soon after these achievements Kissinger was stymied in an effort to achieve an agreement between Israel and Jordan when, in the fall of 1974, the Arab Summit meeting at Rabat, Morocco, designated the Palestine Liberation Organization (PLO), that had been established a decade earlier, as the "sole legitimate representative" of the Palestinian people. Neither Israel nor the United States would agree to negotiate with the PLO. Egyptian-Israeli negotiations, again with Kissinger's involvement, resulted in the Sinai II accords, and accompanying documents, that moved Israel and Egypt closer to peace.

Egyptian President Anwar Sadat's 1977 initiative broke the long-standing Arab refusal to deal openly, publicly and officially with Israel to achieve peace. The process was assisted by United States President Jimmy Carter and led to a summit at Camp David from which two accords emerged. One led to the subsequent Egypt-Israel Peace Treaty of 1979. The other accord was to lead to negotiations for a just, comprehensive and durable peace in the Middle East, concentrating on the West Bank and Gaza Strip. No appreciable progress was made in this sector even as implementation of the Egypt-Israel Peace Treaty proceeded on schedule.

The deteriorating situation on the Israel-Lebanon frontier erupted into hostilities as a consequence of the PLO using Lebanese territory for raids into Israel. Israel responded with a major strike -- Operation Litani -- in 1978 and the War in Lebanon in 1982. The latter was followed by Israel-Lebanon negotiations, assisted by United States Secretary of State George Shultz, that led to the signing of an agreement on May 17, 1983. It provided for the removal of all foreign troops from Lebanon and established the border between the two parties. In effect it established the basis for a peaceful relationship. Although ratified by both, the agreement was later abrogated by Lebanon under the influence of Syria.

Few efforts to resolve the Arab-Israeli conflict followed the collapse of the Israel-Lebanon arrangements until the *intifada* (the uprising) of the Palestinians that began in the Gaza Strip in December 1987. It was soon thereafter, in the spring of 1988, that George Shultz launched a new effort. Although he was unable to achieve any agreements, he refocused attention on the issues and this, in turn, had its effects later in the year.

A new element was introduced into the equation in December 1988 when Yasser Arafat pronounced the PLO's position on the three items that would permit the inauguration of a dialogue between the US and the PLO. He proclaimed PLO acceptance of UN Security Council Resolution 242 and of Israel's right to exist, and renounced terrorism. The outgoing Reagan administration, noting the Arafat statement, designated the United States Ambassador in Tunisia as the channel of official discourse between the United States and the PLO.

The Bush administration began its tenure with an effort to generate Israeli-Palestinian negotiations. Under American influence, the Israeli government, in the spring of 1989, put forth an initiative to launch a negotiation process. Despite various efforts, particularly by the United States and Egypt, the process was essentially moribund by the summer of 1990 when Iraq invaded Kuwait, the prelude to the Gulf War of 1991.

During the Gulf War, Saddam Hussein sought to use the Arab-Israeli conflict as a mechanism to split the anti-Iraq coalition and argued that his actions in

Kuwait were, in part, in support of the Palestinian cause. He launched Scud missiles against Israel and gained support from the PLO as well as some other Arab leaders in his efforts to portray himself as a defender of Arab rights against the West. Although the direct connection was tenuous, the end of the Gulf War created new opportunities in the Middle East and beyond.

The end of hostilities presented the possibilities for creating what President George Bush and Secretary of State James Baker labelled a new world order, among the elements of which was resolution of the Arab-Israeli conflict based on changed conditions and circumstances. The effort was begun by Baker in the spring of 1991 with the first of a number of trips to the region. A series of visits, often marked by United States shuttle diplomacy among the various potential parties, finally led to an agreement to convene a breakthrough peace conference in Madrid, Spain, co-chaired by the United States and the Soviet Union (later, Russia).

The Madrid conference itself marked an important breakthrough in that it was the first public, official meeting between Israel and its Arab neighbors (except Egypt). By marrying bilateral and multilateral peace-making efforts, it was conceptually different from previous attempts to resolve the conflict. Bilateral negotiations begun in Madrid were continued in Washington, D.C. between Israel and delegations of Syrians, Lebanese and Jordanians-Palestinians. At the same time a series of multilateral meetings convened in various world capitals to discuss water, the environment, economic development, arms and security, and refugees. The multilateral talks involved numerous participants from the Middle East and elsewhere and began to make some progress in defining and addressing the technical and functional issues within their purview.

The bilateral talks in Washington moved ahead at a slow pace in 1992. In the spring of 1993, secret Israeli-PLO negotiations in Oslo, Norway, began to yield results. By the summer an agreement had been reached and this was signed on the White House lawn in Washington, D.C., on September 13, 1993 by Israel's Foreign Minister, Shimon Peres, and the PLO's negotiator, Mahmoud Abbas (Abu Mazen). This was followed by the Rabin-Arafat handshake that symbolized the significance of the Israel-PLO Declaration of Principles (DOP) that had been signed that day. The next day Israel and Jordan signed a Common Agenda to guide their negotiations.

The months after the signing of the DOP were replete with efforts to produce the agreements needed to implement it, as well as the work of opponents seeking to prevent movement toward full implementation of the DOP. Parallel with those talks were the Israel-Jordan negotiations that resulted in the Washington Declaration of July 1994 and, subsequently the Israel-Jordan Peace Treaty of 1994 signed in the desert on the border between the two states. Negotiations between Israel and Syria, focusing on the trade of land (that is, the Golan Heights) for peace continued.

Israel and the PLO reached a number of agreements on economic and financial issues as well as the early empowerment of the Palestinian Authority in the Gaza Strip and Jericho. Nevertheless, progress toward conciliation and peace was fraught with difficulties and complications as each issue engendered discord and debate, and opponents of the process sought to undermine the progress and the accords with acts of terror and violence.

A BRIEF CHRONOLOGY OF THE ARAB-ISRAELI CONFLICT

1516-1918	Ottoman rule over Palestine.
1882	Beginning of first aliyah to Palestine.
1896	Theodor Herzl publishes *Der Judenstaat*.
1897	First Zionist Congress meets in Basle, Switzerland. World Zionist Organization is created.
1915-1916	Hussein-McMahon correspondence pledges support for an independent Arab state in return for an Arab revolt against Ottoman Turkey in World War I.
1916 May 16	Sykes-Picot Agreement.
1917 November 2	Balfour Declaration published.
1917 December	British forces capture Palestine.
1919	Feisal-Weizmann correspondence. Paris Peace Conference. King-Crane Commission sent to region.
1920	San Remo Conference grants Britain Mandate for Palestine.
1921 March	Transjordan becomes separate entity; Abdullah established as emir.
1922 June	Churchill White Paper.
1922 July	Palestine Mandate ratified by League of Nations.
1930	Shaw Commission Report. Hope-Simpson Report. British issue Passfield White Paper limiting Jewish immigration into and Jewish land purchases in Palestine.
1931 February	MacDonald letter negates White Paper provisions.
1937	Peel Commission Report; first proposal to partition Palestine.
1939 May 17	British White Paper limits Jewish immigration and

	Zionist land purchases.
1942 May	Biltmore Program promulgated.
1945 March 22	Arab League founded.
1945 November	Anglo-American Committee of Inquiry established.
1945-1946	Jewish-Arab communal tensions in Palestine increase.
1946 May	Independent Kingdom of Trans-Jordan is created; Abdullah becomes King.
1946 July 22	British headquarters in King David Hotel, Jerusalem, bombed.
1947 February 14	British foreign secretary announces that his government has decided to turn the Palestine problem over to the United Nations.
1947 April 28	Opening of United Nations General Assembly special session on Palestine.
1947 May	United Nations Special Committee on Palestine (UNSCOP) is created.
1947 November 29	United Nations adopts Palestine partition plan, Resolution 181 (II), which calls for the establishment of a Jewish and an Arab state in Palestine.
1947 Dec - 1948 May	Intense Jewish-Arab communal warfare in Palestine.
1948 January	Arab Liberation Army enters Palestine.
1948 March 19	U.S. proposes UN trusteeship in Palestine.
1948 April 9	Jewish attack on Deir Yassin.
1948 April 13	Arab attack on bus convoy to Mt. Scopus.
1948 May	Termination of British Mandate.
1948 May 14	Israel proclaims its independence. U.S. President Harry Truman extends de facto recognition. David Ben-Gurion becomes first Prime Minister of Israel. First Arab-Israeli War begins.
1948 May 17	USSR extends full recognition to Israel.
1948 September 17	UN mediator Count Folke Bernadotte is assassinated in Jerusalem.
1948 December 11	UN General Assembly adopts resolution 194 (III).
1949 January 31	U.S. extends full recognition to Israel and Transjordan.
1949 February 24	Egypt and Israel sign armistice agreement at Rhodes.
1949 March 23	Israel and Lebanon sign armistice at Rhodes.
1949 April 3	Israel and Jordan sign armistice at Rhodes.
1949 July 20	Israel and Syria sign armistice at Rhodes.
1949 December	King Abdullah of Jordan annexes the West Bank and East Jerusalem.
1950 April 24	Jordanian parliament ratifies annexation of West Bank and East Jerusalem.
1950 May 25	Tripartite Declaration (Britain, France and U.S.)

	regulates arms flows to the Middle East.
1950 July 5	Knesset approves Law of Return.
1951 July 20	King Abdullah is assassinated in Jerusalem.
1952 July 23	Free Officers coup overthrows Egyptian monarchy.
1952	Yasser Arafat among the organizers of Palestinian Students' Union in Cairo.
1952 August 11	King Talal is replaced by King Hussein in Jordan.
1953 October 14	Israeli troops attack Kibya, Jordan.
1954	Johnston Plan for sharing Jordan River water proposed. Gamal Abdul Nasser becomes Prime Minister and President of Egypt.
1955 February 28	Israel raids Gaza Strip in retaliation for guerilla activity against Israel.
1956 March 1	King Hussein of Jordan dismisses British General John Bagot Glubb.
1956 July 26	Egypt nationalizes Suez Canal.
1956 October 29	Israel invades Sinai Peninsula.
1956 November 5	Britain and France invade Suez Canal zone.
1956 November 6/7	Britain, France, and Israel agree to cease-fire.
1956 December	Anglo-French withdrawal from Suez Canal Zone is completed. Replaced by United Nations Emergency Force (UNEF) troops.
1957 January 5	Eisenhower Doctrine announced.
1957 March	Egypt agrees to deployment of UNEF on border between Gaza Strip and Israel and at Sharm el-Sheikh. U.S. Congress approves Eisenhower Doctrine.
1958 February	United Arab Republic (UAR) of Egypt and Syria created.
1958 July 14	Revolution in Iraq overthrows the monarchy.
1964 January	Palestine Liberation Organization (PLO) is created in Cairo; Ahmed Shukairi becomes first chairman.
1964 May	First Palestine National Council meets in Jerusalem.
1964 June	Israel's National Water carrier begins operation; crisis erupts over Jordan River waters.
1965 January 1	Fatah is established and launches its first attack against Israel.
1966 November	Egypt and Syria sign defense pact.
1966 November 13	Israel responds to killing of Israelis with attack at es-Samu, Jordan.
1967 April 7	Six Syrian MiG's are shot down in an air clash with Israel.
1967 May 13	USSR tells Egypt of impending Israeli attack on Syria.
1967 May 17	Nasser declares alert, remilitarizes the Sinai Peninsula.

1967 May 18	Nasser asks for withdrawal of UNEF troops.
1967 May 23	Nasser announces blockade of Strait of Tiran, closing Gulf of Aqaba to Israeli shipping.
1967 May 30	Egypt and Jordan sign defense pact. Arabs and Israel mobilize for war.
1967 June 5-10	Six Day War. Israel captures West Bank and East Jerusalem from Jordan, the Sinai Peninsula and Gaza Strip from Egypt, and the Golan Heights from Syria.
1967 August	Arab Summit at Khartoum declares "three nos" -- no recognition, no negotiation, no peace with Israel.
1967 November 22	UN Security Council Resolution 242 is adopted.
1967 December 24	Ahmed Shukairi resigns as head of PLO.
1968 March 21	Israel attacks Karameh.
1968 July	PLO Covenant revised.
1968 October	Hafez al-Assad becomes leader of Syria.
1968 December	Israel raids Beirut International Airport in retaliation for Palestinian aircraft hijackings.
1969 February 1-4	Arafat is elected Chairman of the PLO.
1969 Spring	War of Attrition begins along the Suez Canal. Maturation of PLO state-within-a-state in Jordan.
1969 December 9	U.S. Secretary of State William Rogers outlines plan.
1970 June 25	Rogers announces Egypt-Israel cease-fire.
1970 August 7	Cease-fire ends War of Attrition.
1970 September	Civil war in Jordan between the armed forces and the PLO. The PLO is ousted from Jordan.
1970 September 28	Nasser dies; Anwar al-Sadat becomes president of Egypt.
1971 May	Sadat solidifies power as president of Egypt.
1971 May 27	Soviet-Egyptian Treaty of Friendship is signed.
1971 November 28	Jordanian Prime Minister Wasfi Tell is assassinated in Cairo by Black September.
1972 March	King Hussein proposes United Kingdom plan of confederation of West Bank and Jordan.
1971 July	Sadat expels Soviet advisors from Egypt.
1973 October 6-22	The Yom Kippur/Ramadan War.
1973 October 22	UNSC resolution 338 passes.
1973 November 11	Israel-Egypt cease-fire signed at Kilometer 101.
1973 December 21	Geneva Peace Conference convenes.
1974 January 17	Israel-Egypt disengagement agreement, brokered by U.S. Secretary of State Henry Kissinger, is signed at Kilometer 101.
1974 May 31	Israeli-Syrian disengagement brokered by Kissinger is signed in Geneva.
1974 June 12	U.S. President Richard Nixon visits the Middle East.

1974 October	PLO adopts phased program for liberation of Palestine. Arab League designates PLO as "sole legitimate representative of the Palestinian people" at the Rabat Summit.
1974 November 13	Yasser Arafat addresses UN General Assembly. PLO later granted observer status.
1975 April	Lebanese civil war begins.
1975 September	Sinai II agreement between Israel and Egypt is reached; U.S. pledges to Israel that it will not deal with the PLO unless it endorses United Nations Security Council Resolution 242 and recognizes Israel's right to exist.
1975 November 10	United Nations General Assembly resolution 3379 (XXX) declares Zionism to be a form of racism.
1975 December 4	United Nations Security Council allows PLO to participate in debate on Arab-Israeli question.
1977 October 1	U.S.-Soviet Union joint communique is issued.
1977 November 9	Sadat states he is prepared to go to Israeli Knesset if necessary to achieve peace.
1977 November 19-20	Sadat meets Israeli leaders in Jerusalem and addresses the Knesset.
1977 December 25-26	Israeli Prime Minister Menachem Begin meets Sadat in Ismailia, Egypt.
1978 January 4	Jimmy Carter issues Aswan Declaration.
1978 March 11	Palestinians attack an Israeli bus, killing 37.
1978 March 14	Israel launches Operation Litani into south Lebanon.
1978 June 13	Israel completes withdrawal from Lebanon.
1978 September 5-17	Carter, Begin and Sadat meet at Camp David.
1978 September 17	Begin and Sadat sign the Camp David Accords.
1978 November 5	Arab Summit in Baghdad denounces Camp David Accords and criticizes Egypt.
1978 December 10	Nobel Peace Prize awarded jointly to Sadat and Begin.
1979 March 7-13	Carter travels to Egypt and Israel to facilitate the peace negotiations.
1979 March 26	Egypt-Israel Peace Treaty is signed in Washington.
1979 March 31	Egypt is expelled from Arab League, which moves headquarters to Tunis.
1979 May 25	Israel begins withdrawal from Sinai Peninsula.
1980 June 13	European Community issues Venice Declaration.
1980 July 30	Israel adopts Basic Law: Jerusalem, Capital of Israel.
1980 October	Soviet-Syrian Treaty of Friendship and Cooperation signed.
1981 June 7	Israel bombs Iraqi nuclear reactor at Osirak.

1981 August	Crown Prince Fahd of Saudi Arabia outlines peace plan.
1981 October 6	Anwar Sadat is assassinated in Cairo by Islamic fundamentalists; Hosni Mubarak becomes President.
1981 December 14	Israel extends its law and jurisdiction to the Golan Heights.
1982 April 25	Israel completes withdrawal from Sinai Peninsula.
1982 June 6	Israel invades Lebanon (Operation Peace for Galilee).
1982 July-August	Israeli siege of Beirut.
1982 August	Multinational peacekeeping force enters Beirut to oversee PLO evacuation from Lebanon. PLO forces are dispersed in a number of Arab countries. Arafat and his aides are established in Tunisia.
1982 September 1	Reagan announces an initiative for peace.
1982 September 9	Fez Arab Summit adopts peace plan.
1982 September 14	President-elect Bashir Gemayal of Lebanon is assassinated.
1982 September 15	Israel breaks ceasefire and enters Beirut.
1982 September 17-18	Christian Phalange attack Sabra and Shatilla camps outside Beirut and kill hundreds of Palestinians.
1982 September 20	Amin Gemayel becomes President of Lebanon.
1982 September 28	Multinational Force reenters Lebanon.
1982 October 9	King Hussein and Yasser Arafat begin talks on a joint Palestinian-Jordanian response to the Reagan proposals.
1983 February 8	Israel's Kahan Commission of Inquiry releases its report on the massacres at Sabra and Shatilla.
1983 April 10	PLO-Jordanian negotiations break down.
1983 April 28	U.S. States Secretary of State George Shultz begins shuttle diplomacy to work out the final details of Israel-Lebanon accord.
1983 May 17	Lebanon and Israel sign an agreement. Syria rejects it.
1983 September 16	Israel begins first phase of withdrawal from Lebanon.
1984 January 19	Islamic Conference Organization readmits Egypt.
1984 February 21	U.S. peacekeeping force departs Lebanon.
1984 March 5	Lebanon formally abrogates May 17, 1983 agreement.
1985 February 11	Agreement between King Hussein and Yasser Arafat to move together toward achievement of a just settlement of the Middle East crisis.
1985 July	Israel completes withdrawal from Lebanon except for security zone on the Israel-Lebanon frontier.
1986 March	King Hussein breaks relations with Yasser Arafat.
1986 July	Israeli Prime Minister Shimon Peres meets King Hassan II in Morocco.

1987 April	Arafat abrogates agreement with King Hussein.
1987 December 8	An Israeli truck hits a Palestinian car in Gaza killing four people. Anti-Israeli violence erupts throughout the Gaza Strip.
1987 December 9	Intifada begins.
1988 February	HAMAS is created in the Gaza Strip.
1988 April 16	Khalil al-Wazir (Abu Jihad) is assassinated in Tunis.
1988 July 31	King Hussein announces severing of most Jordanian administrative and legal ties to the West Bank, and declares "Jordan is not Palestine."
1988 September 29	Taba is awarded to Egypt by an international arbitration panel.
1988 November 15	Palestine National Council (PNC) in Algiers declares independent Palestinian state.
1988 December 13	Arafat addresses United Nations in Geneva.
1988 December 14	Arafat clarifies position and recognizes Israel's right to exist, accepts UNSC Resolutions 242 and 338, and renounces terrorism. U.S. announces it will begin a dialogue with PLO in Tunisia.
1989 April 6	Israeli Prime Minister Yitzhak Shamir announces election plan for the occupied territories.
1989 May	U.S. accepts Israeli plan as basis for peace process.
1989 May 22	Egypt readmitted to Arab League.
1989 June 27	European Community issues Madrid statement.
1989 September	Egyptian President Hosni Mubarak introduces ten point plan to clarify and advance Israel's proposal.
1989 October	U.S. Secretary of State James Baker suggests five point plan.
1990 March	Shamir government falls after parliamentary vote of no confidence.
1990 June 20	New Shamir government established.
1990 June 20	President George Bush suspends U.S. dialogue with PLO.
1990 August	Iraq invades and occupies Kuwait.
1990 October 8	Palestinians are killed in clashes with Israeli police after a stone throwing incident at the Western Wall.
1990 October 12	United Nations Security Council unanimously adopts resolution 672 condemning the Israeli action.
1990-1991	Arafat supports Saddam Hussein.
1991 January 16	Allied forces launch a massive air campaign against Iraq (Operation Desert Storm). Iraq launches Scud missiles against Israel and Saudi Arabia.
1991 February 23	Allied ground attack against Iraq commences.
1991 February 27	Bush announces the liberation of Kuwait and the sus-

	pension of allied attacks.
1991 March/September	Baker makes a series of visits to the region to pursue an Arab-Israeli settlement.
1991 October 30	Arab-Israeli peace conference begins in Madrid.
1991 December 10	Washington rounds of bilateral Arab-Israeli negotiations begin.
1991 December 16	United Nations General Assembly repeals "Zionism is racism" resolution.
1992 July	Yitzhak Rabin forms coalition government in Israel.
1993 Spring	Secret negotiations between Israel and PLO in Oslo, Norway.
1993 July	Israel launches Operation Accountability in Lebanon.
1993 September 13	Israel-PLO Declaration of Principles (DOP) signed in Washington, D.C.
1993 September 14	Israel and Jordan sign a Common Agenda for negotiations.
1993 October 1	The Conference to Support Middle East Peace (the Donors Conference) meets in Washington.
1993 October 13	Israel and the PLO open talks in Egypt on implementation of the DOP.
1994 February 25	Jewish settler kills Palestinian worshippers in Hebron massacre. Israel-PLO talks suspended.
1994 March 31	Israel-PLO talks resume.
1994 April 29	An agreement establishing a framework for economic ties between Israel and the areas under Palestinian autonomy is signed in Paris.
1994 May 4	An agreement on the details of self-rule for the Gaza Strip and Jericho is signed by Rabin and Arafat.
1994 May 18	Last Israeli troops withdraw from Palestinian areas in Gaza.
1994 June 26	Israel's Shamgar commission issues its report on the Hebron massacre.
1994 July 25	Summit meeting in Washington, D.C., between Prime Minister Yitzhak Rabin and King Hussein of Jordan. Washington Declaration is issued.
1994 July 26	Rabin and Hussein address a joint session of the United States Congress.
1994 August 29	Israel and the Palestinians sign an agreement on early empowerment providing for the transfer of some civil responsibilities to the Palestinians.
1994 September 13	Oslo Declaration issued in Oslo, Norway.
1994 October 1	The Gulf Cooperation Council (GCC) announces the end of the secondary and tertiary boycotts of Israel.
1994 October 9	Two Arab gunmen kill 2 and wound 13 in Jerusalem.

	HAMAS takes responsibility. Members of HAMAS kidnap an Israeli soldier and threaten to kill him. He dies in a rescue attempt five days later.
1994 October 19	A HAMAS suicide-bomber detonates explosives on a crowded bus in Tel Aviv, killing 22 people and wounding 26.
1994 October 26	Israel and Jordan sign a Treaty of Peace.
1994 November 2	Hani Abed is killed by a car bomb. Islamic Jihad blames Israel and vows revenge.
1994 November 10	King Hussein and Yitzhak Rabin exchange ratified copies of the Israel-Jordan Peace Treaty on the shores of the Sea of Galilee during King Hussein's first official public visit to Israel.
1994 November 11	An Islamic Jihad suicide bomber kills three Israeli officers at a military checkpoint.
1994 November 18	Palestinian police fire on demonstrators near a mosque in Gaza City, killing at least 12 people.
1994 November 27	Israel and Jordan declare the establishment of diplomatic relations at the ambassadorial level.
1994 December	Israeli and Syrian Chiefs of Staff, Ehud Barak and Hikmat Shihabi, and their aides meet in Washington.
1994 December 10	Yitzhak Rabin, Shimon Peres and Yasser Arafat receive the 1994 Nobel Peace Prize in Oslo, Norway.
1994 December 26	Israeli Prime Minister Rabin visits Oman and meets with Sultan Qaboos. The Knesset passes a measure that bans political activity by "the Palestinian Authority and other Palestinians" in Jerusalem.
1994 December 29	At the end of a two-day summit meeting in Alexandria, Egypt, Egyptian President Hosni Mubarak, Saudi Arabia's King Fahd and Syrian President Hafez al-Assad issue a joint statement expressing support for "Syria's valid demand for a full Israeli withdrawal from the Golan Heights as a condition to a peace treaty with Israel."
1995 January-June	High-level meetings to achieve implementation of the Israel-PLO DOP continue. Israel-Syria negotiations resume after a hiatus.
1995 January 22	19 Israelis are killed and 62 are wounded in an Islamic Jihad terrorist strike at the Beit Lid junction.
1995 February 2	Rabin, King Hussein, Arafat, and Mubarak meet at the summit in cairo to discuss the peace process. In a joint statement they "reaffirmed their determination to continue the Middle East peace process towards the fulfillment of a just, lasting and comprehensive peace

in the region."

1995 February 12   After a follow-up meeting in Washington, at which Egypt, Israel, Jordan and the Palestinian Authority are joined by United States representatives, a Blair House Joint Communique is issued in which "the five participants reaffirmed their determination to consolidate the breakthroughs achieved in the Arab-Israeli peace process, to overcome obstacles and disputes, and to push forward toward a just, lasting and comprehensive peace in the region based on United Nations Security Council Resolutions 242 and 338...."

1995 June 27-29   Israeli and Syrian Chiefs of Staff, Amnon Shahak and Hikmat Shihabi, and their aides, meet in Washington to continue discussions of the security arrangements on the Golan Heights and related issues in Israel-Syrian negotiations. Dates for future meetings are established.

1995 July 1   Despite progress in their negotiations, Israel and the PLO fail to meet their July 1 deadline date for agreement on expansion of the Palestinian self-rule authority beyond Gaza and Jericho into other locations in the West Bank. The process continues.

DOCUMENTS

DER JUDENSTAAT (FEBRUARY 14, 1896)

Modern political Zionism which sought the creation of a Jewish state in Palestine derives from Theodor Herzl. He was the driving force behind the creation of the political ideology and worldwide movement whose basic concepts are contained in Der Judenstaat (The Jewish State), which was published in Vienna on February 14, 1896. In it Herzl assessed the situation of the Jews and proposed a practical plan for resolution of the Jewish Question by creating a state in which Jews would reconstitute their national life in a territory of their own. Herzl's pamphlet was the catalyst for a campaign to influence European statesmen on behalf of the Zionist cause.

The idea which I have developed in this pamphlet is a very old one; it is the restoration of the Jewish State.

The world resounds with outcries against the Jews, and these outcries have awakened the slumbering idea. ... I shall therefore clearly and emphatically state that I believe in the practical outcome of my scheme, though without professing to have discovered the shape it may ultimately take. The Jewish State is essential to the world; it will therefore be created. ...

It depends on the Jews themselves whether this political pamphlet remains for the present a political romance. ... The Jews who wish for a State shall have it, and they will deserve to have it. ...

The Jewish question still exists. It would be foolish to deny it. ... The Jewish question exists wherever Jews live in perceptible numbers. Where it does not exist, it is carried by Jews in the course of their migrations. We naturally move to those places where we are not persecuted, and there our presence produces persecution. This is the case in every country, and will remain so, even in those highly civilized -- for instance, France -- until the Jewish question finds a solution on a political basis.

... I think the Jewish question is no more a social than a religious one. ... It is a national question, which can only be solved by making it a political world-question to be discussed and settled by the civilized nations of the world in council.

We are a people -- one people. ...

No one can deny the gravity of the situation of the Jews. Wherever they live in perceptible numbers, they are more or less persecuted.

... The nations in whose midst Jews live are all either covertly or openly Anti-Semitic.

The artificial means heretofore employed to overcomes the troubles of Jews have been either too petty -- such as attempts at colonization -- or attempts to convert the Jews into peasants in their present homes.

... I merely wanted to indicate clearly how futile had been past attempts -- most of them well intentioned -- to solve the Jewish Question.

We are one people -- our enemies have made us one without our consent, as repeatedly happens in history. Distress binds us together, and, thus united, we suddenly discover our strength. Yes, we are strong enough to form a State, and, indeed, a model State. We possess all human and material resources necessary for the purpose.

The whole plan is in its essence perfectly simple ....

Let the sovereignty be granted us over a portion of the globe large enough to satisfy the rightful requirements of a nation; the rest we shall manage for ourselves. ...

Let all who are willing to join us, fall in behind our banner and fight for our cause with voice and pen and deed. ...

Shall we choose Palestine or Argentine? We shall take what is given us, and what is selected by Jewish public opinion. ...

Palestine is our ever-memorable historic home. The very name of Palestine would attract our people with a force of marvelous potency.

BASLE PROGRAM (AUGUST 23, 1897)

On August 23, 1897, in Basle (or Basel), Switzerland, Theodor Herzl convened the first World Zionist Congress representing Jewish communities and organizations throughout the world. The congress established the World Zionist Organization (WZO) and founded an effective, modern, political, Jewish national movement with its goal, enunciated in the Basel Program (the original official program of the WZO), that sought the creation of a Jewish state. Zionism rejected other solutions to the Jewish Question and was a political response to centuries of discrimination, persecution, and oppression.

The aim of Zionism is to create for the Jewish people a home in Palestine secured by public law. The Congress contemplates the following means to the attainment of this end:

1. The promotion, on suitable lines, of the colonization of Palestine by Jewish agricultural and industrial workers.

2. The organization and binding together of the whole of Jewry by means of appropriate institutions, local and international, in accordance with the laws of each country.

3. The strengthening and fostering of Jewish national sentiment and consciousness.

4. Preparatory steps towards obtaining Government consent, where necessary, to the attainment of the aim of Zionism.

HUSSEIN-MCMAHON CORRESPONDENCE (JULY 14, 1915-MARCH 10, 1916)

The Hussein-McMahon Correspondence was a series of letters exchanged by Sherif Hussein, the Amir of Mecca, and Sir Henry McMahon, Great Britain's High Commissioner in Egypt, between July 14, 1915 and March 10, 1916, containing British pledges to support post-war Arab independence and the creation of an Arab state in exchange for Arab military support against Ottoman Turkey. The exchanges, and the accompanying negotiations led to a military arrangement that satisfied both parties but the political understandings were ambiguous.

In his letter to Hussein, dated October 24, 1915, McMahon pledges to "... recognize and support the independence of the Arabs in all the regions within the limits demanded by the Sherif of Mecca" subject to certain modifications. Palestine was never directly addressed in the correspondence.

In constructing the post-war peace arrangements, the Arabs cited the Hussein-McMahon correspondence as evidence of Britain's pledges for Arab independence and the boundaries of the Arab state. Britain claimed that the whole of Palestine west of the Jordan river had been excluded from Arab rule as part of the portions of Syria lying west of Damascus excluded by McMahon's pledge.

LETTER FROM THE SHERIF HUSSEIN TO MCMAHON, JULY 14, 1915.

Whereas the whole of the Arab nation without any exception have decided in these last years to live, and to accomplish their freedom, and grasp the reins of their administration both in theory and practice; and whereas they have found and felt that it is to the interest of the Government of Great Britain to support them and aid them to the attainment of their firm and lawful intentions (which are based upon the maintenance of the honour and dignity of their life) without any ulterior motives whatsoever unconnected with this object;

And whereas it is to their (the Arabs') interest also to prefer the assistance of the Government of Great Britain in consideration of their geographical position and economic interests, and also of the attitude of the above-mentioned Government, which is known to both nations and therefore need not be emphasized;

For these reasons the Arab nation see fit to limit themselves, as time is short, to asking the Government of Great Britain, if it should think fit, for the approval, through her deputy or representative, of the following fundamental propositions, leaving out all things considered secondary in comparison with these, so that it may prepare all means necessary for attaining this noble purpose, until such time as it finds occasion for making the actual negotiations:

Firstly. -- England to acknowledge the independence of the Arab countries, bounded on the north by Mersina and Adana up to 37° of latitude, on which degree fall Birijik, Urfa, Mardin, Midiat, Jezirat (Ibn 'Umar), Amadia, up to the border of Persia; on the east by the borders of Persia up to the Gulf of Basra; on the south by the Indian Ocean, with the exception of the position of Aden to remain as it is; on the west by the Red Sea, the Mediterranean Sea up to Mersina. England to approve of the proclamation of an Arab Khalifate of Islam.

Secondly. -- The Arab Government of the Sherif to acknowledge that England shall have the preference in all economic enterprises in the Arab countries whenever conditions of enterprises are otherwise equal.

Thirdly. -- For the security of this Arab independence and the certainty of such preference of economic enterprises, both high contracting parties to offer mutual assistance, to the best ability of their military and naval forces, to face any foreign Power which may attack either party. Peace not to be decided without agreement of both parties.

Fourthly. -- If one of the parties enters upon an aggressive conflict, the other party to assume a neutral attitude, and in case of such party wishing the other to join forces, both to meet and discuss the conditions.

Fifthly. -- England to acknowledge the abolition of foreign privileges in the Arab countries, and to assist the Government of the Sherif in an International Convention for confirming such abolition.

Sixthly. -- Articles 3 and 4 of this treaty to remain in vigour for fifteen years, and if either wishes it to be renewed, one year's notice before lapse of treaty to be given.

Consequently, and as the whole of the Arab nation have (praise to be God) agreed and united for the attainment, at all costs and finally, of this noble object, they beg the Government of Great Britain to answer them positively or negatively in a period of thirty days after receiving this intimation; and if this period should also lapse before they receive an answer, they reserve to themselves complete freedom of action. Moreover, we (the Sherif's family) will consider themselves free in word and deed from the bonds of our previous declaration which we made through Ali Effendi.

LETTER FROM MCMAHON TO THE SHERIF OF MECCA, AUGUST 30, 1915.

... We have the honour to thank you for your frank expressions of the sincerity of your feeling towards England. We rejoice, moreover, that your Highness and your people are of one opinion -- that Arab interests are English interests and English Arab. To this intent we confirm to you the terms of Lord Kitchener's message, which reached you by the hand of Ali Effendi, and in which was stated clearly our desire for the independence of Arabia and its inhabitants, together with our approval of the Arab Khalifate when it should be proclaimed. We declare once more that His Majesty's Government would welcome the resumption of the Khalifate by an Arab of true race. With regard to the questions of limits and boundaries, it would appear to be premature to consume our time in discussing such details in the heat of war, and while, in many portions of them, the Turk is up to now in effective occupation: especially as we have learned, with surprise and regret, that some of the Arabs in those very parts, far from assisting us, are neglecting this their supreme opportunity and are lending their arms to the German and the Turk, to the new despoiler and the old oppressor. ...

LETTER FROM HUSSEIN TO MCMAHON, SEPTEMBER 9, 1915.

... With great cheerfulness and delight I received your letter dated the 19th Shawal, 1333 (the 30th August, 1915), and have given it great consideration and regard, in spite of the impression I received from it of ambiguity and its tone of coldness and hesitation with regard to our essential point. ...

Your Excellency will pardon me and permit me to say clearly that the coolness and hesitation which you have displayed in the question of the limits and boundaries by saying that the discussion of these at present is of no use and is a loss of time, and that they are still in the hands of the Government which is ruling them, &c., might be taken to infer an estrangement or something of the sort.

As the limits and boundaries demanded are not those of one person whom we should satisfy and with whom we should discuss them after the war is over, but out peoples have seen that the life of their new proposal is bound at least by these limits and their word is united on this.

Therefore, they have found it necessary first to discuss this point with the Power in whom they now have their confidence and trust as a final appeal, viz., the illustrious British Empire.

Their reason for this union and confidence is mutual interest, the necessity of regulating territorial divisions and the feelings of their inhabitants, so that they may know how to base their future and life, so not to meet her (England?) or any of her Allies in opposition to their resolution which would produce a contrary issue, which God forbid. ...

With reference to your remark in your letter above mentioned that some of our people are still doing their utmost in promoting the interests of Turkey, your goodness (lit. "perfectness") would not permit you to make this an excuse for the tone of coldness and hesitation with regard to our demands, demands which I cannot admit that you, as a man of sound opinion, will deny to be necessary for our existence; nay, they are the essential essence of our life, material and moral.

... In order to reassure your Excellency I can declare that the whole country, together with those who you say are submitting themselves to Turco-German orders, are all waiting the result of these negotiations, which are dependent only on your refusal or acceptance of the question of the limits and on your declaration of safeguarding their religion first and then the rest of rights from any harm or danger. ...

LETTER FROM MCMAHON TO THE SHERIF OF MECCA, OCTOBER 24, 1915.

... I regret that you should have received from my last letter the impression that I regarded the question of the limits and boundaries with coldness and hesitation; such was not the case, but it appeared to me that the time had not yet come when that question could be discussed in a conclusive manner.

I have realised, however, from your last letter that you regard this question as one of vital and urgent importance. I have, therefore, lost no time in informing the Government of Great Britain of the contents of your letter, and it is with great pleasure that I communicate to you on their behalf of following statement, which I am confident you will receive with satisfaction: --

The two districts of Mersina and Alexandretta and portions of Syria lying to the west of the districts of Damascus, Homs, Hama and Aleppo cannot be said to be purely Arab, and should be excluded from the limits demanded.

With the above modification, and without prejudice to our existing treaties with Arab chiefs, we accept those limits.

As for those regions lying within those frontiers wherein Great Britain is free to act without detriment to the interests of her ally, France. I am empowered in the name of the Government of Great Britain to give the following assurances and make the following reply to your letter: --

(1) Subject to the above modifications, Great Britain is prepared to recognise and support the independence of the Arabs in all the regions within the limits demanded by the Sherif of Mecca.

(2) Great Britain will guarantee the Holy Places against all external aggression and will recognise their inviolability.

(3) When the situation admits, Great Britain will give to the Arabs her advice and will assist them to establish what may appear to be the most suitable forms of government in those various territories.

(4) On the other hand, it is understood that the Arabs have decided to seek the advice and guidance of Great Britain only, and that such European advisers and officials as may be required for the formation of a sound form of administration will be British.

(5) With regard to the *vilayets* of Baghdad and Basra, the Arabs will

recognise that established position and interests of Great Britain necessitate special administrative arrangements in order to secure these territories from foreign aggression, to promote the welfare of the local populations and to safeguard our mutual economic interests. ...

LETTER FROM THE SHERIF OF MECCA TO MCMAHON, NOVEMBER 5, 1915.

... l. In order to facilitate an agreement and to render a service to Islam, and at the same time to avoid all that may cause Islam troubles and hardships -- seeing moreover that we have great consideration for the distinguished qualities and dispositions of the Government of Great Britain -- we renounce our insistence on the inclusion of the *vilayets* of Mersina and Adana in the Arab Kingdom. But the two *vilayets* of Aleppo and Beirut and their seacoasts are purely Arab *vilayets*, and there is no difference between a Moslem and a Christian Arab: they are both descendants of one forefather. ...

2. As the Iraqi *vilayets* are parts of the pure Arab Kingdom, and were in fact the seat of its Government in the time of Ali ibn Abu Talib, and in the time of all the Khalifs who succeeded him; and as in them began the civilisation of the Arabs, and as their towns were the first towns built in Islam where the Arab power became so great; therefore they are greatly valued by all Arabs far and near, and their traditions cannot be forgotten by them. Consequently, we cannot satisfy the Arab nations or make them submit to give us such a title to nobility. But in order to render an accord easy, and taking into consideration the assurances mentioned in the fifth article of your letter to keep and guard our mutual interests in that country as they are one and the same, for all these reasons we might agree to leave under the British administration for a short time those districts now occupied by the British troops without the rights of either party being prejudiced thereby (especially those of the Arab nation: which interests are to it economic and vital), and against a suitable sum paid as compensation to the Arab Kingdom for the period of occupation, in order to meet the expenses which every new kingdom is bound to support; at the same time respecting your agreements with the Sheikhs of those districts, and especially those which are essential. ...

4. The Arab nation has a strong belief that after this war is over the Turks under German influence will direct their efforts to provoke the Arabs and violate their rights, both material and moral, to wipe out their mobility and honour and reduce them to utter submission as they are determined to ruin them entirely. The reasons for the slowness shown in our action have already been stated.

5. When the Arabs know the Government of Great Britain is their ally who will not leave them to themselves at the conclusion of peace in the face of Turkey and Germany, and that she will support and will effectively defend them, then to enter the war at once will, no doubt, be in conformity with the general interest of the Arabs.

6. Out letter dated the 29th Shauâl, 1333 (the 9th September, 1915), saves

us the trouble of repeating our opinions as to articles 3 and 4 of your honoured last letter regarding administration, Government advisers and officials, especially as you have declared, exalted Minister, that you will not interfere with internal affairs. ...

LETTER FROM MCMAHON TO THE SHERIF OF MECCA, DECEMBER 14, 1915.

... I am gratified to observe that you agree to the exclusion of the districts of Mersina and Adana from Boundaries of the Arab territories.

I also note with great pleasure and satisfaction your assurances that the Arabs are determined to act in conformity with the precepts laid down by Omar Ibn Khattab and the early Khalifs, which secure the rights and privileges of all religions alike.

In stating that the Arabs are ready to recognise and respect all our treaties with Arab chiefs, it is, of course, understood that this will apply to all territories included in the Arab Kingdom, as the Government of Great Britain cannot repudiate engagements which already exist.

With regard to the *vilayets* of Aleppo and Beirut, the Government of Great Britain have fully understood and taken careful note of your observations, but, as the interests of our ally, France, are involved in them both, the question will require careful consideration and a further communication on the subject will be addressed to you in due course.

The Government of Great Britain, as I have already informed you, are ready to give all guarantees of assistance and support within their power to the Arab Kingdom, but their interests demand, as you yourself have recognised, a friendly and stable administration in the *vilayet* of Baghdad, and the adequate safeguarding of these interests calls for a much fuller and more detailed consideration than the present situation and the urgency of these negotiations permit.

We fully appreciate your desire for caution, and have no wish to urge you to hasty action, which might jeopardise the eventual success of your projects, but, in the meantime, it is most essential that you should spare no effort to attach all the Arab peoples to our united cause and urge them to afford no assistance to our enemies.

It is on the success of these efforts and on the more active measures which the Arabs may hereafter take in support of our cause, when the time for action comes, that the permanence and strength of our agreement must depend.

Under these circumstances I am further directed by the Government of Great Britain to inform you that you may rest assured that Great Britain has no intention of concluding any peace in terms of which the freedom of the Arab peoples from German and Turkish domination does not form an essential condition. ...

LETTER FROM THE SHERIF OF MECCA TO MCMAHON, JANUARY 1, 1916.

... With regard to what had been stated in your honoured communication concerning El Iraq as to the matter of compensation for the period of occupation, we, in order to strengthen the confidence of Great Britain in our attitude and in our words and actions, really and veritably, and in order to give her evidence of our certainty and assurance in trusting her glorious Government, leave the determination of the amount to the perception of her wisdom and justice.

As regards the northern parts and their coasts, we have already stated in our previous letter what were the utmost possible modifications, and all this was only done so to fulfill those aspirations whose attainment is desired by the will of the Blessed and Supreme God. It is this same feeling and desire which impelled us to avoid what may possibly injure the alliance of Great Britain and France and the agreement made between them during the present wars and calamities; yet we find it our duty that the eminent minister should be sure that, at the first opportunity after this war is finished, we shall ask you (what we avert our eyes from to-day) for what we now leave to France in Beirut and its coasts.

I do not find it necessary to draw your attention to the fact that our plan is of greater security to the interests and protection of the rights of Great Britain than it is to us, and will necessarily be so whatever may happen, so that Great Britain may finally see her friends in that contentment and advancement which she is endeavouring to establish for them now, especially as her Allies being neighbours to us will be the germ of difficulties and discussion with which there will be no peaceful conditions. In addition to which the citizens of Beirut will decidedly never accept such dismemberment, and they may oblige us to undertake new measures which may exercise Great Britain, certainly not less than her present troubles, because of our belief and certainty in the reciprocity and indeed the identity of our interests, which is the only cause that caused us never to care to negotiate with any other Power but you. Consequently, it is impossible to allow any derogation that gives France, or any other Power, a span of land in those regions. ...

LETTER FROM MCMAHON TO THE SHERIF OF MECCA, JANUARY 25, 1916.
... We take note of your remarks concerning the *vilayet* of Baghdad, and will take the question into careful consideration when the enemy has been defeated and the time for peaceful settlement arrives.

As regards the northern parts, we note with satisfaction your desire to avoid anything which might possibly injure the alliance of Great Britain and France. It is, as you know, our fixed determination that nothing shall be permitted to interfere in the slightest degree with our united prosecution of this war to a victorious conclusion. Moreover, when the victory has been won, the friendship of Great Britain and France will become yet more firm and enduring, cemented by the blood of Englishmen and Frenchmen who have died side by side fighting for the cause of right and liberty. ...

SYKES-PICOT AGREEMENT (MAY 15-MAY 16, 1916)

In late 1914 Turkey entered World War I on the side of the Central Powers. Soon thereafter Great Britain, France, and Russia began to consider the disposition of the Ottoman Empire's territory in the Middle East. Britain and France began secret negotiations over the disposition of the Ottoman territory in 1915, which were completed in January 1916. Britain's negotiator was Sir Mark Sykes, a member of Parliament and an Arabist. France was represented by Francois-Georges Picot, a French diplomat who had served as Consul General in Beirut. The two countries officially ratified the agreement in May 1916 in an exchange of letters from British Foreign Secretary Sir Edward Grey to France's Ambassador to Great Britain, Paul Cambon. The agreement defined areas of British and French control as well as spheres of interest and the division of Ottoman Empire territories under the League of Nations Mandate system generally followed its terms.

BRITISH FOREIGN MINISTER SIR EDWARD GREY TO FRENCH AMBASSADOR TO LONDON PAUL CAMBON, 15 MAY 1916.

I shall have the honour to reply fully in a further note to your Excellency's note of the 9th instant, relative to the creation of an Arab State, but I should meanwhile be grateful if your Excellence could assure me that in those regions which, under the conditions recorded in that communication, become entirely French, or in which French interests are recognised as predominant, any existing British concessions, rights of navigation or development, and the rights and privileges of any British religious, scholastic, or medical institutions will be maintained.

His Majesty's Government are, of course, ready to give a reciprocal assurance in regard to the British area.

GREY TO CAMBON, 16 MAY 1916.

I have the honour to acknowledge the receipt of your Excellency's note of the 9th instant, stating that the French Government accept the limits of a future Arab State, or Confederation of States, and of those parts of Syria where French interests predominate, together with certain conditions attached thereto, such as they result from recent discussions in London and Petrograd on the subject.

I have the honour to inform your Excellency in reply that the acceptance of the whole project, as it now stands, will involve the abdication of considerable British interests, but since His Majesty's Government recognise the advantage to the general cause of the Allies entailed in producing a more favourable internal political situation in Turkey, they are ready to accept the arrangement now arrived at, provided that the co-operation of the Arabs is secured, and that the Arabs fulfill the conditions and obtain the towns of Homs, Hama, Damascus, and Aleppo.

It is accordingly understood between the French and British Governments

-- 1. That France and Great Britain are prepared to recognise and protect an independent Arab State or a Confederation of Arab States in the areas (A) and (B) marked on the annexed map, under the suzerainty of an Arab chief. That in area (A) France, and in area (B) Great Britain, shall have priority of right of enterprise and local loans. That in area (A) France, and in area (B) Great Britain, shall alone supply advisers or foreign functionaries at the request of the Arab State or Confederation of Arab States. 2. That in the blue area France, and in the red area Great Britain, shall be allowed to establish such direct or indirect administration or control as they desire and as they may think fit to arrange with the Arab State or Confederation of Arab States. 3. That in the brown area there shall be established an international administration, the form of which is to be decided upon after consultation with Russia, and subsequently in consultation with the other Allies, and the representatives of the Shereef of Mecca. 4. That Great Britain be accorded (1) the ports of Haifa and Acre, (2) guarantee of a given supply of water from the Tigris and Euphrates in area (A) for area (B). His Majesty's Government, on their part, undertake that they will at no time enter into negotiations for the cession of Cyprus to any third Power without the previous consent of the French Government. 5. That Alexandretta shall be a free port as regards the trade of the British Empire, and that there shall be no discrimination in port charges or facilities as regards British shipping and British goods; that there shall be freedom of transit for British goods through Alexandretta and by railway through the blue area, whether those goods are intended for or originate in the red area, or (B) area, or area (A); and there shall be no discrimination, direct or indirect, against British goods on any railway or against British goods or ships at any port serving the areas mentioned.

That Haifa shall be a free port as regards the trade of France, her dominions and protectorates, and there shall be no discrimination in port charges or facilities as regards French shipping and French goods. There shall be freedom of transit for French goods through Haifa and by the British railway through the brown area, whether those goods are intended for or originate in the blue area, area (A), or area (B), and there shall be no discrimination, direct or indirect, against French goods on any railway, or against French goods or ships at any port serving the areas mentioned. 6. That in area (A) the Bagdad Railway shall not be extended southwards beyond Mosul, and in area (B) northwards beyond Samarra, until a railway connecting Bagdad with Aleppo via the Euphrates Valley has been completed,and then only with the concurrence of the two Governments. 7. That Great Britain has the right to build, administer, and be sole owner of a railway connecting Haifa with area (B), and shall have a perpetual right to transport troops along such a line at all times.

It is to be understood by both Governments that this railway is to facilitate the connexion of Bagdad with Haifa by rail, and it is further understood that, if the engineering difficulties and expense entailed by keeping this connecting line in the brown area only make the project unfeasible, that the French Government shall be prepared to consider that the line in question may also traverse the polygon Banias-Keis Marib-Salkhad Tell Otsda-Mesmie before reaching area (B). 8. For a period of twenty years the existing Turkish customs tariff shall remain in force throughout the whole of the blue and red areas, as well as in areas (A) and (B), and no increase in the rates of duty or conversion from *ad valorem* to specific rates shall be made except by agreement between the two powers.

There shall be no interior customs barriers between any of the above-mentioned areas. The customs duties leviable on goods destined for the interior shall be collected at the port of entry and handed over to the administration of the area of destination. 9. It shall be agreed that the French Government will at no time enter into any negotiations for the cession of their rights and will not cede such rights in the blue area to any third Power, except the Arab State or Confederation of Arab States, without the previous agreement of His Majesty's Government, who, on their part, will give a similar undertaking to the French Government regarding the red area. 10. The British and French Government, as the protectors of the Arab State, shall agree that they will not themselves acquire and will not consent to a third Power acquiring territorial possessions in the Arabian peninsula, nor consent to a third Power installing a naval base either on the east coast, or on the islands, of the Red Sea. This, however, shall not prevent such a adjustment of the Aden frontier as may be necessary in consequence of recent Turkish aggression. 11. The negotiations with the Arabs as to the boundaries of the Arab States shall be continued through the same channel as heretofore on behalf of the two Powers. 12. It is agreed that measures to control the importation of arms into the Arab territories will be considered by the two Governments.

I have further the honour to state that, in order to make the agreement complete, His Majesty's Government are proposing to the Russian Government to exchange notes analogous to those exchanged by the latter and your Excellency's Government on the 26th April last. Copies of these notes will be communicated to your Excellency as soon as exchanged.

I would also venture to remind your Excellency that the conclusion of the present agreement raises, for practical consideration, the question of the claims of Italy to a share in any partition or rearrangement of Turkey in Asia, as formulated in article 9 of the agreement of the 26th April, 1915, between Italy and the Allies.

His Majesty's Government further consider that the Japanese Government should be informed of the arrangements now concluded.

BALFOUR DECLARATION (NOVEMBER 2, 1917)

The declaration, issued by the British government on November 2, 1917, took the form of a letter from Arthur James Balfour, the foreign secretary, to Lord Rothschild, a prominent British Zionist leader. Substantial effort by the Zionist organization, with a special role played by Chaim Weizmann, preceded the government's decision, after lengthy discussion and some division. The declaration was vague and sought to assuage the concerns and fears of prominent Jews in England as well as those of the non-Jewish inhabitants of Palestine. Nevertheless, it engendered much controversy, then and since. Among the problems was the Balfour Declaration's apparent conflict with arrangements made by the British with the French in the Sykes-Picot Agreement and with the Arabs primarily in the Hussein-McMahon Correspondence concerning the future of the Middle East after the termination of hostilities. The declaration provided a basis for Zionist claims to Palestine.

I have much pleasure in conveying to you, on behalf of His Majesty's Government, the following declaration of sympathy with Jewish Zionist aspirations which has been submitted to, and approved by, the Cabinet:

"His majesty's government view with favour the establishment in Palestine of a national home for the Jewish people, and will use their best endeavours to facilitate the achievement of this object, it being clearly understood that nothing shall be done which may prejudice the civil and religious rights of existing non-Jewish communities in Palestine, or the rights and political status enjoyed by Jews in any other country."

I should be grateful if you would bring this declaration to the knowledge of the Zionist Federation.

FEISAL-WEIZMANN AGREEMENT (JANUARY 3, 1919)

Chaim Weizmann went to Aqaba in May 1918 to meet Feisal ibn Hussein and to seek closer cooperation between the Zionists and the Arabs under the leadership of Sherif Hussein and his son Feisal. Feisal assured Weizmann of his good will toward Zionist aspirations and attributed past misunderstandings between the Arabs and the Jews to the machinations of the Ottoman Turks. On a number of subsequent occasions Feisal claimed that he shared Weizmann's objectives. These exchanges of sentiment and perspective were formalized in a document signed on January 3, 1919 in which Feisal and Weizmann pledged to work with each other to achieve the goals of both the Zionists and the Arabs. Feisal renounced any claim to Palestine which would become the territory of the Jews and would be separate from the new Arab state. He appended a statement that this agreement would be valid only if the Arabs obtained their independence as formulated by him in an earlier memorandum for the British. Relations between the two deteriorated thereafter and effectively ended by the end of the year.

His Royal Highness the Emir Feisal, representing and acting on behalf of the Arab Kingdom of Hedjaz, and Dr. Chaim Weizmann, representing and acting on behalf of the Zionist Organization, mindful of the racial kinship and ancient bonds existing between the Arabs and the Jewish people, and realising that the surest means of working out the consummation of their natural aspirations is through the closest possible collaboration in the development of the Arab State and Palestine, and being desirous further of confirming the good understanding which exists between them, have agreed upon the following Articles: --

Article I. The Arab State and Palestine in all their relations and undertakings shall be controlled by the most cordial goodwill and understanding, and to this end Arab and Jewish duly accredited agents shall be established and maintained in the respective territories.

Article II. Immediately following the completion of the deliberations of the Peace Conference, the definite boundaries between the Arab State and Palestine shall be determined by a Commission to be agreed upon by the parties hereto.

Article III. In the establishment of the Constitution and Administration of Palestine all such measures shall be adopted as will afford the fullest guarantees for carrying into effect the British Government's Declaration of the 2nd of November, 1917.

Article IV. All necessary measures shall be taken to encourage and stimulate immigration of Jews into Palestine on a large scale, and as quickly as possible to settle Jewish immigrants upon the land through closer settlement and intensive cultivation of the soil. In taking such measures the Arab peasant and tenant farmers shall be protected in their rights, and shall be assisted in forwarding their economic development.

Article V. No regulation or law shall be made prohibiting or interfering in any way with the free exercise of religion; and further, the free exercise and enjoyment of religious profession and worship, without discrimination or preference, shall forever be allowed. No religious test shall ever be required for the exercise of civil or political rights.

Article VI. The Mohammedan Holy Places shall be under Mohammedan control.

Article VII. The Zionist Organisation proposes to send to Palestine a Commission of experts to make a survey of the economic possibilities of the country, and to report upon the best means for its development. The Zionist Organisation will place the aforementioned Commission at the disposal of the Arab State for the purpose of a survey of the economic possibilities of the Arab State and to report upon the best means for its development. The Zionist Organisation will use its best efforts to assist the Arab State in providing the means for developing the natural resources and economic possibilities thereof.

Article VIII. The parties hereto agree to act in complete accord and harmony on all matters embraced herein before the Peace Congress.

Article IX. Any matters of dispute which may arise between the contracting parties shall be referred to the British Government for arbitration.

Given under our hand at London, England, the third day of January, one thousand nine hundred and nineteen.

Reservation by the Emir Feisal:

If the Arabs are established as I have asked in my manifesto of 4 January, addressed to the British Secretary of State for Foreign Affairs, I will carry out what is written in this agreement. If changes are made, I cannot be answerable for failing to carry out this agreement.

CHURCHILL WHITE PAPER (JULY 1, 1922)

The Churchill White Paper is an official British statement of policy regarding the geographical boundaries of Palestine and the idea of "a Jewish National Home in Palestine as contained in the Balfour Declaration." It was published by the British government on July 1, 1922, was accepted on July 6 by the House of Commons, and by the Council of the League of Nations on September 29, 1922. The phrase, "a Jewish National Home in Palestine," as used in the 1917 Balfour Declaration was vague and since the League of Nations was in the process of assigning Palestine as a mandated territory to Great Britain and since the Balfour Declaration was in contradiction of promises made by McMahon to Sherif Hussein regarding the future of Palestine, a clarification of British policy was necessary.

The Zionists, although unhappy with the new restrictions on the Jewish National Home, accepted the White Paper because it ultimately guaranteed them a role in the Mandate of Palestine. The Arabs rejected it because it gave the Zionists assurances of a future in Palestine and deprived them of their positions west of the Jordan River.

The Secretary of State for the Colonies has given renewed consideration to the existing political situation in Palestine, with a very earnest desire to arrive at a settlement of the outstanding questions which have given rise to uncertainty and unrest among certain sections of the population. After consultation with the High Commissioner for Palestine the following statement has been drawn up. It summarises the essential parts of the correspondence that has already taken place between the Secretary of State and a Delegation from the Moslem Christian Society of Palestine, which has been for some time in England, and it states the further conclusions which have since been reached.

The tension which has prevailed from time to time in Palestine is mainly due to apprehensions, which are entertained both by sections of the Arab and by sections of the Jewish population. These apprehensions, so far as the Arabs are concerned, are partly based upon exaggerated interpretations of the meaning of the Declaration favouring the establishment of a Jewish National Home in Palestine, made on behalf of His Majesty's Government on 2nd November, 1917. Unauthorised statements have been made to the effect that the purpose in view is to create wholly Jewish Palestine. Phrases have been used such as that Palestine is to become "as Jewish as England is English." His Majesty's Government regard any such expectation as impracticable and have no such aim in view. Nor have they at any time contemplated, as appears to be feared by the Arab Delegation, the disappearance or the subordination of the Arabic population, language or culture in Palestine. They would draw attention to the fact that the terms of the Declaration referred to do not contemplate that Palestine as a whole should be converted into a Jewish National Home, but that such a Home should be founded *in Palestine.* In this connection it has been observed with satisfaction that at the meeting of the Zionist Congress, the supreme governing body of the Zionist Organisation, held at Carlsbad in September, 1921, a resolution was passed expressing as the official statement of Zionist aims "the determination of the Jewish people to live with the Arab people on terms of unity and mutual respect, and together with them to make the common home into a flourishing community, the upbuilding of which may assure to each of its peoples an undisturbed national development."

It is also necessary to point out that the Zionist Commission in Palestine, now termed the Palestine Zionist Executive, has not desired to possess, and does not possess, any share in the general administration to possess, and does not possess, any share in the general administration of the country. Nor does the special position assigned to the Zionist Organisation in Article IV of the Draft Mandate for Palestine imply any such functions. That special position relates to the measures to be taken in Palestine affecting the Jewish population, and contemplates that the Organisation may assist in the general development of the country, but does not entitle it to share in any degree in its Government.

Further, it is contemplated that the status of all citizens of Palestine in the eyes of the law shall be Palestinian, and it has never been intended that they, or any section of them, should posses any other juridical status.

So far as the Jewish population of Palestine are concerned, it appears that some among them are apprehensive that His Majesty's Government may depart from the policy embodied in the Declaration of 1917. It is necessary, therefore, once more to affirm that these fears are unfounded, and that that Declaration, re-affirmed by the Conference of the Principal Allied Powers at San Remo and again in the Treaty of Sèvres, is not susceptible of change.

During the last two or three generations the Jews have created in Palestine a community, now numbering 80,000, of whom about one-fourth are farmers or workers upon the land. This community has its own political organs; an elected assembly for the direction of its domestic concerns; elected councils in the towns; and an organisation for the control of its schools. It has its elected Chief Rabbinate and Rabbinical Council for the direction of its religious affairs. Its

tion has transferred to a Supreme Council elected by the Moslem community of Palestine the entire control of Moslem religious endowments (Wakfs), and of the Moslem religious Courts. To this Council the Administration has also voluntarily restored considerable revenues derived from ancient endowments which has been sequestrated by the Turkish Government. The Education Department is also advised by a committee representative of all sections of the population, and the Department of Commerce and Industry has the benefit of the co-operation of the Chambers of Commerce which have been established in the principal centres. It is the intention of the Administration to associate in an increased degree similar representative committees with the various Departments of the Government.

The Secretary of State believes that a policy upon these lines, coupled with the maintenance of the fullest religious liberty in Palestine and with the scrupulous regard for the rights of each community with reference to its Holy Places, cannot but commend itself to the various sections of the population, and that upon this basis may be built up that spirit of co-operation upon which the future progress and prosperity of the Holy Land must largely depend.

PALESTINE MANDATE (JULY 24, 1922)

At the end of World War I the great powers dismantled the Ottoman Empire. Great Britain was granted control over Palestine under the League of Nations Mandate System and retained control of the territory from 1922 to 1948. Its mandatory obligations were to promote those conditions which would enable the indigenous population to achieve self-government. The Mandate was formulated with Zionist interests in view: among other items it included the text of the Balfour Declaration.

The Council of the League of Nations:

Whereas the Principal Allied Powers have agreed, for the purpose of giving effect to the provisions of Article 22 of the Covenant of the League of Nations, to entrust to a Mandatory selected by the said Powers the administration of the territory of Palestine, which formerly belonged to the Turkish Empire, within such boundaries as may be fixed by them; and

Whereas the Principal Allied Powers have also agreed that the Mandatory should be responsible for putting into effect the declaration originally made on November 2nd, 1917, by the establishment in Palestine of a national home for the Jewish people, it being clearly understood that nothing should be done which might prejudice the civil and religious rights of existing non-Jewish communities in Palestine, or the rights and political status enjoyed by Jews in any other country; and

Whereas recognition has thereby been given to the historical connection of the Jewish people with Palestine and to the grounds for reconstituting their national home in that country; and

Whereas the Principal Allied Powers have selected His Britannic Majesty as the Mandatory for Palestine; and

Whereas the mandate in respect of Palestine has been formulated in the following terms and submitted to the Council of the League for approval; and

Whereas His Britannic Majesty has accepted the mandate in respect of Palestine and undertaken to exercise it on behalf of the League of Nations in conformity with the following provisions; and

Whereas by the aforementioned Article 22 (paragraph 8) it is provided that the degree of authority, control or administration to be exercised by the Mandatory, not having been previously agreed upon by the Members of the League, shall be explicitly defined by the Council of the League of Nations;

Confirming the said mandate, defines its terms as follows:

Article 1. The Mandatory shall have full powers of legislation and of administration, save as they may be limited by the terms of this mandate.

Article 2. The Mandatory shall be responsible for placing the country under such political, administrative and economic conditions as will secure the establishment of the Jewish national home, as laid down in the preamble, and the development of self-governing institutions, and also for safeguarding the civil and religious rights of all the inhabitants of Palestine, irrespective of race and religion.

Article 3. The Mandatory shall, so far as circumstances permit, encourage local autonomy.

Article 4. An appropriate Jewish agency shall be recognised as a public body for the purpose of advising and co-operating with the Administration of Palestine in such economic, social and other matters as may affect the establishment of the Jewish national home and the interests of the Jewish population in Palestine, and, subject always to the control of the Administration, to assist and take part in the development of the country.

The Zionist organisation, so long as its organisation and constitution are in the opinion of the Mandatory appropriate, shall be recognised as such agency. It shall take steps in consultation with His Britannic Majesty's Government to secure the co-operation of all Jews who are willing to assist in the establishment of the Jewish national home.

Article 5. The Mandatory shall be responsible for seeing that no Palestine territory shall be ceded or leased to, or in any way placed under the control of, the Government of any foreign Power.

Article 6. The Administration of Palestine, while ensuring that the rights and position of other sections of the population are not prejudiced, shall facilitate Jewish immigration under suitable conditions and shall encourage, in co-operation with the Jewish agency referred to in Article 4, close settlement by Jews on the land, including State lands and waste lands not required for public purposes.

Article 7. The Administration of Palestine shall be responsible for enacting a nationality law. There shall be included in this law provisions framed so as to facilitate the acquisition of Palestinian citizenship by Jews who take up their permanent residence in Palestine.

Article 8. The privileges and immunities of foreigners, including the benefits of consular jurisdiction and protection as formerly enjoyed by capitulation or usage in the Ottoman Empire, shall not be applicable in Palestine.

Unless the Powers whose nationals enjoyed the afore-mentioned privileges and immunities on August 1st, 1914, shall have previously renounced the right to their re-establishment, or shall have agreed to their non-application for a specified period, these privileges and immunities shall, at the expiration of the mandate, be immediately re-established in their entirety or with such modifications as may have been agreed upon between the Powers concerned.

Article 9. The Mandatory shall be responsible for seeing that the judicial system established in Palestine shall assure to foreigners, as well as to natives, a complete guarantee of their rights.

Respect for the personal status of the various peoples and communities and for their religious interests shall be fully guaranteed. In particular, the control and administration of Wakfs shall be exercised in accordance with religious law and the dispositions of the founders.

Article 10. Pending the making of special extradition agreements relating to Palestine, the extradition treaties in force between the Mandatory and other foreign Powers shall apply to Palestine.

Article 11. The Administration of Palestine shall take all necessary measures to safeguard the interests of the community in connection with the development of the country, and, subject to any international obligations accepted by the Mandatory, shall have full power to provide for public ownership or control of any of the natural resources of the country or of the public works, services and utilities established or to be established therein. It shall introduce a land system appropriate to the needs of the country, having regard, among other things, to the desirability of promoting the close settlement and intensive cultivation of the land.

The Administration may arrange with the Jewish agency mentioned in Article 4 to construct or operate, upon fair and equitable terms, any public works, services and utilities, and to develop any of the natural resources of the country, in so far as these matters are not directly undertaken by the Administration. Any such arrangements shall provide that no profits distributed by such agency, directly or indirectly, shall exceed a reasonable rate of interest on the capital, and any further profits shall be utilised by it for the benefit of the country in a manner approved by the Administration.

Article 12. The Mandatory shall be entrusted with the control of the foreign relations of Palestine and the right to issue exequaturs to consuls appointed by foreign Powers. He shall also be entitled to afford diplomatic and consular protection to citizens of Palestine when outside its territorial limits.

Article 13. All responsibility in connection with the Holy Places and religious buildings or sites in Palestine, including that of preserving existing rights and of securing free access to the Holy Places, religious buildings and sites and the free exercise of worship, while ensuring the requirements of public order and decorum, is assumed by the Mandatory, who shall be responsible solely to the League of Nations in all matters connected herewith, provided that nothing in this article shall prevent the Mandatory from entering into such arrangements as he may deem reasonable with the Administration for the purpose of carrying the provisions of this article into effect; and provided also that nothing in this mandate shall be construed as conferring upon the Mandatory authority to interfere with the fabric or the management of purely Moslem sacred shrines, the immunities of which are guaranteed.

Article 14. A special Commission shall be appointed by the Mandatory to study, define and determine the rights and claims in connection with the Holy Places and the rights and claims relating to the different religious communities in Palestine. The method of nomination, the composition and the functions of this Commission shall be submitted to the Council of the League for its approval, and the Commission shall not be appointed or enter upon its functions without the approval of the Council.

Article 15. The Mandatory shall see that complete freedom of conscience and the free exercise of all forms of worship, subject only to the maintenance of public order and morals, are ensured to all. No discrimination of any kind shall be made between the inhabitants of Palestine on the ground of race, religion or language. No person shall be excluded from Palestine on the sole ground of his religious belief.

The right of each community to maintain its own schools for the education of its own members in its own language, while conforming to such educational requirements of a general nature as the Administration may impose, shall not be denied or impaired.

Article 16. The Mandatory shall be responsible for exercising such supervision over religious or eleemosynary bodies of all faiths in Palestine as may be required for the maintenance of public order and good government. Subject to such supervision, no measures shall be taken in Palestine to obstruct or interfere with the enterprise of such bodies or to discriminate against any representative or member of them on the ground of his religion or nationality.

Article 17. The Administration of Palestine may organise on a voluntary basis the forces necessary for the preservation of peace and order, and also for the defence of the country, subject, however, to the supervision of the Mandatory, but shall not use them for purposes other than those above specified save with the consent of the Mandatory. Except for such purposes, no military, naval or air forces shall be raised or maintained by the Administration of Palestine

Nothing in this article shall preclude the Administration of Palestine from contributing to the cost of the maintenance of the forces of the Mandatory in Palestine.

The Mandatory shall be entitled at all times to use the roads, railways and ports of Palestine for the movement of armed forces and the carriage of fuel and supplies.

Article 18. The Mandatory shall see that there is no discrimination in Palestine against the nationals of any State Member of the League of Nations (including companies incorporated under its laws) as compared with those of the Mandatory or of any foreign State in matters concerning taxation, commerce or navigation, the exercise of industries or professions, or in the treatment of merchant vessels or civil aircraft. Similarly, there shall be no discrimination in Palestine against goods originating in or destined for any of the said States, and there shall be freedom of transit under equitable conditions across the mandated area.

Subject as aforesaid and to the other provisions of this mandate, the Administration of Palestine may, on the advice of the Mandatory, impose such taxes and Customs duties as it may consider necessary, and take such steps as it may think best to promote the development of the natural resources of the country and to safeguard the interests of the population. It may also, on the advice of the Mandatory, conclude a special Customs agreement with any State the territory of which in 1914 was wholly included in Asiatic Turkey or Arabia.

Article 19. The Mandatory shall adhere on behalf of the Administration of Palestine to any general international conventions already existing, or which may be concluded hereafter with the approval of the League of Nations, respecting the slave traffic, the traffic in arms and ammunition, or the traffic in drugs, or relating to commercial equality, freedom of transit and navigation, aerial navigation and postal, telegraphic and wireless communication or literary, artistic or industrial property.

Article 20. The Mandatory shall co-operate on behalf of the Administration of Palestine, so far as religious, social and other conditions may permit, in the execution of any common policy adopted by the League of Nations for preventing and combating disease, including diseases of plants and animals.

Article 21. The Mandatory shall secure the enactment within twelve months from this date, and shall ensure the execution of a Law of Antiquities based on the following rules. This law shall ensure equality of treatment in the matter of excavations and archaeological research to the nations of all States Members of the League of Nations. 1. "Antiquity" means any construction or any product of human activity earlier than the year 1700 P.D. 2. The Law for the protection of antiquities shall proceed by encouragement rather than by threat.

Any person who, having discovered an antiquity without being furnished with the authorisation referred to in paragraph 5, reports the same to an official of the competent Department, shall be rewarded to the value of the discovery.

3. No antiquity may be disposed of except to the competent Department, unless this Department renounces the acquisition of any such antiquity.

No antiquity may leave the country without an export license from the said Department. 4. Any person who maliciously or negligently destroys or damages an antiquity shall be liable to a penalty to be fixed. 5. No clearing of ground or digging with the object of finding antiquities shall be permitted, under penalty of fine, except to persons authorised by the competent Department. 6. Equitable terms shall be fixed for expropriation, temporary or permanent, of lands which might be of historical or archaeological interest. 7. Authorisation to excavate shall only be granted to persons who show sufficient guarantees or archaeological experience. The Administration of Palestine shall not, in granting these authorisations, act in such a way as to exclude scholars of any nation without good grounds. 8. The proceeds of excavations may be divided between the excavator and the competent Department in a proportion fixed by that Department. If division seems impossible for scientific reasons, the excavator shall receive a fair indemnity in lieu of a part of the find.

Article 22. English, Arabic and Hebrew shall be the official languages of Palestine. Any statement or inscription in Arabic on stamps or money in Palestine shall be repeated in Hebrew and any statement or inscription in Hebrew shall be repeated in Arabic.

Article 23. The Administration of Palestine shall recognise the holy days of the respective communities in Palestine as legal days of rest for the members of such communities.

Article 24. The mandatory shall make to the Council of the League of Nations an annual report to the satisfaction of the Council as to the measures taken during the year to carry out the provisions of the mandate. Copies of all laws and regulations promulgated or issued during the year to carry out the provisions of the mandate. Copies of all laws and regulations promulgated or issued during the year shall be communicated with the report.

Article 25. In the territories lying between the Jordan and the eastern boundary of Palestine as ultimately determined, the Mandatory shall be entitled, with the consent of the Council of the League of Nations, to postpone or withhold application of such provisions of this mandate as he may consider inapplicable to the existing local conditions, and to make such provision for the administration of the territories as he may consider suitable to those conditions, provided that no action shall be taken which is inconsistent with the provisions of Articles 15, 16 and 18.

Article 26. The Mandatory agrees that, if any dispute whatever should arise between the Mandatory and another Member of the League of Nations relating to the interpretation or the application of the provisions of the mandate, such dispute, if it cannot be settled by negotiations, shall be submitted to the Permanent Court of International Justice provided for by Article 14 of the Covenant of the League of Nations.

Article 27. The consent of the Council of the League of Nations is required for any modification of the terms of this mandate.

Article 28. In the event of the termination of the mandate hereby conferred upon the Mandatory, the Council of the League of Nations shall make such arrangements as may be deemed necessary for safeguarding in perpetuity, under guarantee of the League, the rights secured by Articles 13 and 14, and shall use its influence for securing, under the guarantee of the League, that the Government of Palestine will fully honour the financial obligations legitimately incurred by the Administration of Palestine during the period of the mandate, including the rights of public servants to pensions or gratuities.

The present instrument shall be deposited in original in the archives of the League of Nations and certified copies shall be forwarded by the Secretary-General of the League of Nations to all Members of the League.

Done at London the twenty-fourth day of July, one thousand nine hundred and twenty-two.

PUBLIC RESOLUTION NO. 73, 67TH CONGRESS, SECOND SESSION (SEPTEMBER 21, 1922)

In its earliest years the United States was not active in the politics and diplomacy of the Middle East. Throughout much of the period prior to World War I, and even later, American interests and involvement in the area were primarily private in nature, focusing on non-political activities.

This American involvement was expanded by the beginning of the twentieth century when the United States, inaugurating its role as a power concerned with international developments, altered its approach to a number of areas and issues, including the Middle East. Despite its role in World War I and in the creation of the League of Nations, the United States had little knowledge of, and participation in, the events and agreements that later had a significant effect on the future of the Arab-Israeli conflict such as the Hussein-McMahon correspondence, the Sykes-Picot Agreement, and the Balfour Declaration. Eventually, however, President Woodrow Wilson endorsed the Balfour Declaration. He also sent an investigating commission (King-Crane) to the region to elucidate local opinion and report its findings, although its report had no meaningful effect. The United States reverted to a position of political-diplomatic nonparticipation by the 1920s. Nevertheless, in 1922 the Congress unanimously approved a joint resolution endorsing the Balfour Declaration that had originally been introduced in the Senate by Senator Henry Cabot Lodge and in the House by Congressman Hamilton Fish.

Resolved by the Senate and House of Representatives of the United States of America in Congress Assembled.

That the United States of America favors the establishment in Palestine of a national home for the Jewish people, it being clearly understood that nothing shall be done which may prejudice the civil and religious rights of Christian and all other non-Jewish communities in Palestine, and that the holy places and religious buildings and sites in Palestine shall be adequately protected.

BRITISH POLICY IN PALESTINE (1922-1939)

For several years after the establishment of the Mandate, Palestine was relatively calm. In 1928 and 1929 there were disturbances and riots associated with the Wailing Wall, and Jews were killed in Jerusalem, Hebron and Safed, with more injured there and elsewhere. The British government established a commission of inquiry in September 1929 headed by Sir Walter Shaw to investigate the cause of the anti-Jewish riots and to suggest policies that might prevent such occurrences in the future. The Shaw Commission report (March 1930) suggested that the disturbances resulted from Arab fears of Jewish domination of Palestine through Zionist immigration and land purchases. It recommended that the British government issue a clear statement of policy on the meaning of the Mandate provisions that were intended to provide for the rights of the non-Jewish populations and that it provide explicit policy on issues such as land tenure and immigration, the latter with the goal of preventing a repeat of the "excessive immigration of 1925-1926." The report also called for a special commission to determine the rights of Arabs and Jews with regard to the Wailing Wall. The government appointed a new commission under Sir John Hope-Simpson to focus on the economic dimension of the land and immigration questions.

The Hope-Simpson Report was submitted to the British government in August 1930 and was published at the same time as the Passfield White Paper in October 1930. Concerned with the economic and social plight of the Palestinian Arabs noted in the Shaw Report, Sir John Hope-Simpson examined the questions of immigration, land settlement and development. His report, as characterized in the Passfield White Paper, stated that "at the present time and with the present methods of Arab cultivation there remains no margin of land available for agricultural settlement by new immigrants, with the exception of such undeveloped land as the various Jewish agencies hold in reserve." The Hope-Simpson Report called for the coordination of Jewish immigration with unemployment figures in Palestine. "The economic capacity of the country to absorb new immigrants must therefore be judged with reference to the position of Palestine as a whole in regard to unemployment." The Report called for the suspension of Jewish Immigration Certificates to Palestine. The analysis and recommendations of the John Hope-Simpson Report were incorporated into the Passfield White Paper.

The Ramsay MacDonald government's Colonial Secretary, Sidney Webb (Lord

Passfield), was strongly anti-Zionist. On October 21, 1930, he issued a statement of policy on Palestine which reinterpreted the Balfour Declaration in light of available land for cultivation in Palestine and criticized the colonization policies and immigration practices of the Histadrut (Jewish labor federation) that focused on Jewish labor. The White Paper suggested that increased Jewish immigration would leave the Arabs landless. Parliament debated the policy on November 18, 1930 and MacDonald's government was subjected to intense criticism. Its recommendations aroused a great furor among the Zionists. The MacDonald cabinet was shaken. In a letter sent by the Prime Minister to Chaim Weizmann, and read on the floor of the Commons by MacDonald on February 13, 1931, he confirmed the British government's desire to encourage Jewish settlement in Palestine, and noted that such immigration could take place without endangering the rights of the Arab population. In effect he repudiated the Passfield White Paper.

For several years afterward Palestine remained relatively calm.

In November 1935, the Arabs in Palestine petitioned the British Mandatory authorities to halt land transfers to the Jews, to establish a form of democratic leadership, and to terminate further Jewish immigration until there was an evaluation of the absorptive capacity of the country. Their demands were rejected and, in April 1936, the Arab Higher Committee called for a general strike. The Arab revolt soon escalated into violence as marauding bands of Arabs attacked Jewish settlements and Jewish groups responded. After appeals from Arab leaders in the surrounding states, the committee called off the strike in October 1936.

The British government appointed a commission under Lord Robert Peel to assess the situation, to determine the causes of, and to find a solution for, the Arab revolt. It began its hearings in Jerusalem in November 1936. Discouraged and distrustful of previous British promises, the Arabs of Palestine boycotted them. They did not appear until its last week and then only because they had been persuaded to do so by the rulers in the neighboring Arab states.

The Peel report, published as a White Paper in July 1937, noted that the British gained the support of both the Arabs and Jews during World War I and in return made promises to each. Although the British had believed that both Arabs and Jews could find a degree of compatibility under the Mandate, this belief had not been justified nor would it be in the future. However, Britain would not renounce its obligations; it was responsible for the welfare of the Mandate and would strive to make peace. "In the light of experience and of the arguments adduced by the Commission [His Majesty's Government] are driven to the conclusions that there is an irreconcilable conflict between the aspirations of Arabs and Jews in Palestine, that these aspirations cannot be satisfied under the terms of the present Mandate, and that a scheme of partition on the general lines recommended by the Commission represents the best and most hopeful solution to the deadlock."

Cantonization was examined as a possible solution and found wanting because it would not resolve the matter of self-government. The Commission suggested partition with Palestine divided into three zones -- the Jewish zone, the Arab section, and a corridor from Tel Aviv-Jaffa to Jerusalem and Bethlehem that would continue under a British Mandate. The protection of the Holy Places were to be guaranteed by the League of Nations. The drawbacks of partition would be outweighed by the advantages of peace and security. The Mandate would be replaced by a treaty system identical to that of Iraq and Syria. The guiding principle was the separation of Jewish areas of settlement from those completely or mostly occupied by the Arabs. The plan was a reversal of British policy on both the Mandate and the Balfour Declaration and engendered protests from the Arabs and the Zionists. The Arabs did not want to have to give up any land to the Jews, and the Zionists felt betrayed in their pursuit of all of Palestine as a National Home. Britain endorsed the Peel plan. After reviewing report in July/August 1937, the League of Nation's Permanent Mandates Commission in Geneva objected to the partition. The Jewish Agency accepted the plan even though it was not happy with the exclusion of Jerusalem and with the amount of territory allotted to the Jewish state. The Arabs rejected the plan and a new and more violent phase of the Arab revolt began.

In December 1937 the British government appointed a four member technical commission to investigate the feasibility of the recommendations. Headed by Sir John Woodhead, the Commission arrived in Palestine in April 1938. It was subjected to pressures from within the British government. The Colonial Office contended that the British had to demonstrate resolve not to succumb to the pressures of terrorist threats and any policy statement should help moderate Arab leadership. Furthermore, Britain had a responsibility to maintain its promises to the Jews. The Foreign Office, however, contended that a pro-Zionist policy would increase Arab support for the Axis powers. The commission's report was published in October 1938. It held that the Peel Commission's proposals were not feasible -- primarily because they would leave a large Arab minority within the boundaries of a Jewish state, which also would be surrounded by other Arab states. The commission offered two alternative proposals for partition. One would have reduced the size of the Jewish state by annexing an area south of Jerusalem to the Arab state and including Galilee in a mandatory territory. The second alternative would have left a Jewish state as a coastal strip. Because the commission could not reach agreement, it stated that it could not recommend boundaries for states created from the mandatory territory. It concluded that there were no feasible boundaries for self-supporting Arab and Jewish states in Palestine. Nevertheless, it suggested a number of partition plans. The government issued a White Paper on November 9, 1938 noting that partition was impracticable: "His Majesty's Government ... have reached the conclusion that ... the political, administrative and financial difficulties involved in the proposal to create independent Arab and Jewish States inside Palestine are so great that this solution of the problem is impracticable."

On February 7, 1939 the British Government convened the St. James

Conference in London to see if a solution could be developed through negotiations with the Arabs and the Jews. The failure of the conference led to a White Paper of May 17, 1939, that called for severe restrictions on Jewish immigration, while it acknowledged the Woodhead Commission's findings that the partition of Palestine was not feasible. "His Majesty's Government believe that the framers of the Mandate in which the Balfour Declaration was embodied could not have intended that Palestine should be converted into a Jewish State against the will of the Arab population of the country." It called therefore for the establishment of a Jewish National Home in an independent Palestinian state. Jewish immigration would be restricted, as would be land transfers. The White Paper foresaw an independent Palestinian state within 10 years. Both the Arabs and the Jews rejected the White Paper. The House of Commons debated the White Paper on May 22, 1939 and it was approved by a vote of 268 to 179. The House of Lords also approved it. There was outrage in both Arab and Jewish communities. The Arabs wanted an immediate end to all Jewish immigration and the review of all immigrants who had entered Palestine since 1918. The Zionists felt that the British had backed away from previous agreements to work toward a Jewish homeland and that this policy as a breach of faith. Peace in Palestine seemed improbable.

PEEL WHITE PAPER (JUNE 22, 1937)

The Force of Circumstances. ...

2. Under the stress of the World War the British Government made promises to Arab and Jews in order to obtain their support. On the strength of those promises both parties formed certain expectations.

3. The application to Palestine of the Mandate System in general and of the specific Mandate in particular implied the belief that the obligations thus undertaken towards the Arabs and the Jews respectively would prove in course of time to be mutually compatible owing to the conciliatory effect on the Palestinian Arabs of the material prosperity which Jewish immigration would bring to Palestine as a whole. That belief has not been justified, and we see no hope of its being justified in the future.

4. On that account it might conceivably be argued that Britain is now entitled to renounce its obligations. But we have no doubt that the British people would repudiate any such suggestion. ... We are responsible for the welfare of the country. Its government is in our hands. We are bound to strive to the utmost to do justice and make peace.

5. What are the existing circumstances? An irrepressible conflict has arisen between two national communities within the narrow bounds of one small country. About 1,000,000 Arabs are in strife, open or latent, with some 400,000 Jews. There is no common ground between them. The Arab community is

predominantly Asiatic in character, the Jewish community predominantly European. They differ in religion and in language. Their cultural and social life, their ways of thought and conduct, are as incompatible as their national aspirations. ... The War and its sequel have inspired all Arabs with the hope of reviving in a free and united Arab world the traditions of the Arab golden age. The Jews similarly are inspired by their historic past. They mean to show what the Jewish nation can achieve when restored to the land of its birth. ...

6. This conflict was inherent in the situation from the outset. ...

7. The conflict has grown steadily more bitter. It has been marked by a series of five Arab outbreaks, culminating in the rebellion of last year. ...

8. This intensification of the conflict will continue. ...

9. The conflict is primarily political, though the fear of economic subjection to the Jews is also in Arab minds. ...

10. Meanwhile the "external factors" will continue to play the part they have played with steadily increasing force from the beginning. On the one hand, Saudi Arabia, the Yemen, 'Iraq and Egypt are already recognized as sovereign states, and Trans-Jordan as an "independent government." In less than three years' time Syria and the Lebanon will attain their national sovereignty. The claim of the Palestinian Arabs to share in the freedom of the Asiatic Arabia will thus be reinforced. ...

11. On the other hand, the hardships and anxieties of the Jews in Europe are not likely to grow less in the near future. The pressure on Palestine will continue and might at any time be accentuated. ... The Mandatory will be urged unceasingly to admit as many Jews into Palestine as the National Home can provide with a livelihood and to protect them when admitted from Arab attacks.

12. Thus, for internal and external reasons, it seems probable that the situation, bad as it now is, will grow worse. The conflict will go on, the gulf between Arabs and Jews will widen. ...

14. In these circumstances, we are convinced that peace, order and good government can only be maintained in Palestine for any length of time by a rigorous system of repression. ... The lesson is plain, and nobody, we think, will now venture to assert that the existing system offers any real prospect of reconciliation between the Arabs and the Jews. ...

17. ... To put it in one sentence, we cannot -- in Palestine as it now is -- both concede the Arab claim to self-government and secure the establishment of the Jewish National Home. ...

19. Manifestly the problem cannot be solved by giving either the Arabs or the Jews all they want. The answer to the question "Which of them in the end will govern Palestine?" must surely be "Neither". ... But, while neither race can justly rule all Palestine, we see no reason why, if it were practicable, each race should not rule part of it.

20. No doubt the idea of Partition as a solution of the problem has often occurred to students of it, only to be discarded. There are many who would have

felt an instinctive dislike to cutting up the Holy Land. The severance of Trans-Jordan, they would have thought, from historic Palestine was bad enough. ...

Cantonisation.

1. The political division of Palestine could be effected in a less final and thorough-going manner than by Partition. It could be divided as federal States are divided into provinces or cantons; and this method has been so often mentioned and so ably advocated under the name of "Cantonisation" as a means of solving the Palestine problem that it is incumbent on us to discuss it before setting out the plan for Partition which we ourselves have to propose. ...

A Plan of Partition.

1. We return, then, to Partition as the only method we are able to propose for dealing with the root of the trouble.

2. ... we feel justified in recommending that Your Majesty's Government should take the appropriate steps for the termination of the present Mandate on the basis of Partition.

3. ... There seem to us to be three essential features of such a [partition] plan. It must be practicable. It must conform to our obligations. It must do justice to the Arabs and the Jews.

1. A Treaty System.

4. The Mandate for Palestine should terminate and be replaced by a Treaty System in accordance with the precedent set in Iraq and Syria.

5. A new Mandate for the Holy Places should be instituted ...

6. Treaties of Alliance should be negotiated by the Mandatory with the Government of Trans-Jordan and representatives of the Arabs of Palestine on the one hand and with the Zionist Organisation on the other. These Treaties would declare that within as short a period as may be convenient, two sovereign independent States would be established -- the one an Arab State, consisting of Trans-Jordan united with that part of Palestine which lies to the east and south of a frontier such as we suggest in Section 3 below; the other a Jewish State consisting of that part of Palestine which lies to the north and west of that frontier.

7. The Mandatory would undertake to support any requests for admission to the League of Nations which the Governments of the Arab and the Jewish States might make in accordance with Article I of the Covenant.

8. The Treaties would include strict guarantees for the protection of minorities in each State, and the financial and other provisions to which reference will be made in subsequent Sections.

9. Military Conventions would be attached to the Treaties, dealing with the maintenance of naval, military and air forces, the upkeep and use of ports, roads and railways, the security of the oil pipe line and so forth.

2. The Holy Places.

10. The partition of Palestine is subject to the overriding necessity of keeping the sanctity of Jerusalem and Bethlehem inviolate and of ensuring free and safe access to them for all the world. That, in the fullest sense of the mandatory phrase, is "a sacred trust of civilization" -- a trust on behalf not merely of the peoples of Palestine but of multitudes in other lands to whom those places, one or both, are Holy Places.

11. A new Mandate, therefore, should be framed with the execution of this trust as its primary purpose. An enclave should be demarcated extending from a point north of Jerusalem to a point south of Bethlehem, and access to the sea should be provided by a corridor extending to the north of the main road and to the south of the railway, including the towns of Lydda and Ramle, and terminating at Jaffa.

12. We regard the protection of the Holy Places as a permanent trust, unique in its character and purpose, and not contemplated by Article 22 of the Covenant of the League of Nations. ...

13. Guarantees as to the rights of the Holy Places and free access thereto (as provided in Article 13 of the existing Mandate), as to transit across the mandated area, and as to non-discrimination in fiscal, economic and other matters should be maintained in accordance with the principles of the Mandate System. ...

14. We think it would accord with Christian sentiment in the world at large if Nazareth and the Sea of Galilee (Lake Tiberias) were also covered by this Mandate. ...

15. The Mandatory should similarly be charged with the protection of religious endowments and of such buildings, monuments and places in the Arab and Jewish States as are sacred to the Jews and the Arabs respectively. ...

3. The Frontier.

17. The natural principle for the Partition of Palestine is to separate the areas in which the Jews have acquired land and settled from those which are wholly or mainly occupied by Arabs. ... the Jewish lands and colonies are mostly to be found in the Maritime Plain between Al Majdal and Mount Carmel, in the neighbourhood of Haifa, in the Plain of Esdraelon and the Valley of Jezreel, and in the east of Galilee, i.e., south of Tiberias, on the shores of the Lake, near Safad, and in the Huleh Basin. The rest of Galilee and the northern part of the plain of Acre are almost wholly in Arab occupation. So also is the central hill-country of old Samaria and Judaea -- except for Jerusalem and its vicinity. The towns of Nablus, Jenin and Tulkarm, the last an outpost on the edge of the Maritime Plain, are centres of Arab nationalism. Except in and near Jerusalem and at Hebron, there are practically no Jews between Jenin and Beersheba. This Arab block extends eastwards to the River Jordan between the Dead Sea and Beisan. In the area stretching south and south-east of Beersheba to the Egyptian frontier, the Jews have bought some isolated blocks of land but the population is entirely Arab.

18. This existing separation of the area of Jewish land and settlement from that of wholly or mainly Arab occupation seems to us to offer a fair and practicable basis for Partition, provided that, in accordance with the spirit of our obligations, (1) a reasonable allowance is made within the boundaries of the Jewish State for the growth of population and colonization, and (2) reasonable compensation is given to the Arab State for the loss of land and revenue. ...

21. In terms of the present administrative divisions of Palestine, this frontier would mean the inclusion in the Jewish Area of the Sub-Districts of Acre, Safad, Tiberias, Nazareth and Haifa and parts of the Sub-Districts of Jenin, Tulkarm, the Sub-Districts of Nablus, Ramallah, Jericho, Hebron, Gaza and Beersheba, and parts of the Sub-Districts of Beisan, Jenin, Tulkarm, Jaffa, Ramle, Jerusalem and Bethlehem.

22. We make the following observations and recommendations with regard to the proposed frontier and to questions arising from it: (i) No frontier can be drawn which separates all Arabs and Arab-owned land from all Jews and Jewish-owned land. (ii) The Jews have purchased substantial blocks of land in the Gaza Plain and near Beersheba and obtained options for the purchase of other blocks in this area. The proposed frontier would prevent the utilization of those lands for the southward expansion of the Jewish National Home. On the other hand, the Jewish lands in Galilee, and in particular the Huleh basin ... would be in the Jewish Area. (iii) The proposed frontier necessitates the inclusion in the Jewish Area of the Galilee highlands between Safad and the Plain of Acre. ... At Tiberias, on the other hand (which contains 6,150 Jews and 3,550 Arabs) and at Safad (which contains 2,000 Jews and 7,900 Arabs) the outbreak of last year has led to serious friction. There has been trouble also, though not so acute, in the two other "mixed" towns in the Jewish Area -- Haifa (about 50,000 Jews and 48,000 Arabs) and Acre (8,550 Arabs and 250 Jews). We believe that it would greatly promote the successful operation of Partition in its early stages and in particular help to ensure the execution of the Treaty guarantees for the protection of minorities, if those four towns were kept for a period under Mandatory administration. (iv) Jaffa is an essentially Arab town in which the Jewish minority has recently been dwindling. We suggest that it should form part of the Arab State. ... (v) While the Mediterranean would be accessible to the Arab State at Jaffa and at Gaza, we think that in the interests of Arab trade and industry the Arab State should also have access for commercial purposes to Haifa, the only existing deep-water port on the coast. ...

4. Inter-State Subvention.

23. ... the Jews contribute more *per capita* to the revenues of Palestine than the Arabs, and the Government has thereby been enabled to maintain public services for the Arabs at a higher level than would otherwise have been possible. Partition would mean, on the one hand, that the Arab Area would no longer profit from the taxable capacity of the Jewish Area. On the other hand, (1) the

Jews would acquire a new right of sovereignty in the Jewish Area: (2) that Area, as we have defined it, would be larger than the existing area of Jewish land and settlement: (3) the Jews would be freed from their present liability for helping to promote the welfare of Arabs outside that Area. It seems to us, therefore, not unreasonable to suggest that the Jewish State should pay a subvention to the Arab State when Partition comes into effect. ...

5. British Subvention.

25. The Inter-State Subvention would adjust the financial balance in Palestine; but it must be remembered that the plan we are submitting involves the inclusion of Trans-Jordan in the Arab State. The taxable capacity of Trans-Jordan is very low and its revenues have never sufficed to meet the cost of its administration. ...

26. The Mandate for Trans-Jordan ought not in our opinion to be relinquished without securing, as far as possible, that the standard of administration should not fall too low through lack of funds to maintain it; and it is in this matter, we submit, that the British people might fairly be asked to do their part in facilitating a settlement. ... And apart from any such considerations we think that the British people, great as their financial burdens now are, would agree to a capital payment in lieu of their present annual liability, as a means towards honouring their obligations and making peace in Palestine. ...

6. Tariffs and Ports.

28. The Arab and Jewish States, being sovereign independent States, would determine their own tariffs. Subject to the terms of the Mandate, the same would apply to the Mandatory Government. ...

7. Nationality.

32. All persons domiciled in the Mandated Area (including Haifa, Tiberias, Safad, and the enclave on the Gulf of Aqaba, as long as they remain under Mandatory administration) who now possess the status of British protected persons would retain it; but apart from this all Palestinians would become the nationals of the States in which they are domiciled. ...

10. Exchange of Land and Population.

... 36. If Partition is to be effective in promoting a final settlement it must mean more than drawing a frontier and establishing two States. Sooner or later there should be a transfer of land and, as far as possible, an exchange of population. ...

39. The political aspect of the land-problem is still more important. Owing to the fact that there has been no census since 1931 it is impossible to calculate with precision the distribution of population between the proposed Arab and Jewish areas, but, according to an approximate estimate supplied to us, in the area allocated in our plan to the Jewish State (excluding the urban districts which we suggest should be retained for a period under Mandatory administration) there are now about 225,000 Arabs. In the area allotted to the Arab State there are only some 1,250 Jews: but in Jerusalem and Haifa there are about 125,000 Jews

as against 85,000 Arabs. The existence of these minorities clearly constitutes the most serious hindrance to the smooth and successful operation of Partition. ...

42. The immediate need, therefore, is for those areas to be surveyed and an authoritative estimate made of the practical possibilities of irrigation and development. This, we suggest, should be undertaken at once, and the requisite staff and funds provided for its completion in the shortest possible time. If, as a result, it is clear that a substantial amount of land could be made available for the re-settlement of Arabs living in the Jewish area, the most strenuous efforts should be made to obtain an agreement for the exchange of land and population.

... 47. Such is the plan of Partition which we submit to the consideration of Your Majesty's Government. We believe that it fulfils the essential conditions of Partition and demonstrates that, if Palestine ought to be divided, it can be divided. ...

49. The following, then, are our recommendations for the period of transition. (1) *Land.* Steps should be taken to prohibit the purchase of land by Jews within the Arab Area (i.e., the area of the projected Arab State) or by Arabs within the Jewish Area (i.e., the area of the projected Jewish State). The settlement of the plain-lands of the Jewish Area should be completed within two years. (2) *Immigration.* Instead. of the political "high-level" recommended in Chapter X, paragraph 97, there should be a territorial restriction on Jewish immigration. No Jewish immigration into the Arab Area should be permitted. Since it would therefore not affect the Arab Area and since the Jewish State would soon become responsible for its results, the volume of Jewish immigration should be determined by the economic absorptive capacity of Palestine less the Arab Area. (3) *Trade.* ... (4) *Advisory Council.* The Advisory Council should, if possible, be enlarged by the nomination of Arab and Jewish representatives; but, if either party refused to serve, the Council should continue as at present. (5) *Local Government.* ... (6) *Education.* A vigorous effort should be made to increase the number of Arab schools. ...

Conclusion.

1. "Half a loaf is better than no bread" is a peculiarly English proverb; and, considering the attitude which both the Arab and the Jewish representatives adopted in giving evidence before us, we think it improbable that either party will be satisfied at first sight with the proposals we have submitted for the adjustment of their rival claims. For Partition means that neither will get all it wants. It means that the Arabs must acquiesce in the exclusion from their sovereignty of a piece of territory, long occupied and once ruled by them. It means that the Jews must be content with less than the Land of Israel they once ruled and have hoped to rule again. But it seems to us possible that on reflection both parties will come to realize that the drawbacks of Partition are outweighed by its advantages. For, if it offers neither party all it wants, if offers each what it wants most, namely freedom and security.

2. The advantages to the Arabs of Partition on the lines we have proposed may be summarized as follows: (i) They obtain their national independence and can co-operate on an equal footing with the Arabs of the neighbouring countries in the cause of Arab unity and progress. (ii) They are finally delivered from the fear of being "swamped" by the Jews and from the possibility of ultimate subjection to Jewish rule. (iii) In particular, the final limitation of the Jewish National Home within a fixed frontier and the enactment of a new Mandate for the protection of the Holy Places, solemnly guaranteed by the League of Nations, removes all anxiety lest the Holy Places should ever come under Jewish control. (iv) As a set-off to the loss of territory the Arabs regard as their, the Arab State will receive a subvention from the Jewish State. It will also, in view of the backwardness of Trans-Jordan, obtain a grant of £2,000,000 from the British Treasury; and, if an arrangement can be made for the exchange of land and population, a further grant will be made for the conversion, as far as may prove possible, of uncultivable land in the Arab State into productive land from which the cultivators and the State alike will profit.

3. The advantages of Partition to the Jews may be summarized as follows: (i) Partition secures the establishment of the Jewish National Home and relieves it from the possibility of its being subjected in the future to Arab rule. (ii) Partition enables the Jews in the fullest sense to call their National Home their own: for it converts it into a Jewish State. Its citizens will be able to admit as many Jews into it as they themselves believe can be absorbed. They will attain the primary objective of Zionism -- a Jewish nation, planted in Palestine, giving its nationals the same status in the world as other nations give their. They will cease at last to live a "minority life."

4. To both Arabs and Jews Partition offers a prospect -- and we see no such prospect in any other policy -- of obtaining the inestimable boon of peace. ...

5. There was a time when Arab statesmen were willing to concede little Palestine to the Jews, provided that the rest of Arab Asia were free. That condition was not fulfilled then, but it is on the eve of fulfilment now. ...

6. There is no need to stress the advantage to the British people of a settlement in Palestine. We are bound to honour to the utmost of our power the obligations we undertook in the exigencies of war towards the Arabs and the Jews. ... Partition offers a possibility of finding a way through them, a possibility of obtaining a final solution of the problem which does justice to the rights and aspirations of both the Arabs and the Jews and discharges the obligations we undertook towards them twenty years ago to the fullest extent that is practicable in the circumstances of the present time.

7. Nor is it only the British people, nor only the nations which conferred the Mandate or approved it, who are troubled by what has happened and is happening in Palestine. Numberless men and women all over the world would feel a sense of deep relief if somehow an end could be put to strife and bloodshed in a thrice hallowed land.

ALL OF WHICH WE HUMBLY SUBMIT FOR YOUR MAJESTY'S GRACIOUS CONSIDERATION.

BILTMORE PROGRAM (MAY 11, 1942)

After World War I Britain was the focus of Zionist political and diplomatic endeavor. However, during and after World War II, political necessity and reality resulted in a shift to the United States. The Biltmore Program, adopted by the Extraordinary Zionist Conference at the Biltmore Hotel in New York on May 11, 1942, in response to Britain's policy toward the Jewish national home (particularly the restrictions on land sales and immigration), became the basis for Zionist effort until Israel's independence. The program called for the fulfillment of the Balfour Declaration and the mandate, urging that "Palestine be established as a Jewish Commonwealth." It reflected the urgency of the situation in which the Jewish leadership found itself as a consequence of the Holocaust and the need to provide for the displaced Jews of Europe.

1. American Zionists assembled in this Extraordinary Conference reaffirm their unequivocal devotion to the cause of democratic freedom and international justice to which the people of the United States, allied with the other United Nations, have dedicated themselves, and give expression to their faith in the ultimate victory of humanity and justice over lawlessness and brute force.

2. This Conference offers a message of hope and encouragement to their fellow Jews in the Ghettos and concentration camps of Hitler-dominated Europe and prays that their hour of liberation may not be far distant.

3. The Conference sends its warmest greetings to the Jewish Agency Executive in Jerusalem, to the Va'ad Leumi, and to the whole Yishuv in Palestine, and expresses its profound admiration for their steadfastness and achievements in the face of peril and great difficulties. The Jewish men and women in field and factory, and the thousands of Jewish soldiers of Palestine in the Near East who have acquitted themselves with honor and distinction in Greece, Ethiopia, Syria, Libya and on other battlefields, have shown themselves worthy of their people and ready to assume the rights and responsibilities of nationhood.

4. In our generation, and in particular in the course of the past twenty years, the Jewish people have awakened and transformed their ancient homeland; from 50,000 at the end of the last war their numbers have increased to more then 500,000. They have made the waste places to bear fruit and the desert to blossom. Their pioneering achievements in agriculture and in industry, embodying new patterns of cooperative endeavor, have written a notable page in the history of colonization.

5. In the new values thus created, their Arab neighbors in Palestine have shared. The Jewish people in its own work of national redemption welcomes the economic, agricultural and national development of the Arab peoples and states. The Conference reaffirms the stand previously adopted at Congresses of the World Zionist Organization, expressing the readiness and the desire of the Jewish people for full cooperation with their Arab neighbors.

6. The Conference calls for the fulfilment of the original purpose of the Balfour Declaration and the Mandate which *"recognizing the historical connection of the Jewish people with Palestine"* was to afford them the opportunity, as stated by President Wilson, to found there a Jewish Common-wealth.

The Conference affirms its unalterable rejection of the White Paper of May 1939 and denies its moral or legal validity. The White Paper seeks to limit, and in fact to nullify Jewish rights to immigration and settlement in Palestine, and, as stated by Mr. Winston Churchill in the House of Commons in May 1939, constitutes "a breach and repudiation of the Balfour Declaration." The policy of the White Paper is cruel and indefensible in its denial of sanctuary to Jews fleeing from Nazi persecution; and at a time when Palestine has become a focal point in the war front of the United Nations, and Palestine Jewry must provide all available manpower for farm and factory and camp, it is in direct conflict with the interests of the allied war effort.

7. In the struggle against the forces or aggression and tyranny, of which Jews were the earliest victims, and which now menace the Jewish National Home, recognition must be given to the right of the Jews of Palestine to play their full part in the war effort and in the defense of their country, through a Jewish military force fighting under its own flag and under the high command of the United Nations.

8. The Conference declares that the new world order that will follow victory cannot be established on foundations of peace, justice and equality, less the problem of Jewish homelessness is finally solved.

The Conference urges that the gates of Palestine be opened; that the Jewish Agency be vested with control of immigration into Palestine and with the necessary authority for upbuilding the country, including the development of its unoccupied and uncultivated lands; and that Palestine be established as a Jewish Commonwealth integrated in the structure of the new democratic world.

Then and only then will the age-old wrong to the Jewish people be righted.

LEAGUE OF ARAB STATES (MARCH 22, 1945)

The League of Arab States was founded March 22, 1945 in Alexandria, Egypt to coordinate increased Arab economic, cultural, and political unity. The Arab

League Council is the highest decision-making body, composed of the heads of member states and based on equal representation.

The formation of an Arab coordinating body had been encouraged by Britain in line with its policies to gain influence in the Near East and assistance against Germany during World War II. Anthony Eden, then Secretary of State for Foreign Affairs, in a May 22, 1941 speech at Mansion House and in comments to the House of Commons on February 24, 1943 stated British support for Arab unity. Later that year (July 31-August 5), the Prime Minister of Egypt, Nahhas Pasha, and Iraq, Nuri al-Said, met to discuss issues of federation and collaboration between Arab states. A conference in Alexandria concluded on October 10, 1944 with Egypt, Syria, Transjordan, Iraq, and Lebanon signing a protocol to establish a League of Arab states. The league would deal with common issues and strengthen inter-Arab relations. On March 22, 1945 the Charter was signed by Egypt, Iraq, Syria, Lebanon, Saudi Arabia, Transjordan, and Yemen.

The Arab League considered the Palestine issue shortly after its founding and decided to boycott "Zionist goods". The Arab League rejected (December 17, 1947) the partition plan, called for an independent Arab state in Palestine, and resolved (February 9, 1948) to prevent the birth of the Jewish state. However, competing national interests hindered military and political coordination before the 1948 war and limited the League's effectiveness during the fighting.

Article 1. The League of the Arab States is composed of the independent Arab States which have signed this pact.

Any independent Arab State has the right to become a member of the League. If it desires to do so, it shall submit a request which will be deposited with the permanent Secretariat-General and submitted to the Council at the first meeting held after submission of the request.

Article 2. The League has as its purpose the strengthening of the relations between the member states; the coordination of their policies in order to achieve cooperation between them and to safeguard their independence and sovereignty; and a general concern with the affairs and interests of the Arab countries. It has also as its purpose the close cooperation of the member states, with due regard to the organization and circumstances of each state, on the following matters: A. Economic and financial affairs, including commercial relations, customs, currency, and questions of agriculture and industry. B. Communications: this includes railroads, roads, aviation, navigation, telegraphs, and posts. C. Cultural affairs. D. Nationality, passports, visas, execution of judgments, and extradition of criminals. E. Social affairs. F. Health problems.

Article 3. The League shall possess a Council composed of the representatives of the member state of the League; each state shall have a single vote, irrespective of the number of its representatives.

It shall be the task of the Council to achieve the realization of the objectives of the League and to supervise the execution of agreements which the member states have concluded on the questions enumerated in the preceding article, or on any other questions.

It likewise shall be the Council's task to decide upon the means by which the League is to cooperate with the international bodies to be created in the future in order to guarantee security and peace and regulate economic and social relations.

Article 4. For each of the questions listed in Article 2 there shall be set up a special committee in which the member states of the League shall be represented. These committees shall be charged with the task of laying down the principles and extent of cooperation. Such principles shall be formulated as draft agreements, to be presented to the Council for examination preparatory to their submission to the aforesaid states.

Representatives of the other Arab countries may take part in the work of the aforesaid committees. The Council shall determine the conditions under which these representatives may be permitted to participate and the rules governing such representation.

Article 5. Any resort to force in order to resolve disputes arising between two or more member states of the League is prohibited. If there should arise among them a difference which does not concern a state's independence, sovereignty, or territorial integrity, and if the parties to the dispute have recourse to the Council for the settlement of the difference, the decision of the Council shall then be enforceable and obligatory.

In such a case, the states between whom the difference has arisen shall not participate in the deliberations and decisions of the Council.

The Council may lend its good offices for the settlement of all differences which threaten to lead to war between two member states, or a member state and a third state, with a view to bringing about their reconciliation.

Decisions of arbitration and mediation shall be taken by majority vote.

Article 6. In case of aggression or threat of aggression by one state against a member state, the state which has been attacked or threatened with aggression may demand the immediate convocation of the Council.

The Council shall by unanimous decision determine the measures necessary to repulse the aggression. If the aggressor is a member state, his vote shall not be counted in determining unanimity.

If, as a result of the attack, the government of the state attacked finds itself unable to communicate with the Council, that state's representative in the Council shall have the right to request the convocation of the Council for the purpose indicated in the foregoing paragraph. In the event that this representative is unable to communicate with the Council, any member state of the League shall have the right to request the convocation of the Council.

Article 7. Unanimous decisions of the Council shall be finding upon all member states of the League; majority decisions shall be binding only upon those states which have accepted them.

In either case the decisions of the Council shall be enforced in each member state according to its respective fundamental laws.

Article 8. Each member state shall respect the systems of government established in the other member states and regard them as exclusive concerns of those states. Each shall pledge to abstain from any action calculated to change established systems of government.

Article 9. States of the League which desire to establish closer cooperation and stronger bonds than are provided by this Pact may conclude agreements to that end.

Article 10. The permanent seat of the League of Arab States is established in Cairo. The Council may, however, assemble at any other place it may designate.

Article 1l. The Council of the League shall convene in ordinary session twice a year, in March and in October. It shall convene in extraordinary session upon the request of two member states of the League whenever the need arises.

Article 12. The League shall have a permanent Secretariat-General which shall consist of a Secretary-General, Assistant Secretaries, and an appropriate number of officials.

The Council of the League shall appoint the Secretary-General by a majority of two-thirds of the states of the League. The Secretary-General, with the approval of the Council, shall appoint the Assistant Secretaries and the principal officials of the League.

The Council of the League shall establish an administrative regulation for the functions of the Secretariat-General and matters relating to the staff.

The Secretary-General shall have the rank of Ambassador and the Assistant Secretaries that of Ministers Plenipotentiary.

The first Secretary-General of the League is named in an Annex to this Pact.

Article 13. The Secretary-General shall prepare the draft budget of the League and shall submit it to the Council for approval before the beginning of each fiscal year.

The Council shall fix the share of the expenses to be borne by each state of the League. This share may be reconsidered if necessary.

Article 14. The members of the Council of the League as well as the members of the committees and the officials who are to be designated in the administrative regulation shall enjoy diplomatic privileges and immunity when engaged in the exercise of their functions.

The buildings occupied by the organs of the League shall be inviolable.

Article 15. The first meeting of the Council shall be convened at the invitation of the Head of the Egyptian Government. Thereafter it shall be convened at the invitation of the Secretary-General.

The representatives of the member States of the League shall alternatively assume the Presidency of the Council at each of its ordinary sessions.

Article 16. Except in cases specifically indicated in this Pact, a majority vote of the Council shall be sufficient to make enforceable decisions on the following matters: A. Matters relating to personnel. B. Adoption of the budget of the League. C. Establishment of the administrative regulations for the Council, the committees, and the Secretariat-General. D. Decisions to adjourn the sessions.

Article 17. Each member State of the League shall deposit with the Secretariat-General one copy of every treaty or agreement concluded or to be concluded in the future between itself and another member state of the League or a third state.

Article 18. If a member state contemplates withdrawal from the League, it shall inform the Council of its intention one year before such withdrawal is to go into effect.

The Council of the League may consider any state which fails to fulfill its obligations under this Pact as having become separated from the League, this to go into effect upon a unanimous decision of the States, not counting the state concerned.

Article 19. This Pact may be amended with the consent of two thirds of the state belonging to the League, especially in order to make firmer and stronger the ties between the member states, to create an Arab Tribunal of Arbitration, and to regulate the relations of the League with any international bodies to be created in the future to guarantee security and peace.

Final action on an amendment cannot be taken prior to the session following the session in which the motion was initiated.

If a state does not accept such an amendment it may withdraw at such time as the amendment goes into effect, without being bound by the provisions of he preceding article.

Article 20. This Pact and its Annexes shall be ratified according to the basic laws in force among the High Contracting Parties.

The instruments of ratification shall be deposited with the Secretariat-General of the Council and the Pact shall become operative as regards each ratifying state fifteen days after the Secretariat-General has received the instruments of ratification from four states.

This Pact has been drawn up in Cairo in the Arabic language on the 8th day of Rabi II, thirteen hundred and sixty-four (22 March 1945), in one copy which shall be deposited in the safe keeping of the Secretariat-General.

An identical copy shall be delivered to each state of the League.

(1) *Annex Regarding Palestine.* Since the termination of the last great war the rule of the Ottoman Empire over the Arab countries, among them Palestine, which had become detached from that Empire, has come to an end. She has come to be independent in herself, not subordinate to any other state.

The Treaty of Lausanne proclaimed that her future was to be settled by the parties concerned.

However, even though she was as yet unable to control her own affairs, the Covenant of the League (of Nations) in 1919 made provision for a regime based upon recognition of her independence.

Her international existence and independence in the legal sense cannot, therefore, be questioned, any more than could the independence of the other Arab countries.

Although the outward manifestations of this independence have remained obscured for reasons beyond her control, this should not be allowed to interfere with her participation in the work of the Council of the League.

The States signatory to the Pact of the Arab League are therefore of the opinion that, considering the special circumstances of Palestine, and until that country can effectively exercise its independence, the Council of the League should take charge of the selection of an Arab representative from Palestine to take part in its work.

(2) *Annex Regarding Cooperation With Countries Which Are Not Members of the Council of the League.* Whereas the member states of the League will have to deal in the Council as well as in the committees with matters which will benefit and affect the Arab world at large:

And Whereas the Council has to take into account the aspirations of the Arab countries which are not members of the Council and has to work toward their realization;

Now therefore, it particularly behooves the states signatory to the Pact of the Arab League to enjoin the Council of the League, when considering the admission of those countries to participation in the committees referred to in the Pact, that it should do its utmost to cooperate with them, and furthermore, that it should spare no effort to learn their needs and understand their aspirations and hopes; and that it should work thenceforth for their best interests and the safeguarding of their future with all the political means at its disposal.

(3) *Annex Regarding the Appointment of a Secretary-General of the League.* The states signatory to this Pact have agreed to appoint His Excellency Abd-ul-Rahman 'Azzam Bey, to be Secretary-General of the League of Arab States.

This appointment is made for two years. The Council of the League shall hereafter determine the new regulations for the Secretariat-General.

ANGLO-AMERICAN COMMITTEE OF INQUIRY (APRIL 20, 1946)

With the end of World War II, the Palestine problem took on new and urgent dimensions. The United States and Britain now saw the issue from different perspectives. An Anglo-American Committee of Inquiry was established to study the issue and to seek to establish a common approach to Palestine. This would require a compromise of the British leaning toward the Arab position and the

Truman administration's focus on the plight of European Jewish displaced persons and refugees, as well as its sensitivity to Zionist entreaties and efforts which had, with the Biltmore conference, increasingly focused its efforts in the United States rather than Europe.

The establishment of the committee and its terms of reference were made public on November 13, 1945. The Committee's recommendations straddled the views and positions of the two governments. The report was not formally accepted by either government although Truman welcomed the recommendation concerning 100,000 Jews and certain other provisions.

Recommendation No. 1. We have to report that such information as we received about countries other than Palestine gave no hope of substantial assistance in finding homes for Jews wishing or impelled to leave Europe.

But Palestine alone cannot meet the emigration needs of the Jewish victims of Nazi and Fascist persecution. The whole world shares responsibility for them and indeed for the resettlement of all "Displaced Persons."

We therefore recommend that our governments together, and in association with other countries, should endeavour immediately to find new homes for all such "Displaced Persons," irrespective of creed or nationality, whose ties with their former communities have been irreparably broken.

Though emigration will solve the problems of some victims of persecution, the overwhelming majority, including a considerable number of Jews, will endeavour to secure that immediate effect is given to the provision of the United Nations Charter calling for "Universal respect for, and observance of, human rights and fundamental freedoms for all without distinction as to race, sex, language, or religion."

Recommendation No. 2. We recommend (A) that 100,000 certificates be authorised immediately for the admission into Palestine of Jews who have been the victims of Nazi and Fascist persecution; (B) that these certificates be awarded as far as possible in 1946 and that actual immigration be pushed forward as rapidly as conditions will permit.

Recommendation No. 3. In order to dispose, once and for all, of the exclusive claims of Jews and Arabs to Palestine, we regard it as essential that a clear statement of the following principles should be made:

I. That Jew shall not dominate Arab and Arab shall dominate Jew in Palestine. II. That Palestine shall be neither a Jewish state nor an Arab state. III. That the form of government ultimately to be established, shall, under International Guarantees, fully protect and preserve the interests in the Holy Land of Christendom and of the Moslem and Jewish faiths.

Thus Palestine must ultimately become a state which guards the rights and interests of Moslems, Jews and Christians alike: and accords to the inhabitants, as a whole, the fullest measure of self-government, consistent with the three paramount principles set forth above.

Recommendation No. 4. We have reached the conclusion that the hostility between Jews and Arabs and, in particular, the determination of each to achieve domination, if necessary by violence, make it certain that, now and for some time to come, any attempt to establish either an independent Palestinian state or independent Palestinian states would result in civil strife such as might threaten the peace of the world. We therefore recommend that, until this hostility disappears, the Government of Palestine be continued as at present under mandate pending the execution of a Trusteeship Agreement under the United Nations.

Recommendation No. 5. Looking towards a form of ultimate self-government, consistent with the three principles laid down in Recommendation No. 3, we recommend that the Mandatory or Trustee should proclaim the principle that Arab economic, educational and political advancement in Palestine is of equal importance with that of the Jews, and should at once prepare measures designed to bridge the gap which now exists and raise the Arab standard of living to that of the Jews: and so bring the two peoples to a full appreciation of their common interest and common destiny in the land where both belong.

Recommendation No. 6. We recommend that pending the early reference to the United Nations and the execution of a trusteeship agreement, the Mandatory should administer Palestine according to the mandate which declares with regard to immigration that "the administration of Palestine, while ensuring that the rights and position of other sections of the population are not prejudiced, shall facilitate Jewish immigration under suitable conditions."

Recommendation No. 7. (A) We recommend that the Land Transfers Regulations of 1940 be rescinded and replaced by regulations based on a policy of freedom in the sale, lease or use of land, irrespective of race, community or creed; and providing adequate protection for the interests of small owners and tenant cultivators. (B) We further recommend that steps be taken to render nugatory and to prohibit provisions in conveyances, leases and agreements relating to land which stipulate that only members of one race, community or creed may be employed on or about or in connection therewith. (C) We recommend that the government should exercise such close supervision over he Holy Places and localities such as the Sea of Galilee and its vicinity as will protect them from desecration and from uses which offend the conscience of religious people; and that such laws as are required for this purpose be enacted forthwith.

Recommendation No. 8. Various plans for large-scale agricultural and industrial development in Palestine have been presented for our consideration; these projects, if successfully carried into effect, could not only greatly enlarge the capacity of the country to support an increasing population, but also raise the living standards of Jew and Arab alike.

We are not in a position to assess the soundness of these specific plans; but we cannot state too strongly that, however technically feasible they may be, they will fail unless there is peace in Palestine. Moreover their full success requires the willing co-operation of adjacent Arab States, since they are not merely Palestinian projects. We recommend therefore, that the examination, discussion and execution of these plans be conducted, from the start and throughout, in full consultation and co-operation not only with the Jewish Agency but also with the governments of the neighbouring Arab States directly affected.

Recommendation No. 9. We recommend that, in the interests of the conciliation of the two peoples and of general improvement of the Arab standard of living, the educational system of both Jews and Arabs be reformed including the introduction of compulsory education within a reasonable time.

Recommendation No. 10. We recommend that, if this report is adopted, it should be made clear beyond all doubt to both Jews and Arabs that any attempt from either side, by threats of violence, by terrorism, or by the organisation or use of illegal armies to prevent its execution, will be resolutely suppressed.

Furthermore, we express the view that the Jewish Agency should at once resume active co-operation, and in the maintenance of that law and order throughout Palestine which is essential for the good of all, including the new immigrants.

UNITED NATIONS GENERAL ASSEMBLY RESOLUTION 181 (II) (NOVEMBER 29, 1947)

After World War II, Britain sought to reassess its policy in various locations, including Palestine. After some efforts to negotiate the situation with the Arabs and the Zionists, the Labor government decided to refer the Palestine issue to the United Nations General Assembly. At the request of the United Kingdom, the General Assembly met in special session from April 28 to May 15, 1947 and it established the United Nations Special Committee on Palestine (UNSCOP). UNSCOP was composed of 11 member states and charged to ascertain facts and to investigate all questions and issues relevant to the problem of Palestine and then to prepare a report and submit proposals not later than September 1, 1947.

On November 29, 1947, the United Nations General Assembly adopted Resolution 181 (II), the partition plan for Palestine, by a vote of 33 in favor, 13 against, 10 abstentions, and one absent. It divided the Palestine Mandate into an Arab state, a Jewish state, and an internationalized sector including Jerusalem. It provided the basis for Israel's independence and for the Arab-Israeli conflict. In general, the Zionists accepted the decision as the best attainable given the political circumstances. The Palestinians and the Arab states rejected the decision as unfair and pledged to restore the rights of the Arabs of Palestine. These reactions ensured that attempts to implement the plan would lead to conflict.

The General Assembly, Having met in special session at the request of the mandatory Power to constitute and instruct a Special Committee to prepare for the consideration of the question of the future Government of Palestine at the second regular session; *Having Constituted* a Special Committee and instructed it to investigate all questions and issues relevant to the problem of Palestine, and to prepare proposals for the solution of the problem, and *Having received and examined* the report of the Special Committee (document A/364) including a number of unanimous recommendations and a plan of partition with economic union approved by the majority of the Special Committee, *Considers* that the present situation in Palestine is one which is likely to impair the general welfare and friendly relations among nations; *Takes note* of the declaration by the mandatory Power that it plans to complete its evacuation of Palestine by 1 August 1948; *Recommends* to the United Kingdom, as the mandatory Power for Palestine, and to all other Members of the United Nations the adoption and implementation, with regard to the future Government of Palestine, of the Plan of Partition with Economic Union set out below; *Requests* that (a) The Security Council take the necessary measures as provided for in the plan for its implementation; (b) The Security Council consider, if circumstances during the transitional period require such consideration, whether the situation in Palestine constitutes a threat to the peace. If it decides that such a threat exists, and in order to maintain international peace and security, the Security Council should supplement the authorization of the General Assembly by taking measures, under Articles 39 and 41 of the Charter, to empower the United Nations Commission, as provided in this resolution, to exercise in Palestine the functions which are assigned to it by this resolution; (c) The Security Council determine as a threat to the peace, breach of the peace or act of aggression, in accordance with Article 39 of the Charter, any attempt to alter by force the settlement envisaged by this resolution; (d) The Trusteeship Council be informed of the responsibilities envisaged for it in this plan; *Calls upon* the inhabitants of Palestine to take such steps as may be necessary on their part to put this plan into effect; *Appeals* to all Governments and all peoples to refrain from taking any action which might hamper or delay the carrying out of these recommendations, and *Authorizes* the Secretary-General to reimburse travel and subsistence expenses of the members of the Commission referred to in Part 1, Section B, Paragraph 1 below, on such basis and in such form as he may determine most appropriate in the circumstances, and to provide the Commission with the necessary staff to assist in carrying out the functions assigned to the Commission by the General Assembly.

The General Assembly, Authorizes the Secretary-General to draw from the Working Capital Fund a sum not to exceed 2,000,000 dollars for the purposes set forth in the last paragraph of the resolution on the future government of Palestine.

PLAN OF PARTITION WITH ECONOMIC UNION. PART I. FUTURE CONSTITUTION AND GOVERNMENT OF PALESTINE. A. TERMINATION

OF MANDATE, PARTITION AND INDEPENDENCE. 1. The Mandate for Palestine shall terminate as soon as possible but in any case not later than 1 August 1948. 2. The armed forces of the mandatory Power shall be progressively withdrawn from Palestine, the withdrawal to be completed as soon as possible but in any case not later than 1 August 1948. The mandatory Power shall advise the Commission, as far in advance as possible, of its intention to terminate the mandate and to evacuate each area. The mandatory Power shall use its best endeavours to ensure that an area situated in the territory of the Jewish State, including a seaport and hinterland adequate to provide facilities for a substantial immigration, shall be evacuated at the earliest possible date and in any event not later than 1 February 1948. 3. Independent Arab and Jewish States and the Special International Regime for the City of Jerusalem, set forth in Part III of this Plan, shall come into existence in Palestine two months after the evacuation of the armed forces of the mandatory Power has been completed but in any case not later than 1 October 1948. The boundaries of the Arab State, the Jewish State, and the City of Jerusalem shall be as described in Parts II and III below. 4. The period between the adoption by the General Assembly of its recommendation on the question of Palestine and the establishment of the independence of the Arab and Jewish States shall be a transitional period.

B. STEPS PREPARATORY TO INDEPENDENCE. 1. A Commission shall be set up consisting of one representative of each of five Member States. The Members represented on the Commission shall be elected by the General Assembly on as broad a basis, geographically and otherwise, as possible. 2. The administration of Palestine shall, as the mandatory Power withdraws its armed forces, be progressively turned over to the Commission, which shall act in conformity with the recommendations of the General Assembly, under the guidance of the Security Council. The mandatory Power shall to the fullest possible extent coordinate its plans for withdrawal with the plans of the Commission to take over and administer areas which have been evacuated. In the discharge of this administrative responsibility the Commission shall have authority to issue necessary regulations and take other measures as required. The mandatory Power shall not take any action to prevent, obstruct or delay the implementation by the Commission of the measures recommended by the General Assembly. 3. On its arrival in Palestine the Commission shall proceed to carry out measures for the establishment of the frontiers of the Arab and Jewish States and the City of Jerusalem in accordance with the general lines of the recommendations of the General Assembly on the partition of Palestine. Nevertheless, the boundaries as described in Part II of this Plan are to be modified in such a way that village areas as a rule will not be divided by state boundaries unless pressing reasons make that necessary. 4. The Commission, after consultation with the democratic parties and other public organizations of the Arab and Jewish States, shall select and establish in each State as rapidly as possible a Provisional Council of Government. The activities of both the Arab and Jewish Provisional

Councils of Government shall be carried out under the general direction of the Commission. If by 1 April 1948 a Provisional Council of Government cannot be selected for either of the States, or, if selected, cannot carry out its functions, the Commission shall communicate that fact to the Security Council for such action with respect to that State as the Security Council may deem proper, and to the Secretary-General for communication to the Members of the United Nations. 5. Subject to the provisions of these recommendations, during the transitional period the Provisional Councils of Government, acting under the Commission, shall have full authority in the areas under their control including authority over matters of immigration and land regulation. 6. The Provisional Council of Government of each State, acting under the Commission, shall progressively receive from the Commission full responsibility for the administration of that State in the period between the termination of the Mandate and the establishment of the State's independence. 7. The Commission shall instruct the Provisional Councils of Government of both the Arab and Jewish States, after their formation, to proceed to the establishment of administrative organs of government, central and local. 8. The Provisional Council of Government of each State shall, within the shortest time possible, recruit an armed militia from the residents of that State, sufficient in number to maintain internal order and to prevent frontier clashes. This armed militia in each State shall, for operational purposes, be under the command of Jewish or Arab officers resident in that State, but general political and military control, including the choice of the militia's High Command, shall be exercised by the Commission. 9. The Provisional Council of Government of each State shall, not later than two months after the withdrawal of the armed forces of the mandatory Power, hold elections to the Constituent Assembly which shall be conducted on democratic lines. The election regulations in each State shall be drawn up by the Provisional Council of Government and approved by the Commission. Qualified voters for each State for this election shall be persons over eighteen years of age who are (a) Palestinian citizens residing in that State; and (b) Arabs and Jews residing in the State, although not Palestinian citizens, who, before voting, have signed a notice of intention to become citizens of such State. Arabs and Jews residing in the City of Jerusalem who have signed a notice of intention to become citizens, the Arabs of the Arab State and the Jews of the Jewish State, shall be entitled to vote in the Arab and Jewish States respectively. Women may vote and be elected to the Constituent Assemblies. During the transitional period no Jew shall be permitted to establish residence in the area of the proposed Arab State, and no Arab shall be permitted to establish residence in the area of the proposed Jewish State, except by special leave of the Commission. 10. The Constituent Assembly of each State shall draft a democratic constitution for its State and choose a provisional government to succeed the Provisional Council of Government appointed by the Commission. The Constitutions of the States shall embody Chapters 1 and 2 of the Declaration provided for in section C below and include, inter alia, provisions for: (a) Establishing in each State a legislative body elected by universal suffrage and by secret ballot on the basis of proportional representation, and an executive body responsible to the legislature; (b) Settling all international disputes in which the State may be involved by peaceful means in such a manner that international peace and security, and justice, are not endangered; (c) Accepting the obligation of the State to refrain in its international relations from the threat or use of force against the territorial integrity or political independence of any State, or in any other manner inconsistent with the purpose of the United Nations; (d) Guaranteeing to all persons equal and non-discriminatory rights in civil, political, economic and religious matters and the enjoyment of human rights and fundamental freedoms, including freedom of religion, language, speech and publication, education, assembly and association; (e) Preserving freedom of transit and visit for all residents and citizens of the other State in Palestine and the City of Jerusalem, subject to considerations of national security, provided that each State shall control residence within its borders. 11. The Commission shall appoint a preparatory economic commission of three members to make whatever arrangements are possible for economic co-operation, with a view to establishing, as soon as practicable, the Economic Union and the Joint Economic Board, as provided in section D below. 12. During the period between the adoption of the recommendations on the question of Palestine by the General Assembly and the termination of the Mandate, the mandatory Power in Palestine shall maintain full responsibility for administration in areas from which it has not withdrawn its armed forces. The Commission shall assist the mandatory Power in the carrying out of these functions. Similarly the mandatory Power shall co-operate with the Commission in the execution of its functions. 13. With a view to ensuring that there shall be continuity in the functioning of administrative services and that, on the withdrawal of the armed forces of the mandatory Power, the whole administration shall be in the charge of the Provisional Councils and the Joint Economic Board, respectively, acting under the Commission, there shall be a progressive transfer, from the mandatory Power to the Commission, of responsibility for all the functions of government, including that of maintaining law and order in the areas from which the forces of the mandatory Power have been withdrawn. 14. The Commission shall be guided in its activities by the recommendations of the General Assembly and by such instructions as the Security Council may consider necessary to issue. The measures taken by the Commission, within the recommendations of the General Assembly, shall become immediately effective unless the Commission has previously received contrary instructions from the Security Council. The Commission shall render periodic monthly progress reports, or more frequently if desirable, to the Security Council. 15. The Commission shall make its final report to the next regular session of the General Assembly and to the Security Council simultaneously.

C. DECLARATION. A declaration shall be made to the United Nations by the Provisional Government of each proposed State before independence. It shall contain, inter alia, the following clauses: General Provision. The stipulations contained in the Declaration are recognized as fundamental laws of the State and no law, regulation or official action shall conflict or interfere with these stipulations, nor shall any law, regulation or official action prevail over them.

CHAPTER 1: *Holy Places, religious buildings and sites.* 1. Existing rights in respect of Holy Places and religious buildings or sites shall not be denied or impaired. 2. In so far as Holy Places are concerned, the liberty of access, visit, and transit shall be guaranteed, in conformity with existing rights, to all residents and citizen of the other State and of the City of Jerusalem, as well as to aliens, without distinction as to nationality, subject to requirements of national security, public order and decorum. Similarly, freedom of worship shall be guaranteed in conformity with existing rights, subject to the maintenance of public order and decorum. 3. Holy Places and religious buildings or sites shall be preserved. No act shall be permitted which may in an way impair their sacred character. If at any time it appears to the Government that any particular Holy Place, religious, building or site is in need of urgent repair, the Government may call upon the community or communities concerned to carry out such repair. The Government may carry it out itself at the expense of the community or community concerned if no action is taken within a reasonable time. 4. No taxation shall be levied in respect of any Holy Place, religious building or site which was exempt from taxation on the date of the creation of the State. No change in the incidence of such taxation shall be made which would either discriminate between the owners or occupiers of Holy Places, religious buildings or sites, or would place such owners or occupiers in a position less favourable in relation to the general incidence of taxation than existed at the time of the adoption of the Assembly's recommendations. 5. The Governor of the City of Jerusalem shall have the right to determine whether the provisions of the Constitution of the State in relation to Holy Places, religious buildings and sites within the borders of the State and the religious rights appertaining thereto, are being properly applied and respected, and to make decisions on the basis of existing rights in cases of disputes which may arise between the different religious communities or the rites of a religious community with respect to such places, buildings and sites. He shall receive full co-operation and such privileges and immunities as are necessary for the exercise of his functions in the State.

CHAPTER 2: *Religious and minority rights.* 1. Freedom of conscience and the free exercise of all forms of worship, subject only to the maintenance of public order and morals, shall be ensured to all. 2. No discrimination of any kind shall be made between the inhabitants on the ground of race, religion, language or sex. 3. All persons within the jurisdiction of the State shall be entitled to equal protection of the laws. 4. The family law and personal status of the various minorities and their religious interests, including endowments, shall be respected. 5. Except as may be required for the maintenance of public order and good government, no measure shall be taken to obstruct or interfere with the enterprise of religious or charitable bodies of all faiths or to discriminate against any representative or member of these bodies on the ground of his religion or nationality. 6. The State shall ensure adequate primary and secondary education for the Arab and Jewish minority, respectively, in its own language and its cultural traditions. The right of each community to maintain its own schools for the education of its own members in its own language, while conforming to such educational requirements of a general nature as the State may impose, shall not be denied or impaired. Foreign educational establishments shall continue their activity on the basis of their existing rights. 7. No restriction shall be imposed on the free use by any citizen of the State of any language in private intercourse, in commerce, in religion, in the Press or in publications of any kind, or at public meetings. 8. No expropriation of land owned by an Arab in the Jewish State (by a Jew in the Arab State) shall be allowed except for public purposes. In all cases of expropriation full compensation as fixed by the Supreme Court shall be said previous to dispossession.

CHAPTER 3: *Citizenship, international conventions and financial obligations.* 1. CITIZENSHIP. Palestinian citizens residing in Palestine outside the City of Jerusalem, as well as Arabs and Jews who, not holding Palestinian citizenship, reside in Palestine outside the City of Jerusalem shall, upon the recognition of independence, become citizens of the State in which they are resident and enjoy full civil and political rights. Persons over the age of eighteen years may opt, within one year from the date of recognition of independence of the State in which they reside, for citizenship of the other State, providing that no Arab residing in the area of the proposed Arab State shall have the right to opt for citizenship in the proposed Jewish State and no Jew residing in the proposed Jewish State shall have the right to opt for citizenship in the proposed Arab State. The exercise of this right of option will be taken to include the wives and children under eighteen years of age of persons so opting. Arabs residing in the area of the proposed Jewish State and Jews residing in the area of the proposed Arab State who have signed a notice of intention to opt for citizenship of the other State shall be eligible to vote in the elections to the Constituent Assembly of that State, but not in the elections to the Constituent Assembly of the State in which they reside. 2. *International conventions.* (a) The State shall be bound by all the international agreements and conventions, both general and special, to which Palestine has become a party. Subject to any right of denunciation provided for therein, such agreements and conventions shall be respected by the State throughout the period for which they were concluded. (b) Any dispute about the applicability and continued validity of international conventions or treaties signed or adhered to by the mandatory Power on behalf of Palestine shall be referred to the International Court of Justice in accordance with the provisions of the Statute of the Court. 3. *Financial obligations.* (a) The State shall respect and fulfil all financial obligations of whatever nature assumed on behalf of

Palestine by the mandatory Power during the exercise of the Mandate and recognized by the State. This provision includes the right of public servants to pensions, compensation or gratuities. (b) These obligations shall be fulfilled through participation in the Joint Economic Board in respect of those obligations applicable to Palestine as a whole, and individually in respect of those applicable to, and fairly apportionable between, the States. (c) A Court of Claims, affiliated with the Joint Economic Board, and composed of one member appointed by the United Nations, one representative of the United Kingdom and one representative of the State concerned, should be established. Any dispute between the United Kingdom and the State respecting claims not recognized by the latter should be referred to that Court. (d) Commercial concessions granted in respect of any part of Palestine prior to the adoption of the resolution by the General Assembly shall continue to be valid according to their terms, unless modified by agreement between the concession-holders and the State.

CHAPTER 4: *Miscellaneous provisions.* 1. The provisions of chapters 1 and 2 of the declaration shall be under the guarantee of the United Nations, and no modifications shall be made in them without the assent of the General Assembly of the United Nations. Any Member of the United Nations shall have the right to bring to the attention of the General Assembly any infraction or danger of infraction of any of these stipulations, and the General Assembly may thereupon make such recommendations as it may deem proper in the circumstances. 2. Any dispute relating to the application or interpretation of this declaration shall be referred, at the request of either party, to the International Court of Justice, unless the parties agree to another mode of settlement.

D. ECONOMIC UNION AND TRANSIT. 1. The Provisional Council of Government of each State shall enter into an undertaking with respect to Economic Union and Transit. This undertaking shall be drafted by the Commission provided for in section B, paragraph 1, utilizing to the greatest possible extent the advice and cooperation of representative organizations and bodies from each of the proposed States. It shall contain provisions to establish the Economic Union of Palestine and provide for other matters of common interest. If by 1 April 1948 the Provisional Councils of Government have not entered into the undertaking, the undertaking shall be put into force by the Commission. *The Economic Union of Palestine.* 2. The objectives of the Economic Union of Palestine shall be: (a) A customs union; (b) A joint currency system providing for a single foreign exchange rate; (c) Operation in the common interest on a non-discriminatory basis of railways inter-State highways; postal, telephone and telegraphic services and ports and airports involved in international trade and commerce; (d) Joint economic development, especially in respect of irrigation, land reclamation and soil conservation; (e) Access for both States and for the City of Jerusalem on a non-discriminatory basis to water and power facilities. 3. There shall be established a Joint Economic Board, which shall consist of three representatives of each of the two States and three foreign members appointed by the Economic and Social Council of the United Nations. The foreign members shall be appointed in the first instance for a term of three years; they shall serve as individuals and not as representatives of States. 4. The functions of the Joint Economic Board shall be to implement either directly or by delegation the measures necessary to realize the objectives of the Economic Union. It shall have all powers of organization and administration necessary to fulfil its functions. 5. The States shall bind themselves to put into effect the decisions of the Joint Economic Board. The Board's decisions shall be taken by a majority vote. 6. In the event of failure of a State to take the necessary action the Board may, by a vote of six members, decide to withhold an appropriate portion of the part of the customs revenue to which the State in question is entitled under the Economic Union. Should the State persist in its failure to cooperate, the Board may decide by a simple majority vote upon such further sanctions, including disposition of funds which it has withheld, as it may deem appropriate. 7. In relation to economic development, the functions of the Board shall be planning, investigation and encouragement of joint development projects, but it shall not undertake such projects except with the assent of both States and the City of Jerusalem, in the event that Jerusalem is directly involved in the development project. 8. In regard to the joint currency system, the currencies circulating in the two States and the City of Jerusalem shall be issued under the authority of the Joint Economic Board, which shall be the sole issuing authority and which shall determine the reserves to be held against such currencies. 9. So far as is consistent with paragraph 2(b) above, each State may operate its own central bank, control its own fiscal and credit policy, its foreign exchange receipts and expenditures, the grant of import licences, and may conduct international financial operations on its own faith and credit. During the first two years after the termination of the Mandate, the Joint Economic Board shall have the authority to take such measures as may be necessary to ensure that -- to the extent that the total foreign exchange revenues of the two States from the export of goods and services permit, and provided that each State takes appropriate measures to conserve its own foreign exchange resources -- each State shall have available, in any twelve months' period, foreign exchange sufficient to assure the supply of quantities of imported goods and services for consumption in its territory equivalent to the quantities of such goods and services consumed in that territory in the twelve months' period ending 31 December 1947. 10. All economic authority not specifically vested in the Joint Economic Board is reserved to each State. 11. There shall be a common customs tariff with complete freedom of trade between the States, and between the States and the City of Jerusalem. 12. The tariff schedules shall be drawn up by a Tariff Commission, consisting of representatives of each of the States in equal numbers, and shall be submitted to the Joint Economic Board for approval by a majority vote. In case of disagreement in the Tariff Commission, the Joint Economic Board shall arbitrate the points of difference. In the event that the Tariff Commission fails to draw up any schedule by a date to be fixed, the Joint Economic Board shall determine the tariff schedule. 13. The following items shall be a first charge on the customs and other common revenue of the Joint Economic Board: (a) The expenses of the customs service and of the operation of the joint services; (b) The administrative expenses of the Joint Economic Board; (c) The financial obligations of the Administration of Palestine, consisting of: (i) The service of the outstanding public debt; (ii) The cost of superannuation benefits, now being paid or falling due in the future, in accordance with the rules and to the extent established by paragraph 3 of chapter 3 above. 14. After these obligations have been met in full, the surplus revenue from the customs and other common services shall be divided in the following manner: not less than 5 per cent and not more than 10 per cent to the City of Jerusalem; the residue shall be allocated to each State by the Joint Economic Board equitably, with the objective of maintaining a sufficient and suitable level of government and social services in each State, except that the share of either State shall not exceed the amount of that State's contribution to the revenues of the Economic Union by more than approximately four million pounds in any year. The amount granted may be adjusted by the Board according to the price level in relation to the prices prevailing at the time of the establishment of the Union. After five years, the principles of the distribution of the joint revenue may be revised by the Joint Economic Board on a basis of equity. 15. All international conventions and treaties affecting customs tariff rates, and those communications services under the jurisdiction of the Joint Economic Board, shall be entered into by both States. In these matters, the two States shall be bound to act in accordance with the majority of the Joint Economic Board. 16. The Joint Economic Board shall endeavour to secure for Palestine's exports fair and equal access to world markets. 17. All enterprises operated by the Joint Economic Board shall pay fair wages on a uniform basis. *Freedom of transit and visit.* 18. The undertaking shall contain provisions preserving freedom of transit and visit for all residents or citizens of both States and of the City of Jerusalem, subject to security considerations; provided that each State and the City shall control residence within its borders. *Termination, modification and interpretation of the undertaking.* 19. The undertaking and any treaty issuing therefrom shall remain in force for a period of ten years. It shall continue in force until notice of termination, to take effect two years thereafter, is given by either of the parties. 20. During the initial ten-year period, the undertaking and any treaty issuing therefrom may not be modified except by consent of both parties and with the approval of the General Assembly. 21. Any dispute relating to the application or the interpretation of the undertaking and any treaty issuing therefrom shall be referred, at the request of either party, to the International Court Of Justice, unless the parties agree to another mode of settlement.

E. Assets. 1. The movable assets of the Administration of Palestine shall be allocated to the Arab and Jewish States and the City of Jerusalem on an equitable basis. Allocations should be made by the United Nations Commission referred to iii section B, paragraph 1, above. Immovable assets shall become the property of the government of the territory in which they are situated. 2. During the period between the appointment of the United Nations Commission and the termination of the Mandate, the mandatory Power shall, except in respect of ordinary operations, consult with the Commission on any measure which it may contemplate involving the liquidation, disposal or encumbering of the assets of the Palestine Government, such as the accumulated treasury surplus, the proceeds of Government bond issues, State lands or any other asset.

F. Admission to Membership in the United Nations. When the independence of either the Arab or the Jewish State as envisaged in this plan has become effective and the declaration and undertaking, as envisaged in this plan, have been signed by either of them, sympathetic consideration should be given to its application for admission to membership in the United Nations in accordance with article 4 of the Charter of the United Nations.

PART II. BOUNDARIES. A. The Arab State. [Here follows a detailed description of the boundary] B. The Jewish State. The north-eastern sector of the Jewish State (Eastern Galilee) is bounded on the north and west by the Lebanese frontier and on the east by the frontiers of Syria and Trans-jordan. It includes the whole of the Huleh Basin, Lake Tiberias, the whole of the Beisan Sub-District, the boundary line being extended to the crest of the Gilboa mountains and the Wadi Malih. From there the Jewish State extends north-west, following the boundary described in respect of the Arab State. The Jewish section of the coastal plain extends from a point between Minat El-Qila and Nabi Yunis in the Gaza Sub-District and includes the towns of Haifa and Tel-Aviv, leaving Jaffa as an enclave of the Arab State. The eastern frontier of the Jewish State follows the boundary described in respect of the Arab State. The Beersheba area comprises the whole of the Beersheba Sub-District, including the Negeb and the eastern part of the Gaza Sub-District, but excluding the town of Beersheba and those areas described in respect of the Arab State. It includes also a strip of land along the Dead Sea stretching from the Beersheba-Hebron Sub-District boundary line to 'Ein Geddi, as described in respect of the Arab State. C. The city of Jerusalem. The boundaries of the City of Jerusalem are as defined in the recommendations on the City of Jerusalem. (See Part III, section B, below).

PART III. CITY OF JERUSALEM. A. Special regime. The City of Jerusalem shall be established as a corpus separatum under a special international regime and shall be administered by the United Nations. The Trusteeship Council shall be designated to discharge the responsibilities of the Administering Authority on behalf of the United Nations. B. Boundaries of the city. The City of Jerusalem shall include the present municipality of Jerusalem plus the surrounding villages and towns, the most eastern of which shall be Abu Dis; the most southern, Bethlehem; the most western, 'Ein Karim (including also the built-up area of Motsa); and the most northern Shu'fat, as indicated on the attached sketch-map (annex B). C. Statute of the city. The Trusteeship Council shall, within five months of the approval of the present plan, elaborate and approve a detailed statute of the City which shall contain, inter alia, the substance of the following provisions: 1. *Government machinery; special objectives.* The Administering Authority in discharging its administrative obligations shall pursue the following special objectives: a) To protect and to preserve the unique spiritual and religious interests located in the city of the three great monotheistic faiths throughout the world, Christian, Jewish and Moslem; to this end to ensure that order and peace, and especially religious peace, reign in Jerusalem; b) To foster cooperation among all the inhabitants of the city in their own interests as well as in order to encourage and support the peaceful development of the mutual relations between the two Palestinian peoples throughout the Holy Land; to promote the security, well-being and any constructive measures of development of the residents having regard to the special circumstances and customs of the various peoples and communities. 2. *Governor and administrative staff.* A Governor of the City of Jerusalem shall be appointed by the Trusteeship Council and shall be responsible to it. He shall be selected on the basis of special qualifications and without regard to nationality. He shall not, however, be a citizen of either State in Palestine. The Governor shall represent the United Nations in the City and shall exercise on their behalf all powers of administration, including the conduct of external affairs. He shall be assisted by an administrative staff classed as international officers in the meaning of Article 100 of the Charter and chosen whenever practicable from the residents of the city and of the rest of Palestine on a non-discriminatory basis. A detailed plan for the organization of the administration of the city shall be submitted by the Governor to the Trusteeship Council and duly approved by it. 3. *Local autonomy.* a) The existing local autonomous units in the territory of the city (villages, townships and municipalities) shall enjoy wide powers of local government and administration. b) The Governor shall study and submit for the consideration and decision of the Trusteeship Council a plan for the establishment of special town units consisting, respectively, of the Jewish and Arab sections of new Jerusalem. The new town units shall continue to form part the present municipality of Jerusalem. 4. *Security measures.* a) The City of Jerusalem shall be demilitarized; neutrality shall be declared and preserved, and no para-military formations, exercises or activities shall be permitted within its borders. b) Should the administration of the City of Jerusalem be seriously obstructed or prevented by the non-cooperation or interference of one or more sections of the population the Governor shall have authority to take such measures as may be necessary to restore the effective functioning of administration. c) To assist in the maintenance of internal law and order, especially for the protection of the Holy Places and religious buildings and sites in the city, the Governor shall organize a special police force of adequate strength, the members of which shall be recruited outside of Palestine. The Governor shall be empowered to direct such budgetary provision as may be necessary for the maintenance of this force. 5. *Legislative organization.* A Legislative Council, elected by adult residents of the city irrespective of nationality on the basis of universal and secret suffrage and proportional representation, shall have powers of legislation and taxation. No legislative measures shall, however, conflict or interfere with the provisions which will be set forth in the Statute of the City, nor shall any law, regulation, or official action prevail over them. The Statute shall grant to the Governor a right of vetoing bills inconsistent with the provisions referred to in the preceding sentence. It shall also empower him to promulgate temporary ordinances in case the Council fails to adopt in time a bill deemed essential to the normal functioning of the administration. 6. *Administration of justice.* The Statute shall provide for the establishment of an independent judiciary system, including a court of appeal. All the inhabitants of the city shall be subject to it. 7. *Economic union and economic regime.* The City of Jerusalem shall be included in the Economic Union of Palestine and be bound by all stipulations of the undertaking and of any treaties issued therefrom, as well as by the decisions of the Joint Economic Board. The headquarters of the Economic Board shall be established in the territory City. The Statute shall provide for the regulation of economic matters not falling within the regime of the Economic Union, on the basis of equal treatment and non-discrimination for all members of the United Nations and their nationals. 8. *Freedom of transit and visit: control of residents.* Subject to considerations of security, and of economic welfare as determined by the Governor under the directions of the Trusteeship Council, freedom of entry into, and residence within the borders of the City shall be guaranteed for the residents or citizens of the Arab and Jewish States. Immigration into, and residence within, the borders of the city for nationals of other States shall be controlled by the Governor under the directions of the Trusteeship Council. 9. *Relations with Arab and Jewish States.* Representatives of the Arab and Jewish States shall be accredited to the Governor of the City and charged with the protection of the interests of their States and nationals in connection with the international administration of the City. 10. *Official languages.* Arabic and Hebrew shall be the official languages of the city. This will not preclude the adoption of one or more additional working languages, as may be required. 11. *Citizenship.* All the residents shall become ipso facto citizens of the City of Jerusalem unless they opt for citizenship of the State of which they have been citizens or, if Arabs or Jews, have filed notice of intention to become citizens of the Arab or Jewish State respectively, according to Part 1, section B, paragraph 9, of this Plan. The Trusteeship Council shall make arrangements for consular protection of the citizens of the City outside its territory. 12. *Freedoms of citizens.* a) Subject only to the requirements of public order and morals, the inhabitants of the City shall be ensured the enjoyment of human rights and fundamental freedoms, including freedom of conscience, religion and worship, language, education, speech and press, assembly and association, and petition. b) No discrimination of any kind shall be made between the inhabitants on the grounds of race, religion, language or sex. c) All persons within the City shall be entitled to equal protection of the laws. d) The family law and personal status of the various persons and communities and their religious interests, including endowments, shall be respected. e) Except as may be required for the maintenance of public order and good government, no measure shall be taken to obstruct or interfere with the enterprise of religious or charitable bodies of all faiths or to discriminate against any representative or member of these bodies on the ground of his religion or nationality. f) The City shall ensure adequate primary and secondary education for the Arab and Jewish communities respectively, in their own languages and in accordance with their cultural traditions. The right of each community to maintain its own schools for the education of its own members in its own language, while conforming to such educational requirements of a general nature as the City may impose, shall not be denied or impaired. Foreign educational establishments shall continue their activity on the basis of their existing rights. g) No restriction shall be imposed on the free use by any inhabitant of the City of any language in private intercourse, in commerce, in religion, in the Press or in publications of any kind, or at public meetings. 13. *Holy Places* a) Existing rights in respect of Holy Places and religious buildings or sites shall not be denied or impaired. b) Free access to the Holy Places and religious buildings or sites and the free exercise of worship shall be secured in conformity with existing rights and subject to the requirements of public order and decorum. c) Holy Places and religious buildings or sites shall be preserved. No act shall be permitted which may in any way impair their sacred character. If at any time it appears to the Governor that any particular Holy Place, religious building or site is in need of urgent repair, the Governor may call upon the community or communities concerned to carry out such repair. The Governor may carry it out himself at the expense of the community or communities concerned if no action is taken within a reasonable time. d) No taxation shall be levied in respect of any Holy Place, religious building or site which was exempt from taxation on the date of the creation of the City. No change in the incidence of such taxation shall be made which would either discriminate between the owners or occupiers of Holy Places, religious buildings or sites or would place such owners or occupiers in a position less favourable in relation to the general incidence of taxation than existed at the time of the adoption of the Assembly's recommendations. 14. *Special powers of the Governor in respect of the Holy Places, religious buildings and sites in the City and in any part of Palestine.* a) The protection of the Holy Places, religious buildings and sites located in the City of Jerusalem shall be a special concern of the Governor. b) With relation to such places, buildings and sites in Palestine outside the city, the Governor shall determine, on the ground of powers granted to him by the Constitution of both States, whether the provisions of the Constitution of the Arab and Jewish States in Palestine dealing therewith and the religious rights appertaining thereto are being properly applied and respected. c) The Governor shall also be empowered to make decisions on the basis of existing rights in cases of disputes which may arise between the different religious communities or the rites of a religious community in respect of the Holy Places, religious buildings and sites in any part of Palestine. In this task he may be assisted by a consultative council of representatives of different denominations acting in an advisory capacity. D. Duration of the special regime. The Statute elaborated by the Trusteeship Council the aforementioned principles shall come into force not later than 1 October 1948. It shall remain in force in the first instance for a period of ten years, unless the Trusteeship Council finds it necessary to undertake a re-examination of these provisions at an earlier date. After the expiration of this period the whole scheme shall be subject to examination by the Trusteeship Council in the light of experience acquired with its functioning. The residents the City shall be then free to express by means of a referendum their wishes as to possible modifications of regime of the City.

PART IV. CAPITULATIONS. States whose nationals have in the past enjoyed in Palestine the privileges and immunities of foreigners, including the benefits of consular jurisdiction and protection, as formerly enjoyed by capitulation or usage in the Ottoman Empire, are invited to renounce any right pertaining to them to the re-establishment of such privileges and immunities in the proposed Arab and Jewish States and the City of Jerusalem.

DECLARATION OF THE ESTABLISHMENT OF THE STATE OF ISRAEL (MAY 14, 1948)

On May 14, 1948, when the British Mandate over Palestine expired, the Jewish People's Council gathered at the Tel Aviv Museum, and approved the following proclamation, declaring the establishment of the State of Israel.

ERETZ-ISRAEL (the Land of Israel) was the birthplace of the Jewish people. Here their spiritual, religious and political identity was shaped. Here they first attained to statehood, created cultural values of national and universal significance and gave to the world the eternal Book of Books.

After being forcibly exiled from their land, the people kept faith with it throughout their Dispersion and never ceased to pray and hope for their return to it and for the restoration in it of their political freedom.

Impelled by this historic and traditional attachment, Jews strove in every successive generation to re-establish themselves in their ancient homeland. In recent decades they returned in their masses. Pioneers, ma'pilim (immigrants coming to Eretz-Israel in defiance of restrictive legislation) and defenders, they made deserts bloom, revived the Hebrew language, built villages and towns, and created a thriving community controlling its own economy and culture, loving peace but knowing how to defend itself, bringing the blessings of progress to all the country's inhabitants, and aspiring towards independent nationhood.

In the year 5657 (1897), at the summons of the spiritual father of the Jewish State, Theodore Herzl, the First Zionist Congress convened and proclaimed the right of the Jewish people to national rebirth in its own country.

This right was recognized in the Balfour Declaration of the 2nd November, 1917, and re-affirmed in the Mandate of the League of Nations which, in particular, gave international sanction to the historic connection between the Jewish people and Eretz-Israel and to the right of the Jewish people to rebuild its National Home.

The catastrophe which recently befell the Jewish people -- the massacre of millions of Jews in Europe -- was another clear demonstration of the urgency of solving the problem of its homelessness by re-establishing in Eretz-Israel the Jewish State, which would open the gates of the homeland wide to every Jew and confer upon the Jewish people the status of a fully-privileged member of the community of nations.

Survivors of the Nazi holocaust in Europe, as well as Jews from other parts of the world, continued to migrate to Eretz-Israel, undaunted by difficulties, restrictions and dangers, and never ceased to assert their right to a life of dignity, freedom and honest toil in their national homeland.

In the Second World War, the Jewish community of this country contributed its full share to the struggle of the freedom- and peace-loving nations against the forces of Nazi wickedness and, by the blood of its soldiers and its war effort, gained the right to be reckoned among the peoples who founded the United Nations.

On the 29th November, 1947, the United Nations General Assembly passed a resolution calling for the establishment of a Jewish State in Eretz-Israel; the General Assembly required the inhabitants of Eretz-Israel to take such steps as were necessary on their part for the implementation of that resolution. This recognition by the United Nations of the right of the Jewish people to establish their State is irrevocable.

This right is the natural right of the Jewish people to be masters of their own fate, like all other nations, in their own sovereign State.

ACCORDINGLY WE, MEMBERS OF THE PEOPLE'S COUNCIL, REPRE-SENTATIVES OF THE JEWISH COMMUNITY OF ERETZ-ISRAEL AND OF THE ZIONIST MOVEMENT, ARE HERE ASSEMBLED ON THE DAY OF THE TERMINATION OF THE BRITISH MANDATE OVER ERETZ-ISRAEL AND, BY VIRTUE OF OUR NATURAL AND HISTORIC RIGHT AND ON THE STRENGTH OF THE RESOLUTION OF THE UNITED NATIONS GENERAL ASSEMBLY, HEREBY DECLARE THE ESTABLISHMENT OF A JEWISH STATE IN ERETZ-ISRAEL, TO BE KNOWN AS THE STATE OF ISRAEL.

WE DECLARE that, with effect from the moment of the termination of the Mandate being tonight, the eve of Sabbath, the 6th Iyar, 5708 (15th May, 1948), until the establishment of the elected, regular authorities of the State in accordance with the Constitution which shall be adopted by the Elected Constituent Assembly not later than the 1st October 1948, the People's Council shall act as a Provisional Council of State, and its executive organ, the People's Administration, shall be the Provisional Government of the Jewish State, to be called "Israel".

THE STATE OF ISRAEL will be open for Jewish immigration and for the Ingathering of the Exiles; it will foster the development of the country for the benefit of all its inhabitants; it will be based on freedom, justice and peace as envisaged by the prophets of Israel; it will ensure complete equality of social and political rights to all its inhabitants irrespective of religion, race or sex; it will guarantee freedom of religion, conscience, language, education and culture; it will safeguard the Holy Places of all religions; and it will be faithful to the principles of the Charter of the United Nations.

THE STATE OF ISRAEL is prepared to cooperate with the agencies and representatives of the United Nations in implementing the resolution of the General Assembly of the 29th November, 1947, and will take steps to bring about the economic union of the whole of Eretz-Israel.

WE APPEAL to the United Nations to assist the Jewish people in the building-up of its State and to receive the State of Israel into the comity of nations.

WE APPEAL -- in the very midst of the onslaught launched against us now for months -- to the Arab inhabitants of the State of Israel to preserve peace and participate in the upbuilding of the State on the basis of full and equal citizenship and due representation in all its provisional and permanent institutions.

WE EXTEND our hand to all neighbouring states and their peoples in an offer of peace and good neighbourliness, and appeal to them to establish bonds of cooperation and mutual help with the sovereign Jewish people settled in its own land. The State of Israel is prepared to do its share in a common effort for the advancement of the entire Middle East.

WE APPEAL to the Jewish people throughout the Diaspora to rally round the Jews of Eretz-Israel in the tasks of immigration and upbuilding and to stand by them in the great struggle for the realization of the age-old dream -- the redemption of Israel.

PLACING OUR TRUST IN THE ALMIGHTY, WE AFFIX OUR SIGNA-TURES TO THIS PROCLAMATION AT THIS SESSION OF THE PROVI-SIONAL COUNCIL OF STATE, ON THE SOIL OF THE HOMELAND, IN THE CITY OF TEL-AVIV, ON THIS SABBATH EVE, THE 5TH DAY OF IYAR, 5708 (14TH MAY, 1948).

UNITED NATIONS GENERAL ASSEMBLY RESOLUTION 194 (III) (DECEMBER 11, 1948)

On December 11, 1948 the United Nations General Assembly adopted this resolution to resolve the Palestine problem. The Assembly declared that refugees wishing to return to their homes and live at peace with their neighbors should be permitted to do so and those choosing not to return should be compensated. It also called for the demilitarization and internationalization of Jerusalem and for the protection of, and free access to, the holy places. The resolution provided for the establishment of a three member United Nations Conciliation Commission for Palestine to assist the parties in achieving a final settlement on outstanding questions.

The General Assembly, Having considered further the situation in Palestine, 1. *Expresses* its deep appreciation of the progress achieved through the good offices of the late United Nations Mediator in promoting a peaceful adjustment of the future situation of Palestine, for which cause he sacrificed his life; and *Extends* its thanks to the Acting Mediator and his staff for their continued efforts and devotion to duty in Palestine; 2. *Establishes* a Conciliation Commission consisting of three States Members of the United Nations which shall have the following functions: (a) To assume, in so far as it considers necessary in existing circumstances, the functions given to the United Nations Mediator on Palestine by the resolution of the General Assembly of 14 May 1948; (b) To carry out the specific functions and directives given to it by the present resolution and such additional functions and directives as may be given to it by the General Assembly or by the Security Council; (c) To undertake, upon the request of the Security Council, any of the functions now assigned to the United Nations Mediator on Palestine or to the United Nations Truce Commission by resolutions of the Security Council; upon such request to the Conciliation Commission by the Security Council with respect to all the remaining functions of the United Nations Mediator on Palestine under Security Council resolutions, the office of the Mediator shall be terminated; 3. *Decides* that a Committee of the Assembly, consisting of China, France, the Union of Soviet Socialist Republics, the United Kingdom and the United States of America, shall present, before the end of the first part of the present session of the General Assembly, for the approval of the Assembly a proposal concerning the names of the three States which will constitute the Conciliation Commission; 4. *Requests* the Commission to begin its functions at once, with a view to the establishment of contact between the parties themselves and the Commission at the earliest possible date; 5. *Calls upon* the Governments and authorities concerned to extend the scope of the negotiations provided for in the Security Council's resolution of 16 November 1948 and to seek agreement by negotiations conducted either with the Conciliation Commission or directly with a view to the final settlement of all questions outstanding between them; 6. *Instructs* the Conciliation Commission to take steps to assist the Governments and authorities concerned to achieve a final settlement of all questions outstanding between them; 7. *Resolves* that the Holy Places -- including Nazareth -- religious buildings and sites in Palestine should be protected and free access to them assured, in accordance with existing rights and historical practice; that arrangements to this end should be under effective United Nations supervision; that the United Nations Conciliation Commission, in presenting to the fourth regular session of the General Assembly its detailed proposal for a permanent international regime for the territory of Jerusalem, should include recommendations concerning the Holy Places in that territory; that with regard to the Holy Places in the rest of Palestine the Commission should call upon the political authorities of the areas concerned to give appropriate formal guarantees as to the protection of the Holy Places and access to them; and that these undertakings should be presented to the General Assembly for approval; 8. *Resolves* that, in view of its association with three world religions, the Jerusalem area, including the present municipality of Jerusalem plus the surrounding villages and towns, the most Eastern of which shall be Abu Dis; the most Southern, Bethlehem; the most Western, Ein Karim (including also the built-up area of Motsa); and the most Northern Shu'fat, should be accorded special and separate treatment from the rest of Palestine and should be placed under effective United Nations control; *Requests* the Security Council to take further steps to ensure the demilitarization of Jerusalem at the earliest possible date; *Instructs* the Conciliation Commission to present to the fourth regular session of the General Assembly detailed proposals for a permanent international regime for the Jerusalem area which will provide for the maximum local autonomy for distinctive groups consistent with the special international status of the Jerusalem area; The Conciliation Commission is authorized to appoint a United Nations representatives who shall cooperate with the local authorities with respect to the interim administration of the Jerusalem area; 9. *Resolves* that, pending agreement on more detailed arrangements among the Governments and authorities concerned, the freest possible access to Jerusalem by road, rail or air should be accorded to all inhabitants of Palestine; *Instructs* the Conciliation Commission to report immediately to the Security Council, for appropriate action by that organ, any attempt by any party to impede such access; 10. *Instructs* the Conciliation Commission to seek arrangements among the Governments and authorities concerned which will facilitate the economic development of the area, including arrangements for access to ports and airfields and the use of transportation and communication facilities; 11. *Resolves* that the refugees wishing to return to their homes and live at peace with their neighbours should be permitted to do so at the earliest practicable date, and that compensation should be paid for the property of those choosing not to return and for loss of or damage to property which, under principles of international law or in equity, should be made good by the Governments or authorities responsible; *Instructs* the

Conciliation Commission to facilitate the repatriation, resettlement and economic and social rehabilitation of the refugees and the payment of compensation, and to maintain close relations with the Director of the United Nations Relief for Palestine Refugees and, through him, with the appropriate organs and agencies of the United Nations; 12. *Authorizes* the Conciliation Commission to appoint such subsidiary bodies and to employ such technical experts, acting under its authority, as it may find necessary for the effective discharge of its functions and responsibilities under the present resolution; The Conciliation Commission will have its official headquarters at Jerusalem. The authorities responsible for maintaining order in Jerusalem will be responsible for taking all measures necessary to ensure the security of the Commission. The Secretary-General will provide a limited number of guards for the protection of the staff and premises of the Commission; 13. *Instructs* the Conciliation Commission to render progress reports periodically to the Secretary-General for transmission to the Security Council and to the Members of the United Nations; 14. *Calls Upon* all Governments and authorities concerned to cooperate with the Conciliation Commission and to take all possible steps to assist in the implementation of the present resolution; 15. *Requests* the Secretary-General to provide the necessary staff and facilities and to make appropriate arrangements to provide the necessary funds required in carrying out the terms of the present resolution.

ARMISTICE AGREEMENTS (1949)

The termination of the British Mandate over Palestine and the Israeli Declaration of Independence were accompanied by the entry of the regular armed forces of the Arab League member states into what had been Palestine. The Secretary General of the Arab League formally notified the United Nations Secretary General of this on May 15, 1948. Thus began the first of the Arab-Israeli wars, generally known as Israel's War of Independence and often referred to in the Arab world as al-Nakba (the disaster or the catastrophe). By early 1949 it became clear that the military hostilities should give way to negotiations for armistice agreements to terminate the fighting and to prepare for movement for resolution of the broader issues. Negotiations on the island of Rhodes were conducted under the auspices of Ralph Bunche, the United Nations Acting Mediator for Palestine.

Beginning in early 1949 Israel and each of the neighboring states signed an armistice agreement terminating the hostilities of the first Arab-Israeli War that followed the end of the British Mandate. Iraq, although a participant in the conflict, refused to do so. The agreements were to end the hostilities and pave the way for peace negotiations, but the latter did not occur. Egypt signed its armistice agreement with Israel on February 24, 1949; Lebanon on March 23, 1949; Jordan on April 3, 1949; and Syria on July 20, 1949.

Each of the agreements was based on several principles: that no military or political advantage should be gained under the truce; that no changes in military positions should be made by either side after the armistice; and that the provisions of the armistices were a consequence of purely military considerations -- they were temporary pending the negotiation of more binding arrangements. Each agreement set up a mixed armistice commission to observe and maintain the cease-fire. The text of the Egypt-Israel agreement follows.

PREAMBLE. The Parties to the present Agreement, responding to the Security Council resolution of 16 November 1948 calling upon them, as a further provisional measure under Article 40 of the Charter of the United Nations and in order to facilitate the transition from the present truce to permanent peace in Palestine, to negotiate an Armistice; having decided to enter into negotiations under United Nations Chairmanship concerning the implementation of the Security Council resolutions of 4 and 16 November 1948; and having appointed representatives empowered to negotiate and conclude an Armistice Agreement:

The undersigned representatives, in the full authority entrusted to them by their respective Governments, have agreed upon the following provisions:

Article I. With a view to promoting the return to permanent peace in Palestine and in recognition of the importance in this regard of mutual assurances concerning the future military operations of the Parties, the following principles, which shall be fully observed by both Parties during the Armistice, are hereby affirmed:

1. The injunction of the Security Council against resort to military force in the settlement of the Palestine question shall henceforth be scrupulously respected by both Parties.

2. No aggressive action by the armed forces -- land, sea, or air -- of either Party shall be undertaken, planned, or threatened against the people or the armed forces of the other; it being understood that the use of the term "planned" in this context has no bearing on normal staff planning as generally practiced in military organizations.

3. The right of each Party to its security and freedom from fear of attack by the armed forces of the other shall be fully respected.

4. The establishment of an armistice between the armed forces of the two Parties is accepted as an indispensable step toward the liquidation of armed conflict and the restoration of peace in Palestine.

Article II. 1. In pursuance of the foregoing principles and of the resolutions of the Security Council of 4 and 16 November 1948, a general armistice between the armed forces of the two Parties -- land, sea and air -- is hereby established.

2. No element of the land, sea or air military or para-military forces of either Party, including non-regular forces, shall commit any warlike to hostile act against the military or para-military forces of the other Party, or against civilians in territory under the control of the Party; or shall advance beyond or pass over

for any purpose whatsoever the Armistice Demarcation Line set forth in Article VI of this Agreement except as provided in Article III of this Agreement; and elsewhere shall not violate the international frontier; or enter into or pass through the air space of the other Party or through the waters within three miles of the coastline of the other Party.

Article III. 1. In pursuance of the Security Council's resolution of 4 November 1948, and with a view to the implementation of the Security Council's resolution of 16 November 1948, the Egyptian Military Forces in the AL FALUJA area shall be withdrawn.

2. This withdrawal shall begin on the day after that which follows the signing of this Agreement, at 0500 hours GMT, and shall be beyond the Egypt-Palestine frontier.

3. The withdrawal shall be under the supervision of the United Nations and in accordance with the Plan of Withdrawal set forth in Annex I to this Agreement.

Article IV. With specific reference to the implementation of the resolutions of the Security Council of 4 and 16 November 1948, the following principles and purposes are affirmed:

1. The principle that no military or political advantage should be gained under the truce ordered by the Security Council is recognized.

2. It is also recognized that the basic purposes and spirit of the Armistice would not be served by the restoration of previously held military positions, changes from those now held other than as specifically provided for in this Agreement, or by the advance of the military forces of either side beyond positions held at the time this Armistice Agreement is signed.

3. It is further recognized that rights, claims or interests of a non-military character in the area of Palestine covered by this Agreement may be asserted by either Party, and that these, by mutual agreement being excluded from the Armistice negotiations, shall be, at the discretion of the Parties, the subject of later settlement. It is emphasized that it is not the purpose of this Agreement to establish, to recognize, to strengthen, or to weaken or nullify, in any way, any territorial, custodial or other rights, claims or interests which may be asserted by either Party in the area of Palestine or any part or locality thereof covered by this Agreement, whether such asserted rights, claims or interests derive from Security Council resolutions, including the resolution of 4 November 1948 and the Memorandum of 13 November 1948 for its implementation, or from any other source. The provisions of this Agreement are dictated exclusively by military considerations and are valid only for the period of the Armistice.

Article V. 1. The line described in Article VI of this Agreement shall be designated as the Armistice Demarcation Line and is delineated in pursuance of the purpose and intent of the resolutions of the Security Council of 4 and 16 November 1948.

2. The Armistice Demarcation Line is not to be construed in any sense

as a political or territorial boundary, and is delineated without prejudice to rights, claims and positions of either Party to the Armistice as regards ultimate settlement of the Palestine question.

3. The basic purpose of the Armistice Demarcation Line is to delineate the line beyond which the armed forces of the respective Parties shall not move except as provided in Article III of this Agreement.

4. Rules and regulations of the armed forces of the Parties, which prohibit civilians from crossing the fighting lines or entering the area between the lines, shall remain in effect after the signing of this Agreement with application to the Armistice Demarcation Line defined in Article VI.

Article VI. 1. In the GAZA-RAFAH area the Armistice Demarcation Line shall be as delineated in paragraph 2.B (i) of the Memorandum of 13 November 1948 on the implementation of the Security Council resolution of 2 November 1948, namely by a line from the coast at the mouth of the Wadi Hasi in an easterly direction through Deir Suneid and across the Gaza-Al Majdal Highway to a point 3 kilometres east of the Highway, then in a southerly direction parallel to the Gaza-Al Madjal Highway, and continuing thus to the Egyptian frontier.

2. Within this line Egyptian forces shall nowhere advance beyond their present positions, and this shall include Beit Hanun and its surrounding area from which Israeli forces shall be withdrawn to north of the Armistice Demarcation Line, and any other positions within the line delineated in paragraph 1 shall be evacuated by Israeli forces as set forth in paragraph 3.

3. Israeli outposts, each limited to platoon strength, may be maintained in this area at the following points: Deir Suneid, on the north side of the Wadi (MR 10751090); 700 SW of Sa'ad (MR 10500982); Sulphur Quarries (MR 09870924); Tall-Jamma (MR 09720887); and KH AL Ma'in (MR 09320821). The Israeli outpost maintained at the Cemetery (MR 08160723) shall be evacuated on the day after that which follows the signing of this Agreement. The Israeli outpost at Hill 79 (MR 10451017) shall be evacuated not later than four weeks following the day on which this Agreement is signed. Following the evacuation of the above outposts, new Israeli outpost may be established at MR 08360700, and at a point due east of Hill 79 east of the Armistice Demarcation Line.

4. In the Bethlehem-Hebron area, wherever positions are held by Egyptian forces, the provisions of this Agreement shall apply to the forces of both Parties in each locality, except that the demarcation of the Armistice Line and reciprocal arrangements for withdrawal and reduction of forces shall be undertaken in such manner as amy be decided by the Parties, at such time as an Armistice Agreement may be concluded covering military forces in that area other than those of the Parties to this Agreement, or sooner at the will of the Parties.

Article VII. 1. It is recognized by the Parties to this Agreement that in certain sectors of the total area involved, the proximity of the forces of a third party not covered by this Agreement makes impractical the full application of all provisions of the Agreement to such sectors. For this reason alone, therefore, and pending the conclusion of an Armistice Agreement in place of the existing truce with that third party, the provisions of this Agreement relating to reciprocal reduction and withdrawal of forces shall apply only to the western front and not to the eastern front.

2. The areas comprising the western and eastern fronts shall be as defined by the United Nations Chief of Staff of the Truce Supervision Organization, on the basis of the deployment of forces against each other and past military activity or the future possibility thereof in the area. This definition of the western and eastern fronts is set forth in Annex II of this Agreement.

3. In the area of the western front under Egyptian control. Egyptian defensive forces only may be maintained. All other Egyptian forces shall be withdrawn from this area to a point or points no further east than El Arish-Abou Aoueigila.

4. In the area of the western front under Israeli control, Israeli defensive forces only, which shall be based on the settlements, may be maintained. All other Israeli forces shall be withdrawn from this area to a point or points north of the line delineated in paragraph 2.A of the Memorandum of 13 November 1948 on the implementation of the resolution of the Security Council of 4 November 1948.

5. The defensive forces referred to in paragraphs 3 and 4 above shall be as defined in Annex III to this Agreement.

Article VIII. 1. The area comprising the village of El Auja and vicinity, as defined in paragraph 2 of this Article, shall be demilitarized, and both Egyptian and Israeli armed forces shall be totally excluded therefrom. The Chairman of the Mixed Armistice Commission established in Article X of this Agreement and United Nations Observers attached to the Commission shall be responsible for ensuring the full implementation of this provision.

2. The area thus demilitarized shall be as follows: From a point on the Egypt-Palestine frontier five (5) kilometres north-west of the intersection of the Rafah-El Auja road and the frontier (MR 08750468), south-east to Khashm El Mamdud (MR 09650414), thence south-east to Hill 405 (MR 10780285), thence south-west to a point on the Egypt-Palestine frontier five (5) kilometres south-east of the intersection of the old railway tracks and the frontier (MR 09950145), thence returning north-west along the Egypt-Palestine frontier to the point of origin.

3. On the Egyptian side of the frontier, facing the El Auja area, no Egyptian defensive positions shall be closer to El Auja than El Qouseima and Abou Aoueigila.

4. The road Taba-Qouseima-Auja shall not be employed by any military forces whatsoever for the purpose of entering Palestine.

The movement of armed forces of either Party to this Agreement into any part of the area defined in paragraph 2 of this Article, for any purpose, or failure by either Party to respect or fulfil any of the other provisions of this Article, when confirmed by the United Nations representatives, shall constitute a flagrant violation of this Agreement.

Article IX. All prisoners of war detained by either Party to this Agreement and belonging to the armed forces, regular or irregular, of the other Party shall be exchanged as follows:

1. The exchange of prisoners of war shall be under United Nations supervision and control throughout. The exchange shall begin within ten days after the signing of this Agreement and shall be completed not later than twenty-one days following. Upon the signing of this Agreement, the Chairman of the Mixed Armistice Commission established in Article X of this Agreement, in consultation with the appropriate military authorities of the Parties, shall formulate a plan for the exchange of prisoners of war within the above period, defining the date and places of exchange and all other relevant details.

2. Prisoners of war against whom a penal prosecution may be pending, as well as those sentenced for crime or other offence, shall be included in this exchange of prisoners.

3. All articles of personal use, valuables, letters, documents, identification marks, and other personal affects of whatever nature, belonging to prisoners of war who are being exchanged, shall be returned to them, or, if they have escaped or died, to the Party to whose armed forces they belonged.

4. All matters not specifically regulated in this Agreement shall be decided in accordance with the principles laid down in the International Convention relating to the Treatment of Prisoners of War, signed at Geneva on 27 July 1929.

5. The Mixed Armistice Commission established in Article X of this Agreement shall assume responsibility for locating missing persons, whether military or civilian, within the areas controlled by each Party, to facilitate their expeditious exchange. Each Party undertakes to extent to the Commission full co-operation and assistance in the discharge of this function.

Article X. 1. The execution of the provisions of this Agreement shall be supervised by a Mixed Armistice Commission composed of seven members, of whom each Party to this Agreement shall designate three, and whose Chairman shall be the United Nations Chief of Staff of the Truce Supervision Organization or a senior officer from the Observer personnel of that Organization designed by him following consultation with both Parties to this Agreement.

2. The Mixed Armistice Commission shall maintain its headquarters at El Auja, and shall hold its meetings at such places and at such times as it may deem necessary for the effective conduct of its work.

3. The Mixed Armistice Commission shall be convened in its first meeting by the United Nations Chief of Staff of the Truce Supervision Organization not later than one week following the signing of this Agreement.

4. Decisions of the Mixed Armistice Commission, to the extent possible, shall be based on the principle of unanimity. In the absence of unanimity, decisions shall be taken by a majority vote of the members of the Commission present and voting. On questions of principle, appeal shall lie to a Special Committee, composed of the United Nations Chief of Staff of the Truce Supervision Organization and one member each of the Egyptian and Israeli Delegations to the Armistice Conference at Rhodes or some other senior officer, whose decisions on all such questions shall be final. If no appeal against a decision of the Commission is filed within one week from the date of said decision, that decision shall be taken as final. Appeals to the Special Committee shall be presented to the United Nations Chief of Staff of the Truce Supervision Organization, who shall convene the Committee at the earliest possible date.

5. The Mixed Armistice Commission shall formulate its own rules of procedure. Meetings shall be held only after due notice to the members by the Chairman. The quorum for its meetings shall be a majority of its members.

6. The Commission shall be empowered to employ Observers, who may be from among the military organizations of the Parties or from the military personnel of the United Nations Truce Supervision Organization, or from both, in such numbers as may be considered essential to the performance of its functions. In the event United Nations Observers should be so employed, they shall remain under the command of the United Nations Chief of Staff of the Truce Supervision Organization. Assignments of a general or special nature given to United Nations Observers attached to the Mixed Armistice Commission shall be subject to approval by the United Nations Chief of Staff or his designated representative on the Commission, whichever is serving as Chairman.

7. Claims or complaints presented by either Party relating to the application of this Agreement shall be referred immediately to the Mixed Armistice Commission through its Chairman. The Commission shall take such action on all such claims or complaints by means of its observation and investigation machinery as it may deem appropriate, with a view to equitable and mutually satisfactory settlement.

8. Where interpretation of the meaning of a particular provision of this Agreement is at issue, the Commission's interpretation shall prevail, subject to the right of appeal as provided in paragraph 4. The Commission, in its discretion and as the need arises, may from time to time recommend to the Parties modifications in the provisions of this Agreement.

9. The Mixed Armistice Commission shall submit to both Parties reports on its activities as frequently as it may consider necessary. A copy of each such report shall be presented to the Secretary-General of the United Nations for transmission to the appropriate organ or agency of the United Nations.

10. Members of the Commission and its Observers shall be accorded such freedom of movement and access in the areas covered by this Agreement as the Commission may determine to be necessary, provided that when such

decisions of the Commission are reached by a majority vote United Nations Observers only shall be employed.

11. The expenses of the Commission, other than those relating to United Nations Observers, shall be apportioned in equal shares between the two Parties to this Agreement.

Article XI. No provision of this Agreement shall in any way prejudice the rights, claims and positions of either Party hereto in the ultimate peaceful settlement of the Palestine question.

Article XII. The present Agreement is not subject to ratification and shall come into force immediately upon being signed.

2. This Agreement, having been negotiated and concluded in pursuance of the resolution of the Security Council of 16 November 1948 calling for the establishment of an armistice in order to eliminate the threat to the peace in Palestine and to facilitate the transition from the present truce to permanent peace in Palestine, shall remain in force until a peaceful settlement between the Parties is achieved, except as provided in paragraph 3 of this Article.

3. The Parties to this Agreement may, by mutual consent, revise this Agreement or any of its provisions, or may suspend its application, other than Articles I and II, at any time. In the absence of mutual agreement and after this Agreement has been in effect for one year from the date of its signing, either of the Parties may call upon the Secretary-General of the United Nations to convoke a conference of representatives of the two Parties for the purpose of reviewing, revising or suspending any of the provisions of this Agreement other than Articles I and II. Participation in such conference shall be obligatory upon the Parties.

If the conference provided for in paragraph 3 of this Article does not result in an agreed solution of a point in dispute, either Party may bring the matter before the Security Council of the United Nations for the relief sought on the grounds that this Agreement has been concluded in pursuance of Security Council action toward the end of achieving peace in Palestine.

5. This Agreement supersedes the Egyptian-Israeli General Cease-Fire Agreement entered into by the Parties on 24 January 1949.

6. This Agreement is signed in quintuplicate, of which one copy shall be retained by each Party, two copies communicated to the Secretary-General of the United Nations for transmission to the Security Council and to the United Nations Conciliation Commission on Palestine, and one copy to the Acting Mediator on Palestine.

TRIPARTITE DECLARATION (MAY 25, 1950)

The end of the first Arab-Israeli war and the armistice agreements that followed did not lead to peace. Arms deliveries by Great Britain to Egypt, Jordan and Iraq were resumed and the Arab world spoke of a new round of war against Israel. Israel purchased military equipment when available and produced some. The three Western powers sought to control the developing regional arms race and to prevent renewal of Arab-Israeli, or other, hostilities. To this end, the United States, France and the United Kingdom issued a declaration on May 25, 1950 in which they proposed limiting arms supplies to the region to those needed for security.

The Governments of the United Kingdom, France, and the United States, having had occasion during the recent Foreign Ministers meeting in London to review certain questions affecting the peace and stability of the Arab states and of Israel, and particularly that of the supply of arms and war material to these states, have resolved to make the following statements:

1. The three Governments recognize that the Arab states and Israel all need to maintain a certain level of armed forces for the purposes of assuring their internal security and their legitimate self-defense and to permit them to play their part in the defense of the area as a whole. All applications for arms or war material for these countries will be considered in the light of these principles. In this connection the three Governments wish to recall and reaffirm the terms of the statement made by their representatives on the Security Council on August 4, 1949, in which they declared their opposition to the development of an arms race between the Arab states and Israel.

2. The three Governments declare that assurances have been received from all the states in question, to which they permit arms to be supplied from their countries, that the purchasing state does not intend to undertake any act of aggression against any other state. Similar assurances will be requested from any other state in the area to which they permit arms to be supplied in the future.

3. The three Governments take this opportunity of declaring their deep interest in and their desire to promote the establishment and maintenance of peace and stability in the area and their unalterable opposition to the use of force or threat of force between any of the states in that area. The three Governments, should they find that any of these states was preparing to violate frontiers or armistice lines, would, consistently with their obligations as members of the United Nations, immediately take action, both within and outside the United Nations, to prevent such violation.

LAW OF RETURN (JULY 5, 1950)

On July 5, 1950 the Israeli parliament, the Knesset, passed the Law of Return that assured virtually unlimited and unfettered Jewish immigration to Israel by providing that every Jew has the right to immigrate to Israel to settle there unless the applicant is engaged in an activity "directed against the Jewish people" or one that may "endanger public health or the security of the state." An amendment in 1954 also restricted those likely to endanger public welfare. The 1950 law has provided the formal basis for the substantial immigration (aliya) that has taken place since independence. The concept of unlimited immigration has been reinforced by the programs and actions of successive governments and has had overwhelming support in parliament and from Israel's Jewish population. The text includes the amendments of 1954 and 1970.

1. Every Jew has the right to come to this country as an oleh [Jew immigrating to Israel].

2. (a) Aliyah [immigration of Jews to Israel] shall be by oleh's visa. (b) An oleh's visa shall be granted to every Jew who has expressed his desire to settle in Israel, unless the Minister of the Interior is satisfied that the applicant (1) is engaged in an activity directed against the Jewish people; or (2) is likely to endanger public health or the security of the State; or (3) is a person with a criminal past, likely to endanger public welfare.

3. (a) A Jew who has come to Israel and subsequent to his arrival has expressed his desire to settle in Israel may, while still in Israel, receive an oleh's certificate. (b) The restrictions specified in section 2(b) shall apply also to the grant of an oleh's certificate, but a person shall not be regarded as endangering public health on account of an illness contracted after his arrival in Israel.

4. Every Jew who has immigrated into this country before the coming into force of this Law, and every Jew who was born in this country, whether before or after the coming into force of this Law, shall be deemed to be a person who has come to this country as an oleh under this Law. 4A. (a) The rights of a Jew under this Law and the rights of an oleh under the Nationality Law, 5712-1952, as well as the rights of an oleh under any other enactment, are also vested in a child and a grandchild of a Jew, the spouse of a Jew, the spouse of a child of a Jew and the spouse of a grandchild of a Jew, except for a person who has been a Jew and has voluntarily changed his religion. (b) It shall be immaterial whether or not a Jew by whose right a right under subsection (a) is claimed is still alive and whether or not he has immigrated to Israel. (c) The restrictions and conditions prescribed in respect of a Jew or an oleh by or under this Law or by the enactments referred to in subsection (a) shall also apply to a person who claims a right under subsection (a). 4B. For the purposes of this Law, "Jew" means a person who was born of a Jewish mother or has become converted to Judaism and who is not a member of another religion.

5. The Minister of Immigration is charged with the implementation of this Law and may make regulations as to any matter relating to such implementation and also as to the grant of oleh's visas and oleh's certificates to minors up to the age of 18 years.

JERUSALEM PROGRAM (AUGUST 30, 1951)

After the independence of Israel in 1948, the Basle Program no longer correspond-ed with reality. At the twenty-third Zionist Congress, which met in Jerusalem from August 14 to 30, 1951, the status of the Zionist movement after the establishment of Israel was the central issue and the Jerusalem Program was adopted. It noted that "The task of Zionism is the consolidation of the State of Israel, the ingathering of the exiles in Eretz Israel and the fostering of the unity of the Jewish people." At the twenty-seventh Congress, held in Jerusalem between June 9 and 19, 1968, the Jerusalem Program was modified and additional elements were added to it. These included references to the unity of the Jewish people, the centrality of Israel in the life of the Jewish people, and the ingathering of the Jewish people in its historic homeland through aliyah. The principles of the Jerusalem Program reconfirmed the relationship between Israel, Zionism, and the Jewish people.

The aims of Zionism are: The Unity of the Jewish People and the centrality of Israel in its life; the ingathering of the Jewish People in its historic homeland, Eretz Yisrael, through aliya from all lands; the strengthening of the State of Israel, founded on the Prophetic ideals of justice and peace: the preservation of the identity of the Jewish People through the fostering of Jewish and Hebrew education and of Jewish spiritual and cultural values; the protection of Jewish rights everywhere.

UNITED STATES AIDE-MÉMOIRE (FEBRUARY 11, 1957)

As part of the reassurances that led to Israel's withdrawal from the Sinai Peninsula and the Gaza Strip after the Sinai War of 1956, United States Secretary of State John Foster Dulles presented an aide-mémoire to Israeli Ambassador Abba Eban, on February 11, 1957, in which the United States noted its belief that the Gulf of Aqaba "comprehends international waters and that no nation has the right to prevent free and innocent passage in the Gulf and through the Straits giving access thereto." When, in May 1967, Egyptian President Gamal Abdul Nasser announced the blockade of the Strait of Tiran, Israel sought reassurances based on this pledge from the United States that the action would not stand.

The United Nations General Assembly has sought specifically, vigorously, and almost unanimously, the prompt withdrawal from Egypt of the armed forces of Britain, France and Israel. Britain and France have complied unconditionally. The forces of Israel have been withdrawn to a considerable extent but still hold Egyptian territory at Sharm el Shaikh at the entrance to the Gulf of Aqaba. They also occupy the Gaza Strip which is territory specified by the Armistice arrangements to be occupied by Egypt.

We understand that it is the position of Israel that (1) it will evacuate its military forces from the Gaza Strip provided Israel retains the civil administration and police in some relationship to the United Nations; and (2) it will withdraw from Sharm el Shaikh if continued freedom of passage through the Straits is assured.

With respect to (1) the Gaza Strip -- it is the view of the United States that the United Nations General Assembly has no authority to require of either Egypt or Israel a substantial modification of the Armistice Agreement, which, as noted, now gives Egypt the right and responsibility of occupation. Accordingly, we believe that Israeli withdrawal from Gaza should be prompt and unconditional, leaving the future of the Gaza Strip to be worked out through the efforts and good offices of the United Nations.

We recognize that the area has been a source of armed infiltration and reprisals back and forth contrary to the Armistice Agreement and is a source of great potential danger because of the presence there of so large a number of Arab refugees -- about 200,000. Accordingly, we believe that the United Nations General Assembly and the Secretary General should seek that the United Nations Emergency Force, in the exercise of its mission, move into this area and be on the boundary between Israel and the Gaza Strip.

The United States will use its best efforts to help to assure this result, which we believe is contemplated by the Second Resolution of February 2, 1957.

With respect to (2) the Gulf of Aqaba and access thereto -- the United States believes that the Gulf comprehends international waters and that no nation has the right to prevent free and innocent passage in the Gulf and through the Straits giving access thereto. We have in mind not only commercial usage, but the passage of pilgrims on religious missions, which should be fully respected.

The United States recalls that on January 28, 1950, the Egyptian Ministry of Foreign Affairs informed the United States that the Egyptian occupation of the two islands of Tiran and Senafir at the entrance of the Gulf of Aqaba was only to protect the islands themselves against possible damage or violation and that "this occupation being in no way conceived in a spirit of obstructing in any way innocent passage through the stretch of water separating these two islands from the Egyptian coast of Sinai, it follows that the passage, the only practicable one, will remain free as in the past, in conformity with international practice and recognized principles of the law of nations."

In the absence of some overriding decision to the contrary, as by the International Court of Justice, the United States, on behalf of vessels of United States registry, is prepared to exercise the right of free and innocent passage and to join with others to secure general recognition of this right.

It is of course clear that the enjoyment of a right of free and innocent passage by Israel would depend upon its prior withdrawal in accordance with the

United Nations Resolutions. The United States has no reason to assume that any littoral state would under these circumstances obstruct the right of free and innocent passage.

The United States believes that the United Nations General Assembly and the Secretary General should, as a precautionary measure, seek that the United Nations Emergency Force move into the Straits area as the Israeli forces are withdrawn. This again we believe to be within the contemplation of the Second Resolution of February 2, 1957.

(3) The United States observes that the recent resolutions of the United Nations General Assembly call not only for the prompt and unconditional withdrawal of Israel behind the Armistice lines but call for other measures.

We believe, however, that the United Nations has properly established an order of events and an order or urgency and that the first requirement is that forces of invasion and occupation should withdraw.

The United States is prepared publicly to declare that it will use its influence, in concert with other United Nations members, to the end that, following Israel's withdrawal, these other measures will be implemented.

We believe that our views and purposes in this respect are shared by many other nations and that a tranquil future for Israel is best assured by reliance upon the fact, rather than by an occupation in defiance of the overwhelming judgment of the world community.

PALESTINE NATIONAL COVENANT (JUNE 1964)

The Palestine National Covenant was adopted by the Palestine National Council meeting at which the Palestine Liberation Organization (PLO) was created in June 1964. It was revised by the Palestine National Council in Cairo in July 1968. At the core is Article 20 which declares that the "Balfour Declaration, the Mandate for Palestine and everything that has been based upon them, are deemed null and void." Although various Palestinian and other Arab leaders have suggested that the covenant has been superseded in part by subsequent statements and declarations, the Covenant remained formally unchanged even after the Israel-PLO Declaration of Principles of September 13, 1993.

Article 1: Palestine is the homeland of the Arab Palestinian people; it is an indivisible part of the Arab homeland, and the Palestinian people are an integral part of the Arab nation.

Article 2: Palestine, with the boundaries it had during the British Mandate, is an indivisible territorial unit.

Article 3: The Palestinian people possess the legal right to their homeland and have the right to determine their destiny after achieving the liberation of their country in accordance with their wishes and entirely of their own accord and will.

Article 4: The Palestinian identity is a genuine, essential and inherent characteristic; it is transmitted from parents to children. The Zionist occupation and the dispersal of the Palestinian Arab people, through the disasters which befell them, do not make them lose their Palestinian identity and their membership of the Palestinian community, nor do they negate them.

Article 5: The Palestinians are those Arab nationals who, until 1947, normally resided in Palestine regardless of whether they were evicted from it or have stayed there. Anyone born, after that date, of a Palestinian father -- whether inside Palestine or outside it -- is also a Palestinian.

Article 6: The Jews who had normally resided in Palestine until the beginning of the Zionist invasion will be considered Palestinians.

Article 7: That there is a Palestinian community and that it has material, spiritual and historical connections with Palestine are indisputable facts. It is a national duty to bring up individual Palestinians in an Arab revolutionary manner. All means of information and education must be adopted in order to acquaint the Palestinian with his country in the most profound manner, both spiritual and material, that is possible. He must be prepared for the armed struggle and ready to sacrifice his wealth and his life in order to win back his homeland and bring about its liberation.

Article 8: The phase in their history, through which the Palestinian people are now living, is that of national (watani) struggle for the liberation of Palestine. Thus the conflicts among the Palestinian national forces are secondary, and should be ended for the sake of the basic conflict that exists between the forces of Zionism and of imperialism on the one hand, and the Palestinian Arab people on the other. On this basis the Palestinian masses, regardless of whether they are residing in the national homeland or in diaspora (mahajir) constitute -- both their organization and the individuals -- one national front working for the retrieval of Palestine and its liberation through armed struggle.

Article 9: Armed struggle is the only way to liberate Palestine. Thus it is the overall strategy, not merely a tactical phase. The Palestinian Arab people assert their absolute determination and firm resolution to continue their armed struggle and to work for an armed popular revolution for the liberation of their country and their return to it. They also assert their right to normal life in Palestine and to exercise their right to self-determination and sovereignty over it.

Article 10: Commando action constitutes the nucleus of the Palestinian popular liberation war. This requires its escalation, comprehensiveness and mobilization of all the Palestinian popular and educational efforts and their organization and involvement in the armed Palestinian revolution. It also requires the achieving of unity for the national (watani) struggle among the different groupings of the Palestinian people, and between the Palestinian people and the Arab masses so as to secure the continuation of the revolution, its escalation and victory.

Article 11: The Palestinians will have three mottoes: national (wataniyya) unity, national (qawmiyya) mobilization and liberation.

Article 12: The Palestinian people believe in Arab unity. In order to contribute their share towards the attainment of that objective, however, they must, at the present stage of their struggle, safeguard their Palestinian identity and develop their consciousness of that identity, and oppose any plan that may dissolve or impair it.

Article 13: Arab unity and the liberation of Palestine are two complementary objectives, the attainment of either of which facilitates the attainment of the other. Thus, Arab unity leads to the liberation of Palestine; the liberation of Palestine leads to Arab unity; and work towards the realization of one objective proceeds side by side with work towards the realization of the other.

Article 14: The destiny of the Arab nation, and indeed Arab existence itself, depends upon the destiny of the Palestinian cause. From this interdependence springs the Arab nation's pursuit of, and striving for, the liberation of Palestine. The people of Palestine play the role of the vanguard in the realization of this sacred national (qawmi) goal.

Article 15: The liberation of Palestine, from an Arab viewpoint, is a national (qawmi) duty and it attempts to repel the Zionist and imperialist aggression against the Arab homeland, and aims at the elimination of Zionism in Palestine. Absolute responsibility for this falls upon the Arab nation -- peoples and governments -- with the Arab people of Palestine in the vanguard.

Accordingly the Arab nation must mobilize all its military, human, and moral and spiritual capabilities to participate actively with the Palestinian people in the liberation of Palestine. It must, particularly in the phase of the armed Palestinian revolution; offer and furnish the Palestinian people with all possible help, and material and human support, and make available to them the means and opportunities that will enable them to continue to carry out their leading role in the armed revolution, until they liberate their homeland.

Article 16: The liberation of Palestine, from a spiritual point of view, will provide the Holy Land with an atmosphere of safety and tranquility, which in turn will safeguard the country's religious sanctuaries and guarantee freedom of worship and of visit to all, without discrimination of race, color, language, or religion. Accordingly, the people of Palestine look to all spiritual forces in the world for support.

Article 17: The liberation of Palestine, from a human point of view, will restore to the Palestinian individual his dignity, pride and freedom. Accordingly the Palestinian Arab people look forward to the support of all those who believe in the dignity of man and his freedom in the world.

Article 18: The liberation of Palestine, from an international point of view, is a defensive action necessitated by the demands of self-defence. Accordingly, the Palestinian people, desirous as they are of the friendship of all people, look to freedom-loving, justice-loving and peace-loving states for support in order to restore their legitimate rights in Palestine, to re-establish peace and security in the country, and to enable its people to exercise national sovereignty and freedom.

Article 19: The partition of Palestine in 1947 and the establishment of the State of Israel are entirely illegal, regardless of the passage of time, because they were contrary to the will of the Palestinian people and to their natural right in their homeland, and inconsistent with the principles embodied in the Charter of the United Nations, particularly the right to self-determination.

Article 20: The Balfour Declaration, the Mandate for Palestine and everything that has been based upon them, are deemed null and void. Claims of historical or religious ties of Jews with Palestine are incompatible with the facts history and the true conception of what constitutes statehood. Judaism, being a religion, is not an independent nationality. Nor do Jews constitute a single nation with an identity of its own; they are citizens of the states to which they belong.

Article 21: The Arab Palestinian people, expressing themselves by the armed Palestinian revolution, reject all solutions which are substitutes for the total liberation of Palestine and reject all proposals aiming at the liquidation of the Palestinian problem, or its internationalization.

Article 22: Zionism is a political movement organically associated with international imperialism and antagonistic to all action for liberation and to progressive movements in the world. It is racist and fanatic in its nature, aggressive, expansionist and colonial in its aims, and fascist in its methods. Israel is the instrument of the Zionist movement, and a geographical base for world imperialism placed strategically in the midst of the Arab homeland to combat the hopes of the Arab nation for liberation, unity and progress. Israel is a constant source of threat *vis-à-vis* peace in the Middle East and the whole world. Since the liberation of Palestine will destroy the Zionist and imperialist presence and will contribute to the establishment of peace in the Middle East, the Palestinian people look for the support of all the progressive and peaceful forces and urge them all, irrespective of their affiliations and beliefs, to offer the Palestinian people all aid and support in their just struggle for the liberation of their homeland.

Article 23: The demands of security and peace, as well as the demands of right and justice, require all states to consider Zionism an illegitimate movement, to outlaw its existence, and to ban its operations, in order that friendly relations among peoples may be preserved, and the loyalty of citizens to their respective homelands safeguarded.

Article 24: The Palestinian people believe in the principles of justice, freedom, sovereignty, self-determination, human dignity, and in the right of all peoples to exercise them.

Article 25: For the realization of the goals of this Charter and its principles, the Palestinian Liberation Organization will perform its role in the liberation of

Palestine in accordance with the Constitution of this Organization.

Article 26: The Palestine Liberation Organization, representative of the Palestinian revolutionary forces, is responsible for the Palestinian Arab people's movement in its struggle -- to retrieve its homeland, liberate and return to it and exercise the right to self-determination in it -- in all military, political and financial fields and also for whatever may be required by the Palestinian case on the inter-Arab and international levels.

Article 27: The Palestinian Liberation Organization shall cooperate with all Arab states, each according to its potentialities; and will adopt a neutral policy among them in the light of the requirements of the war of liberation; and on this basis it shall not interfere in the internal affairs of any Arab State.

Article 28: The Palestinian Arab people assert the genuineness and independence of their national (wataniyya) revolution and reject all forms of intervention, trusteeship and subordination.

Article 29: The Palestinian people possess the fundamental and genuine legal right to liberate and retrieve their homeland. The Palestinian people determine their attitude towards all states and forces on the basis of the stands they adopt *vis-à-vis* the Palestinian case and the extent of the support they offer to the Palestinian revolution to fulfill the aims of the Palestinian people.

Article 30: Fighters and carriers of arms in the war of liberation are the nucleus of the popular army which will be the protective force for the gains of the Palestinian Arab people.

Article 31: The Organization shall have a flag, an oath of allegiance and an anthem. All this shall be decided upon in accordance with a special regulation.

Article 32: Regulations, which shall be known as the Constitution of the Palestine Liberation Organization, shall be annexed to this Charter. It shall lay down the manner in which the Organization, and its organs and institutions, shall be constituted; the respective competence of each; and the requirements of its obligations under the Charter.

Article 33: This Charter shall not be amended save by (vote of) a majority of two-thirds of the total membership of the National Congress of the Palestine Liberation Organization (taken) at a special session convened for that purpose.

JOHNSON'S FIVE PRINCIPLES OF PEACE (JUNE 19, 1967)

Following the end of the Six Day War, June 5-11, 1967, diplomatic efforts were made by the Arab states and the Soviet bloc to force Israel to withdraw from the territory it had occupied during the hostilities. A United Nations General Assembly Emergency Session was called by the Soviet Union and it was convened on June 19, 1967 with Soviet Premier Aleksei Kosygin in attendance. On the same day, United States President Lyndon Johnson addressed the State Department's Foreign Policy Conference for Educators to detail the United States' position. Johnson articulated five principles of peace but no specific program of negotiation incorporating the principles was put forward and Johnson noted that "we are ready ... to see any method tried, and we believe that none should be excluded altogether. Perhaps all of them will be useful and all will be needed."

... Now, finally, let me turn to the Middle East -- and to the tumultuous events of the past months.

Those events have proved the wisdom of five great principles of peace in the region.

The first and the greatest principle is that every nation in the area has a fundamental right to live, and to have this right respected by its neighbors.

For the people of the Middle East, the path to hope does not lie in threats to end the life of any nation. Such threats have become a burden to the peace, not only of that region but a burden to the peace of the entire world.

In the same way, no nation would be true to the United Nations Charter, or to its own true interests, if it should permit military success to blind it to the fact that its neighbors have rights and its neighbors have interests of their own. Each nation, therefore, must accept the right of others to live.

Second, this last month, I think, shows us another basic requirement for settlement. It is a human requirement: justice for the refugees.

A new conflict has brought new homelessness. The nations of the Middle East must at last address themselves to the plight of those who have been displaced by war. In the past, both sides have resisted the best efforts of outside mediators to restore the victims of conflict to their homes, or to find them other proper places to live and work. There will be no peace for any party in the Middle East unless this problem is attacked with new energy by all, and certainly, primarily by those who are immediately concerned.

A third lesson from this last month is that maritime rights must be respected. Our Nation has long been committed to free maritime passage through international waterways, and we, along with other nations, were taking the necessary steps to implement this principle when hostilities exploded. If a single act of folly was more responsible for this explosion than any other, I think it was the arbitrary and dangerous announced decision that the Straits of Tiran would be closed. The right of innocent maritime passage must be preserved for all nations.

Fourth, this last conflict has demonstrated the danger of the Middle Eastern arms race of the last 12 years. Here the responsibility must rest not only on those in the area -- but upon the larger states outside the area. We believe that scarce resources could be used much better for technical and economic development. We have always opposed this arms race, and our own military shipments to the area have consequently been severely limited.

Now the waste and futility of the arms race must be apparent to all the peoples of the world. And now there is another moment of choice. The United States of America, for its part, will use every resource of diplomacy, and every counsel of reason and prudence, to try to find a better course.

As a beginning, I should like to propose that the United Nations immediately call upon all of its members to report all shipments of all military arms into this area, and to keep those shipments on file for all the peoples of the world to observe.

Fifth, the crisis underlines the importance of respect for political independence and territorial integrity of all the states of the area. We reaffirmed that principle at the height of this crisis. We reaffirm it again today on behalf of all.

This principle can be effective in the Middle East only on the basis of peace between the parties. The nations of the region have had only fragile and violated truce lines for 20 years. What they now need are recognized boundaries and other arrangements that will give them security against terror, destruction, and war. Further, there just must be adequate recognition of the special interest of three great religions in the holy places of Jerusalem.

These five principles are not new, but we do think they are fundamental. Taken together, they point the way from uncertain armistice to durable peace. We believe there must be progress toward all of them if there is to be progress toward any.

There are some who have urged, as a single, simple solution, an immediate return to the situation as it was on June 4. As our distinguished and able Ambassador, Mr. Arthur Goldberg, has already said, this is not a prescription for peace, but for renewed hostilities.

Certainly troops must be withdrawn, but there must also be recognized rights of national life, progress in solving the refugee problem, freedom of innocent maritime passage, limitation of the arms race, and respect for political independence and territorial integrity.

But who will make this peace where all others have failed for 20 years or more?

Clearly the parties to the conflict must be the parties to the peace. Sooner or later it is they who must make a settlement in the area. It is hard to see how it is possible for nations to live together in peace if they cannot learn to reason together.

But we must still ask, who can help them? Some say it should be the United Nations; some call for the use of other parties. We have been first in our support of effective peacekeeping in the United Nations, and we also recognize the great values to come from mediation.

We are ready this morning to see any method tried, and we believe that none should be excluded altogether. Perhaps all of them will be useful and all will be needed.

So, I issue an appeal to all to adopt no rigid view on these matters. I offer assurance to all that this Government of ours, the Government of the United States, will do its part for peace in every forum, at every level, at every hour.

Yet there is no escape from this fact: The main responsibility for the peace of the region depends upon its own leaders of that region. What will be truly decisive in the Middle East will be what is said and what is done by those who live in the Middle East.

They can seek another arms race, if they have not profited from the experience of this one, if they want to. But they will seek it at a terrible cost to their own people -- and to their very long-neglected human needs. They can live on a diet of hate -- though only at the cost of hatred in return. Or they can move toward peace with one another.

The world this morning is watching, watching for the peace of the world, because that is really what is at stake. It will look for patience and justice, it will look for humility and moral courage. It will look for signs of movement from prejudice and the emotional chaos of conflict to the gradual, slow shaping steps that lead to learning to live together and learning to help mold and shape peace in the area and in the world.

The Middle East is rich in history, rich in its people and its resources. It has no need to live in permanent civil war. It has the power to build its own life, as one of the prosperous regions of the world in which we live.

If the nations of the Middle East will turn toward the works of peace, they can count with confidence upon the friendship, and the help, of all the people of the United States of America.

In a climate of peace, we here will do our full share to help with a solution for the refugees. We here will do our full share in support of regional coopera- tion. We here will do our share, and do more, to see that the peaceful promise of nuclear energy is applied to the critical problems of desalting water and helping to make the desert bloom.

Our country is committed -- and we here reiterate that commitment today -- to a peace that is based on five principles:

-- first, the recognized right of national life;

-- second, justice for the refugees;

-- third, innocent maritime passage;

-- fourth, limits on the wasteful and destructive arms race; and

-- fifth, political independence and territorial integrity for all.

This is a time not for malice, but for magnanimity; not for propaganda, but for patience; not for vituperation, but for vision.

On the basis of peace, we offer our help to the people of the Middle East. That land, known to every one of us since childhood as the birthplace of great religions and learning, can flourish once again in our time. We here in the United States shall do all in our power to help make it so. ...

KHARTOUM ARAB SUMMIT RESOLUTIONS (SEPTEMBER 1, 1967)

At the Khartoum Arab Summit on September 1, 1967, the Arab states articulated their policy after the Six Day War and the established the framework of subsequent Arab policy on the conflict. They agreed to unite their efforts "to eliminate the effects of the [Israeli] aggression" in the Six Day War and to secure Israeli withdrawal from the occupied territories.

... The Arab heads of state have agreed to unite their political efforts on the international and diplomatic level to eliminate the effects of the aggression and to ensure the withdrawal of the aggressive Israeli forces from the Arab lands which have been occupied since the 5 June aggression. This will be done within the framework of the main principle to which the Arab states adhere, namely: no peace with Israel, no recognition of Israel, no negotiations with it, and adherence to the rights of the Palestinian people in their country.

UNSC RESOLUTION 242 (NOVEMBER 22, 1967)

After months of diplomatic-political discussions dealing with the consequences of the Six Day War in both the General Assembly and the Security Council, as well as in other bilateral and multilateral venues, the United Nations Security Council, on November 22, 1967, adopted a British-sponsored resolution, designed to achieve a solution to the Arab-Israeli conflict, that was deliberately vague but emphasized an exchange of territory for peace. The resolution has been the basis of all subsequent peace efforts. Gunnar Jarring, then Sweden's Ambassador to Moscow, was appointed by the United Nations Secretary General in November 1967 to implement the resolution, but ultimately he failed to secure meaningful movement toward peace.

The Security Council, Expressing its continuing concern with the grave situation in the Middle East, *Emphasizing* the inadmissibility of the acquisition of territory by war and the need to work for a just and lasting peace in which every State in the area can live in security, *Emphasizing further* that all Member States in their acceptance of the Charter of the United Nations have undertaken a commitment to act in accordance with Article 2 of the Charter, 1. *Affirms* that the fulfillment of Charter principles requires the establishment of a just and lasting peace in the Middle East which should include the application of both the following principles: (i) Withdrawal of Israeli armed forces from territories occupied in the recent conflict; (ii) Termination of all claims or states of belligerency and respect for and acknowledgement of the sovereignty, territorial integrity and political independence of every State in the area and their right to live in peace within secure and recognized boundaries free from threats or acts of force; 2. *Affirms further* the necessity (a) For guaranteeing freedom of navigation through international waterways in the area; (b) For achieving a just settlement of the refugee problem; (c) For guaranteeing the territorial inviolability and political independence of every State in the area, through measures including the establishment of demilitarized zones; 3. *Requests* the Secretary--General to designate a Special Representative to proceed to the Middle East to establish and maintain contacts with the States concerned in order to promote agreement and assist efforts to achieve a peaceful and accepted settlement in accordance with the provisions and principles in this resolution; 4. *Requests* the Secretary-General to report to the Security Council on the progress of the efforts of the Special Representative as soon as possible.

ROGERS PLAN (DECEMBER 9, 1969)

In the spring of 1969 the United States entered into quadripartite discussions with the United Kingdom, France, and the Soviet Union, and bilateral discussions with the Soviet Union, in an effort to achieve an agreed interpretation of United Nations Security Council Resolution 242 for Ambassador Jarring's use as a means of resolving the Arab-Israeli conflict. On December 9, 1969, United States Secretary of State William P. Rogers in a speech before the 1969 Galaxy Conference on Adult Education entitled "A Lasting Peace in the Middle East: An American View," publicly presented what later became known as the Rogers Plan (or Rogers Plan A): a policy statement on the situation in the Middle East and the US proposals presented earlier to the Soviet Union on October 28, 1969 as part of the two and four-power talks begun in the spring of 1969, in order to aid Ambassador Gunnar Jarring in his United Nations sponsored peace effort as outlined in UNSC Resolution 242. Secretary Rogers' address of December 9, 1969, reflected U.S. thinking during these talks and provided formulas for a solution to the Egyptian-Israeli part of the dispute.

The plan was rejected by Israel, Egypt, and the Soviet Union.

I am going to speak tonight about the situation in the Middle East. I want to refer to the policy of the United States as it relates to that situation in the hope that there may be a better understanding of that policy and the reasons for it.

Following the third Arab-Israeli war in 20 years, there was an upsurge of hope that a lasting peace could be achieved. That hope has unfortunately not been realized. There is no area of the world today that is more important, because it could easily again be the source of another serious conflagration.

When this administration took office, one of our first actions in foreign affairs was to examine carefully the entire situation in the Middle East. It was obvious that a continuation of the unresolved conflict there would be extremely dangerous, that the parties to the conflict alone would not be able to overcome their legacy of suspicion to achieve a political settlement, and that international efforts to help needed support.

The United States decided it had a responsibility to play a direct role in seeking a solution.

Thus, we accepted a suggestion put forward both by the French Government and the Secretary General of the United Nations. We agreed that the major powers -- the United States, the Soviet Union, the United Kingdom, and France -- should cooperate to assist the Secretary-General's representative, Ambassador Jarring, in working out a settlement in accordance with the resolution of the Security Council of the United Nations of November 1967. We also decided to consult directly with the Soviet Union, hoping to achieve as wide an area of agreement as possible between us.

These decisions were made in full recognition of the following important factors:

First, we knew that nations not directly involved could not make a durable peace for the peoples and governments involved. Peace rests with the parties to the conflict. The efforts of major powers can help, they can provide a catalyst, they can stimulate the parties to talk, they can encourage, they can help define a realistic framework for agreement; but an agreement among other powers cannot be a substitute for agreement among the parties themselves.

Second, we know that a durable peace must meet the legitimate concerns of both sides.

Third, we were clear that the only framework for a negotiated settlement was one in accordance with the entire text of the U.N. Security Council resolution. That resolution was agreed upon after long and arduous negotiations; it is carefully balanced; it provides the basis for a just and lasting peace -- a final settlement -- not merely an interlude between wars.

Fourth, we believe that a protracted period of no war, no peace, recurrent violence, and spreading chaos would serve the interests of no nation, in or out of the Middle East.

For 8 months we have pursued these consultations in four-power talks at the United Nations and in bilateral discussions with the Soviet Union. ...

The substance of the talks that we have had with the Soviet Union has been conveyed to the interested parties through diplomatic channels. This process has served to highlight the main roadblocks to the initiation of useful negotiations among the parties.

On the one hand, the Arab leaders fear that Israel is not in fact prepared to withdraw from Arab territory occupied in the 1967 war.

On the other hand, Israeli leaders fear that the Arab states are not in fact prepared to live in peace with Israel.

Each side can cite from its viewpoint considerable evidence to support its fears. Each side has permitted its attention to be focused solidly and to some extent solely on these fears.

What can the United States do to help to overcome these roadblocks?

We have friendly ties with both Arabs and Israelis. To call for Israeli withdrawal as envisaged in the U.N. resolution without achieving agreement on peace would be partisan toward the Arabs. To call on the Arabs to accept peace without Israeli withdrawal would be partisan toward Israel. Therefore, our policy is to encourage the Arabs to accept a permanent peace based on a binding agreement and to urge the Israelis to withdraw from occupied territory when their territorial integrity is assured as envisaged by the Security Council resolution.

In an effort to broaden the scope of discussion we have recently resumed four-power negotiations at the United Nations.

Let me outline our policy on various elements of the Security Council resolution. The basic and related issues might be described as peace, security, withdrawal, and territory.

Peace Between the Parties. The resolution of the Security Council makes clear that the goal is the establishment of a state of peace between the parties instead of the state of belligerency which has characterized relations for over 20 years. We believe the conditions and obligations of peace must be defined in specific terms. For example, navigation rights in the Suez Canal and in the Strait of Tiran should be spelled out. Respect for sovereignty and obligations of the parties to each other must be made specific.

Egypt

But peace, of course, involves much more than this. It is also a matter of the attitudes and intentions of the parties. Are they ready to coexist with one another? Can a live-and-let-live attitude replace suspicion, mistrust, and hate? A peace agreement between the parties must be based on clear and stated intentions and a willingness to bring about basic changes in the attitudes and conditions which are characteristic of the Middle East today.

Security. A lasting peace must be sustained by a sense of security on both sides. To this end, as envisaged in the Security Council resolution, there should be demilitarized zones and related security arrangements more reliable than those which existed in the area in the past. The parties themselves, with Ambassador Jarring's help, are in the best position to work out the nature and the details of such security arrangements. It is, after all, their interests which are at stake and their territory which is involved. They must live with the results.

Withdrawal and Territory. The Security Council resolution endorses the principle of the nonacquisition of territory by war and calls for withdrawal of Israeli armed forces from territories occupied in the 1967 war. We support this part of the resolution, including withdrawal, just as we do its other elements.

The boundaries from which the 1967 war began were established in the 1949 armistice agreements and have defined the areas of national jurisdiction in the Middle East for 20 years. Those boundaries were armistice lines, not final political borders. The rights, claims, and positions of the parties in an ultimate peaceful settlement were reserved by the armistice agreements.

The Security Council resolution neither endorses nor precludes these armistice lines as the definitive political boundaries. However, it calls for withdrawal from occupied territories, the nonacquisition of territory by war, and the establishment of secure and recognized boundaries.

We believe that while recognized political boundaries must be established and agreed upon by the parties, any changes in the preexisting lines should not reflect the weight of conquest and should be confined to insubstantial alterations required for mutual security. We do not support expansionism. We believe troops must be withdrawn as the resolution provides. We support Israel's security and the security of the Arab states as well. We are for a lasting peace that requires security for both.

By emphasizing the key issues of peace, security, withdrawal, and territory, I do not want to leave the impression that other issues are not equally important. Two in particular deserve special mention: the questions of refugees and of Jerusalem.

There can be no lasting peace without a just settlement of the problem of those Palestinians whom the wars of 1948 and 1967 have made homeless. This human dimension of the Arab-Israeli conflict has been of special concern to the United States for over 20 years. During this period the United States has contributed about $500 million for the support and education of the Palestinian refugees. We are prepared to contribute generously along with others to solve this problem. We believe its just settlement must take into account the desires and aspirations of the refugees and the legitimate concerns of the governments in the area.

The problem posed by the refugees will become increasingly serious if their future is not resolved. There is a new consciousness among the young Palestinians who have grown up since 1948 which needs to be channeled away from bitterness and frustration toward hope and justice.

The question of the future status of Jerusalem, because it touches deep emotional, historical, and religious wellsprings, is particularly complicated. We have made clear repeatedly in the past two and a half years that we cannot accept unilateral actions by any party to decide the final status of the city. We believe its status can be determined only through the agreement of the parties concerned, which in practical terms means primarily the Governments of Israel and Jordan, taking into account the interests of other countries in the area and the international community. We do, however, support certain principles which we believe would provide an equitable framework for a Jerusalem settlement.

Specifically, we believe Jerusalem should be a unified city within which there would no longer be restrictions on the movement of persons and goods.

There should be open access to the unified city for persons of all faiths and nationalities. Arrangements for the administration of the unified city should take into account the interests of all its inhabitants and of the Jewish, Islamic, and Christian communities. And there should be roles for both Israel and Jordan in the civic, economic, and religious life of the city.

It is our hope that agreement on the key issues of peace, security, withdrawal, and territory will create a climate in which these questions of refugees and of Jerusalem, as well as other aspects of the conflict, can be resolved as part of the overall settlement.

During the first weeks of the current United Nations General Assembly the efforts to move matters toward a settlement entered a particularly intensive phase. Those efforts continue today.

I have already referred to our talks with the Soviet Union. In connection with those talks there have been allegations that we have been seeking to divide the Arab states by urging the U.A.R. to make a separate peace. These allegations are false. It is a fact that we and the Soviets have been concentrating on the questions of a settlement between Israel and the United Arab Republic. We have been doing this in the full understanding on both our parts that, before there can be a settlement of the Arab-Israeli conflict, there must be agreement between the parties on other aspects of the settlement -- not only those related to the United Arab Republic but also those related to Jordan and other states which accept the Security Council resolution of November 1967.

We started with the Israeli-United Arab Republic aspect because of its inherent importance for future stability in the area and because one must start somewhere.

We are also ready to pursue the Jordanian aspect of a settlement; in fact the four powers in New York have begun such discussions. Let me make it perfectly clear that the U.S. position is that implementation of the overall settlement would begin only after complete agreement had been reached on related aspects of the problem.

In our recent meetings with the Soviets we have discussed some new formulas in an attempt to find common positions. They consist of three principal elements:

First, there should be a binding commitment by Israel and the United Arab Republic to peace with each other, with all the specific obligations of peace spelled out, including the obligation to prevent hostile acts originating from their respective territories.

Second, the detailed provisions of peace relating to security safeguards on the ground should be worked out between the parties, under Ambassador Jarring's auspices, utilizing the procedures followed in negotiating the armistice agreements under Ralph Bunche in 1949 at Rhodes. This formula has been previously used with success in negotiations between the parties on Middle Eastern problems. A principal objective of the four-power talks, we believe, should be to help Ambassador Jarring engage the parties in a negotiating process under the Rhodes formula.

So far as a settlement between Israel and the United Arab Republic goes, these safeguards relate primarily to the area of Sharm al-Shaykh controlling access to the Gulf of Aqaba, the need for demilitarized zones as foreseen in the Security Council resolution, and final arrangements in the Gaza Strip.

Third, in the context of peace and agreement on specific security safeguards, withdrawal of Israeli forces from Egyptian territory would be required.

Such an approach directly addresses the principal national concerns of both Israel and the U.A.R. It would require the U.A.R. to agree to a binding and specific commitment to peace. It would require withdrawal of Israeli armed forces from U.A.R. territory to the international border between Israel [or Mandated Palestine] and Egypt which has been in existence for over a half century. It would also require the parties themselves to negotiate the practical security arrangements to safeguard the peace.

We believe that this approach is *balanced* and fair. ...

ROGERS PLAN B -- THE CEASEFIRE/STANDSTILL PROPOSAL (JUNE 19, 1970)

Fighting in the Suez Canal Zone rapidly escalated during the spring of 1970 as Egypt introduced advanced Soviet surface-to-air missiles (SAMs) and Israel executed a series of deep penetration air raids into Egypt. In June the United States launched an initiative to secure a cease-fire and reactivate the Jarring talks, dormant since the spring of 1969. In late July, the United Arab Republic, Jordan, and Israel accepted the U.S. proposal. The cease-fire/standstill agreement became effective on August 7, 1970.

In similar letters to United Arab Republic Foreign Minister Mahmoud Riad and Jordanian Foreign Minister Zaid Rifai from United States Secretary of State William P. Rogers dated June 19, 1970, an initiative was outlined. A copy was also presented to Israel. These letters presented Rogers Plan B or the Second Rogers Initiative. It also came to be known as the "stop shooting, start talking" proposal. The letters stated that the United States was interested in a lasting peace, the framework for its establishment being United Nations Security Council Resolution 242, to be implemented under the auspices of United Nations Ambassador Gunnar Jarring. The letters went on to suggest that the first step toward a lasting peace would be the reinstatement of the cease-fire between Israel and the United Arab Republic to be agreed upon for at least a limited period.

On July 22, 1970, UAR Foreign Minister Riad accepted the proposal with qualifications, followed by Jordan on July 26. On July 31 Israel agreed to accept the plan, and communicated its intention on August 4, 1970. At 2200 GMT,

August 7, 1970, Israel and the United Arab Republic began observing a cease-fire. The talks envisioned by the plan began on August 25, 1970. Due to cease-fire violations by Egypt and United States reluctance to support Israeli claims, the Israeli ambassador to the United Nations refused to enter into a second round of talks.

DEAR MR. FOREIGN MINISTER: I have read carefully President Nasser's statement of May 1 and your subsequent remarks to Mr. Bergus [Donald C. Bergus, Counselor of Embassy and Consul General, U.S. Special Interests Section, Spanish Embassy, Cairo] Mr. Sisco [Joseph J. Sisco, Assistant Secretary of State for Near Eastern and South Asian Affairs] has also reported fully on his conversations with President Nasser and you, and we have been giving serious thought to what can be done about the situation in the Near East. I agree that the situation is at a critical point and I think it is in our joint interest that the United States retain and strengthen friendly ties with all the peoples and states of the area. We hope this will prove possible and are prepared to do our part. We look to others concerned, and in particular to your government, which has so important a role to play to move with us to seize this opportunity. If it is lost, we shall all suffer the consequences and we would regret such an outcome very much indeed. In this spirit, I urge that your government give the most careful consideration to the thoughts which I set forth below.

We are strongly interested in a lasting peace, and we would like to help the parties achieve it. We have made serious and practical proposals to that end, and we have counseled all parties on the need for compromise, and on the need to create an atmosphere in which peace is possible. By the latter we mean a reduction of tensions as well as clarifications of positions to give both Arabs and Israelis some confidence that the outcome will preserve their essential interests.

In our view, the most effective way to agree on a settlement would be for the parties to begin to work out under Ambassador Jarring's auspices the detailed steps necessary to carry out Security Council Resolution 242. Foreign Minister Eban of Israel has recently said that Israel would be prepared to make important concessions once talks got started. At the same time, Egyptian participation in such talks would go far towards overcoming Israeli doubts that your government does in fact seek to make peace with it. I understand the problems that direct negotiations pose for you, and we have made it clear from the beginning that we were not proposing such an arrangement be put into effect at the outset, although, depending on the progress of discussions, we believe the parties will find it necessary to meet together at some point if peace is to be established between them.

With the above thoughts in mind, the US puts forward the following proposal for consideration of the UAR.

(a) that both Israel and the UAR· subscribe to a restoration of the ceasefire for a least a limited period;

(b) that Israel and the UAR (as well as Israel and Jordan) subscribe to the following statement which would be in the form of a report from Ambassador Jarring to the Secretary General U Thant:

The UAR (Jordan) and Israel advise me that they agree:

(a) that having accepted and indicated their willingness to carry out Resolution 242 in all its parts, they will designate representatives to discussions to be held under my auspices, according to such procedure and at such places and times as I may recommend, taking into account as appropriate each side's preference as to method of procedure and previous experience between the parties;

(b) that the purpose of the aforementioned discussions is to reach agreement on the establishment of a just and lasting peace between them based on (1) mutual acknowledgment by the UAR (Jordan) and Israel of each other's sovereignty, territorial integrity and political independence, and (2) Israeli withdrawal from territories occupied in the 1967 conflict, both in accordance with Resolution 242;

(c) that to facilitate my task of promoting agreement as set forth in Resolution 242, the parties will strictly observe, effective July 1 until at least October 1, the ceasefire resolutions of the Security Council.

We hope the UAR will find this proposal acceptable; we are also seeking Israeli acceptance. In the meantime, I am sure you will share my conviction that everything be done to hold these proposals in confidence so as not to prejudice the prospects for their acceptance.

I am sending a similar message to Foreign Minister Rifai [Abd al-Munin Ar-Rifai, Foreign Minister of Jordan].

ROGERS PLAN C -- INTERIM SUEZ CANAL PROPOSAL (OCTOBER 4, 1971)

As part of an address before the United Nations General Assembly on October 4, 1971, United States Secretary of State William P. Rogers outlined the United States position concerning an interim Suez Canal agreement between Egypt and Israel. This plan, known as Rogers Plan C, or the Third Rogers Initiative, and the Rogers Six-Point Program, capped a summer of diplomatic efforts. Rogers stated the ultimate goal of the plan to be a lasting peace, pursued within the framework of United Nations Security Council Resolution 242. However, for the purposes of establishing an atmosphere of confidence and trust, he urged the immediate acceptance of an interim Suez Canal agreement that would allow the reopening of the canal as well as some disengagement of opposing military forces.

Israel rejected it on October 12, 1971, but reversed this decision on February 2, 1972 and agreed to "close proximity" talks with Egypt with the United States acting as mediator. This approach was rejected by Egypt.

... The other place where progress is urgently required is in the Middle East. Over several years, the United Nations has made determined and persistent efforts to achieve a lasting peace in that critical area. Nonetheless, the opportunities for success and the risks of failure remain in precarious balance.

Security Council Resolution 242, establishing the principles for a durable peace, was the first major step toward reason after 18 years of belligerency and a fragile, often violated armistice.

The cease-fire along the Suez Canal, now nearing its 15th month, was the second major step away from war.

It is time for a third major step toward peace.

For 4 years Ambassador Jarring [U.N. Special Representative Gunnar Jarring] has worked diligently to secure the agreement called for in Security Council Resolution 242. We support his efforts. We believe his mission remains the best path to an overall settlement and to lasting peace. Our views on such a final peace settlement remain those expressed in President Nixon's foreign policy report earlier this year and in my statement of December 9, 1969.

Both sides to the conflict are committed to the fundamental and reciprocal principles to which the Jarring Mission is dedicated; living in peace with each other and withdrawal from territories occupied in the 1967 conflict as set forth in Security Council Resolution 242. Despite those commitments, a deep gulf of suspicion and distrust remains.

Each side is convinced of the justice of its cause. Each is concerned about its future security. A political settlement based on mutual accommodation could assure both. An attempt to achieve these ends by force will destroy all possibilities for either.

This is why we believe a third major step toward peace is essential: -- A step which can be taken now; -- A step that is practical; -- A step that could help create the confidence and trust which are now lacking; -- A step toward full and complete implementation of Resolution 242.

That step is an interim Suez Canal agreement. That is why the United States has welcomed the interest of both Egypt and Israel in such an agreement. That is why, at the request of the parties, the United States has undertaken to play a constructive role in the process of arriving at an agreement.

In order to explore the positions of each side, we have discussed concrete and specific ideas designed to meet the legitimate needs and concerns of both sides. Those ideas, given willingness and good intentions on both sides, could become the basis for a breakthrough. They require further quiet discussions with the parties, an undertaking we now hope can be expedited along the following lines:

A first point is the relationship between an interim agreement and an overall settlement. A fair approach should be founded on two basic principles:

-- That a Suez Canal agreement is merely a step toward complete and full implementation of Resolution 242 within a reasonable period of time and not an end in itself. That has to be clearly established in any agreement.

-- That neither side can realistically expect to achieve, as part of an interim agreement, complete agreement on the terms and conditions of an overall settlement. If it could, there would be no necessity for an interim agreement. Those final terms and conditions will have to be worked out through negotiations under Ambassador Jarring's auspices. And we would hope that if an interim agreement is reached, active negotiations under Ambassador Jarring's auspices could be renewed.

A second point is the matter of the cease-fire. Its maintenance is in the interest of all of us, of everyone concerned, of everyone in this room -- in fact, in the interest of the whole world. The ultimate objective, of course, is a permanent end to belligerency as part of a final binding peace agreement. But such a commitment is not realizable in the context of an interim agreement. Neither would a cease-fire of short duration be realistic. With good will on both sides, it should be possible to find common understanding between the parties on this issue.

Third is the zone of withdrawal. There are, of course, very important strategic considerations involved in this key point. However, based on our discussions, we believe it should be possible to meet the principal concerns of both sides. Without going into the details, I would merely say that I believe that in the long run the most significant aspect of an interim agreement might prove to be that it established the principle of withdrawal looking to an overall settlement as a fact rather than as a theory.

Fourth is the nature of the supervisory arrangements. Both sides must have confidence that the agreement will not be violated and that adequate machinery will be provided for prompt detection of any infractions. We are confident that the ways reassuring to both Israel and Egypt can be found for altering and strengthening the supervisory mechanisms that have existed in the area for the past two decades.

Fifth is the question of an Egyptian presence east of the Suez Canal. The reopening and operation of the Suez Canal would require Egyptian personnel east of the canal. It is understandable, too, that normal activities should be pursued in as much of the zone evacuated as possible. The question of an Egyptian military presence east of the canal is one on which the parties hold opposite views. But here, too, based on our discussion, we believe that there are possibilities for compromise on this issue.

Sixth is the use of the Suez Canal. The United States has long held that the canal should be open to passage for all nations without discrimination. This principle is clear in the Security Council resolution of November 1967. What is at present at issue in considering an interim agreement is principally the timing at which this right could be exercised. We believe an accommodation on this point is quite possible.

With those six points in mind let me say this: Because the parties have asked us, we intend to continue our determined effort to assist them in arriving at an interim agreement. This effort, we believe, is imperative because -- and I think it is important to keep this in mind -- there is no more realistic and hopeful alternative to pursue.

There are risks to peace; but the greater risk is inaction, unwillingness to face up to the hard decisions.

A practical step now -- an interim agreement -- would make the next step toward peace less difficult for all the parties to take.

It would restore the use of the Suez Canal as a waterway for international shipping.

It would reestablish Egypt's authority over a major national asset.

It would separate the combatants.

It would produce the first Israeli withdrawal.

It would extend the cease-fire.

It would diminish the risk of major-power involvement.

It would be an important step toward the complete implementation of Security Council Resolution 242.

I submit that the logic for such an agreement is overwhelming. If the leaders of the area would grasp this opportunity, they would give new hope to their peoples for tranquillity, for progress, and for peace. ...

SOVIET-EGYPTIAN TREATY OF FRIENDSHIP AND COOPERATION (MAY 27, 1971)

On May 27, 1971, Soviet President Nikolai Podgornyi and Egyptian President Anwar Sadat signed a fifteen year Treaty of Friendship and Cooperation that declared an unbreakable friendship between the two countries and cooperation in political, economic, scientific, technological, and cultural fields. The treaty was a direct result of Moscow's increasingly strained relationship with Egypt's new president, following the death of Nasser. Sadat purged pro-Nasserist and pro-Soviet elements from the government and made overtures in the international arena indicating a change in Egypt's position on the Arab-Israeli conflict. Throughout 1971, his so-called "year of decision," Sadat's main priority was the restoration of Egyptian territory occupied by Israel. He proposed an interim agreement on the Suez Canal and in early May he met with United States Secretary of State William Rogers to discuss a peace settlement. Although the talks were inconclusive, they represented the highest level of communication between the two countries since the early 1950s. Mistrustful of Sadat's intentions, the Soviets sought to salvage an increasingly tenuous relationship through a formal treaty. It was the first Soviet treaty with an Arab country. Moscow hoped to gain greater influence over Sadat and his actions, while Sadat saw the treaty as a means to acquire the arms necessary for war. Despite his numerous requests, Moscow consistently failed to supply Sadat with aircraft and missiles. Increasingly frustrated Sadat publicly expelled Soviet military advisors from Egypt on July 18, 1972. Sadat later admitted that his disagreement with the Soviets stemmed from their failure to deliver requested arms, their disapproval over his plans to wage war against Israel, and the existing era of super-power dénte. In March 1976, Sadat unilaterally abrogated the Soviet-Egyptian Treaty of Friendship and Cooperation.

The Union of Soviet Socialist Republics and the United Arab Republic,

Being firmly convinced that the further development of friendship and all-around cooperation between the Union of Soviet Socialist Republics and the United Arab Republic is responsive to the interests of the peoples of both states and serves the cause of strengthening universal peace,

Being inspired by the ideals of the struggle against imperialism and colonialism, and for the freedom, independence and social progress of peoples,

Being determined to wage persistently the struggle for the consolidation of international peace and security in accordance with the invariable course of their peace-loving foreign policies,

Reaffirming their loyalty to the aims and principles of the United Nations Charter,

And being motivated by the aspiration to strengthen and consolidate the traditional relations of sincere friendship and cooperation and thus creating a basis for their further development,

Have agreed on the following:

Article 1. The High contracting parties solemnly declare that unbreakable friendship will always exist between the two countries and their peoples. They will continue to develop and strengthen the existing relations of friendship and all-round cooperation between them in the political, economic, scientific, technological, cultural and other fields on the basis of the principles of respect for sovereignty, territorial integrity, non-interference in one another's internal affairs, equality and mutual benefit.

Article 2. The Union of Soviet Socialist Republics, as a socialist state, and the United Arab Republic, which has set itself the aim of the socialist reconstruction of society, will cooperate closely and in all fields in ensuring conditions for preserving and further developing the social and economic gains of their peoples.

Article 3. Guided by the aspiration to promote in every way the maintenance of international peace and the security of peoples, the Union of Soviet Socialist Republics and the United Arab Republic will continue with the utmost determination to exert efforts toward achieving and ensuring a lasting and just peace in the Middle East in accordance with the aims and principles of the United Nations Charter.

In conducting a peace-loving foreign policy, the high contracting parties will come out in favor of peace, the relaxation of international tension, the achieving of general and complete disarmament and the prohibition of nuclear and other types of weapons of mass destruction.

Article 4. Guided by the ideals of the freedom and equality of all peoples, the high contracting parties condemn imperialism and colonialism in all their forms and manifestations. They will continue to come out against imperialism and for the complete and final liquidation of colonialism in pursuance of the U.N. Declaration on the Granting of Independence to All Colonial Countries and Peoples, and will wage an unswerving struggle against racism and apartheid.

Article 5. The high contracting parties also will continue to expand and deepen all-round cooperation and the exchange of experience in the economic, scientific and technological fields -- in industry, agriculture, water conservation, irrigation, the development of natural resources, the development of power engineering, the training of national cadres, and other branches of the economy.

The two sides will expand trade and maritime shipping between the two states on the basis of the principles of mutual benefit and most favored nation treatment.

Article 6. The high contracting parties will promote further cooperation between them in the fields of science, the arts, literature, education, public health, the press, radio, television, cinema, tourism, physical education, and other fields. The parties will promote wider cooperation and direct contacts between political and social organizations of the working people, enterprises and cultural and scientific institutions for the purpose of achieving a deeper mutual acquaintance with the life, work and achievements of the peoples of the two countries.

Article 7. Being deeply interested in ensuring peace and the security of peoples and attaching great importance to the concerted nature of their actions in the international arena in the struggle for peace, the high contracting parties will, for this purpose, regularly consult each other at various levels on all important questions affecting the interests of both states.

In the event of situations arising which, in the opinion of both sides, create a danger to peace or a breach of peace, they will contact each other without delay in order to concert their positions with a view to removing the threat that has arisen or restoring peace.

Article 8. In the interests of strengthening the defense capability of the United Arab Republic, the high contracting parties will continue to develop cooperation in the military field on the basis of appropriate agreements between them. Such cooperation will provide, in particular, for assistance in the training of UAR military personnel and in mastering the armaments and equipment supplied to the United Arab Republic for the purpose of strengthening its capability in the cause of eliminating the consequences of aggression as well as increasing its ability to stand up to aggression in general.

Article 9. Proceeding from the purposes and principles of the Treaty,

Each of the high contracting parties states that it will not enter into alliances or take part in any groupings of states, or in actions or measures directed against the other high contracting party.

Article 10. Each of the high contracting parties declares that its obligations under existing international treaties are not in contradiction with the provisions of this Treaty and it undertakes not to enter into any international agreements incompatible with it.

Article 11. The present Treaty shall be valid for 15 years from the day it enters into force.

If neither of the high contracting parties announces, a year before the expiry of this term, its desire to terminate the Treaty, it shall remain in force for the next five years and so henceforward, until one of the high contracting parties, a year before the expiry of the current five-year period, gives a written warning of its intention to terminate its validity.

Article 12. The present Treaty is subject to ratification and shall enter into force on the day of the exchange of the instruments of ratification, which will take place in Moscow in the very near future.

The present Treaty is done in two copies, each in Russian and Arabic, both texts being equally authentic.

DONE in the city of Cairo on May 27, 1971, which corresponds to 3 Rabia as-Sani, 1391, Hidjra.

HUSSEIN PROPOSAL FOR A UNITED ARAB KINGDOM (MARCH 15, 1972)

In March 1972 King Hussein of Jordan proposed the establishment of a United Arab Kingdom to incorporate the East Bank as the Jordan region and the West Bank (and other liberated Palestinian territories) as the Palestine region.

We are happy to declare that the bases of the proposed formula for the new phase are as follows: 1. The Hashimite Kingdom of the Jordan shall become a United Arab Kingdom and shall bear this name. 2. The United Arab Kingdom shall consist of two regions: a. The Palestine region which will consist of the West Bank and any other Palestinian territories which are liberated and whose inhabitants desire to join it. b. The Jordan region which will consist of the East Bank. 3. Amman shall be the central capital of the kingdom as well as the capital of the Jordan region. 4. Jerusalem shall be the capital of the Palestine region. 5. The head of the state shall be the king, who will assume the central executive authority with the held of a central cabinet. The central legislative authority shall be vested in the king and an assembly to be known as the national assembly.

Members of this assembly shall be elected by direct secret ballot. Both regions shall be equally represented in this assembly. 6. The central judicial authority shall be vested in a central supreme court. 7. The kingdom shall have unified armed forces whose supreme commander is the king. 8. The responsibilities of the central executive authority shall be confined to affairs connected with the kingdom as an international entity to guarantee the kingdom's safety, stability and prosperity. 9. The executive authority in each region shall be assumed by a governor general from among its sons and a regional cabinet from among its sons as well. 10. Legislative authority in each region shall be assumed by a council to be called the people's council. It shall be elected by direct secret voting. This council will elect the region's governor general. 11. The judicial authority in the region shall be in the hands of the region's courts, and no one will have power over them. 12. The executive authority in each region shall assume responsibility for all the affairs of the region except such affairs as the constitution defines as coming under the jurisdiction of the central executive authority.

Naturally the implementation of this formula and its bases should be according to the constitutional norms in force. It will be referred to the [Jordanian] National Assembly to adopt the necessary measures to prepare a new constitution for the country.

UNSC RESOLUTION 338 (OCTOBER 22, 1973)

On October 22, 1973 the United Nations Security Council adopted Resolution 338 which called for an immediate cease-fire in the Yom Kippur (Ramadan) War and the implementation of United Nations Security Council Resolution 242. This provided the basis for the initial post-war military disengagement negotiations. The resolution was submitted as a joint United States-Soviet Union resolution and was adopted by a vote of 14 to 0. China did not participate in the voting (but did not cast a veto) citing the fact that the text failed to condemn Israel and it was formulated by the United States and the Soviet Union without reference to the Security Council.

The Security Council 1. *Calls Upon* all parties to the present fighting to cease all firing and terminate all military activity immediately, no later than 12 hours after the moment of the adoption of this decision, in the positions they now occupy; 2. *Calls upon* the parties concerned to start immediately after the cease-fire the implementation of Security Council resolution 242 (1967) in all of its parts; 3. *Decides* that, immediately and concurrently with the cease-fire, negotiations start between the parties concerned under appropriate auspices aimed at establishing a just and durable peace in the Middle East.

UNSC RESOLUTION 339 (OCTOBER 23, 1973)

At Egypt's request the United Nations Security Council convened on October 23, 1973 because of the breakdown of the cease-fire agreed to in UNSC Resolution 338. The draft resolution was sponsored jointly by the US and USSR and was adopted by a vote of 14-0 with China not voting.

UNSC Resolution 339 did not secure a cease-fire. On October 24 fighting continued as Israeli forces completed the encirclement of Egypt's Third Army and launched an assault on Suez City.

The Security Council, *Referring* to its resolution 338 (1973) of 22 October 1973, 1. *Confirms* its decision on an immediate cessation of all kinds of firing and of all military action, and urges that the forces of the two sides be returned to the positions they occupied at the moment the cease-fire became effective; 2. *Requests* the Secretary-General to take measures for immediate dispatch of United Nations observers to supervise the observance of the cease-fire between the forces of Israel and the Arab Republic of Egypt, using for this purpose the personnel of the United Nations now in the Middle East and first of all the personnel now in Cairo.

UNSC RESOLUTION 340 (OCTOBER 25, 1973)

The Security Council failed to secure a cease-fire through resolutions 338 and 339. Resolution 340 was adopted by a 14-0 vote on October 25, with China not participating in the voting. Although Resolution 340 secured an unstable cease-fire. U.S. Secretary of State Henry Kissinger, through talks with President Anwar Sadat and Prime Minister Golda Meir, facilitated a six-point agreement signed on November 11, 1993 in which both sides agreed they would "observe scrupulously" the cease-fire.

The Security Council, *Recalling* its resolution 338 (1973) of 22 October 1973 and 339 (1973) of 23 October 1973, Noting with regret the reported repeated violation of the cease-fire in non-compliance with resolutions 338 (1973) and 339 (1973), *Noting with concern* from the Secretary-General's report that the United Nations military observers have not yet been enabled to place themselves on both sides of the cease-fire line, 1. *Demands* that immediate and complete cease-fire be observed and that the parties return to the positions occupied by them at 1650 GMT on 22 October 1973; 2. *Requests* the Secretary-General, as an immediate step, to increase the number of military observers on both sides; 3. *Decides* to set up immediately under its authority a United Nations Emergency Force to be composed of personnel drawn from States Members of the United Nations except the permanent members of the Security Council, and requests the Secretary-General to report within 24 hours on the steps taken to this effect; 4. *Requests* the Secretary-General to report to the Council on an urgent and continuing basis on the state of the implementation of the present resolution, as well as resolution 338 (1973) and 339 (1973); 5. *Requests* all Member States to extend their full co-operation to the United Nations in the implementation of the present resolution, as well as resolutions 338 (1973) and 339 (1973).

EGYPT-ISRAEL SIX POINT AGREEMENT (NOVEMBER 11, 1973)

After the adoption of United Nations Security Council Resolutions 338, 339 and 340, Egyptian and Israeli military officers met at Kilometer 101 on the Cairo-Suez road and on November 11, 1973 an agreement to stabilize the cease-fire was signed. Almost immediately there was disagreement concerning the implementation of various points and negotiations continued to reach accord on the elements of the agreement.

A. Egypt and Israel agree to observe scrupulously the cease-fire called for by the U.N. Security Council.

B. Both sides agree that discussions between them will begin immediately to settle the question of the return to the 22 October positions in the framework of agreement on the disengagement and separation of forces under the auspices of the U.N.

C. The town of Suez will receive daily supplies of food, water, and medicine. All wounded civilians in the town will be evacuated.

D. There shall be no impediment to the movement of non-military supplies to the East Bank.

E. The Israeli checkpoints on the Cairo-Suez road will be replaced by U.N. checkpoints. At the Suez end of the road Israeli officers can participate with the U.N. to supervise the nonmilitary nature of the cargo at the bank of the canal.

F. As soon as the U.N. checkpoints are established on the Cairo-Suez road, there will be an exchange of all prisoners of war, including the wounded.

EGYPT-ISRAEL DISENGAGEMENT OF FORCES AGREEMENT (JANUARY 18, 1974)

Efforts to conclude an agreement on a separation of forces between Israel and Egypt included talks at Kilometer 101 on the Cairo-Suez road, at Geneva, and finally, during negotiations carried out by United States Secretary of State Henry Kissinger. After days of shuttle diplomacy between Egypt and Israel, Kissinger was successful in securing an agreement. On January 17, 1974 an agreement between Egypt and Israel for the disengagement and separation of their military forces was announced simultaneously in Washington, D.C., Cairo and Jerusalem. The following day, it was signed at Kilometer 101 by the Chiefs of Staff of the Israeli (David Elazar) and the Egyptian (Mohammed Abdul Ghani al Gamassy) armed forces.

A. Egypt and Israel will scrupulously observe the cease-fire on land, sea, and air called for by the U.N. Security Council and will refrain from the time of the signing of this document from all military or para-military actions against each other. B. The military forces of Egypt and Israel will be separated in accordance with the following principles: 1. All Egyptian forces on the eastside of the Canal will be deployed west of the line designated as Line A on the attached map. All Israeli forces, including those west of the Suez Canal and the Bitter Lakes, will be deployed east of the line designated as Line B on the attached map. 2. The area between the Egyptian and Israeli lines will be a zone of disengagement in which the United Nations Emergency Force (UNEF) will be stationed. The UNEF will continue to consist of units from countries that are not permanent members of the Security Council. 3. The area between the Egyptian line and the Suez Canal will be limited in armament and forces. 4. The area between the Israeli line (Line B on the attached map) and the line designated as Line C on the attached map, which runs along the western base of the mountains where the Gidi and Mitla Passes are located, will be limited in armament and forces. 5. The limitations referred to in paragraphs 3 and 4 will be inspected by UNEF. Existing procedures of the UNEF, including the attaching of Egyptian and Israel liaison officers to UNEF, will be continued. 6. Air forces of the two sides will be permitted to operate up to their respective lines without interference from the other side. C. The detailed implementation of the disengagement of forces will be worked out by military representatives of Egypt and Israel, who will agree on the stages of this process. These representatives will meet no later that 48 hours after the signature of this agreement at Kilometre 101 under the aegis of the United Nations for this purpose. They will complete this task within five days. Disengagement will begin within 48 hours after the completion of the work of the military representatives and in no event later than seven days after the signature of this agreement. The process of disengagement will be completed not later than 40 days after it begins. D. This agreement is not regarded by Egypt and Israel as a final peace agreement. It constitutes a first step toward a final, just and durable peace according to the provisions of Security Council Resolution 338 and within the framework of the Geneva Conference.

AGRANAT COMMISSION OF INQUIRY INTERIM REPORT (APRIL 1974)

In November 1973 the government of Israel appointed a five-member Commission of Inquiry to investigate the events leading up to the hostilities (including information concerning the enemy's moves and intentions), the assessments and decisions of military and civilian bodies in regard to this information, and the Israel Defense Forces' deployments, preparedness for battle, and actions in the first phase of the fighting in connection with the Yom Kippur War. The commission was composed of Supreme Court Chief Justice Shimon Agranat, Justice Moshe Landau of the Supreme Court, State Comptroller Yitzhak Nebenzahl, and two former chiefs of staff of the Israel Defense Forces, Yigael Yadin and Haim Laskov. It issued an interim report in April 1974 which focused primarily on events prior to the outbreak of hostilities and the conduct of the war during its early stages. Its full report was made public in January 1995. It reaffirmed the conclusion that the intelligence establishment and the government fell victim to a mistaken conception that Egypt and Syria were incapable of starting a war in 1973. Thus, there was difficulty in accepting facts that did not fit the conception.

Chapter 1: Preface. 1. On November 18, 1973, the Cabinet adopted the following resolution: *Resolved*: A) That the following matters, namely: 1. The information, in the days preceding the Yom Kippur War, concerning the enemy's moves and his intentions to open war, as well as the assessments and the decisions of the duly authorized military and civilian bodies with regard to the aforementioned information; 2. The Israel Defence Forces' deployment for battle in general, its preparedness in the days preceding the Yom Kippur War and its actions up to the containment of the enemy .... B) That an Inquiry Commission shall be set up to investigate the aforementioned matters and report to the Cabinet. ...

Chapter 2: The Principal Conclusions of the Commission on the Subjects of Information, Its Evaluation and Readiness of the IDF. ... 10. The opening of the war by Egypt and Syria on Yom Kippur, October 6, 1973, at approximately 14.00 hours, took the Israel Defence Forces by surprise in that until the early morning hours of that day the IDF's Supreme Command and the political leadership did not evaluate that total war was about to commence -- and on the morning of that day, when it was already clear to them that the war would break out, the Supreme Command mistakenly assumed that it would break out only at 18.00 hours. Responsibility for these mistaken evaluations should be placed primarily on the Director of Military Intelligence [DMI] and on his Principal Assistant in charge of the Intelligence Branch's Research Department, which is the only body in the country engaged in intelligence research. They failed by providing the IDF with totally insufficient warning: It was only about 4.30 a.m. on Yom Kippur that the DMI, on the strength of fresh intelligence he had received, notified that the enemy would open war at 18.00 hours on both fronts. This brief warning did not allow for mobilization of the reserves in an orderly fashion, and involved the hasty mobilization of the land forces, contrary to the regular timetables and mobilization procedures. The additional error of four hours, between 18.00 and 14.00, further reduced the interval between the call-up of the reserves and the opening of fire by the enemy. This second error caused further, disruptions in the readiness of the regular forces at the fronts and their correct deployment, particularly on the Canal front. 11. There were three reasons for the failure of the authorities responsible for evaluation: Firstly, their obdurate adherence to what was known as "the conception," according to which a) Egypt would not launch war against Israel before she had first ensured sufficient air power to attack Israel in depth, and in particular Israel's principal airfields, so as to paralyse the Israel air force, and b) that Syria would only launch an all-out attack on Israel simultaneously with Egypt. ... This "conception" had, therefore, in practice become obsolete. Secondly, the Director of Military Intelligence assured the IDF that he would be able to give advance warning of any enemy intention to launch all-out war in good time to allow for the orderly callup of the reserves. This undertaking was assumed as the firm foundation for the defence plans of the IDF. We find there were no grounds for giving the IDF such an absolute undertaking. Thirdly, in the days preceding the Yom Kippur War, the Intelligence Branch (Research) had received numerous warning reports.... The Research Division of the Intelligence and the Director of Military Intelligence did not correctly evaluate the warnings contained in these reports, owing to their doctrinaire adherence to the "conception" and the fact that they were prepared to explain the enemy deployment along the front lines, which was without precedent in the size of the forces and in their orientation towards the fronts, on the assumption that all this testified only to a defensive deployment in Syria and the holding of a multiarm "exercise" in Egypt, similar to exercises held there in the past.

For this reason the Director of Military Intelligence also displayed exaggerated caution in the circumstances by failing to take additional measures that were at his disposal and which might have revealed important complementary information. The enemy thus succeeded in misleading the IDF and taking them by surprise under the guise of an exercise supposedly taking place in Egypt. Only on the morning of Friday, October 5, did the confidence of the Intelligence Branch in the correctness of its evaluation begin to be shaken.... And yet the correct conclusion was still not drawn, and the summary of the evaluation of the Intelligence Branch continued to be: "Low probability" and even "Lower than low" probability of the enemy launching a war. Only early in the morning of Saturday, Yom Kippur, after further ambiguous reports were received, did the Director of Military Intelligence come to the conclusion that war would break out the same day. ...

13. The mistakes of the Intelligence Branch were not the only mistakes

disrupting the IDF's moves at the beginning of the war. In addition, there were errors in the working of the state of readiness during the days preceding the war. There was an unjustified delay in the mobilization of the reserves. It is our opinion that, on the basis of the data in his possession, the Chief of Staff should already have recommended partial mobilization of the land forces at the beginning of the week preceding the war, to maintain the right proportions between the enemy forces, which were at full alert and prepared for action against us, and our own forces. At the very latest, he should have recommended -- in view of reports received -- extensive mobilization on the morning of Friday, October 5, even assuming that the enemy's intentions were still not clear at that time.

Secondly, we have found that, in total reliance on the Intelligence Branch's assurance that it could always give the IDF sufficient warning for orderly mobilization of the reserves, no defence plan properly worked out in detail was prepared for the eventuality that the regular forces would have to check, on their own, an all-out attack by the enemy on the Egyptian and Syrian fronts simultaneously -- with the IDF being caught by surprise as they were.

Thirdly, even after receipt of the warning on Saturday morning, the regular armoured forces on the Canal front were not optimally deployed in time, under the circumstances created, in accordance with the plan that existed for the defensive deployment of the regular forces. Furthermore, no clear directive was given that morning to the GOC Southern Command and from him also to the lower echelons, as to how they were to prepare for the attack, and lack of clarity prevailed in issuing operational orders and ensuring their implementation. ...

Chapter 3: Conclusions and Recommendations of the Commission on the Institutional Level. ... 17. We have learned from the evidence before us that there is a lack of clear definition as to the division of authority, duties and responsibilities concerning security matters amongst the three authorities dealing with these matters: the Government and the Prime Minister; the Minister of Defence; and the Chief of Staff, who heads the IDF; and in the determination of the relationship between the political leadership and the IDF High Command. Particularly vital is such a clear definition of authority in cases wherein the initiative lies in the hands of the enemy. Furthermore, we have found no explicit authority in the law for the practice whereby the Chief of Staff is appointed by the Government on the recommendation of the Minister of Defence. The unclarity in all these respects is evidently of historic origin -- dating back to the time when the late David Ben-Gurion served both as Prime Minister and Minister of Defence, and his strong personality affected the lack of definition on this important subject. One thing, however, is clear from the constitutional aspect: It has never been decided that the Minister of Defence is a "Super Chief of Staff" who is required to guide the Chief of Staff in the latter's area of responsibility on operational matters, or a kind of supreme commander of the IDF by virtue of his being Minister of Defence. The inadequate definition of powers prevailing in the present situation in the field of security, the vital importance of which is unsurpassed, hampers the effectiveness of the work, detracts from the focusing of legal responsibility, and causes uncertainty and frustration amongst the public. ... 22. *Intelligence Community -- Intelligence Evaluation.* A) As noted above, the factual situation on the eve of the Yom Kippur War -- and over a period of many years before then -- was that only one body in the intelligence community, namely, the General Staff's Intelligence Branch, engaged in intelligence evaluation, research and evaluation of reports. This intelligence evaluation was, thus, the only one submitted to the Chief of Staff, the Defence Minister, the Prime Minister and the Cabinet. This system of evaluation in the intelligence community had grave reflections on the evaluation of the intelligence information by the governmental authorities on the eve of the war. ...

Chapter 4: Conclusions About Office-Holders. 23. *The Director of Military Intelligence, Major-General Eliyahu Ze'ira*, testified before us very frankly and showed himself to be an officer of outstanding intellectual ability, enjoying great authority over his subordinates and highly regarded by his superiors in the IDF and the higher political echelons. He had served in his position for only a year before the outbreak of the war, and was confronted with patterns of thought which were determined in the Intelligence Branch's research before his appointment. But he adopted the "conception," which, through its rigidity, deadened the necessary openness and the willingness always to contend anew with the information which flowed into the Intelligence Branch, and he even played his part in strengthening it. He displayed a prominent tendency to take unqualified decisions as an officer stemming from great self-confidence and readiness to act as final arbiter in Intelligence matters in Israel. ...

Our opinion is that in the light of his serious failure Major-General Ze'ira can no longer continue to serve in his position as Director of Military Intelligence. 24. In the hands of *Brigadier-General Arye Shalev*, as assistant to the Director of Military Intelligence in charge of research, was concentrated the subject of research and evaluation in the Intelligence Branch -- that subject in which the Intelligence Branch failed so grievously. He had served in this capacity, previously under the title of Head of the Research Department, for a long time, since September-October 1967. He played an important part in moulding methods of research, analysis, evaluation and preparation of the information for distribution from this department in recent years. According to his testimony before us his approach to the "conception" was flexible: he was prepared to assess its fundamental validity from time to time. But from the documents produced by his department and from statements made by him during various discussions, it is clear that his evaluations never deviated from the framework of the "conception." He bears heavy responsibility for the most grievous mistake of the department he headed and we therefore believe that he cannot continue to serve in the Intelligence Branch. ... 28. *The Chief of Staff's Responsibility*: We have reached the conclusion that the Chief of Staff, Lt.-

General David Elazar, bears personal responsibility for what happened on the eve of the war with regard to both evaluation of the situation and the question of the IDF's preparedness. We state this with particular regret as it involves a soldier who has served the State with devotion and distinction for many years and has splendid achievements to his credit during and before the Six Day War. ... In the light of what has been stated above we regard it as our duty to recommend the termination of Lt.-General David Elazar's appointment as Chief of Staff. 30. *Personal Responsibility at the Government Level.* In determining the responsibility of the Ministers for acts of commission or omission in which they played a personal part it is our duty to stress that we deemed ourselves free to draw conclusions on the basis of our findings only so far as direct responsibility is concerned. We did not consider it to be our task to express an opinion as to the implications of their parliamentary responsibility. ... 31. (1) With regard to the question of the Defence Minister's direct personal responsibility, we must point out that in this partial report we are considering only the subjects of the information and the state of readiness and the Defence Minister's part therein. ... (3) We have carefully considered these matters and reached the conclusion that, by the criterion of reasonable conduct required of the bearer of the post of Minister of Defence, the Minister was not obliged to order additional or different precautionary measures [to] those recommended to him by the General Staff of the IDF, according to the joint assessment and the advice of the Director of Military Intelligence and the Chief of Staff. 32. With respect to the Prime Minister, what we have stated above (para. 30) as regards personal responsibility at Cabinet level likewise holds good. ... It is greatly to the Prime Minister's credit that, under the circumstances, during the emergency of Saturday morning, she made proper use of the authority vested in her to make decisions. She decided wisely, with common sense the speedily in favour of the full mobilization of the reserves, despite weighty political considerations, thereby performing a most important service for the defence of the State.

Conclusion. 33. In concluding this partial report, the Commission considers itself bound to reiterate that, despite the fact that it has not yet concluded the hearing of testimony on every matter relating to the conduct of the war up to conclusion of the containment stage, it is already in possession of much evidence clearly attesting that in the Yom Kippur War, the IDF was confronted by one of the most difficult challenges which could possibly confront any army -- and emerged victorious. Despite the difficult initial position from which the IDF started out in the war, and despite the errors committed at this stage -- partly detailed above, and partly to be detailed in the reasoning on this report -- not only did it succeed in mobilizing the reserves at unprecedented speed, with all their complex formations, but at the same time it also blocked the massive invasion of enemy armies which had planned and trained for this onslaught over many years and, in the opening stages, had enjoyed the benefit of surprise. The IDF's success was secured at the cost of heavy and irreplaceable casualties, and thanks to the supreme heroism of all ranks, the endless powers of improvisation of its commanders, and the stability and strength of its basic organizational structure. These facts reinforce the Commission in its opinion that not only does the IDF possess the capacity to absorb criticism and draw the painful conclusions implied, but that it will thereby increase and enhance its strength.

ISRAEL-SYRIA DISENGAGEMENT OF FORCES AGREEMENT (MAY 31, 1974)

Negotiations for the separation and disengagement of forces between Israel and Syria following the Yom Kippur War were held in February and March 1974, when Israeli and Syrian representatives came to Washington and presented their respective initial positions to U.S. Secretary of State Henry Kissinger. Kissinger spent May in the Middle East, shuttling between Jerusalem and Damascus. His efforts to formulate an agreement were successful and it was subsequently signed in Geneva on May 31 by senior military officers of both sides.

A. Israel and Syria will scrupulously observe the cease-fire on land, sea and air and will refrain from all military actions against each other, from the time of the signing of the document, in implementation of United Nations Security Council resolution 338 dated October 22, 1973.

B. The military forces of Israel and Syria will be separated in accordance with the following principles:

1. All Israeli military forces will be west of the line designated as Line A on the map attached hereto, except in the Kuneitra area, where they will be west of line A-1.

2. All territory east of Line A will be under Syrian administration, and the Syrian civilians will return to this territory.

3. The area between Line A and the Line designated as Line B on the attached map will be an area of separation. In this area will be stationed the United Nations Disengagement Observer Force established in accordance with the accompanying protocol.

4. All Syrian military forces will be east of the line designated as Line B on the attached map.

5. There will be two equal areas of limitation in armament and forces, one west of Line A and one east of Line B as agreed upon.

6. Air forces of the two sides will be permitted to operate up to their respective lines without interference from the other side.

C. In the area between Line A and Line A-1 on the attached map there shall be no military forces.

D. This agreement and the attached map will be signed by the military representatives of Israel and Syria in Geneva not later than May 31, 1974, in the Egyptian-Israeli military working group of the Geneva Peace Conference under the aegis of the United Nations, after that group has been joined by a Syrian military representative, and with the participation of representatives of the United States and the Soviet Union. The precise delineation of a detailed map and a plan for the implementation of the disengagement of forces will be worked by military representatives of Israel and Syria in the Egyptian-Israeli military working group, who will agree on the stages of this process. The military working group described above will state their work for this purpose in Geneva under the aegis of the United Nations within 24 hours after the signing of this agreement. They will complete this task within five days. Disengagement will begin within 24 hours after the completion of the task of the military working group. The process of disengagement will be completed not later than twenty days after it begins.

E. The provisions of paragraph A, B, and C shall be inspected by personnel of the United Nations Disengagement Observer Force under this agreement.

F. Within 24 hours after the signing of this agreement in Geneva all wounded prisoners of war which each side holds of the other as certified by the ICRC will be repatriated. The morning after the completion of the task of the military working group, all remaining prisoners of war will be repatriated.

G. The bodies of all dead soldiers held by either side will be returned for burial in their respective countries within 10 days after the signing of this agreement.

H. This agreement is not a peace agreement. It is a step toward a just and durable peace on the basis of Security Council Resolution 338 dated October 22, 1973.

PROTOCOL CONCERNING THE UNITED NATIONS DISENGAGEMENT OBSERVER FORCE

Israel and Syria agree that:

The function of the United Nations Disengagement Observer Force (UNDOF) under that agreement will be to use its best efforts to maintain the cease-fire and to see that it is scrupulously observed. It will supervise the agreement and protocol thereto with regard to the area of separation and limitation. In carrying out its mission, it will comply with generally applicable Syrian laws and regulations and still not hamper the functioning of local civil administration. It will enjoy freedom of movement and communication and other facilities that are necessary for its mission. It will be mobile and provided with personal weapons of a defensive character and shall use such weapons only in self-defence. The number of the UNDOF shall be about 1,250, who will be selected by the Secretary-General of the United Nations in consultation with the parties from members of the United Nations who are not permanent members of the Security Council.

The UNDOF will be under the command of the United Nations vested in the Secretary-General under the authority of the Security Council. The UNDOF shall carry out inspections under the agreement and report thereon to the parties on a regular basis not less often than once every 15 days and in addition when requested by either party.

It shall mark on the ground the respective lines shown on the map attached to the agreement. Israel and Syria will support a resolution of the United Nations Security Council which will provide for the UNDOF contemplated by the agreement. The initial authorization will be for six months subject to renewal by further resolution of the Security Council.

UNITED NATIONS DISENGAGEMENT OBSERVER FORCE (UNDOF) (MAY 31, 1974)

After the Yom Kippur War, there were periodic clashes between Israeli and Syrian forces on the Golan Heights and these became increasingly serious during April 1974. The disengagement agreement of May 1974 created an "area of separation" on the Golan Heights between Israeli and Syrian forces. The parties also agreed to limit their forces and armaments in two equal "areas of limitation" on either side of the area of separation. On May 31, 1974, the United Nations Security Council adopted resolution 350 which established the UNDOF along the same lines as the United Nations Emergency Force II stationed in the Sinai Peninsula. Under the agreement and the accompanying protocol, Israeli and Syrian forces were to be separated by a buffer zone manned by a United Nations Disengagement Observer Force of about 1,250. The Secretary General drew troops from the existing forces in the area, especially UNEF II. In addition to the contingents from UNEF, approximately 90 of the UNTSO Military Observers already deployed in the area were transferred to UNDOF. Israel and Syria agreed that UNDOF's function would be to use its best efforts to maintain the ceasefire and to see that it is scrupulously observed, and to supervise the agreement with regard to areas of separation and limitation of forces and armament. The UNDOF area of operations extends 80 miles from Mount Hermon in the north to the Jordan River in the south. It consists of an area of separation (a buffer zone varying in width from less than a kilometer to 8 kilometers) and three zones of limitation established at 10, 20, and 25 kilometers on each side of the area of separation. In each of the areas of limitations there are restrictions on the numbers of soldiers and quantities and types of equipment permitted. UNDOF's original mandate was for six months but it has been extended every six months since 1974.

The Security Council, Having considered the report of the Secretary-General contained in documents S/11302 and Add.1. and having heard his statement made at the 1773rd meeting of the Security Council, 1. *Welcomes* the Agreement on Disengagement between Israeli and Syrian Forces, negotiated in implementation of Security Council resolution 338 (1973) of 22 October 1973; 2. *Takes note* of the Secretary-General's report and the annexes thereto and his statement; 3. *Decides* to set up immediately under its authority a United Nations Disengagement Observer Force, and requests the Secretary-General to take the necessary steps to this effect in accordance with his above-mentioned report and the annexes thereto; the Force shall be established for an initial period of six months, subject to renewal by further resolution of the Security Council; 4. *Requests* the Secretary-General to keep the Security Council fully informed of further developments.

PLO PHASED PLAN (JUNE 1974)

After the Yom Kippur War, the PLO adopted, in June 1974, in Cairo, Egypt, a two-stage program to restore the Palestinians to Palestine. The first stage was to create a Palestinian state in any territory vacated by Israel. The second phase was to launch a military assault from that state against Israel.

The Palestinian National Council:

On the basis of the Palestinian National Charter and the Political Programme drawn up at the eleventh session, held from January 6-12, 1973; and from its belief that it is impossible for a permanent and just peace to be established in the area unless our Palestinian people recover all their national rights and, first and foremost, their rights to return and to self-determination on the whole of the soil of their homeland; and in the light of a study of the new political circumstances that have come into existence in the period between the Council's last and present sessions, resolves the following:

1. To reaffirm the Palestine Liberation Organization's previous attitude to Resolution 242, which obliterates the national right of our people and deals with the cause of our people as a problem of refugees. The Council therefore refuses to have anything to do with this resolution at any level, Arab or international, including the Geneva Conference.

2. The Liberation Organization will employ all means, and first and foremost armed struggle, to liberate Palestinian territory and to establish the independent combatant national authority for the people over every part of Palestinian territory that is liberated. This will require further changes being effected in the balance of power in favour of our people and their struggle.

3. The Liberation Organization will struggle against any proposal for a Palestinian entity the price of which is recognition, peace, secure frontiers,

renunciation of national rights and the deprival of our people of their right to return and their right to self-determination on the soil of their homeland.

4. Any step taken towards liberation is a step towards the realization of the Liberation Organization's strategy of establishing the democratic Palestinian state specified in the resolutions of previous Palestinian National Councils.

5. Struggle along with the Jordanian national forces to establish a Jordanian-Palestinian national front whose aim will be to set up in Jordan a democratic national authority in close contact with the Palestinian entity that is established through the struggle.

6. The Liberation Organization will struggle to establish unity in struggle between the two peoples and between all the forces of the Arab liberation movement that are in agreement on this programme.

7. In the light of this programme, the Liberation Organization will struggle to strengthen national unity and to raise it to the level where it will be able to perform its national duties and tasks.

8. Once it is established, the Palestinian national authority will strive to achieve a union of the confrontation countries, with the aim of completing the liberation of all Palestinian territory, and as a step along the road to comprehensive Arab unity.

9. The Liberation Organization will strive to strengthen its solidarity with the socialist countries, and with forces of liberation and progress throughout the world, with the aim of frustrating all the schemes of Zionism, reaction and imperialism.

10. In light of this programme, the leadership of the revolution will determine the tactics which will serve and make possible the realization of these objectives.

The Executive Committee of the Palestine Liberation Organization will make every effort to implement this programme, and should a situation arise affecting the destiny and the future of the Palestinian people, the National Assembly will be convened in extraordinary session.

RABAT ARAB SUMMIT RESOLUTIONS (OCTOBER 28, 1974)

At the Arab summit conference in Rabat, Morocco, in October 1974, the representatives unanimously recognized the Palestine Liberation Organization "... as the sole, legitimate representative of the Palestine people." Jordan's King Hussein appeared to alter his position when he joined his fellow delegates in accepting the PLO's claim to negotiate for the West Bank. The Rabat summit further affirmed the right of the Palestinians to return to their homeland and self-determination. The resolutions clouded the prospects for Arab-Israeli negotiations, since Israel had declared it would not negotiate with the PLO and the PLO had consistently refused to recognize Israel's right to exist. It also raised doubts about the viability of Henry Kissinger's step-by-step approach to resolution of the Arab-Israeli conflict.

The conference of the Arab Heads of State: 1. Affirms the right of the Palestinian people to return to their homeland and to self-determination. 2. Affirms the right of the Palestinian people to establish an independent national authority, under the leadership of the PLO in its capacity as the sole legitimate representative of the Palestine people, over all liberated territory. The Arab States are pledged to uphold this authority, when it is established, in all spheres and at all levels. 3. Supports the PLO in the exercise of its national and international responsibilities, within the context of the principle of Arab solidarity. 4. Invites the Kingdom of Jordan, Syria and Egypt to formalize their relations in the light of these decisions and in order that they may be implemented. 5. Affirms the obligation of all Arab States to preserve Palestinian unity and not to interfere in Palestinian internal affairs.

UNGA RESOLUTION 3210 (XXIX) (OCTOBER 14, 1974)

On October 14, 1974 the United Nations General Assembly adopted this resolution, by a vote of 105 in favor, 4 against, and 20 abstaining, inviting the Palestine Liberation Organization to participate in the deliberations of the General Assembly.

The General Assembly, *Considering* that the Palestinian people is the principal party to the question of Palestine, *Invites* the Palestine Liberation Organization, the representative of the Palestinian people, to participate in the deliberations of the General Assembly on the question of Palestine in plenary meetings.

UNGA RESOLUTION 3236 (XXIX) (NOVEMBER 22, 1974)

This resolution was adopted, by a vote in the General Assembly of 89 in favor, 7 against, and 37 abstentions, on November 22, 1974 in response to a discussion of the Palestine problem. It reaffirmed the inalienable rights of the Palestinian people, including the right of self-determination without external interference, the right to national independence and sovereignty, and the right to return to their homes and property.

The General Assembly, Having considered the question of Palestine, *Having heard* the statement of the Palestine Liberation Organization, the representative of the Palestinian people, *Having also heard* other statements made during the debate, *Deeply concerned* that no just solution to the problem of Palestine has yet been achieved and recognizing that the problem of Palestine continues to endanger international peace and security, *Recognizing* that the Palestinian people is entitled to self-determination in accordance with the Charter of the United Nations, *Expressing its grave concern* that the Palestinian people has been prevented from enjoying its inalienable rights, in particular its right to self-determination, *Guided* by the purposes and principles of the Charter, *Recalling* its relevant resolutions which affirm the right of the Palestinian people to self-determination, 1. *Reaffirms* the inalienable rights of the Palestinian people in Palestine, including: (a) The right of self-determination without external interference; (b) The right to national independence and sovereignty; 2. *Reaffirms* also the inalienable right of the Palestinians to return to their homes and property from which they have been displaced and uprooted, and calls for their return; 3. *Emphasizes* that full respect for and the realization of these inalienable rights of the Palestinian people are indispensable for the solution of the question of Palestine; 4. *Recognizes* that the Palestinian people is a principal party in the establishment of a just and durable peace in the Middle East; 5. *Further recognizes* the right of the Palestinian people to regain its rights by all means in accordance with the purposes and principles of the Charter of the United Nations; 6. *Appeals* to all States and international organizations to extend their support to the Palestinian people in its struggle to restore its rights, in accordance with the Charter; 7. *Requests* the Secretary-General to establish contacts with the Palestine Liberation Organization on all matters concerning with question of Palestine; 8. *Requests* the Secretary-General to report to the General Assembly at its thirtieth session on the implementation of the present resolution; 9. *Decides* to include the item "Question of Palestine" in the provisional agenda of its thirtieth session.

OBSERVER STATUS FOR THE PLO -- UNGA RESOLUTION 3237 (XXIX) (NOVEMBER 22, 1974)

In November 1974, the United Nations General Assembly, by a vote of 95 in favor, 17 opposed (including the United States and Israel) and 19 abstentions, passed this resolution granting observer status to the Palestine Liberation Organization (PLO). The resolution stressed a previous UN resolution, UNGA 3102 (XXVIII), which stated that the Palestinians are entitled to equal rights and self-determination and to membership in several other UN organizations. The operative clauses called for PLO participation in all sessions and workings of all international conferences convened under the auspices of the UN.

The General Assembly, Having considered the question of Palestine, *Taking into consideration* the universality of the United Nations prescribed in the Charter, *Recalling* its resolution 3102 (XXVII) of 12 December 1973, *Taking into account* Economic and Social Council resolutions 1835 (LVI) of 14 May 1974 and 1840 (LVI) of 15 May 1974, *Noting* that the Diplomatic Conference on the Reaffirmation and Development of International Humanitarian Law Applicable in Armed Conflicts, the World Population Conference and the World Food Conference have in effect invited the Palestine Liberation Organization to participate in their respective deliberations, *Noting also* that the Third United Nations Conference on the Law of the Sea has invited the Palestine Liberation Organization to participate in its deliberations as an observer, 1. *Invites* the Palestine Liberation Organization to participate in the sessions and the work of the General Assembly in the capacity of observer; 2. *Invites* the Palestine Liberation Organization to participate in the sessions and work of all international conferences convened under the auspices of the General Assembly in the capacity of observer; 3. *Considers* that the Palestine Liberation Organization is entitled to participate as an observer in the sessions and the work of all international conferences convened under the auspices of other organs of the United Nations. 4. *Requests* the Secretary-General to take the necessary steps for the implementation of the present resolution.

SINAI II ACCORDS (SEPTEMBER 1, 1975)

After intensive shuttle diplomacy by United States Secretary of State Henry Kissinger, Egypt and Israel agreed, in September 1975, to a partial pullback of Israeli troops in the Sinai Peninsula from the Mitla and Gidi passes, return of the Abu Rudeis oil fields in exchange for a mutual pledge to refrain from the threat or use of force or military blockade, and the unimpeded passage of nonmilitary cargoes destined for Israel through the Suez Canal. There was a formal agreement between the two parties, an annex, and a proposal for an American presence in the Sinai Peninsula in connection with an early-warning system. This was more than a simple disengagement of military forces as they agreed that "the conflict between them and in the Middle East shall not be resolved by military force but by peaceful means." These were the first steps toward increased accommodation between the parties and it moved in the direction of a peace settlement. There were memoranda of agreement between the United States and Israel and United States assurances to Israel and to Egypt. It was in the Memorandum of Agreement between the United States and Israel regarding the Geneva Peace Conference that the United States pledged that it "will continue to adhere to its present policy with respect to the Palestine Liberation Organization, whereby it will not recognize or negotiate with the Palestine Liberation Organization so long as the Palestine Liberation Organization does not recognize Israel's right to exist and does not accept Security Council Resolutions 242 and 338."

This agreement, which followed upon the January 1974 Egypt-Israel Separation of Forces Agreement, was initialled in Jerusalem and Alexandria on September 1 and officially signed in Geneva on September 4.

The Government of the Arab Republic of Egypt and the Government of Israel have agreed that:

Article I. The conflict between them and in the Middle East shall not be resolved by military force but by peaceful means.

The Agreement concluded by the parties on 18 January 1974, within the framework of the Geneva Peace Conference, constituted a first step towards a just and durable peace according to the provisions of Security Council Resolution 338 of 22 October 1973.

They are determined to reach a final and just peace settlement by means of negotiations called for by Security Council Resolution 338, this Agreement being a significant step towards that end.

Article II. The parties hereby undertake not to resort to the threat or use of force or military blockade against each other.

Article III. The parties shall continue scrupulously to observe the cease-fire on land, sea and air and to refrain from all military or para-military actions against each other. The parties also confirm that the obligations contained in the annex and, when concluded, the Protocol shall be an integral part of this Agreement.

Article IV. A. The military forces of the parties shall be deployed in accordance with the following principles: (1) All Israel forces shall be deployed east of the lines designated as lined J and M on attached map. (2) All Egyptian forces shall be deployed west of the line designated as line E on the attached map. (3) The area between the lines designated on the attached map as lines E and F and the area between the lines designated on the attached map as lines J and K shall be limited in armament and forces. (4) The limitations on armament and forces in the areas described by paragraph (3) above shall be agreed as described in the attached annex. (5) The zone between the lines designated on the attached map as lines E and J will be a buffer zone. In this zone the United Nations Emergency Force will continue to perform its functions as under the Egyptian-Israeli Agreement of 18 January 1974. (6) In the area south from line E and west from line M, as defined on the attached map, there will be no military forces, as specified in the attached annex. B. The details concerning the new lines, the redeployment of the forces and its timing, the limitation on armaments and forces, aerial reconnaissance, the operation of the early warning and surveillance installations and the use of the roads, the United Nations functions and other arrangements will all be in accordance with the provisions of the annex and map which are an integral part of this Agreement and of the protocol which is to result from negotiations pursuant to the annex and which, when concluded, shall become an integral part of this Agreement.

Article V. The United Nations Emergency Force is essential and shall continue its functions and its mandate shall be extended annually.

Article VI. The parties hereby establish a joint commission for the duration of this Agreement. It will function under the aegis of the chief co-ordinator of the United Nations peace-keeping missions in the Middle East in order to consider any problem arising from this Agreement and to assist the United Nations Emergency Force in the execution of its mandate. The joint commission shall function in accordance with procedures established in the Protocol.

Article VII. Non-military cargoes destined for or coming from Israel shall be permitted through the Suez Canal.

Article VIII. This Agreement is regarded by the parties as a significant step toward a just and lasting peace. It is not a final peace agreement. The parties shall continue their efforts to negotiate a final peace agreement within the framework of the Geneva peace conference in accordance with Security Council Resolution 338.

Article IX. This Agreement shall enter into force upon signature of the Protocol and remain in force until superseded by a new agreement.

ANNEX TO THE AGREEMENT

Within five days after the signature of the Egypt-Israel Agreement, representatives of the two parties shall meet in the military working group of the Middle East peace conference at Geneva to begin preparation of a detailed Protocol for the implementation of the Agreement. The working group will complete the Protocol within two weeks. In order to facilitate preparation of the Protocol and implementation of the agreement, and to assist in maintaining the scrupulous observance of the cease-fire and other elements of the Agreement, the two parties have agreed on the following principles, which are integral part of the Agreement, as guidelines for the working group.

1. DEFINITIONS OF LINES AND AREA. The deployment lines, areas of limited forces and armaments, buffer zones, the area south from line E and west from line M, other designated areas, road sections for common use and other features referred to in article IV of the Agreement shall be indicated on the attached map (1:100,000 - United States edition). 2. BUFFER ZONES (A) Access to the buffer zones will be controlled by the United Nations Emergency Force, according to procedures to be worked out by the working group and the United Nations Emergency Force. (B) Aircraft of either party will be permitted to fly freely up to the forward line of the party. Reconnaissance aircraft of either party may fly up to the middle line of the buffer zone between E and J on an

agreed schedule. (C) In the buffer zone, between lines E and J, there will be established under article IV of the Agreement an early warning system entrusted to United States civilian personnel as detailed in a separate proposal, which is a part of this Agreement. (D) Authorized personnel shall have access to the buffer zone for transit to and from the early warning system; the manner in which this is carried out shall be worked out by the working group and the United Nations Emergency Force. 3. AREA SOUTH OF LINE E AND WEST OF LINE M. (A) In this area, the United Nations Emergency Force will assure that there are no military or para-military forces of any kind, military fortifications and military installations; it will establish checkpoints and have the freedom of movement necessary to perform this function. (B) Egyptian civilians and third country civilian oil field personnel shall have the right to enter, exit from, work and live in the above indicated area, except for buffer zones 2A, 2B and the United Nations posts. Egyptian civilian police shall be allowed in the area to perform normal civil police functions among the civilian population in such number and with such weapons and equipment as shall be provided for in the Protocol. (C) Entry to and exit from the area, by land, by air or by sea, shall be only through United Nations Emergency Force checkpoints. The United Nations Emergency Force shall also establish checkpoints along the road, the dividing line and at either points, with the precise locations and number to be included in the Protocol. (D) Access to the airspace and the coastal area shall be limited to unarmed Egyptian civilian vessels and unarmed civilian helicopters and transport planes involved in the civilian activities of the areas agreed by the working group. (E) Israel undertakes to leave intact all currently existing civilian installations and infrastructures. (F) Procedures for use of the common sections of the coastal road along the Gulf of Suez shall be determined by the working group and detailed in the Protocol. 4. AERIAL SURVEILLANCE. There shall be a continuation of aerial reconnaissance missions by the United States over the areas covered by the Agreement (the area between lines F and K), following the same procedures already in practice. The missions will ordinarily be carried out at a frequency of one mission every 7 - 10 days, with either party or the United Nations Emergency Force empowered to request an earlier mission. The United States Government will make the mission results available expeditiously to Israel, Egypt and the Chief Coordinator of the United Nations Peace-Keeping Missions in the Middle East. 5. LIMITATION OF FORCES AND ARMAMENTS. (A) Within the areas of limited forces and armaments (the areas between lines J and K and lines E and F) the major limitation shall be as follows: (1) Eight (8) standard infantry battalions. (2) Seventy-five (75) tanks. (3) Seventy-two (72) artillery pieces, including heavy mortars (i.e. with caliber larger than 120 mm.), whose range shall not exceed twelve (12) km. (4) The total number of personnel shall not exceed eight thousand (8,000). (5) Both parties agree not to station or locate in the area weapons which can reach the line of the other side. (6) Both parties agree that in the areas between line A (of the disengagement agreement of 18 January 1974) and line E they will construct no new fortifications or installations for forces of a size greater than that agreed herein. (B) The major limitations beyond the areas of limited forces and armament will be: (1) Neither side will station nor locate any weapon in areas from which they can reach the other line. (2) The parties will not place any anti-aircraft missiles within an area of ten (10) kilometers east of line K and west of line F, respectively. (C) The United Nations Emergency Force will conduct inspections in order to ensure the maintenance of the agreed limitations within these areas. 6. PROCESS OF IMPLEMENTATION. The detailed implementation and timing of the redeployment of forces, turnover of oil fields, and other arrangements called for by the Agreement, annex and Protocol shall be determined by the working group, which will agree on the stages of this process, including the phased movement of Egyptian troops to line E and Israeli troops to line J. The first phase will be the transfer of the oil fields and installations to Egypt. This process will begin within two weeks from the signature of the Protocol with the introduction of the necessary technicians, and it will be completed no later than eight weeks after it begins. The detail of the phasing will be worked out in the military working group. Implementation of the redeployment shall be completed within 5 months after signature of the Protocol.

PROPOSAL. In connection with the early warning system referred to in article IV of the Agreement between Egypt and Israel concluded on this date and as an integral part of that Agreement (hereafter referred to as the basic Agreement), the United States proposes the following: 1. The early warning system to be established in accordance with article IV in the area shown on the map attached to the basic agreement will be entrusted to the United States. It shall have the following elements: A. There shall be two surveillance stations to provide strategic early warning, one operated by Egyptian and one operated by Israeli personnel. Their locations are shown on map attached to the basic Agreement. Each station shall be manned by not more than 250 technical and administrative personnel. They shall perform the functions of visual and electronic surveillance only within their stations. B. In support of these stations, to provide tactical early warning and to verify access to them, three watch stations shall be established by the United States in the Mitla and Giddi Passes as will be shown on the map attached to the basic Agreement. These stations shall be operated by United States civilian personnel. In support of these stations, there shall be established three unmanned electronic sensor fields at both ends of each Pass and in the general vicinity of each station and the roads leading to and from those stations. 2. The United States civilian personnel shall perform the following duties in connection with the operation and maintenance of these stations: A. At the two surveillance stations described in paragraph 1A above, United States civilian personnel will verify that nature of the operations of the stations and all movement into and out of each station and will immediately report any detected divergency from its authorized role of visual and electronic surveillance to the parties to the basic Agreement and to the United Nations Emergency Force. B. At each watch station described in paragraph B above, the United States civilian personnel will immediately report to the parties of the basic Agreement and to the United Nations Emergency Force any movement of armed forces, other than the United Nations Emergency Force, into either Pass and any observed preparations for such movement. C. The total number of United States civilian personnel assigned to functions under this proposal shall not exceed 200. Only civilian personnel shall be assigned to functions under this proposal. 3. No arms shall be maintained at the stations and other facilities covered by this proposal, except for small arms required for their protection. 4. The United States personnel serving the early warning system shall be allowed to move freely within the area of the system. 5. The United States and its personnel shall be entitled to have such support facilities as are reasonably necessary to perform their functions. 6. The United States personnel shall be immune from local criminal, civil, tax and customs jurisdiction and may be accorded any other specific privileges and immunities provided for in the United Nations Emergency Force Agreement of 13 February 1957. 7. The United States affirms that it will continue to perform the functions described above for the duration of the basic Agreement. 8. Notwithstanding any other provision of this proposal, the United States may withdraw its personnel only if it concludes that their safety is jeopardized or that continuation of their role is no longer necessary. In the latter case the parties to the basic Agreement will be informed in advance in order to give them the opportunity to make alternative arrangements. If both parties to the basic Agreement request the United States to conclude its role under this proposal. the United States will consider such requests conclusive. 9. Technical problems including the location of the watch stations will be worked out through consultation with the United States.

/s/ Henry A. Kissinger, Secretary of State

MEMORANDUM OF AGREEMENT BETWEEN THE GOVERNMENTS OF ISRAEL AND THE UNITED STATES. The United States recognizes that the Egypt-Israel Agreement initialed on September 1, 1975, (hereinafter referred to as the Agreement), entailing the withdrawal from vital areas in Sinai, constitutes an act of great significance on Israel's part in the pursuit of final peace. That Agreement has full United States support.

United States-Israeli Assurances. 1. The United States Government will make every effort to be fully responsive, within the limits of its resources and Congressional authorization and appropriation, on an on-going and long-term basis to Israel's military equipment and other defense requirements, to its energy requirements and to its economic needs. The needs specified in paragraphs 2, 3 and 4 below shall be deemed eligible for inclusion within the annual total to be requested in FY76 and later fiscal years.

2. Israel's long-term military supply needs from the United States shall be

the subject of periodic consultations between representatives of the United States and Israeli defense establishments, with agreement reached on specific items to be included in a separate United States-Israeli memorandum. To this end, a joint study by military experts will be undertaken within 3 weeks. In conducting this study, which will include Israel's 1976 needs, the United States will view Israel's requests sympathetically, including its request for advanced and sophisticated weapons.

3. Israel will make its own independent arrangements for oil supply to meet its requirements through normal procedures. In the event Israel is unable to secure its needs in this way, the United States Government, upon notification of this fact by the Government of Israel, will act as follows for five years, at the end of which period either side can terminate this arrangement on one-year's notice.

(a) If the oil Israel needs to meet all its normal requirements for domestic consumption is unavailable for purchase in circumstances where no quantitative restrictions exist on the ability of the United States to procure oil to meet its normal requirements, the United States Government will promptly make oil available for purchase by Israel to meet all of the aforementioned normal requirements of Israel. If Israel is unable to secure the necessary means to transport such oil to Israel, the United States Government will make every effort to help Israel secure the necessary means of transport.

(b) If the oil Israel needs to meet all of its normal requirements for domestic consumption is unavailable for purchase in circumstances where quantitative restrictions through embargo or otherwise also prevent the United States from procuring oil to meet its normal requirements, the United States Government will promptly make oil available for purchase by Israel in accordance with the International Energy Agency conservation and allocation formula as applied by the United States Government, in order to meet Israel's essential requirements. If Israel is unable to secure the necessary means to transport such oil to Israel, the United States Government will make every effort to help Israel secure the necessary means of transport.

Israeli and United States experts will meet annually or more frequently at the request of either party, to review Israel's continuing oil requirement.

4. In order to help Israel meet its energy needs, and as part of the overall annual figure in paragraph 1 above, the United States agrees:

(a) In determining the overall annual figure which will be requested from Congress, the United States Government will give special attention to Israel's oil import requirements and, for a period as determined by Article 3 above, will take into account in calculating that figure Israel's additional expenditures for the import of oil to replace that which would have ordinarily come from Abu Rodeis and Ras Sudar (4.5 million tons in 1975).

(b) To ask Congress to make available funds, the amount to be determined by mutual agreement, to the Government of Israel necessary for a project for the construction and stocking of the oil reserves to be stored in Israel, bringing storage reserve capacity and reserve stocks now standing at approximately six months, up to one-year's need at the time of the completion of the project. The project will be implemented within four years. The construction, operation and financing and other relevant questions of the project will be the subject of early and detailed talks between the two Governments.

The United States Government will not expect Israel to begin to implement the Agreement before Egypt fulfills its undertaking under the January 1974 Disengagement Agreement to permit passage of all Israeli cargoes to and from Israeli ports through the Suez Canal.

6. The United States Government agrees with Israel that the next agreement with Egypt should be a final peace agreement.

7. In case of an Egyptian violation of any of the provisions of the Agreement, the United States Government is prepared to consult with Israel as to the significance of the violation and possible remedial action by the United States Government.

8. The United States Government will vote against any Security Council resolution which in its judgment affects or alters adversely the Agreement.

9. The United States Government will not join in and will seek to prevent efforts by others to bring about consideration of proposals which it and Israel agree are detrimental to the interests of Israel.

10. In view of the long-standing United States commitment to the survival and security of Israel, the United States Government will view with particular gravity threats to Israel's security or sovereignty by a world power. In support of this objective, the United States Government will in the event of such threat consult promptly with the Government of Israel with respect to what support, diplomatic or otherwise, or assistance it can lend to Israel in accordance with its constitutional practices.

11. The United States Government and the Government of Israel will, at the earliest possible time, and if possible, within two months after the signature of this document, conclude the contingency plan for a military supply operation to Israel in an emergency situation.

12. It is the United States Government's position that Egyptian commitments under the Egypt-Israel Agreement, its implementation, validity and duration are not conditional upon any act of developments between the other Arab states and Israel. The United States Government regards the Agreement as standing on its own.

13. The United States Government shares the Israeli position that under existing political circumstances negotiations with Jordan will be directed toward an overall peace settlement.

14. In accordance with the principle of freedom of navigation on the high seas and free and unimpeded passage through and over straits connecting international waters, the United States Government regards the Straits of Bab-el-

Mandeb and the Strait of Gibraltar as international waterways. It will support Israel's right to free and unimpeded passage through such straits. Similarly, the United States Government recognizes Israel's right to freedom of flights over the Red Sea and such straits and will support diplomatically the exercise of that right.

15. In the event that the United Nations Emergency Force or any other United Nations organ is withdrawn without the prior agreement of both Parties to the Egypt-Israel Agreement and the United States before this Agreement is superseded by another agreement, it is the United States view that the Agreement shall remain binding in all its parts.

16. The United States and Israel agree that signature of the Protocol of the Egypt-Israel Agreement and its full entry into effect shall not take place before approval by the United States Congress of the United States role in connection with the surveillance and observation functions described in the Agreement and its Annex. The United States has informed the Government of Israel that it has obtained the Government of Egypt agreement to the above.

/s/ Yigal Allon, Deputy Prime Minister and Minister of Foreign Affairs, For the Government of Israel

/s/ Henry A. Kissinger, Secretary of State, For the Government of the United States

MEMORANDUM OF AGREEMENT BETWEEN THE GOVERNMENTS OF ISRAEL AND THE UNITED STATES. The Geneva Peace Conference. 1. The Geneva Peace Conference will be reconvened at a time coordinated between the United States and Israel.

2. The United States will continue to adhere to its present policy with respect to the Palestine Liberation Organization, whereby it will not recognize or negotiate with the Palestine Liberation Organization so long as the Palestine Liberation Organization does not recognize Israel's right to exist and does not accept Security Council Resolutions 242 and 338. The United States Government will consult fully and seek to concert its position and strategy at the Geneva Peace Conference on this issue with the Government of Israel. Similarly, the United States will consult fully and seek to concert its position and strategy with Israel with regard to the participation of any other additional states. It is understood that the participation at a subsequent phase of the Conference of any possible additional state, group or organization will require the agreement of all the initial participants.

3. The United States will make every effort to ensure at the Conference that all the substantive negotiations will be on a bilateral basis.

4. The United States will oppose and, if necessary, vote against any initiative in the Security Council to alter adversely the terms of reference of the Geneva Peace Conference or to change Resolutions 242 and 338 in ways which are incompatible with their original purpose.

5. The United States will seek to ensure that the role of the cosponsors will be consistent with what was agreed in the Memorandum of Understanding between the United States Government and the Government of Israel of December 20, 1973.

6. The United States and Israel will concert action to assure that the Conference will be conducted in a manner consonant with the objectives of this document and with the declared purpose of the Conference, namely the advancement of a negotiated peace between Israel and each one of its neighbors.

/s/ Yigal Allon, Deputy Prime Minister and Minister of Foreign Affairs, For the Government of Israel

/s/ Henry A. Kissinger, Secretary of State, For the Government of the United States

Assurances from USG to Israel. On the question of military and economic assistance to Israel, the following conveyed by the U.S. to Israel augments what the Memorandum of Agreement states. The United States is resolved to continue to maintain Israel's defensive strength through the supply of advanced types of equipment, such as the F-16 aircraft. The United States Government agrees to an early meeting to undertake a joint study of high technology and sophisticated items, including the Pershing ground-to-ground missiles with conventional warheads, with the view to giving a positive response. The U.S. Administration will submit annually for approval by the U.S. Congress a request for military and economic assistance in order to help meet Israel's economic and military needs.

Assurances from USG to Egypt. 1. The United States intends to make a serious effort to help bring about further negotiations between Syria and Israel, in the first instance through diplomatic channels. 2. In the event of an Israeli violation of the Agreement, the United States is prepared to consult with Egypt as to the significance of the violation and possible remedial action by the United States. 3. The United States will provide technical assistance to Egypt for the Egyptian Early Warning Station. 4. The U.S. reaffirms its policy of assisting Egypt in its economic development, the specific amount to be subject to Congressional authorization and appropriation.

JOINT COMMUNIQUE BY THE GOVERNMENTS OF THE UNITED STATES AND THE UNION OF SOVIET SOCIALIST REPUBLICS (OCTOBER 1, 1977)

United States President Jimmy Carter assigned a priority to the establishment of peace in the Middle East for his administration believing that the existing conditions in the region were ripe for resolution. The Carter administration called for a new approach to replace Henry Kissinger's step-by-step diplomacy. The early foreign policy strategy was based, in part, on a 1975 report entitled Towards

Peace in the Middle East *issued under the auspices of the Brookings Institution in Washington, D.C. The report advocated a comprehensive settlement to the Arab-Israeli conflict. It noted that the United States had moral, political and economic interests in a stable peace, particularly in the security, independence and well-being of both Israel and the Arab states. It recommended that the United States cooperate with the Soviet Union as this would be beneficial should they be willing to participate. Efforts to resume the Geneva Peace Conference, suspended since December 1973, were a focal point of Secretary of State Cyrus Vance's efforts. In discussions with the parties to the conflict, he pursued an appropriate formula that would allow resumption of the Conference. Secretary Vance also reviewed the Arab-Israeli question with Soviet Foreign Minister Andre Gromyko in May and following a meeting at the United Nations in New York in September 1977 the United States and the Soviet Union issued a joint call for a resumption of the Geneva Conference. President Sadat's initiative superseded this effort.*

Having exchanged views regarding the unsafe situation which remains in the Middle East, US Secretary of State Cyrus Vance and Member of the Politbureau of the Central Committee of the CPSU, Minister for Foreign Affairs of the USSR A.A. Gromyko have the following statement to make on behalf of their countries, which are cochairmen of the Geneva Peace Conference on the Middle East:

1. Both governments are convinced that vital interests of the peoples of this area, as well as the interests of strengthening peace and international security in general, urgently dictate the necessity of achieving, as soon as possible, a just and lasting settlement of the Arab-Israeli conflict. This settlement should be comprehensive, incorporating all parties concerned and all questions.

The United States and the Soviet Union believe that, within the framework of a comprehensive settlement of the Middle East problem, all specific questions of the settlement should be resolved, including such key issues as withdrawal of Israeli Armed Forces from territories occupied in the 1967 conflict; the resolution of the Palestinian question, including insuring the legitimate rights of the Palestinian people; termination of the state of war and establishment of normal peaceful relations on the basis of mutual recognition of the principles of sovereignty, territorial integrity, and political independence.

The two governments believe that, in addition to such measures for insuring the security of the borders between Israel and the neighboring Arab states as the establishment of demilitarized zones and the agreed stationing in them of UN troops or observers, international guarantees of such borders as well as of the observance of the terms of the settlement can also be established should the contracting parties so desire. The United States and the Soviet Union are ready to participate in these guarantees, subject to their constitutional processes.

2. The United States and the Soviet Union believe that the only right and effective way for achieving a fundamental solution to all aspects of the Middle

East problem in its entirety is negotiations within the framework of the Geneva peace conference, specially convened for these purposes, with participation in its work of the representatives of all the parties involved in the conflict including those of the Palestinian people, and legal and contractual formalization of the decisions reached at the conference.

In their capacity as cochairmen of the Geneva conference, the United States and the USSR affirm their intention, through joint efforts and in their contacts with the parties concerned, to facilitate in every way the resumption of the work of the conference not later than December 1977. The cochairmen note that there still exist several questions of a procedural and organizational nature which remain to be agreed upon by the participants to the conference.

3. Guided by the goal of achieving a just political settlement in the Middle East and of eliminating the explosive situation in this area of the world, the United States and the USSR appeal to all the parties in the conflict to understand the necessity for careful consideration of each other's legitimate rights and interests and to demonstrate mutual readiness to act accordingly.

SADAT PEACE INITIATIVE (NOVEMBER 9, 1977)

After the breakdown of United States efforts to resolve the impasse in Israeli and Egyptian positions following the Yom Kippur War, and the failure of an October 1977 joint communique by the United States and the Soviet Union to revive the Geneva Conference, President Anwar Sadat of Egypt decided to make a direct approach. In the course of an address to the Egyptian parliament on November 9, 1977, Sadat announced that he was willing to go to Israel to discuss peace. The announcement was a surprise, but not a precipitous action as contacts had taken place through a variety of channels. The Israeli government subsequently extended an invitation for a visit by Sadat. Sadat's arrival in Israel on November 19 was one of the most highly charged moments in Arab-Israeli history, and he delivered a strong speech to Israel's parliament in which he outlined Egypt's conditions for peace: a return to the 1967 borders and justice for the Palestinians. This opened the formal dialogue between the two states. The talks continued with the intervention of various negotiators including President Jimmy Carter, who brought Sadat and Israeli Premier Menachem Begin together at Camp David in September 1978, after the breakdown of bilateral talks.

... Let me now pause for a moment and talk to you and our people and the Arab nation about the latest developments as regards the [Geneva] Conference, which is being proposed at both the Arab and international levels not as an end in itself but as a means that could lead to that end. If we succeed in exploiting our strength so as to face Israel with the choice between a peace based on justice and legality and a confrontation with incalculable consequences, it will be a confrontation in which the Arab nation will employ all its resources, material and moral. You are well aware of what efforts have been made in recent months towards convening the Geneva Conference as soon as possible -- before the end of this year in fact -- on condition that, before it is convened, proper preparations are made to ensure that the aims for which it is convened are realized. ... I say this frankly, in your presence, to our people, to the Arab nation and to the whole world. We are ready to go to Geneva and to sit down on behalf of peace regardless of all the procedural problems raised by Israel in the hope of spoiling our chances or of so exasperating us that we say, as we have done in the past, No, we do not want to go and we shall not go, so that she may appear to the world as the advocate of peace ....

I am ready to agree to any procedural points. When we go to Geneva we shall refuse to give up the territory, the Arab territory occupied in 1967, and neither Israel nor any other power will be able to prevent me demanding the legitimate rights of the Palestinians, their right to self-determination and to establish their state. ...

I am ready to go to Geneva -- and I do not conceal this from you who are the representatives of the people and I say it in the hearing of our people and of the Arab nation. You heard me saying that I am prepared to go to the ends of the earth if my doing so will prevent any of my officers or men being killed or wounded. I really am ready to go to the ends of the earth and Israel will be amazed to hear me say that we do not refuse -- I am prepared to go to their very home, to the Knesset itself and discuss things with them. ...

ASWAN FORMULA (JANUARY 4, 1978)

On January 4, 1978, during a brief stopover in Aswan, Egypt, Jimmy Carter enunciated what became known as the Aswan Declaration or Aswan Formula. Carter praised Egyptian President Anwar Sadat's initiative of November 1977 and stressed the friendship and convergence of goals between the United States and Egypt. He also noted the need for the Egyptian-Israeli peace negotiations to succeed. Carter outlined the principles or bases which would provide the foundation for the achievement of a "just and comprehensive peace."

President Sadat, people of Egypt:

It is an honor and a pleasure for us to be in this great country, led by such a strong and courageous man.

Mr. President, your bold initiative in seeking peace has aroused the admiration of the entire world. One of my most valued possessions is the warm, personal relationship which binds me and President Sadat together and which exemplifies the friendship and the common purpose of the people of Egypt and the people of the United States of America.

The Egyptian-Israeli peace initiative must succeed, while still guarding the sacred and historic principles held by the nations who have suffered so much in this region. There is no good reason why accommodation cannot be reached.

In my own private discussions with both Arab and Israeli leaders, I have been deeply impressed by the unanimous desire for peace. My presence here today is a direct result of the courageous initiative which President Sadat undertook in his recent trip to Jerusalem.

The negotiating process will continue in the near future. We fully support this effort, and we intend to play an active role in the work of the political committee of Cairo, which will soon reconvene in Jerusalem.

We believe that there are certain principles, fundamentally, which must be observed before a just and a comprehensive peace can be achieved. First, true peace must be based on normal relations among the parties to the peace. Peace means more than just an end to belligerency. Second, there must be withdrawal by Israel from territories occupied in 1967 and agreements on secure and recognized borders for all parties in the context of normal and peaceful relations in accordance with United Nations Resolutions 242 and 338. And third there must be a resolution of the Palestinian problem in all its aspects. The problem must recognize the legitimate rights of the Palestinian people and enable the Palestinians to participate in the determination of their own future.

Some flexibility is always needed to ensure successful negotiations and the resolution of conflicting views. We know that the mark of greatness among leaders is to consider carefully the views of others and the greater benefits that can result among the people of all nations which can come from a successful search for peace.

Mr. President, our consultations this morning have reconfirmed our common commitment to the fundamentals which will, with God's help, make 1978 the year for permanent peace in the Middle East.

UNSC RESOLUTION 425 (MARCH 19, 1978)

On March 11, 1978 terrorists attacked two Israeli buses near Tel Aviv killing 37 Israelis and injuring more than 75. The Israel Defense Forces, in Operation Litani, entered southern Lebanon on March 14 in order to eliminate PLO bases and staging areas south of the Litani River. By March 19, 1978 Israel was in control of all of Lebanon south of the Litani River, and Israeli Prime Minister Menachem Begin stated that withdrawal of Israeli forces would be contingent upon the removal of Palestinian guerrillas from the area. The United States proposed that Israeli troops be replaced by an international force and that in time these troops would be replaced by the Lebanese Army. The United Nations Security Council adopted Resolution 425, which created the United Nations Interim Force in Lebanon (UNIFIL), on March 19, 1978. The UNIFIL troops first arrived in southern Lebanon on March 22, 1978 to take up positions between the Israelis and Palestinians. They have remained in southern Lebanon since then.

The Security Council, Taking note of the letters of the Permanent Representative of Lebanon (S/12600 and S/12606) and the Permanent Representative of Israel (S/12607), *Having heard* the statements of the Permanent Representatives of Lebanon and Israel, *Gravely concerned* at the deterioration of the situation in the Middle East, and its consequences to the maintenance of international peace. *Convinced* that the present situation impedes the achievement of a just peace in the Middle East, 1. *Calls for* strict respect for the territorial integrity, sovereignty and political independence of Lebanon within its internationally recognized boundaries; 2. *Calls upon* Israel immediately to cease its military action against Lebanese territorial integrity and withdraw forthwith its forces from all Lebanese territory; 3. *Decides*, in the light of the request of the Government of Lebanon, to establish immediately under its authority a United Nations interim force for southern Lebanon for the purpose of confirming the withdrawal of Israeli forces, restoring international peace and security and assisting the Government of Lebanon in ensuring the return of its effective authority in the area, the force to be composed of personnel drawn from States Members of the United Nations. 4. *Requests* the Secretary-General to report to the Council within twenty-four hours on the implementation of this resolution.

CAMP DAVID ACCORDS (SEPTEMBER 17, 1978)

Egyptian President Anwar Sadat's historic visit to Jerusalem in November 1977 was followed by negotiations in which the United States, and President Jimmy Carter personally, played an active and often crucial role. In September 1978, President Carter, President Sadat, Prime Minister Menachem Begin of Israel, and their senior aides, held an extraordinary series of meetings for thirteen days at the presidential retreat at Camp David, Maryland, during which they discussed the Arab-Israeli conflict. On September 17, 1978, they announced, at the White House, the conclusion of two accords that provided the basis for continuing negotiations for peace: a "Framework for Peace in the Middle East" and "A Framework for the Conclusion of a Peace Treaty Between Egypt and Israel."

The Middle East framework set forth general principles and some specifics to govern a comprehensive peace settlement, focusing on the future of the West Bank and the Gaza Strip. The Egypt-Israel framework called for Israel's withdrawal from the Sinai Peninsula and the establishment of normal, peaceful relations

between the two states. In addition to the two frameworks there was a series of
accompanying letters clarifying the parties' positions on various issues. The
Egyptian cabinet approved the accords on September 19 and on September 28 the
Israeli Knesset voted 84-19 (with 17 abstentions) to endorse them.

THE FRAMEWORK FOR PEACE IN THE MIDDLE EAST

Muhammad Anwar al-Sadat, President of the Arab Republic of Egypt, and
Menachem Begin, Prime Minister of Israel, met with Jimmy Carter, President of
the United States of America, at Camp David from September 5 to September
17, 1978, and have agreed on the following framework for peace in the Middle
East. They invite other parties to the Arab-Israel conflict to adhere to it.

Preamble

The search for peace in the Middle East must be guided by the following:

* The agreed basis for a peaceful settlement of the conflict between Israel and
its neighbors is United Nations Security Council Resolution 242, in all its parts.

* After four wars during 30 years, despite intensive human efforts, the Middle
East, which is the cradle of civilization and the birthplace of three great
religions, does not enjoy the blessings of peace. The people of the Middle East
yearn for peace so that the vast human and natural resources of the region can
be turned to the pursuits of peace and so that this area can become a model for
coexistence and cooperation among nations.

* The historic initiative of President Sadat in visiting Jerusalem and the
reception accorded to him by the parliament, government and people of Israel,
and the reciprocal visit of Prime Minister Begin to Ismailia, the peace proposals
made by both leaders, as well as the warm reception of these missions by the
peoples of both countries, have created an unprecedented opportunity for peace
which must not be lost if this generation and future generations are to be spared
the tragedies of war.

* The provisions of the Charter of the United Nations and the other accepted
norms of international law and legitimacy now provide accepted standards for the
conduct of relations among all states.

* To achieve a relationship of peace, in the spirit of Article 2 of the United
Nations Charter, future negotiations between Israel and any neighbor prepared
to negotiate peace and security with it are necessary for the purpose of carrying
out all the provisions and principles of Resolutions 242 and 338.

* Peace requires respect for the sovereignty, territorial integrity and political
independence of every state in the area and their right to live in peace within
secure and recognized boundaries free from threats or acts of force. Progress
toward that goal can accelerate movement toward a new era of reconciliation in
the Middle East marked by cooperation in promoting economic development, in
maintaining stability and in assuring security.

* Security is enhanced by a relationship of peace and by cooperation between nations which enjoy normal relations. In addition, under the terms of peace treaties, the parties can, on the basis of reciprocity, agree to special security arrangements such as demilitarized zones, limited armaments areas, early warning stations, the presence of international forces, liaison, agreed measures for monitoring and other arrangements that they agree are useful.

Framework

Taking these factors into account, the parties are determined to reach a just, comprehensive, and durable settlement of the Middle East conflict through the conclusion of peace treaties based on Security Council resolutions 242 and 338 in all their parts. Their purpose is to achieve peace and good neighborly relations. They recognize that for peace to endure, it must involve all those who have been most deeply affected by the conflict. They therefore agree that this framework, as appropriate, is intended by them to constitute a basis for peace not only between Egypt and Israel, but also between Israel and each of its other neighbors which is prepared to negotiate peace with Israel on this basis. With that objective in mind, they have agreed to proceed as follows:

A. West Bank and Gaza. 1. Egypt, Israel, Jordan and the representatives of the Palestinian people should participate in negotiations on the resolution of the Palestinian problem in all its aspects. To achieve that objective, negotiations relating to the West Bank and Gaza should proceed in three stages: (a) Egypt and Israel agree that, in order to ensure a peaceful and orderly transfer of authority, and taking into account the security concerns of all the parties, there should be transitional arrangements for the West Bank and Gaza for a period not exceeding five years. In order to provide full autonomy to the inhabitants, under these arrangements the Israeli military government and its civilian administration will be withdrawn as soon as a self-governing authority has been freely elected by the inhabitants of these areas to replace the existing military government. To negotiate the details of a transitional arrangement, Jordan will be invited to join the negotiations on the basis of this framework. These new arrangements should give due consideration both to the principle of self-government by the inhabitants of these territories and to the legitimate security concerns of the parties involved. (b) Egypt, Israel, and Jordan will agree on the modalities for establishing elected self-governing authority in the West Bank and Gaza. The delegations of Egypt and Jordan may include Palestinians from the West Bank and Gaza or other Palestinians as mutually agreed. The parties will negotiate an agreement which will define the powers and responsibilities of the self-governing authority to be exercised in the West Bank and Gaza. A withdrawal of Israeli armed forces will take place and there will be a redeployment of the remaining Israeli forces into specified security locations. The agreement will also include arrangements for assuring internal and external security and public order. A strong local police force will be established, which may include Jordanian citizens. In addition,

Israeli and Jordanian forces will participate in joint patrols and in the manning of control posts to assure the security of the borders. (c) When the self-governing authority (administrative council) in the West Bank and Gaza is established and inaugurated, the transitional period of five years will begin. As soon as possible, but not later than the third year after the beginning of the transitional period, negotiations will take place to determine the final status of the West Bank and Gaza and its relationship with its neighbors and to conclude a peace treaty between Israel and Jordan by the end of the transitional period. These negotiations will be conducted among Egypt, Israel, Jordan and the elected representatives of the inhabitants of the West Bank and Gaza. Two separate but related committees will be convened, one committee, consisting of representatives of the four parties which will negotiate and agree on the final status of the West Bank and Gaza, and its relationship with its neighbors, and the second committee, consisting of representatives of Israel and representatives of Jordan to be joined by the elected representatives of the inhabitants of the West Bank and Gaza, to negotiate the peace treaty between Israel and Jordan, taking into account the agreement reached in the final status of the West Bank and Gaza. The negotiations shall be based on all the provisions and principles of UN Security Council Resolution 242. The negotiations will resolve, among other matters, the location of the boundaries and the nature of the security arrangements. The solution from the negotiations must also recognize the legitimate right of the Palestinian peoples and their just requirements. In this way, the Palestinians will participate in the determination of their own future through: 1) The negotiations among Egypt, Israel, Jordan and the representatives of the inhabitants of the West Bank and Gaza to agree on the final status of the West Bank and Gaza and other outstanding issues by the end of the transitional period. 2) Submitting their agreements to a vote by the elected representatives of the inhabitants of the West Bank and Gaza. 3) Providing for the elected representatives of the inhabitants of the West Bank and Gaza to decide how they shall govern themselves consistent with the provisions of their agreement. 4) Participating as stated above in the work of the committee negotiating the peace treaty between Israel and Jordan. 2. All necessary measures will be taken and provisions made to assure the security of Israel and its neighbors during the transitional period and beyond. To assist in providing such security, a strong local police force will be constituted by the self-governing authority. It will be composed of inhabitants of the West Bank and Gaza. The police will maintain liaison on internal security matters with the designated Israeli, Jordanian, and Egyptian officers. 3. During the transitional period, representatives of Egypt, Israel, Jordan, and the self-governing authority will constitute a continuing committee to decide by agreement on the modalities of admission of persons displaced from the West Bank and Gaza in 1967, together with necessary measures to prevent disruption and disorder. Other matters of common concern may also be dealt with by this committee. 4. Egypt and Israel will work with each other and with other interested parties to establish agreed procedures for a prompt, just and permanent implementation of the resolution of the refugee problem.

B. Egypt-Israel. 1. Egypt-Israel undertake not to resort to the threat or the use of force to settle disputes. Any disputes shall be settled by peaceful means in accordance with the provisions of Article 33 of the U.N. Charter. 2. In order to achieve peace between them, the parties agree to negotiate in good faith with a goal of concluding within three months from the signing of the Framework a peace treaty between them while inviting the other parties to the conflict to proceed simultaneously to negotiate and conclude similar peace treaties with a view the achieving a comprehensive peace in the area. The Framework for the Conclusion of a Peace Treaty between Egypt and Israel will govern the peace negotiations between them. The parties will agree on the modalities and the timetable for the implementation of their obligations under the treaty.

C. Associated Principles. 1. Egypt and Israel state that the principles and provisions described below should apply to peace treaties between Israel and each of its neighbors -- Egypt, Jordan, Syria and Lebanon. 2. Signatories shall establish among themselves relationships normal to states at peace with one another. To this end, they should undertake to abide by all the provisions of the U.N. Charter. Steps to be taken in this respect include: (a) full recognition; (b) abolishing economic boycotts; (c) guaranteeing that under their jurisdiction the citizens of the other parties shall enjoy the protection of the due process of law. 3. Signatories should explore possibilities for economic development in the context of final peace treaties, with the objective of contributing to the atmosphere of peace, cooperation and friendship which is their common goal. 4. Claims commissions may be established for the mutual settlement of all financial claims. 5. The United States shall be invited to participated in the talks on matters related to the modalities of the implementation of the agreements and working out the timetable for the carrying out of the obligations of the parties. 6. The United Nations Security Council shall be requested to endorse the peace treaties and ensure that their provisions shall not be violated. The permanent members of the Security Council shall be requested to underwrite the peace treaties and ensure respect or the provisions. They shall be requested to conform their policies an actions with the undertaking contained in this Framework.

FRAMEWORK FOR THE CONCLUSION OF A PEACE TREATY BETWEEN EGYPT AND ISRAEL

In order to achieve peace between them, Israel and Egypt agree to negotiate in good faith with a goal of concluding within three months of the signing of this framework a peace treaty between them:

It is agreed that: The site of the negotiations will be under a United Nations flag at a location or locations to be mutually agreed.

All of the principles of U.N. Resolution 242 will apply in this resolution of the dispute between Israel and Egypt. Unless otherwise mutually agreed, terms of the peace treaty will be implemented between two and three years after the peace treaty is signed. The following matters are agreed between the parties: (1) the full exercise of Egyptian sovereignty up to the internationally recognized border between Egypt and mandated Palestine; (2) the withdrawal of Israeli armed forces from the Sinai; (3) the use of airfields left by the Israelis near al-Arish, Rafah, Ras en-Naqb, and Sharm el-Sheikh for civilian purposes only, including possible commercial use only by all nations; (4) the right of free passage by ships of Israel through the Gulf of Suez and the Suez Canal on the basis of the Constantinople Convention of 1888 applying to all nations; the Strait of Tiran and Gulf of Aqaba are international waterways to be open to all nations for unimpeded and nonsuspendable freedom of navigation and overflight; (5) the construction of a highway between the Sinai and Jordan near Eilat with guaranteed free and peaceful passage by Egypt and Jordan; and (6) the stationing of military forces listed below.

Stationing of Forces. No more than one division (mechanized or infantry) of Egyptian armed forces will be stationed within an area lying approximately 50 km. (30 miles) east of the Gulf of Suez and the Suez Canal.

Only United Nations forces and civil police equipped with light weapons to perform normal police functions will be stationed within an area lying west of the international border and the Gulf of Aqaba, varying in width from 20 km. (12 miles) to 40 km. (24 miles).

In the area within 3 km. (1.8 miles) east of the international border there will be Israeli limited military forces not to exceed four infantry battalions and United Nations observers.

Border patrol units not to exceed three battalions will supplement the civil police in maintaining order in the area not included above. The exact demarcation of the above areas will be as decided during the peace negotiations.

Early warning stations may exist to insure compliance with the terms of the agreement.

United Nations forces will be stationed: (1) in part of the area in the Sinai lying within about 20 km. of the Mediterranean Sea and adjacent to the international border, and (2) in the Sharm el-Sheikh area to insure freedom of passage through the Strait of Tiran; and these forces will not be removed unless such removal is approved by the Security Council of the United Nations with a unanimous vote of the five permanent members.

After a peace treaty is signed, and after the interim withdrawal is complete, normal relations will be established between Egypt and Israel, including full recognition, including diplomatic, economic and cultural relations; termination of economic boycotts and barriers to the free movement of goods and people; and mutual protection of citizens by the due process of law.

Interim Withdrawal Between three months and nine months after the signing of the peace treaty, all Israeli forces will withdraw east of a line extending from a point east of El-Arish to Ras Muhammad, the exact location of this line to be determined by mutual agreement.

Annex to the Framework Agreements -- United Nations Security Council Resolutions 242 and 338

EXCHANGES OF LETTERS

LETTER FROM BEGIN TO CARTER, SEPTEMBER 17, 1978

I have the honor to inform you that during two weeks after my return home I will submit a motion before Israel's Parliament (the Knesset) to decide on the following question:

If during the negotiations to conclude a peace treaty between Israel and Egypt all outstanding issues are agreed upon, "are you in favor of the removal of the Israeli settlers from the northern and southern Sinai areas or are you in favor of keeping the aforementioned settlers in those areas?"

The vote, Mr. President, on this issue will be completely free from the usual Parliamentary Party discipline to the effect that although the coalition is being now supported by 70 members out of 120, every member of the Knesset, as I believe, both of the Government and the Opposition benches will be enabled to vote in accordance with his own conscience.

LETTER FROM CARTER TO SADAT, SEPTEMBER 22, 1978

I transmit herewith a copy of a letter to me from Prime Minister Begin setting forth how he proposes to present the issue of the Sinai settlements to the Knesset for the latter's decision. In this connection, I understand from your letter that Knesset approval to withdraw all Israeli settlers from Sinai according to a timetable within the period specified for the implementation of the peace treaty is a prerequisite to any negotiations on a peace treaty between Egypt and Israel.

LETTER FROM SADAT TO CARTER, SEPTEMBER 17, 1978

In connection with the "Framework for a Settlement in Sinai" to be signed tonight, I would like to reaffirm the position of the Arab Republic of Egypt with respect to the settlements: 1. All Israeli settlers must be withdrawn from Sinai according to a timetable within the period specified for the implementation of the peace treaty. 2. Agreement by the Israeli Government and its constitutional institutions to this basic principle is therefore a prerequisite to starting peace negotiations for concluding a peace treaty. 3. If Israel fails to meet this commitment, the "framework" shall be void and invalid.

LETTER FROM CARTER TO BEGIN, SEPTEMBER 22, 1978

I have received your letter of September 17, 1978, describing how you intend to place the question of the future of Israeli settlements in Sinai before the

Knesset for its decision. Enclosed is a copy of President Sadat's letter to me on this subject.

LETTER FROM SADAT TO CARTER, SEPTEMBER 17, 1978

I am writing you to reaffirm the position of the Arab Republic of Egypt with respect to Jerusalem. 1. Arab Jerusalem is an integral part of the West Bank. Legal and historical Arab rights in the city must be respected and restored. 2. Arab Jerusalem should be under Arab sovereignty. 3. The Palestinian inhabitants of Arab Jerusalem are entitled to exercise their legitimate national rights, being part of the Palestinian People in the West Bank. 4. Relevant Security Council resolutions, particularly Resolutions 242 and 267, must be applied with regard to Jerusalem. All the measures taken by Israel to alter the status of the City are null and void and should be rescinded. 5. All peoples must have free access to the City and enjoy the free exercises of worship and the right to visit and transit to the holy places without distinction or discrimination. 6. The holy places of each faith may be placed under the administration and control of their representatives. 7. Essential functions in the City should be undivided and a joint municipal council composed of an equal number of Arab and Israeli members can supervise the carrying out of these functions. In this way, the city shall be undivided.

LETTER FROM BEGIN TO CARTER, SEPTEMBER 17, 1978

I have the honor to inform you, Mr. President, that on 28 June 1967 -- Israel's parliament (The Knesset) promulgated and adopted a law to the effect: "the Government is empowered by a decree to apply the law, the jurisdiction and administration of the State to any part of Eretz Israel (Land of Israel -- Palestine), as stated in that decree." On the basis of this law, the government of Israel decreed in July 1967 that Jerusalem is one city indivisible, the capital of the State of Israel.

LETTER FROM CARTER TO SADAT, SEPTEMBER 22, 1978

I have received your letter of September 17, 1978, setting forth the Egyptian position on Jerusalem. I am transmitting a copy of that letter to Prime Minister Begin for his information. The position of the United States on Jerusalem remains as stated by Ambassador Goldberg in the United Nations General Assembly on July 14, 1967, and subsequently by Ambassador Yost in the United Nations Security Council on July 1, 1969.

LETTER FROM SADAT TO CARTER, SEPTEMBER 17, 1978

In connection with the "Framework for Peace in the Middle East," I am writing you this letter to inform you of the position of the Arab Republic of Egypt, with respect to the implementation of the comprehensive settlement.

To ensure the implementation of the provisions related to the West Bank and Gaza and in order to safeguard the legitimate rights of the Palestinian people,

Egypt will be prepared to assume the Arab role emanating from these provisions, following consultations with Jordan and the representatives of the Palestinian people.

LETTER FROM CARTER TO BEGIN, SEPTEMBER 22, 1978
    I hereby acknowledge that you have informed me as follows: A. In each paragraph of the Agreed Framework Document the expressions "Palestinians" or "Palestinian People" are being and will be construed and understood by you as "Palestinian Arabs." B. In each paragraph in which the expression "West Bank" appears it is being, and will be, understood by the Government of Israel as Judea and Samaria.

BAGHDAD ARAB SUMMIT RESOLUTIONS (NOVEMBER 5, 1978)

After the signing of the Camp David Accords, a majority of Arab leaders met at the summit in Baghdad, Iraq, from November 2-5, 1978, at the initiative of the government of Iraq. The summit's communique rejected the Camp David Accords on the grounds that they harmed the Palestinian cause and contravened resolutions of the Algiers and Rabat summit conferences forbidding unilateral Arab action in settling the Middle East conflict or solving the Palestinian problem. It noted that a solution to the conflict should be based on joint Arab action decided at an Arab summit. Among the decisions was the relocation of the Arab League's headquarters from Cairo to Tunis.

    The conference held discussions with deep awareness of Pan-Arab responsibility and common care for the unity of the Arab stand vis-à-vis the dangers and challenges threatening the Arab nation, particularly following the developments resulting from the signing by the Egyptian Government of the Camp David accords and their effect on the Arab struggle against the Zionist aggression and the interests of the Arab nation. ...
    The conference affirmed a number of principles, including: (1) The cause of Palestine is an Arab fateful cause; it is the essence of the struggle against the Zionist enemy. All the sons and countries of the Arab nation are concerned with this cause and are committed to struggle for it and to make all material and moral sacrifices for it. The struggle for the restoration of Arab rights in Palestine and the occupied Arab territories is a common national responsibility. ... (4) In the light of the above principles it is not permitted for any side to act unilaterally in solving the Palestinian question in particular, and the Arab-Zionist conflict in general. ... (5) No settlement is acceptable unless it is adopted by a resolution of an Arab summit conference held specifically for this purpose.

The conference discussed the two agreements signed by the Egyptian Government at Camp David and considered that they harmed the Palestinian people's rights and the rights of the Arab nation in Palestine and the occupied Arab territory. The conference considered that these agreements have taken place outside the framework of collective Arab responsibility and were opposed to the resolutions of the Arab summit conferences, particularly the resolutions of the Algiers and Rabat summit conferences, the Arab League charter and the UN resolutions on the Palestinian question. ...

The conference decided to call on the Egyptian Government to abrogate these agreements and not to sign any reconciliation treaty with the enemy. The conference hoped that Egypt would return to the fold of joint Arab action and not act unilaterally in the affairs of the Arab-Zionist conflict. ...

EGYPT-ISRAEL PEACE TREATY (MARCH 26, 1979)

On March 26, 1979, Anwar Sadat for the Arab Republic of Egypt and Menachem Begin for the State of Israel, signed a peace treaty in Washington, D.C., witnessed by Jimmy Carter. The treaty, based on the Camp David Accords, contains nine articles, a military annex, an annex dealing with the relations between the parties, and agreed minutes interpreting the main articles of the treaty. There were also letters exchanged among Begin, Carter and Sadat that further amplified the agreement.

Egypt and Israel agreed that negotiations on Palestinian autonomy were to begin in April 1979, with the invited participation of Jordan; failing Jordan's attendance, the two signatories would negotiate alone. A target date of one year later was set for completion of the autonomy talks, following which elections in the West Bank and Gaza should be held and a self-governing authority elected. Once elections were held, the five-year transition period mentioned in the Camp David Accords would begin.

The Government of the Arab Republic of Egypt and the Government of the State of Israel;

PREAMBLE. Convinced of the urgent necessity of the establishment of a just, comprehensive and lasting peace in the Middle East in accordance with Security Council Resolutions 242 and 338; Reaffirming their adherence to the "Framework for Peace in the Middle East Agreed at Camp David," dated September 17, 1978; Noting that the aforementioned Framework as appropriate is intended to constitute a basis for peace not only between Egypt and Israel but also between Israel and each of its other Arab neighbors which is prepared to negotiate peace with it on this basis; Desiring to bring to an end the state of war between them and to establish a peace in which every state in the area can live in security; Convinced that the conclusion of a Treaty of Peace between Egypt and Israel is an important step in the search for comprehensive peace in the area and for the attainment of settlement of the Arab-Israeli conflict in all its aspects; Inviting the other Arab parties to this dispute to join the peace process with Israel guided by and based on the principles of the aforementioned Framework; Desiring as well to develop friendly relations and cooperation between themselves in accordance with the United Nations Charter and the principles of international law governing international relations in times of peace; Agree to the following provisions in the free exercise of their sovereignty, in order to implement the "Framework for the Conclusion of a Peace Treaty Between Egypt and Israel".

Article I. 1. The state of war between the Parties will be terminated and peace will be established between them upon the exchange of instruments of ratification of this Treaty. 2. Israel will withdraw all its armed forces and civilians from the Sinai behind the international boundary between Egypt and mandated Palestine, as provided in the annexed protocol (Annex I), and Egypt will resume the exercise of its full sovereignty over the Sinai. 3. Upon completion of the interim withdrawal provided for in Annex I, the parties will establish normal and friendly relations, in accordance with Article III (3).

Article II. The permanent boundary between Egypt and Israel in the recognized international boundary between Egypt and the former mandated territory of Palestine, as shown on the map at Annex II, without prejudice to the issue of the status of the Gaza Strip. The Parties recognize this boundary as inviolable. Each will respect the territorial integrity of the other, including their territorial waters and airspace.

Article III. 1. The Parties will apply between them the provisions of the Charter of the United Nations and the principles of international law governing relations among states in times of peace. In particular: a. They recognize and will respect each other's sovereignty, territorial integrity and political independence; b. They recognize and will respect each other's right to live in peace within their secure and recognized boundaries; c. They will refrain from the threat or use of force, directly or indirectly, against each other and will settle all disputes between them by peaceful means. 2. Each Party undertakes to ensure that acts or threats of belligerency, hostility, or violence do not originate from and are not committed from within its territory, or by any forces subject to its control or by any other forces stationed on its territory, against the population, citizens or property of the other Party. Each Party also undertakes to refrain from organizing, instigating, inciting, assisting or participating in acts or threats of belligerency, hostility, subversion or violence against the other Party, anywhere, and undertakes to ensure that perpetrators of such acts are brought to justice. 3. The Parties agree that the normal relationship established between them will include full recognition, diplomatic, economic and cultural relations, termination of economic boycotts and discriminatory barriers to the free movement of people and goods, and will guarantee the mutual enjoyment by citizens of the due process of law. The process by which they undertake to achieve such a relationship parallel to the implementation of other provisions of this Treaty is set out in the annexed protocol (Annex III).

Article IV. 1. In order to provide maximum security for both Parties on the basis of reciprocity, agreed security arrangements will be established including limited force zones in Egyptian and Israeli territory, and United Nations forces and observers, described in detail as to nature and timing in Annex I, and other security arrangements the Parties may agree upon. 2. The Parties agree to the stationing of United Nations personnel in areas described in Annex I. The Parties agree not to request withdrawal of the United Nations personnel and that these personnel will not be removed unless such removal is approved by the Security Council of the United Nations, with the affirmative vote of the five Permanent Members, unless the Parties otherwise agree. 3. A Joint Commission will be established to facilitate the implementation of the Treaty, as provided for in Annex I. 4. The security arrangements provided for in paragraphs 1 and 2 of this Article may at the request of either party be reviewed and amended by mutual agreement of the Parties.

Article V. 1. Ships of Israel, and cargoes destined for or coming from Israel, shall enjoy the right of free passage through the Suez Canal and its approaches through the Gulf of Suez and the Mediterranean Sea on the basis of the Constantinople Convention of 1888, applying to all nations, Israeli nationals, vessels and cargoes, as well as persons, vessels and cargoes destined for or coming from Israel, shall be accorded non-discriminatory treatment in all matters connected with usage of the canal. 2. The Parties consider the Strait of Tiran and the Gulf of Aqaba to be international waterways open to all nations for unimpeded and non-suspendable freedom of navigation and overflight. The parties will respect each other's right to navigation and overflight for access to either country through the Strait of Tiran and the Gulf of Aqaba.

Article VI. 1. This Treaty does not affect and shall not be interpreted as affecting in any way the rights and obligations of the Parties under the Charter of the United Nations. 2. The Parties undertake to fulfill in good faith their obligations under this Treaty, without regard to action or inaction of any other party and independently of any instrument external to this Treaty. 3. They further undertake to take all the necessary measures for the application in their relations of the provisions of the multilateral conventions to which they are parties, including the submission of appropriate notification to the Secretary General of the United Nations and other depositaries of such conventions. 4. The Parties undertake not to enter into any obligation in conflict with this Treaty. 5. Subject to Article 103 of the United Nations Charter in the event of a conflict between the obligation of the Parties under the present Treaty and any of their other obligations, the obligations under this Treaty will be binding and implemented.

Article VII. 1. Disputes arising out of the application or interpretation of this

Treaty shall be resolved by negotiations. 2. Any such disputes which cannot be settled by negotiations shall be resolved by conciliation or submitted to arbitration.

Article VIII. The Parties agree to establish a claims commission for the mutual settlement of all financial claims.

Article IX. 1. This Treaty shall enter into force upon exchange of instruments of ratification. 2. This Treaty supersedes the Agreement between Egypt and Israel of September, 1975. 3. All protocols, annexes, and maps attached to this Treaty shall be regarded as an integral part hereof. 4. The Treaty shall be communicated to the Secretary General of the United Nations for registration in accordance with the provisions of Article 102 of the Charter of the United Nations.

Annex I -- Protocol Concerning Israeli Withdrawal and Security Agreements.

Article I. Concept of Withdrawal. 1. Israel will complete withdrawal of all its armed forces and civilians from the Sinai not later than three years from the date of exchange of instruments of ratification of this Treaty. 2. To ensure the mutual security of the Parties, the implementation of phased withdrawal will be accompanied by the military measures and establishment of zones set out in this Annex and in Map 1, hereinafter referred to as "the Zones." 3. The withdrawal from the Sinai will be accomplished in two phases: a. The interim withdrawal behind the line from east of El-Arish to Ras Mohammed as delineated on Map 2 within nine months from the date of exchange of instruments of ratification of this Treaty. b. The final withdrawal from the Sinai behind the international boundary not later than three years from the date of exchange of instruments of ratification of this Treaty. 4. A Joint Commission will be formed immediately after the exchange of instruments of ratification of this Treaty in order to supervise and coordinate movements and schedules during the withdrawal, and to adjust plans and timetables as necessary within the limits established by paragraph 3, above. Details relating to the Joint Commission are set out in Article IV of the attached Appendix. The Joint Commission will be dissolved upon completion of final Israeli withdrawal from the Sinai.

Article II. Determination of Final Lines and Zones. 1. In order to provide maximum security for both Parties after the final withdrawal, the lines and the Zones delineated on Map 1 are to be established and organized as follows: a. Zone A (1) Zone A is bounded on the east by line A (red line) and on the west by the Suez Canal and the east coast of the Gulf of Suez, as shown on Map 1. (2) An Egyptian armed force of one mechanized infantry division and its military installations, and field fortifications, will be in this Zone. (3) The main elements of that Division will consist of: (a) Three mechanized infantry brigades. (b) One armed brigade. (c) Seven field artillery battalions including up to 126 artillery pieces. (d) Seven anti-aircraft artillery battalions including individual surface-to-air missiles and up to 126 anti-aircraft guns of 37 mm and above. (e) Up to 230 tanks. (f) Up to 480 armored personnel vehicles of all types. (g) Up to a total of twenty-two thousand personnel. b. Zone B (1) Zone B is bounded by line B (green line) on the east and by line A (red line) on the west, as shown on Map 1. (2) Egyptian border units of four battalions equipped with light weapons and wheeled vehicles will provide security and supplement the civil police in maintaining order in Zone B. The main elements in the four Border Battalions will consist of up to a total of four thousand personnel. (3) Land based, short range, low power, coastal warning points of the border patrol units may be established on the coast of this Zone. (4) There will be in Zone B field fortifications and military installations for the four border battalions. c. Zone C (1) Zone C is bounded by line B (green line) on the west and the International Boundary and the Gulf of Aqaba on the east, as shown on Map 1. (2) Only United Nations forces and Egyptian civil police will be stationed in Zone C. (3) The Egyptian civil police armed with light weapons will perform normal police functions within this Zone. (4) The United Nations Force will be deployed within Zone C and perform its functions as defined in Article VI of this annex. (5) The United Nations Force will be stationed mainly in camps located within the following stationing areas shown on Map 1, and will establish its precise locations after consultations with Egypt: (a) In that part of the area in the Sinai lying within about 20 Km. of the Mediterranean Sea and adjacent to the International Boundary. (b) In the Sharm el Sheikh area. d. Zone D (1) Zone D is bounded by line D (blue line) on the east and the international boundary on the west, as shown on Map 1. (2) In this Zone there will be an Israeli limited force of four infantry battalions, their military installations, and field fortifications, and United Nations observers. (3) The Israeli forces in Zone D will not include tanks, artillery and anti-aircraft missiles except individual surface-to-air missiles. (4) The main elements of the four Israeli infantry battalions will consist of up to 180 armored personnel vehicles of all types and up to a total of four thousand personnel. 2. Access across the international boundary shall only be permitted through entry check points designated by each Party and under its control. Such access shall be in accordance with laws and regulations of each country. 3. Only those field fortifications, military installations, forces, and weapons specifically permitted by this Annex shall be in the Zones.

Article III. Aerial Military Regime. 1. Flights of combat aircraft and reconnaissance flights of Egypt and Israel shall take place only over Zones A and D, respectively. 2. Only unarmed, non-combat aircraft of Egypt and Israel will be stationed in Zones A and D, respectively. 3. Only Egyptian unarmed transport aircraft will take off and land in Zone B and up to eight such aircraft may be maintained in Zone B. The Egyptian border unit ..., may be equipped with unarmed helicopters to perform their functions in Zone B. 4. The Egyptian civil police may be equipped with unarmed police helicopters to perform normal police functions in Zone C. 5. Only civilian airfields maybe built in the Zones. 6. Without prejudice to the provisions of this Treaty, only those military aerial activities specifically permitted by this Annex shall be allowed in the Zones and the airspace above their territorial waters.

Article IV. Naval Regime. 1. Egypt and Israel may base and operate naval vessels along the coasts of Zones A and D, respectively. 2. Egyptian coast guard boats, lightly armed, may be stationed and operate in the territorial waters of Zone B to assist the border units in performing their functions in this Zone. 3. Egyptian civil police equipped with light boats, lightly armed, shall perform normal police functions within the territorial waters of Zone C. 4. Nothing in this Annex shall be considered as derogating from the right of innocent passage of the naval vessels of either party. 5. Only civilian maritime ports and installations may be built in the Zones. 6. Without prejudice to the provisions of this Treaty, only those naval activities specifically permitted by this Annex shall be allowed in the Zones and in their territorial waters.

Article V. Early Warning Systems. Egypt and Israel may establish and operate early warning systems only in Zones A and D respectively.

Article VI. United Nations Operations. 1. The Parties will request the United Nations to provide forces and observers to supervise the implementation of this Annex and employ their best efforts to prevent any violation of its terms. 2. With respect to these United Nations forces and observers, as appropriate, the Parties agree to request the following arrangements: a. Operation of check points, reconnaissance patrols, and observation posts along the international boundary and line B, and within Zone C. b. Periodic verification of the implementation of the provisions of this Annex will be carried out not less than twice a month unless otherwise agreed by the Parties. c. Additional verifications within 48 hours after the receipt of a request from either Party. d. Ensuring the freedom of navigation through the Strait of Tiran in accordance with Article V of the Treaty of Peace. 3. The arrangements described in this article for each zone will be implemented in ones A, B, and C by the United Nations Force and in Zone D by the United Nations Observers. 4. United Nations verification teams shall be accompanied by liaison officers of the respective Party. 5. The United Nations Force and observers will report their findings to both Parties. 6. The United Nations Force and Observers operating in the Zones will enjoy freedom of movement and other facilities necessary for the performance of their tasks. 7. The United Nations Force and Observers are not empowered to authorize the crossing of the international boundary. 8. The Parties shall agree on the nations from which the United Nations Force and Observers will be drawn. They "ill be drawn from nations other than those which are permanent members of the United Nations Security Council. 9. The Parties agree that the United Nations should make those command arrangements that will best assure the effective implementation of its responsibilities.

Article VII. Liaison System. 1. Upon dissolution of the Joint Commission, a liaison system between the Parties will be established. This liaison system is intended to provide an effective method to assess progress in the implementation

in Article I of this Appendix. 4. Israeli convoys may use the roads south and east of the main road junction east of El Arish to evacuate Israeli forces up to the completion of interim withdrawal. These convoys will proceed in daylight upon four hours notice to the Egyptian liaison group and United Nations forces, will be escorted by United Nations forces, and will be in accordance with schedules coordinated by the Joint Commission. An Egyptian liaison officer will accompany convoys to assure uninterrupted movement. The Joint Commission may approve other arrangements for convoys.

Article III. United Nations Forces. 1. The Parties shall request that United Nations forces be deployed as necessary to perform the functions described in the Appendix up to the time of completion of final Israeli withdrawal. For that purpose, the Parties agree to the redeployment of the United Nations Emergency Force. 2. United Nations forces will supervise the implementation of this Appendix and will employ their best efforts to prevent any violation of its terms. 3. When United Nations forces deploy in accordance with the provisions of Article and II of this Appendix, they will perform the functions of verification in limited force zones in accordance with Article VI of Annex I, and will establish check points, reconnaissance patrols, and observation posts in the temporary buffer zones described in Article II above. Other functions of the United Nations forces which concern the interim buffer zone are described in Article V of this Appendix.

Article IV. Joint Commission and Liaison. 1. The Joint Commission referred to in Article IV of this Treaty will function from the date of exchange of instruments of ratification of this Treaty up to the date of completion of final Israeli withdrawal from the Sinai. 2. The Joint Commission will be composed of representatives of each Party headed by senior officers. This Commission shall invite a representative of the United Nations when discussing subjects concerning the United Nations, or when either Party requests United Nations presence. Decisions of the Joint Commission will be reached by agreement of Egypt and Israel. 3. The Joint Commission will supervise the implementation of the arrangements described in Annex I and this Appendix. To this end, and by agreement of both Parties, it will: a. coordinate military movements described in this Appendix and supervise their implementation; b. address and seek to resolve any problem arising out of the implementation of Annex I and this Appendix, and discuss any violations reported by the United Nations Force and Observers and refer to the Governments of Egypt and Israel any unresolved problems; c. assist the United Nations Force and Observers in the execution of their mandates, and deal with the timetables of the periodic verification when referred to it by the Parties as provided for in Annex I and this Appendix; d. organize the demarcation of the international boundary and all lines and zones described in Annex I and this Appendix; e. supervise the handing over of the main installations in the Sinai from Israel to Egypt; f. agree on necessary arrangements for finding and returning missing bodies of Egyptian and Israeli soldiers; g. organize the setting up and operation of entry check points along the El Arish-Ras Mohammed line in accordance with the provisions of Article 4 of Annex III; h. conduct its operations through the use of joint liaison teams consisting of one Israeli representative and one Egyptian representative, provided from a standing Liaison Group, which will conduct activities as directed by the Joint Commission; i. provide liaison and coordination to the United Nations command implementing provisions of the Treaty, and, through the joint liaison teams, maintain local coordination and cooperation with the United Nations Force stationed in specific areas or United Nations Observers monitoring specific areas for any assistance as needed; j. discuss any other matters which the Parties by agreement may place before it. 4. Meetings of the Joint Commission shall be held at least once a month. In the event that either Party of the Command of the United Nations Force requests a specific meeting, it will be convened within 24 hours. 5. The Joint Committee will meet in the buffer zone until the completion of the interim withdrawal and in El Arish and Beer-Sheba alternately afterwards. The first meeting will be held not later than two weeks after the entry into force of this Treaty.

Article V. Definition of the Interim Buffer Zone and Its Activities. 1. An interim buffer zone, by which the United Nations Force will effect a separation of Egyptian and Israeli elements, will be established west of and adjacent to the interim withdrawal line as shown on Map 2 after implementation of Israeli withdrawal and deployment behind the interim withdrawal line. Egyptian civil police equipped with light weapons will perform normal police functions within this zone. 2. The United Nations Force will operate check points, reconnaissance patrols, and observation posts within the interim buffer zone in order to ensure compliance with the terms of this Article. 3. In accordance with arrangements agreed upon by both Parties and to be coordinated by the Joint Commission, Israeli personnel will operate military technical installations at four specific locations shown on Map 2 and designated as T1 (map central coordinate 57163940), T2 (map central coordinate 59351541), T3 (map central coordinate 5933-1527), and T4 (map central coordinate 61130979) under the following principles: a. The technical installations shall be manned by technical and administrative personnel equipped with small arms required for their protection (revolvers, rifles, sub-machine guns, light machine guns, hand grenades, and ammunition), as follows: T1 -- up to 150 personnel; T2 and T3 -- up to 350 personnel; T4 -- up to 200 personnel. b. Israeli personnel will not carry weapons outside the sites, except officers who may carry personal weapons. c. Only a third party agreed to by Egypt and Israel will enter and conduct inspections within the perimeters of technical installations in the buffer zone. The third party will conduct inspections in a random manner at least once a month. The inspections will verify the nature of the operation of the installations and the weapons and personnel therein. The third party will immediately report to the Parties any divergence from an installation's visual and electronic surveillance or communications role. d. Supply of the installations, visits for technical and administrative purposes, and replacement of personnel and equipment situated in the sites, may occur uninterruptedly from the United Nations check points to the perimeter of the technical installations, after checking and being escorted by only the United Nations forces. e. Israel will be permitted to introduce into its technical installations items required for the proper functioning of the installations and personnel. f. As determined by the Joint Commission, Israel will be permitted to: (1) Maintain in its installations fire-fighting and general maintenance equipment as well as wheeled administrative vehicles and mobile engineering equipment necessary for the maintenance of the sites. All vehicles shall be unarmed. (2) Within the sites and in the buffer zone, maintain roads, water lines, and communications cables which serve the site. At each of the three installation locations (T1, T2 and T3, and T4), this maintenance may be performed with up to two unarmed wheeled vehicles and by up to twelve unarmed personnel with only necessary equipment, including heavy engineering equipment if needed. This maintenance may be performed three times a week, except for special problems, and only after giving the United Nations four hours notice. The teams will be escorted by the United Nations. g. Movement to and from the technical installations will take place only during daylight hours. Access to, and exit from, the technical installations shall be as follows: (1) T1: Through a United Nations check point, and via the road between Abu Aweigila and the intersection of the Abu Aweigila road and the Gebel Libni road (at Km. 161), as shown on Map 2. (2) T2 and T3: through a United Nations checkpoint and via the road constructed across the buffer zone to Gebel Katrina, as shown on Map 2. (3) T2, T3, and T4: via helicopters flying within a corridor at the times, and according to a flight profile, agreed to by the Joint Commission. The helicopters will be checked by the United Nations Force at landing sites outside the perimeter of the installations. h. Israel will inform the United Nations Force at least one hour in advance of each intended movement to and from the installations. i. Israel shall be entitled to evacuate sick and wounded and summon medical experts and medical teams at any time after giving immediate notice to the United Nations Force. 4. The details of the above principles and all other matters in this Article requiring coordination by the Parties will be handled by the Joint Commission. 5. These technical installations will be withdrawn when Israeli forces withdraw from the interim withdrawal line, or at a time agreed by the parties.

Article VI. Disposition of Installations and Military Barriers. Disposition of installations and military barriers will be determined by the Parties in accordance with the following guidelines: 1. Up to three weeks before Israeli withdrawal from any area, the Joint Commission will arrange for Israeli and Egyptian liaison and technical teams to conduct a joint inspection of all appropriate installations to agree upon condition of structures and articles which will be transferred to Egyptian control and to arrange for such transfer. Israel will declare, at that time, its plans for disposition of installations and articles within the installations. 2. Israel undertakes to transfer to Egypt all agreed infrastructures, utilities, and installations intact, inter alia, airfields, roads, pumping stations, and ports. Israel will present to Egypt the information necessary for the maintenance and operation of the facilities. Egyptian technical teams will be permitted to observe and familiarize themselves with the operation of these facilities for a period of up to two weeks prior to transfer. 3. When Israel relinquishes Israeli military water points near El Arish and El Tor, Egyptian technical teams will assume control of those installations and ancillary equipment in accordance with an orderly transfer process arranged beforehand by the Joint Commission. Egypt undertakes to continue to make available at all water supply points the normal quantity of currently available water up to the time Israel withdraws behind the international boundary, unless otherwise agreed in the Joint Commission. 4. Israel will make its best effort to remove or destroy all military barriers, including obstacles and minefields, in the areas and adjacent waters from which it withdraws, according to the following concept: a. Military barriers will be cleared first from areas near populations, roads and major installations and utilities. b. For those obstacles and minefields which cannot be removed or destroyed prior to Israeli withdrawal, Israel will provide detailed maps to Egypt and the United Nations through the Joint Commission not later than 15 days before entry of United Nations forces into the affected areas. c. Egyptian engineers will enter those areas after United Nations forces enter to conduct barrier clearance operations in accordance with Egyptian plans to be submitted prior to implementation.

Article VII. Surveillance Activities. 1. Aerial surveillance activities during the withdrawal will be carried out as follows: a. Both Parties request the United States to continue airborne surveillance flights in accordance with previous agreements until the completion of final Israeli withdrawal. b. Flight profiles will cover the Limited Forces Zones to monitor the limitations on forces and armaments, and to determine that Israeli armed forces have withdrawn from the areas described in Article II of Annex I, Article II of this Appendix, and Maps 2 and 3, and that these forces thereafter remain behind their lines. Special inspection flights may be flown at the request of either Party or of the United Nations. c. Only the main elements in the military organizations of each Party, as described in Annex I and in this Appendix, will be reported. 2. Both Parties request the United States operated Sinai Field Mission to continue its operations in accordance with previous agreements until completion of the Israeli withdrawal from the area east of the Giddi and Mitla Passes. Thereafter, the Mission be terminated.

Article VIII. Exercise of Egyptian Sovereignty. Egypt will resume the exercise of its full sovereignty over evacuated parts of the Sinai upon Israeli withdrawal as provided for in Article I of this Treaty.

Annex III. Protocol Concerning Relations of the Parties.

Article 1. Diplomatic and Consular Relations. The Parties agree to establish diplomatic and consular relations and to exchange ambassadors upon completion of the interim withdrawal.

Article 2. Economic and Trade Relations. 1. The Parties agree to remove all discriminatory barriers to normal economic relations and to terminate economic boycotts of each other upon completion of the interim withdrawal. 2. As soon as possible, and not later than six months after the completion of the interim withdrawal, the Parties will enter negotiations with a view to concluding an agreement on trade and commerce for the purpose of promoting beneficial economic relations.

Article 3. Cultural Relations. 1. The Parties agree to establish normal cultural relations following completion of the interim withdrawal. 2. They agree on the desirability of cultural exchanges in all fields, and shall, as soon as possible and not later than six months after completion of the interim withdrawal, enter into negotiations with a view to concluding a cultural agreement for this purpose.

Article 4. Freedom of Movement. 1. Upon completion of the interim withdrawal, each Party will permit the free movement of the nationals and vehicles of the other into and within its territory according to the general rules applicable to nationals and vehicles of other states. Neither Party will impose discriminatory restrictions on the free movement of persons and vehicles from its territory to the territory of the other. 2. Mutual unimpeded access to places of religious and historical significance will be provided on a non-discriminatory basis.

Article 5. Cooperation for Development and Good Neighborly Relations. 1. The Parties recognize a mutuality of interest in good neighbourly relations and agree to consider means to promote such relations. 2. The Parties will cooperate in promoting peace, stability and development in their region. Each agrees to consider proposals the other may wish to make to this end. 3. The Parties shall seek to foster mutual understanding and tolerance and will, accordingly, abstain from hostile propaganda against each other.

Article 6. Transportation and Telecommunications. 1. The Parties recognize as applicable to each other the rights, privileges and obligations provided for by the aviation agreements to which they are both party, particularly by the Convention on International Civil Aviation, 1944 ("The Chicago Convention") and the International Air Services Transit Agreement, 1944. 2. Upon completion of the interim withdrawal any declaration of national emergency by a party under Article 89 of the Chicago Convention will not be applied to the other party on a discriminatory basis. 3. Egypt agrees that the use of airfields left by Israel near El-Arish, Rafah, Ras El-Nagb and Sharm El-Sheikh shall be for civilian purposes only, including possible commercial use by all nations. 4. As soon as possible and not later than six months after the completion of the interim withdrawal, the

Parties shall enter into negotiations for the purpose of concluding a civil aviation agreement. 5. The Parties will reopen and maintain roads and railways between their countries and will consider further road and rail links. The Parties further agree that a highway will be constructed and maintained between Egypt, Israel and Jordan near Eilat with guaranteed free and peaceful passage of persons, vehicles and goods between Egypt and Jordan, without prejudice to their sovereignty over that part of the highway which falls within their respective territory. 6. Upon completion of the interim withdrawal, normal postal, telephone, telex, data facsimile, wireless and cable communications and television relay services by cable, radio and satellite shall be established between the two Parties in accordance with all relevant international conventions and regulations. 7. Upon completion of the interim withdrawal, each Party shall grant normal access to its ports for vessels and cargoes of the other, as well as vessels and cargoes destined for or coming from the other. Such access will be granted on the same conditions generally applicable to vessels and cargoes of other nations. Article 5 of the Treaty of Peace will be implemented upon the exchange of instruments of ratification of the aforementioned treaty.

Article 7. Enjoyment of Human Rights. The Parties affirm their commitment to respect and observe human rights and fundamental freedoms for all, and they will promote these rights and freedoms in accordance with the United Nations Charter.

Article 8. Territorial Seas. Without prejudice to the provisions of Article 5 of the Treaty of Peace each Party recognizes the right of the vessels of the other Party to innocent passage through its territorial sea in accordance with the rules of international law.

AGREED MINUTES.

Article I. Egypt's resumption of the exercise of full sovereignty over the Sinai provided for in paragraph 2 of Article I shall occur with regard to each area upon Israel's withdrawal from the area.

Article IV. It is agreed between the parties that the review provided for in Article IV (4) will be undertaken when requested by either party, commencing within three months of such a request, but that any amendment can be made only by mutual agreement of both parties.

Article V. The second sentence of paragraph 2 of Article V shall not be construed as limiting the first sentence of that paragraph. The foregoing is not to be construed as contravening the second sentence of paragraph 2 of Article V, which reads as follows: "The Parties will respect each other's right to navigation and overflight for access to either country through the Strait of Tiran and the Gulf of Aqaba."

Article VI (2). The provisions of Article VI shall not be construed in contradiction to the provisions of the framework for peace in the Middle East agreed at Camp David. The foregoing is not to be construed as contravening the provisions of Article VI (2) of the Treaty, which reads as follows: "The Parties undertake to fulfill in good faith their obligations under this Treaty, without regard to action of any other Party and independently of any instrument external to this Treaty."

Article VI (5). It is agreed by the Parties that there is no assertion that this Treaty prevails over other Treaties or agreements or that other Treaties or agreements prevail over this Treaty. The foregoing is not to be construed as contravening the provisions of Article VI (5) of the Treaty, which reads as follows: "Subject to Article 103 of the United Nations Charter, in the event of a conflict between the obligations of the Parties under the present Treaty and any of their other obligations, the obligation under this Treaty will be binding and implemented."

ANNEX I.

Article VI, Paragraph 8, of Annex I provides as follows: "The Parties shall agree on the nations from which the United Nations forces and observers will be drawn. They will be drawn from nations other than those which are permanent members of the United Nations Security Council." The Parties have agreed as follows: "With respect to the provisions of paragraph 8, Article VI, of Annex 1, if no agreement is reached between the Parties, they will accept or support a U.S. proposal concerning the composition of the United Nations force and observers."

ANNEX III. The Treaty of Peace and Annex III thereto provide for establishing normal economic relations between the Parties. In accordance herewith, it is agreed that such relations will include normal commercial sales of oil by Egypt to Israel, and that Israel shall be fully entitled to make bids for Egyptian-origin oil not needed for Egyptian domestic oil consumption, and Egypt and its oil concessionaires will entertain bids made by Israel, on the same basis and terms as apply to other bidders for such oil.

JOINT LETTER FROM PRESIDENT SADAT AND PRIME MINISTER BEGIN TO PRESIDENT CARTER, MARCH 26, 1979

This letter confirms that Israel and Egypt have agreed as follows: The Governments of Israel and Egypt recall that they concluded at Camp David and signed at the White House on September 17, 1978, the annexed documents entitled "A Framework for Peace in the Middle East agreed at Camp David" and "Framework for the Conclusion of a Peace Treaty between Israel and Egypt."

For the purpose of achieving a comprehensive peace settlement in accordance with the above-mentioned Frameworks, Israel and Egypt will proceed with the implementation of those provisions relating to the West Bank and the Gaza Strip. They have agreed to start negotiations within a month after the exchange of the instruments of ratification of the Peace Treaty. In accordance with the

"Framework for Peace in the Middle East," the Hashemite Kingdom of Jordan is invited to join the negotiations. The Delegations of Egypt and Jordan may include Palestinians as mutually agreed. The purpose of the negotiations shall be to agree, prior to the elections, on the modalities for establishing the elected self-governing authority (administrative council), define its powers and responsibilities and agree upon other related issues. In the event Jordan decides not to take part in the negotiations, the negotiations will be held by Israel and Egypt.

The two Governments agree to negotiate continuously and in good faith to conclude these negotiations at the earliest possible date. They also agree that the objective of the negotiations is the establishment of the self-governing authority in the West Bank and Gaza in order to provide full autonomy to the inhabitants.

Israel and Egypt set for themselves the goal of completing the negotiations within one year so that elections will be held as expeditiously as possible after agreement has been reached between the parties. The self-governing authority referred to in the "Framework for Peace in the Middle East" will be established and inaugurated within one month after it has been elected, at which time the transitional period of five years will begin. The Israel military government and its civilian administration will be withdrawn, to be replaced by the self-governing authority, as specified in the "Framework for Peace in the Middle East." A withdrawal of Israeli armed forces will then take place and there will be a redeployment of the remaining Israeli forces into specified security locations.

This letter also confirms our understanding that the United States Government will participate fully in all stages of negotiations.

LETTER FROM PRESIDENT CARTER TO PRIME MINISTER BEGIN ABOUT THE DEPLOYMENT OF A UN OR AN ALTERNATE MULTINATIONAL FORCE

I wish to confirm to you that subject to United States Constitutional processes:

In the event of an actual or threatened violation of the Treaty of Peace between Israel and Egypt, the United States will, on request of one or both of the Parties, consult with the Parties with respect thereto and will take such other action as it may deem appropriate and helpful to achieve compliance with the Treaty.

The United States will conduct aerial monitoring as requested by the Parties pursuant to Annex I of the Treaty. The United States believes that the Treaty provision for permanent stationing of United Nations personnel in the designated limited force zone can and should be implemented by the United Nations Security Council. The United States will exert its utmost efforts to obtain the requisite action by the Security Council. If the Security Council fails to establish and maintain the arrangements called for in the Treaty, the President will be prepared to take those steps necessary to ensure the establishment and maintenance of an acceptable alternative multinational force.

EXCHANGE OF LETTERS BETWEEN PRESIDENT CARTER AND PRIME MINISTER BEGIN REGARDING THE EXCHANGE OF AMBASSADORS BETWEEN EGYPT AND ISRAEL

LETTER OF CARTER TO BEGIN, MARCH 26, 1979

I have received a letter from President Sadat that, within one month after Israel completes its withdrawal to the interim line in Sinai, as provided for in the Treaty of Peace between Egypt and Israel, Egypt will send a resident ambassador to Israel and will receive in Egypt a resident Israeli ambassador.

I would be grateful if you will confirm that this procedure will be agreeable to the Government of Israel.

LETTER FROM BEGIN TO CARTER, MARCH 26, 1979

I am pleased to be able to confirm that the Government of Israel is agreeable to the procedure set out in your letter of March 26, 1979, in which you state: "I have received a letter from President Sadat that, within one month after Israel completes its withdrawal to the interim line in Sinai, as provided for in the Treaty of Peace between Egypt and Israel, Egypt will send a resident ambassador to Israel and will receive in Egypt a resident Israeli ambassador."

VENICE DECLARATION (JUNE 13, 1980)

The nine members of the European Community met in Venice, Italy, in June 1980 to exchange views on the Middle East, among other subjects. They believed "that the traditional ties and common interests" that linked Europe to the Middle East "oblige[d] them to play a special role" to work for peace based on Security Council resolutions 242 and 338. The declaration was a European effort to advance its own political unity and to adopt a consensus approach to the Arab-Israeli conflict. It was rejected by Israel and the PLO and was overshadowed by the Reagan fresh start initiative in September 1982.

1. The Heads of State and Government and the Ministers of Foreign Affairs held a comprehensive exchange of views on all aspects of the present situation in the Middle East, including the state of negotiations resulting from the agreements signed between Egypt and Israel in March 1979. They agreed that growing tensions affecting this region constitute a serious danger and render a comprehensive solution to the Israeli-Arab conflict more necessary and pressing than ever.

2. The nine Member States of the European Community consider that the traditional ties and common interests which link Europe to the Middle East oblige them to play a special role and now require them to work in a more

concrete way towards peace.

3. In this regard, the nine countries of the Community base themselves on Security Council Resolutions 242 and 338 and the positions which they have expressed on several occasions, notably in their Declarations of 29 June 1977, 19 September 1978, 26 March and 18 June 1979, as well as in the speech made on their behalf on 25 September 1979 by the Irish Minister of Foreign Affairs at the 34th United Nations General Assembly.

4. On the bases thus set out, the time has come to promote the recognition and implementation of the two principles universally accepted by the international community: the right to existence and to security of all the States in the region, including Israel, and justice for all the peoples, which implies the recognition of the legitimate rights of the Palestine.

5. All of the countries in the area are entitled to live in peace within secure, recognized and guaranteed borders. The necessary guarantees for a peace settlement should be provided by the UN by a decision of the Security Council and, if necessary, on the basis of other mutually agreed procedures. The Nine declare that they are prepared to participate within the framework of a comprehensive settlement in a system of concrete and binding international guarantees, including (guarantees) on the ground.

6. A just solution must finally be found to the Palestinian problem, which is not simply one of refugees. The Palestinian people, which is conscious of existing as such, must be placed in a position, by an appropriate process defined within the framework of the comprehensive peace settlement, to exercise fully its right to self-determination.

7. The achievement of these objectives requires the involvement and support of all the parties concerned in the peace settlement which the Nine are endeavouring to promote in keeping with the principles formulated in the declaration referred to above. These principles apply to all the parties concerned, and thus the Palestinian people, and to the PLO, which will have to be associated with the negotiations.

8. The Nine recognize the special importance of the role played by the question of Jerusalem for all the parties concerned. The Nine stress that they will not accept any unilateral initiative designed to change the status of Jerusalem and that any agreement on the city's status should guarantee freedom of access for everyone to the Holy Places.

9. The Nine stress the need for Israel to put an end to the territorial occupation which it has maintained since the conflict of 1967, as it has done for part of Sinai. They are deeply convinced that the Israeli settlements constitute a serious obstacle to the peace process in the Middle East. The Nine consider that these settlements, as well as modifications in population and property in the occupied Arab territories, are illegal under international law.

10. Concerned as they are to put an end to violence, the Nine consider that only the renunciation of force or the threatened use of force by all the parties can

create a climate of confidence in the area, and constitute a basic element for a comprehensive settlement of the conflict in the Middle East.

11. The Nine have decided to make the necessary contacts with all the parties concerned. The objective of these contacts would be to ascertain the position of the various parties with respect to the principles set out in this declaration and in the light of the results of this consultation process to determine the form which such an initiative on their part could take.

BASIC LAW: JERUSALEM, CAPITAL OF ISRAEL (JULY 30, 1980)

In May 1980 Egyptian President Anwar Sadat suspended Egyptian participation in the autonomy talks, ostensibly because the Israeli parliament (Knesset) discussed adopting a Basic Law concerning the status of Jerusalem as Israel's capital. The legislation did not meaningfully alter the existing situation but reaffirmed the situation as established either by previous legislation or accepted norms. The autonomy talks resumed in July but were suspended again by Sadat in early August. The stated rationale was that the Knesset had adopted the basic law confirming Jerusalem's status as Israel's "eternal and undivided capital."

On August 20 the United Nations Security Council adopted Resolution 478 which censured Israel for its legislation.

1. Jerusalem, complete and united, is the capital of Israel.

2. Jerusalem is the seat of the President of the State, the Knesset, the Government and the Supreme Court.

3. The Holy Places shall be protected from desecration and any other violation and from anything likely to violate the freedom of access of the members of the different religions to the places sacred to them or their feelings towards those places.

4. (a) The Government shall provide for the development and prosperity of Jerusalem and the well-being of its inhabitants by allocating special funds, including a special annual grant to the Municipality of Jerusalem (Capital City Grant) with the approval of the Finance Committee of the Knesset. (b) Jerusalem shall be given special priority in the activities of the authorities of the State so as to further its development in economic and other matters. (c) The Government shall set up a special body or special bodies for the implementation of this section.

FAHD PLAN (AUGUST 7, 1981)

In an interview with the Saudi Press Agency on August 7, 1981, Crown Prince Fahd of Saudi Arabia outlined the principles for a peaceful settlement of the Arab-Israeli conflict. When asked if the Government of Saudi Arabia has a practical framework for implementing a just and comprehensive settlement of the Palestinian problem, he replied: "Naturally, we cannot indulge ourselves in details here, yet there is a set of principles that can be used as guidelines in our search for a just settlement. They are principles that already have been adopted and reiterated many times by the United Nations during the past few years."

These principles are: (1) Israeli withdrawal from all the Arab territories occupied in 1967, including Arab Jerusalem; (2) Removal of the settlements established by Israel in the Arab territories after 1967; (3) Guaranteeing the freedom of worship and religious practices for all religions in the holy places; (4) Asserting the rights of the Palestinian people to return to their homes and compensating those who do not wish to return; (5) Placing the West Bank and Gaza Strip under the auspices of the United Nations for a transitional period not exceeding several months; (6) Establishing an independent Palestinian state with Jerusalem as its capital; (7) Affirming the right of all the states in the region to live in peace; (8) Guaranteeing the implementation of these principles by the United Nations or some of its member states.

GOLAN HEIGHTS LAW (DECEMBER 14, 1981)

In December 1981 the Knesset extended Israeli law to the Golan Heights by a vote of 63 to 21. In presenting the law, Prime Minister Menachem Begin stated that the time had come to implement the government's policy regarding the Golan Heights citing Syria's implacable hostility to Israel, and the recent deployment of Syrian missiles on Lebanese soil -- a provocation of crisis proportions. He reminded the ministers that the Syrian president had rejected any ties with Israel.

1. The Law, jurisdiction and administration of the state shall apply to the Golan Heights, as described in the Appendix.

2. This Law shall become valid on the day of its passage in the Knesset.

3. The Minister of the Interior shall be charged with the implementation of this Law, and he is entitled, in consultation with the Minister of Justice, to enact regulations for its implementation and to formulate in regulations transitional provisions concerning the continued application of regulations, orders, administrative orders, rights and duties which were in force on the Golan Heights prior to the application of this Law.

REAGAN FRESH START INITIATIVE (SEPTEMBER 1, 1982)

Israel's invasion of Lebanon (Operation Peace for Galilee) on June 6, 1982 was followed by United States efforts to achieve a cease-fire and to arrange for a withdrawal of forces. After Ambassador Philip Habib arranged for the withdrawal of PLO forces from Beirut, the United States moved to achieve a just and lasting peace. In an address to the nation on September 1, 1982, President Ronald Reagan presented his peace proposal, the Fresh Start Initiative, (also known as the Reagan Plan), to settle the Israeli-Palestinian conflict. Secretary of State George P. Shultz was the architect of this plan which was based on Camp David and the principle of the exchange of land for peace set forth in United Nations Security Council Resolution 242. The initiative called on the Palestinians to recognize that their own political aspirations are extricably bound to recognition of Israel's right to a secure future. Reagan asked the Arab states to accept the reality of Israel and that peace and justice are to be gained only through hard, fair, direct negotiations. Jordan was to be empowered to negotiate on behalf of the Palestinians. What appeared to be a positive resolution of the Lebanon crisis, seemed to provide a conducive atmosphere for a new peace initiative to restart the stalled Arab-Israeli peace process.

Jordan's King Hussein gave discreet support and sought to convince Yasser Arafat and the PLO to accept the plan but he was not able to get the PLO to agree to allow Jordan to negotiate on behalf of the Palestinians. By the spring of 1983 he had distanced himself from further involvement. The Lebanese issue moved to the forefront of United States diplomatic efforts.

My fellow Americans, today has been a day that should make us proud. It marked the end of the successful evacuation of the Palestine Liberation Organization (PLO) from Beirut, Lebanon. This peaceful step could never have been taken without the good offices of the United States and, especially, the truly heroic work of a great American diplomat, Ambassador Philip Habib. Thanks to his efforts, I am happy to announce that the U.S. Marine contingent helping to supervise the evacuation has accomplished its mission. Our young men should be out of Lebanon within 2 weeks. They, too, have served the cause of peace with distinction, and we can all be very proud of them.

But the situation in Lebanon is only part of the overall problem of conflict in the Middle East. So, over the past 2 weeks, while events in Beirut dominated the front page, America was engaged in a quiet, behind-the-scenes effort to lay the groundwork for a broader peace in the region. ...

It seemed to me that, with the agreement in Lebanon, we had an opportunity for a more far-reaching peace effort in the region, and I was determined to seize that moment. In the words of the scripture, the time had come to "follow after the things which make for peace."

Tonight, I want to report to you on the steps we have taken, and the prospects they can open up for a just and lasting peace in the Middle East. America has long been committed to bringing peace to this troubled region. For more than a generation, successive U.S. administrations have endeavored to develop a fair and workable process that could lead to a true and lasting Arab-Israeli peace. ...

The Lebanon war, tragic as it was, has left us with a new opportunity for Middle East peace. We must seize it now and bring peace to this troubled area so vital to world stability while there is still time. It was with this strong conviction that over a month ago, before the present negotiations in Beirut has been completed, I directed Secretary of State Shultz to again review our policy and to consult a wide range of outstanding Americans on the best ways to strengthen chances for peace in the Middle East. We have consulted with many of the officials who were historically involved in the process, with Members of the Congress, and with individuals from the private sector, and I have held extensive consultations with my own advisers on the principles I will outline to you tonight. ...

But the opportunities for peace in the Middle East do not begin and end in Lebanon. As we help Lebanon rebuild, we must also move to resolve the root causes of conflict between Arabs and Israelis. The war in Lebanon has demonstrated many things, but two consequences are key to the peace process:

First, the military losses of the PLO have not diminished the yearning of the Palestinian people for a just solution of their claims; and

Second, while Israel's military successes in Lebanon have demonstrated that its armed forces are second to none in the region, they alone cannot bring just and lasting peace to Israel and her neighbors.

The question now is how to reconcile Israel's legitimate security concerns with the legitimate rights of the Palestinians. And that answer can only come at the negotiating table. Each party must recognize that the outcome must be acceptable to all and that true peace will require compromises by all.

So, tonight I am calling for a fresh start. This is the moment for all those directly concerned to get involved -- or lend their support -- to a workable basis for peace. The Camp David agreement remains the foundation of our policy. Its language provides all parties with the leeway they need for successful negotiations.

I call on Israel to make clear that the security for which she yearns can only be achieved through genuine peace, a peace requiring magnanimity, vision, and courage.

I call on the Palestinian people to recognize that their own political aspirations are inextricably bound to recognition of Israel's right to a secure future.

And I call on the Arab states to accept the reality of Israel and the reality that peace and justice are to be gained only through hard, fair, direct negotiation.

I call on the Palestinian people to recognize that their own political aspirations are inextricably bound to recognition of Israel's right to a secure future.

And I call on the Arab states to accept the reality of Israel and the reality that peace and justice are to be gained only through hard, fair, direct negotiation.

In making these calls upon others, I recognize that the United States has a special responsibility. No other nation is in a position to deal with the key parties to the conflict on the basis of trust and reliability.

The time has come for a new realism on the part of all the peoples of the Middle East. The State of Israel is an accomplished fact; it deserves unchallenged legitimacy within the community of nations. But Israel's legitimacy has thus far been recognized by too few countries and has been denied by every Arab state except Egypt. Israel exists; it has a right to exist in peace behind secure and defensible borders; and it has a right to demand of its neighbors that they recognize those facts.

I have personally followed and supported Israel's heroic struggle for survival ever since the founding of the State of Israel 34 years ago. In the pre-1967 borders, Israel was barely 10 miles wide at its narrowest point. The bulk of Israel's population lived within artillery range of hostile Arab armies. I am not about to ask Israel to live that way again.

The war in Lebanon has demonstrated another reality in the region. The departure of the Palestinians from Beirut dramatizes more than ever the homelessness of the Palestinian people. Palestinians feel strongly that their cause is more than a question of refugees. I agree. The Camp David agreement recognized that fact when it spoke of the legitimate rights of the Palestinian people and their just requirements. For peace to endure, it must involve all those who have been most deeply affected by the conflict. Only through broader participation in the peace process -- most immediately by Jordan and by the Palestinians -- will Israel be able to rest confident in the knowledge that its security and integrity will be respected by its neighbors. Only through the process of negotiation can all the nations of the Middle East achieve a secure peace.

These then are our general goals. What are the specific new American positions, and why are we taking them?

In the Camp David talks thus far, both Israel and Egypt have felt free to express openly their views as to what the outcome should be. Understandably, their views have differed on many points.

The United States has thus far sought to play the role of mediator; we have avoided public comment on the key issues. We have always recognized -- and continue to recognize -- that only the voluntary agreement of those parties most directly involved in the conflict can provide an enduring solution. But it has become evident to me that some clearer sense of America's position on the key issues is necessary to encourage wider support for the peace process.

First, as outlined in the Camp David accords, there must be a period of time during which the Palestinian inhabitants of the West Bank and Gaza will have full autonomy over their own affairs. Due consideration must be given to the principle of self-government by the inhabitants of the territories and to the legitimate security concerns of the parties involved.

The purpose of the 5-year period of transition, which would begin after free elections for a self-governing Palestinian authority, is to prove to the Palestinians that they can run their own affairs and that such Palestinian autonomy poses no threat to Israel's security.

The United States will no support the use of any additional land for the purpose of settlements during the transition period. Indeed, the immediate adoption of a settlement freeze by Israel, more than any other action, could create the confidence needed for wider participation in these talks. Further settlement activity is in no way necessary for the security of Israel and only diminishes the confidence of the Arabs that a final outcome can be freely and fairly negotiated.

I want to make the American position well understood: The purpose of this transition period is the peaceful and orderly transfer of authority from Israel to the Palestinian inhabitants of the West Bank and Gaza. At the same time, such a transfer must not interfere with Israel's security requirements.

Beyond the transition period, as we look to the future of the West Bank and Gaza, it is clear to me that peace cannot be achieved by the formation of an independent Palestinian state in those territories. Nor is it achievable on the basis of Israeli sovereignty or permanent control over the West Bank and Gaza.

So the United States will not support the establishment of an independent Palestinian state in the West Bank and Gaza, and we will not support annexation or permanent control by Israel.

There is, however, another way to peace. The final status of these lands must, of course, be reached through the give-and-take of negotiations. But it is the firm view of the United States that self-government by the Palestinians of the West Bank and Gaza in association with Jordan offers the best chance for a durable, just and lasting peace.

We base our approach squarely on the principle that the Arab-Israeli conflict should be resolved through negotiations involving an exchange of territory for peace. This exchange is enshrined in U.N. Security Council Resolution 242 which is, in turn, incorporated in all its parts in the Camp David agreements. U.N. Resolution 242 remains wholly valid as the foundation stone of America's Middle East peace effort.

It is the United States' position that -- in return for peace -- the withdrawal provision of Resolution 242 applies to all fronts, including the West Bank and Gaza.

When the border is negotiated between Jordan and Israel, our view on the extent to which Israel should be asked to give up territory will be heavily affected by the extent of true peace and normalization and the security arrangements offered in return.

Finally, we remain convinced that Jerusalem must remain undivided, but its final status should be decided through negotiations.

In the course of the negotiations to come, the United States will support positions that seem to us fair and reasonable compromises and likely to promote a sound agreement. We will also put forward our own detailed proposals when we believe they can be helpful. And, make no mistake, the United States will oppose any proposal -- from any party and at any point in the negotiating process -- that threatens the security of Israel. America's commitment to the security of Israel is ironclad. And, I might add, so is mine.

During the past few days, our ambassadors in Israel, Egypt, Jordan, and Saudi Arabia have presented to their host governments the proposals in full detail that I have outlined here today. Now I am convinced that these proposals can bring justice, bring security, and bring durability to an Arab-Israeli peace. The United States will stand by these principles with total dedication. They are fully consistent with Israel's security requirements and the aspirations of the Palestinians. We will work hard to broaden participation at the peace table as envisaged by the Camp David accords. And I fervently hope that the Palestinians and Jordan, with the support of their Arab colleagues, will accept this opportunity. ...

These, then, are the principles upon which American policy toward the Arab-Israeli conflict will be based. I have made a personal commitment to see that they endure and, God willing, that they will come to be seen by all reasonable, compassionate people as fair, achievable, and in the interests of all who wish to see peace in the Middle East.

Tonight, on the eve of what can be a dawning of new hope for the people of the troubled Middle East -- and for all the world's people who dream of a just and peaceful future -- I ask you, my fellow Americans, for your support and your prayers in this great undertaking.

FEZ PEACE PLAN (SEPTEMBER 9, 1982)

The Arab summit meeting in Fez, Morocco, in September 1982, adopted a resolution in reaction to the Reagan plan, announced a week earlier, that, in effect, constituted a peace plan. This was based on the principles enunciated a year earlier by Saudi Crown Prince Fahd. The Brezhnev Plan that followed within days clearly draw on this Arab policy statement.

The conference greeted the steadfastness of the Palestine revolutionary forces, the Lebanese and Palestinian peoples and the Syrian Arab Armed Forces and declared its support of the Palestinian people in their struggle for the retrieval of their established national rights.

Out of the conference's belief in the ability of the Arab nation to achieve its legitimate objectives and eliminate the aggression, and out of the principles and basis laid down by the Arab summit conferences, and out of the Arab countries' determination to continue to work by all means for the establishment of peace based on justice in the Middle East and using the plan of President Habib Bourguiba, which is based on international legitimacy, as the foundation for solving the Palestinian question and the plan of His Majesty King Fahd ibn 'Abd al-'Aziz which deals with peace in the Middle East, and in the light of the discussions and notes made by their majesties, excellencies and highnesses the kings, presidents and emirs, the conference has decided to adopt the following principles:

(1) The withdrawal of Israel from all Arab territories occupied in 1967 including Arab al-Kuds (Jerusalem); (2) The dismantling of settlements established by Israel on the Arab territories after 1967; (3) The guarantee of freedom of worship and practice of religious rites for all religions in the holy shrines; (4) The reaffirmation of the Palestinian people's right to self-determination and the exercise of its imprescriptible and inalienable national rights under the leadership of the Palestine Liberation Organization, its sole and legitimate representative, and the indemnification of all those who do not desire to return; (5) Placing the West Bank and Gaza Strip under the control of the UN for a transitory period not exceeding a few months; (6) The establishment of an independent Palestinian state with al-Kuds as its capital; (7) The Security Council guarantees peace among all states of the region including the independent Palestinian state; (8) The Security Council guarantees the respect of these principles.

BREZHNEV PLAN (SEPTEMBER 15, 1982)

On September 15, 1982, in Moscow, General Secretary of the Communist Party of the Soviet Union Leonid Brezhnev put forward proposals concerning the resolution of the Arab-Israeli conflict during talks with general secretary of the Yemeni Socialist Party, Ali Nasser Mohammed. On the basis of United Nations Security Council Resolutions 242 and 338, the plan emphasized securing the Palestinians' right to self-determination and to establish their own state. It stressed that a just and stable Middle East peace could be achieved only with participation of all the sides concerned including the Palestine Liberation Organization (PLO).

1. The strict fulfillment of the principle of inadmissibility of seizure of other's territories by aggression and the necessity to return to the Arabs the territories occupied in 1967, namely the Gòlan Heights, the West Bank of the

Jordan, and the Gaza Strip and Lebanese territories, occupied in 1982. The borders between Israel and its Arab neighbors must be declared inviolable.

2. Ensuring the inalienable right of the Palestinians to self-determination and establishing of their own state on Palestinian territories liberated from the Israeli occupation -- on the West Bank and Gaza Strip. The Palestinian refugees in accordance with the relevant UN resolutions should be given real opportunity to return to their homes in Palestine or to obtain proper compensation for their property left behind.

3. The return to the Arabs of East Jerusalem (occupied by Israel in 1967), an integral part of the Palestinian state. The right of free access to the holy sites of the three religions must be guaranteed in all Jerusalem.

4. The right, reciprocally recognized, of all states of the region to a safe and independent existence and development should be guaranteed.

5. The cessation of the state of war and establishment of peace should be reached between Israel and Arab countries. Meaning that all sides concerned, including Israel and the Palestinian state, should take commitments to respect each other's sovereignty, independence and territorial integrity and settle all problems peacefully by way of negotiations.

6. International guarantees of a Middle East settlement should be worked out and adopted. The role of guarantor should be played by the permanent members of the Security Council of the United Nations or the Security Council as a whole.

KAHAN COMMISSION OF INQUIRY REPORT (FEBRUARY 8, 1983)

After the War in Lebanon, Christian Phalangist forces massacred Palestinians at the Sabra and Shatilla camps in the Beirut area. The resultant anguish within Israel, and consequent public pressure, led to the decision of the Cabinet on September 28, 1982 to establish a Commission of Inquiry. The Commission consisted of Yitzhak Kahan, President of the Supreme Court who served as Commission Chairman, Aharon Barak, Justice of the Supreme Court, and Yona Efrat, a reserve Major General in the Israel Defense Forces. After several months of testimony, it released its findings on February 8, 1983.

The Commission found that while the Phalangist militia bore direct responsibility for the killings, the government of Israel and some of its senior officials had to bear indirect responsibility due to their actions, or lack thereof. Of particular concern was the lack of consideration or indifference on the part of Israeli government officials to the danger that the Phalangists would carry out atrocities against the civilian population in the camps, given their desire for revenge over the killing of their leader Bashir Gemayel and their known antipathy to the Palestinians.

The harshest criticism was reserved for Defense Minister Ariel Sharon and Chief of Staff Rafael Eitan, on whom it laid responsibility for the decision to allow the Phalangists to enter the camps. The Commission questioned Eitan's failure to take into consideration the possibility of the Phalangists taking vengeance against the civilians in the camps; as well as his failure to order measures to avoid such a danger. This was considered a breach of duty by Eitan, but given the fact that he was scheduled to complete his term of office the following month, no punitive action was recommended by the Commission. The Commission charged Sharon with personal responsibility for the decision to allow the Phalangists to enter Sabra and Shatilla. Sharon was charged with nonfulfillment of duty and failure to meet his humanitarian obligation to the occupants of the camps. The Commission recommended that Sharon be removed from office. On February 10, 1983, the Israeli Cabinet voted sixteen to one to oust Ariel Sharon from his position as Minister of Defense. Sharon submitted his resignation, but eventually was reinstated as Minister Without Portfolio.

The commission established that the massacre was perpetrated by the Phalangists and not by any other organized military force. The commission established that hints and accusations to the effect that IDF soldiers were in the camps at the time the massacre was perpetrated were completely groundless and constituted a baseless libel. It established that no conspiracy or plot was entered into between anyone from the Israeli political echelon or from the military echelon in the IDF and the Phalangists with the aim of perpetrating atrocities in the camps.

INTRODUCTION. At a meeting of the Cabinet on 28 September 1982, the Government of Israel resolved to establish a commission of inquiry in accordance with the Commissions of Inquiry Law of 1968. The Cabinet charged the commission as follows: "The matter which will be subjected to inquiry is: all the facts and factors connected with the atrocity carried out by a unit of the Lebanese Forces against the civilian population in the Shatilla and Sabra camps."

In the wake of this resolution, the President of the Supreme Court ... appointed a commission of inquiry comprised as follows: Yitzhak Kahan, President of the Supreme Court, commission chairman; Aharon Barak, Justice of the Supreme Court; Yona Efrat, Major General (Res.). ...

THE DIRECT RESPONSIBILITY. According to the above description of events, all the evidence indicates that the massacre was perpetrated by the Phalangists between the time they entered the camps ...and their departure from the camps.... The victims were found in those areas where the Phalangists were in military control during the aforementioned time period. ... It can be stated with certainty that no organized military force entered the camps at the aforementioned time besides the Phalangists forces. ...

In the course of the events and also thereafter, rumors spread that personnel of Major Haddad were perpetrating a massacre or participating in a massacre. No basis was found for these rumors. ...

Here and there, hints, and even accusations, were thrown out to the effect that I.D.F. soldiers were in the camps at the time the massacre was perpetrated. We have no doubt that these notions are completely groundless and constitute a baseless libel. ...

Contentions and accusations were advanced that even if I.D.F. personnel had not shed the blood of the massacred, the entry of the Phalangists into the camps had been carried out with the prior knowledge that a massacre would be perpetrated there and with the intention that this should indeed take place; and therefore all those who had enabled the entry of the Phalangists into the camps should be regarded as accomplices to the acts of slaughter and sharing in direct responsibility. These accusations too are unfounded. We have no doubt that no conspiracy or plot was entered into between anyone from the Israeli political echelon in the I.D.F. and the Phalangists, with the aim of perpetrating atrocities in the camps. ...

Our conclusion is therefore that the direct responsibility for the perpetration of the acts of slaughter rests on the Phalangist forces. No evidence was brought before us that Phalangist personnel received explicit orders from their command to perpetrate acts of slaughter, but it is evident that the forces who entered the areas were steeped in hatred for the Palestinians, in the wake of the atrocities and severe injuries done to the Christians during the civil war in Lebanon by the Palestinians and those who fought alongside them; and those feelings of hatred were compounded by a longing for revenge in the wake of the assassination of the Phalangists' admired leader Bashir and the killing of several dozen Phalangists two days before their entry into the camps. ...

THE INDIRECT RESPONSIBILITY. To sum up this chapter ... absolutely no direct responsibility devolved upon Israel or upon those who acted in its behalf. At the same time, it is clear from what we have said above that the decision on the entry of the Phalangists into the refugee camps was taken without consideration of the danger ... that the Phalangists would commit massacres and pogroms against the inhabitants of the camps, and without an examinations of the means for preventing this danger. Similarly, it is clear from the course of events that when the reports began to arrive about the actions of the Phalangists in the camps, no proper heed was taken of these reports, the correct conclusions were not drawn from them, and no energetic and immediate actions were taken to restrain the Phalangists and put a stop to their actions. This both reflects and exhausts Israel's indirect responsibility for what occurred in the refugee camps. We shall discuss the responsibility of those who acted in Israel's behalf and in its name in the following chapters.

THE RESPONSIBILITY OF THE POLITICAL ECHELON. ... PERSONAL RESPONSIBILITY. ... The Prime Minister, Mr. Menachem Begin. ... The Prime Minister's lack of involvement in the entire matter casts on him a certain degree of responsibility.

The Minister of Defense, Mr. Ariel Sharon. ... It is our view that responsibility is to be imputed to the Minister of Defense for having disregarded the danger of acts of vengeance and bloodshed by the Phalangists against the population of the refugee camps, and having failed to take this danger into account when he decided to have the Phalangists enter the camps. In addition, responsibility is to be imputed to the Minister of Defense for not ordering appropriate measures for preventing or reducing the danger of massacre as a condition for the Phalangists' entry into the camps. These blunders constitute the non-fulfillment of a duty with which the Defense Minister was charged. ...

The Foreign Minister, Mr. Yitzhak Shamir. ... In our view, the Foreign Minister erred in not taking any measures after the conversation with Minister Zipori in regard to what he had heard from Zipori about the Phalangist actions in the camps.

The Chief of Staff, Lieutenant General Rafael Eitan. ... We find that the Chief of Staff did not consider the danger of acts of vengeance and bloodshed being perpetrated against the population of the refugee camps in Beirut; he did not order the adoption of the appropriate steps to avoid this danger; and his failure to do so is tantamount to a breach of duty that was incumbent upon the Chief of Staff. ... We determine that the Chief of Staff's inaction, described above, and his order to provide the Phalangist forces with tractors, or a tractor, constitute a breach of duty and dereliction of the duty incumbent upon the Chief of Staff.

Director of Military Intelligence, Major General Yehoshua Saguy. ... In our opinion, it was the duty of the director of Military Intelligence ... to demonstrate alertness regarding the role of the Phalangists in the entry to Beirut after Bashir's assassination, to demand an appropriate clarification, and to explicitly and expressly warn all those concerned of the expected danger even prior to receipt of the report on Friday, and certainly after receipt of the report. The fear that his words would not receive sufficient attention, and be rejected does not justify total inaction. This inaction constitutes breach of the duty incumbent on the director of Military Intelligence in this capacity.

Head of the Institute for Intelligence and Special Projects (Mossad). ... It appears to us, that even in the situation described above, the head of the Mossad was obligated to express his opinion at the Cabinet meeting on the entry of the Phalangists and deal in this expression of opinion with the dangers involved in the Phalangists' operations -- especially after he had heard Minister David Levy's remarks. In consideration of all the aforementioned circumstances, it is our opinion that this inaction of the head of the Mossad should not be considered serious.

G.O.C. Northern Command Major General Amir Drori. ... We determine that it was the duty of the G.O.C. to warn the Chief of Staff when the latter arrived in Beirut on 17.9.82 and during the rest of the Chief of Staff's stay in Beirut, that the population in the camps is endangered by the continued presence of the

Phalangist forces in the camps, and that they should be removed from there immediately -- or that at least steps be taken to ensure the safety of the population in the camps or to reduce the danger they face to the barest possible minimum. Major General Drori's refraining from any action regarding the danger facing the civilian population from the Phalangist forces, from the time the Chief of Staff arrived in Beirut and until Saturday, 18.9.82, constitutes, in our opinion, a breach of the duty which was incumbent on Major General Drori.

Division Commander Brigadier General Amos Yaron. ... We determine that by virtue of his failings and actions, detailed above, Brigadier General Yaron committed a breach of the duties incumbent upon him by virtue of his position.

Mr. Avi Duda'i, Personal Aide to The Minister of Defense. ... In view of the entire body of evidence, we do not determine that Duda'i indeed received the report about the 300 people killed on Friday, 17.9.82, and it therefore cannot be determined that he refrained from fulfilling an obligation which was incumbent upon him....

RECOMMENDATIONS AND CLOSING REMARKS. RECOMMENDA-TIONS. With regard to the following recommendations concerning a group of men who hold senior positions in the Government and the Israel Defense Forces, we have taken into account [the fact] that each one of these men has to his credit [the performance of] many public or military services rendered with sacrifice and devotion on behalf of the State of Israel. If nevertheless we have reached the conclusion that it is incumbent upon us to recommend certain measures against some of these men, it is out of recognition that the gravity of the matter and its implications for the underpinnings of public morality in the State of Israel call for such measures.

The Prime Minister, The Foreign Minister, and the Head of the Mossad. We have heretofore established the facts and conclusions with regard to the responsibility of the Prime Minister, the Foreign Minister, and the head of the Mossad. In view of what we have determined with regard to the extent of the responsibility of each of them, we are of the opinion that it is sufficient to determine responsibility and there is no need for any further recommendations.

G.O.C. Northern Command Major General Amir Drori. We have detailed above our conclusions with regard to the responsibility of G.O.C. Northern Command Major General Amir Drori. Major General Drori was charged with many difficult and complicated tasks during the week the I.D.F. entered West Beirut, missions which he had to accomplish after a long period of difficult warfare. He took certain measures for terminating the Phalangists' actions, and his guilt lies in that he did not continue with these actions. Taking into account these circumstances, it appears to us that it is sufficient to determine the responsibility of Major General Drori without recourse to any further recommendation.

The Minister of Defense, Mr. Ariel Sharon. We have found, as has been detailed in this report, that the Minister of Defense bears personal responsibility.

In our opinion, it is fitting that the Minister of Defense draw the appropriate personal conclusions arising out of the defects revealed with regard to the manner in which he discharged the duties of his office -- and if necessary, that the Prime Minister consider whether he should exercise his authority under Section 21-A(a) of the Basic Law: the Government, according to which "the Prime Minister may, after informing the Cabinet of his intention to do so, remove a minister from office."

The Chief of Staff, Lt.-Gen. Rafael Eitan. We have arrived at grave conclusions with regard to the acts and omissions of the Chief of Staff, Lt-Gen. Rafael Eitan. The Chief of Staff is about to complete his term of service in April, 1983. Taking into account the fact that an extension of his term is not under consideration, there is no [practical] significance to a recommendation with regard to his continuing in office as Chief of Staff, and therefore we have resolved that it is sufficient to determine responsibility without making any further recommendation.

The Director of Military Intelligence, Major General Yehoshua Saguy. We have detailed the various extremely serious omissions of the Director of Military Intelligence, Major General Yehoshua Saguy, in discharging the duties of his office. We recommend that Major General Yehoshua Saguy not continue as Director of Military Intelligence.

Division Commander Brigadier General, Amos Yaron. We have detailed above the extent of the responsibility of Brigadier General Amos Yaron. Taking into account all the circumstances, we recommend that Brigadier General Amos Yaron not serve in the capacity of a field commander in the Israel Defense Forces, and that this recommendation not be reconsidered before three years have passed.

In the course of this inquiry, shortcomings in the functioning of [several establishments have been revealed, as described in the chapter dealing with this issue. One must learn the appropriate lessons from these shortcomings, and we recommend that, in addition to internal control in this matter, an investigation into the shortcomings and the manner of correcting them be undertaken by an expert or experts, to be appointed by a Ministerial Defense Committee. If in the course of this investigation it be found that certain persons bear responsibility for these shortcomings, it is fitting that the appropriate conclusions be drawn in their regard, whether in accordance with the appropriate provisions of the military legal code, or in some other manner.

Closing remarks. In the witnesses' testimony and in various documents, stress is laid on the difference between the usual battle ethics of the I.D.F. and the battle ethics of the bloody clashes and combat actions among the various ethnic groups, militias, and fighting forces in Lebanon. The difference is considerable. In the war the I.D.F. waged in Lebanon, many civilians were injured and much loss of life was caused, despite the effort the I.D.F. and its soldiers made not to harm civilians. On more than one occasion, this effort caused I.D.F. troops additional casualties. During the months of the war, I.D.F. soldiers witnessed many sights of killing, destruction, and ruin. From their reactions (about which we have heard) to acts of brutality against civilians, it would appear that despite the terrible sights and experiences of the war and despite the soldier's obligation to behave as a fighter with a certain degree of callousness, I.D.F. soldiers did not lose their sensitivity to atrocities that were perpetrated on non-combatants either out of cruelty or to give vent to vengeful feelings. It is regrettable that the reaction by I.D.F. soldiers to such deeds was not always forceful enough to bring a halt to the despicable acts. It seems to us that the I.D.F. should continue to foster the [consciousness of] basic moral obligations which must be kept even in war conditions, without prejudicing the I.D.F.'s combat ability. The circumstances of combat require the combatants to be tough -- which means to give priority to sticking to the objective and being willing to make sacrifices -- in order to attain the objectives assigned to them, even under the most difficult conditions. But the end never justifies the means, and basic ethical and human values must be maintained in the use of arms.

Among the responses to the commission from the public, there were those who expressed dissatisfaction with the holding of an inquiry on a subject not directly related to Israel's responsibility. The argument was advanced that in previous instances of massacre in Lebanon, when the lives of many more people were taken than those of the victims who fell in Sabra and Shatilla, world opinion was not shocked and no inquiry commissions were established. We cannot justify this approach to the issue of holding an inquiry, and not only for the formal reason that it was not we who decided to hold the inquiry, but rather the Israeli Government resolved thereon. The main purpose of the inquiry was to bring to light all the important facts relating to the perpetration of the atrocities; it therefore has importance from the perspective of Israel's moral fortitude and its functioning as a democratic state that scrupulously maintains the fundamental principles of the civilized world.

We do not deceive ourselves that the results of this inquiry will convince or satisfy those who have prejudices or selective consciences, but this inquiry was not intended for such people. We have striven and have spared no effort to arrive at the truth, and we hope that all persons of good will who will examine the issue without prejudice will be convinced that the inquiry was conducted without any bias. ...

This report was signed on 7 February 1983.

ISRAEL-LEBANON AGREEMENT (MAY 17, 1983)

Following the War in Lebanon, Israel and Lebanon negotiated under the auspices of the United States, concerning the withdrawal of foreign forces from Lebanon and related arrangements. After months of discussion and numerous sessions alternately held in Khalde, Kiryat Shemona and Netanya, starting on December 28, 1982, an agreement was reached. It was signed on May 17, 1983 following the extensive involvement of United States Secretary of State George Shultz who focused on the withdrawal of foreign forces from Lebanon, but also dealt with the broader Reagan initiative.

The Israel-Lebanon agreement did not constitute a "peace treaty" but the countries agreed "to respect the sovereignty, political independence and territorial integrity of each other," and to "confirm that the state of war between Israel and Lebanon has been terminated and no longer exists." The "existing international boundary between Israel and Lebanon" was to be the border between the two states. Israel undertook "to withdraw all its armed forces from Lebanon." Both agreed to refrain from various hostile actions, including hostile propaganda, against each other.

On May 17 Israel and Lebanon signed the agreement, in the Israeli town of Kiryat Shmona and at Khalde in Lebanon, in four languages: English and French (the binding versions), Hebrew, and Arabic. Syria rejected the agreement, and Palestinian leaders, meeting in Damascus, also opposed it. Syria objected to the Israeli security presence in southern Lebanon, claiming that it infringed on Lebanese sovereignty and Syrian security. President Hafez al-Assad wanted to ensure that any negotiations would take Syria's concerns into account and that Syria's leadership of the negotiating team and control of its positions would be assured. Syria also sought to maintain (and enhance) its role and influence in Lebanon.

The Soviet Union's negative reaction was multifaceted. On May 9 it issued a statement in which it charged that the United States and Israel were "grossly violating" Lebanese territory, and it demanded the "unconditional withdrawal" of Israeli troops from Lebanon as the "first and foremost" condition for bringing peace to that country.

Although signed and ratified by both states, Lebanon abrogated the agreement in March 1984 under heavy pressure from Syria.

The Government of the State of Israel and the Government of the Republic of Lebanon: Bearing in mind the importance of maintaining and strengthening international peace based on freedom, equality, justice, and respect for fundamental human rights; Reaffirming their faith in the aims and principles of the Charter of the United Nations and recognizing their right and obligation to live in peace with each other as well as with all states, within secure and recognized boundaries; Having agreed to declare the termination of the state of war between them; Desiring to ensure lasting security for both their States and to avoid threats and the use of force between them; Desiring to establish their mutual relations in the manner provided for in this Agreement; Having delegated their undersigned representative plenipotentiaries, provided with full powers, in order to sign, in the presence of the representative of the United States of America, this Agreement; Have agreed to the following provisions:

ARTICLE 1. 1. The Parties agree and undertake to respect the sovereignty, political independence and territorial integrity of each other. They consider the existing international boundary between Israel and Lebanon inviolable. 2. The Parties confirm that the state of war between Israel and Lebanon has been terminated and no longer exists. 3. Taking into account the provisions of paragraphs 1 and 2, Israel undertakes to withdraw all its armed forces from Lebanon in accordance with the Annex of the present Agreement.

ARTICLE 2. The Parties, being guided by the principles of the Charter of the United Nations and of international law, undertake to settle their disputes by peaceful means in such a manner as to promote international peace and security, and justice.

ARTICLE 3. In order to provide maximum security for Israel and Lebanon, the Parties agree to establish and implement security arrangements, including the creation of a Security Region, as provided for in the Annex of the present Agreement.

ARTICLE 4. 1. The territory of each Party will not be used as a base for hostile or terrorist activity against the other Party, its territory, or its people. 2. Each Party will prevent the existence or organization of irregular forces, armed bands, organizations, bases, offices or infrastructure, the aims and purposes of which include incursions or any act of terrorism into the territory of the other Party, or any other activity aimed at threatening or endangering the security of the other Party and safety of its people. To this end all agreements and arrangements enabling the presence and functioning on the territory of either Party of elements hostile to the other Party are null and void. 3. Without prejudice to the inherent right of self-defense in accordance with international law, each Party will refrain: a. from organizing, instigating, assisting, or participating in threats or acts of belligerency, subversion, or incitement or any aggression directed against the other Party, its population or property, both within its territory and originating therefrom, or in the territory of the other Party. b. from using the territory of the other Party for conducting a military attack against the territory of a third state. c. from intervening in the internal or external affairs of the other Party. 4. Each Party undertakes to ensure that preventive action and due proceedings will be taken against persons or organizations perpetrating acts in violation of this Article.

ARTICLE 5. Consistent with the termination of the state of war and within the framework of their constitutional provisions, the Parties will abstain from any form of hostile propaganda against each other.

ARTICLE 6. Each Party will prevent entry into, deployment in, or passage through its territory, its air space and, subject to the right of innocent passage in accordance with international law, its territorial sea, by military forces, armament, or military equipment of any state hostile to the other Party.

ARTICLE 7. Except as provided in the present Agreement, nothing will preclude the deployment on Lebanese territory of international forces requested and accepted by the Government of Lebanon to assist in maintaining its authority. New contributors to such forces shall be selected from among states having diplomatic relations with both Parties to the present Agreement.

ARTICLE 8. 1. a. Upon entry into force of the present Agreement, a Joint Liaison Committee will be established by the Parties, in which the United States of America will be a participant, and will commence its functions. This Committee will be entrusted with the supervision of the implementation of all areas covered by the present Agreement. In matters involving security arrangements, it will deal with unresolved problems referred to it by the Security Arrangements Committee established in subparagraph c. below. Decisions of this Committee will be taken unanimously. b. The Joint Liaison Committee will address itself on a continuing basis to the development of mutual relations between Israel and Lebanon, inter alia the regulation of the movement of goods, products and persons, communications, etc. c. Within the framework of the Joint Liaison Committee, there will be a Security Arrangements Committee whose composition and functions are defined in the Annex of the present Agreement. d. Subcommittees of the Joint Liaison Committee may be established as the need arises. e. The Joint Liaison Committee will meet in Israel and Lebanon, alternately. f. Each Party, if it so desires and unless there is an agreed change of status, may maintain a liaison office on the territory of the other Party in order to carry out the above-mentioned functions within the framework of the Joint Liaison Committee and to assist in the implementation of the present Agreement. g. The members of the Joint Liaison Committee from each of the Parties will be headed by a senior government official. h. All other matters relating to these liaison offices, their personnel, and the personnel of each Party present in the territory of the other Party in connection with the implementation of the present Agreement will be the subject of a protocol to be concluded between the Parties in the Joint Liaison Committee. Pending the conclusion of this protocol, the liaison offices and the above-mentioned personnel will be treated in accordance with the pertinent provisions of the Convention on Special Missions of December 8, 1969, including those provisions concerning privileges and immunities. The foregoing is without prejudice to the positions of the Parties concerning that Convention. 2. During the six-month period after the withdrawal of all Israeli armed forces from Lebanon in accordance with Article 1 of the present Agreement and the simultaneous restoration of Lebanese governmental authority along the international boundary between Israel and Lebanon, and in the light of the termination of the state of war, the Parties shall initiate, within the Joint Liaison Committee, bona fide negotiations in order to conclude agreements on the movement of goods, products and persons and their implementation on a non-discriminatory basis.

ARTICLE 9. 1. Each of the two Parties will take, within a time limit of one year as of entry into force of the present Agreement, all measures necessary for the abrogation of treaties, laws and regulations deemed in conflict with the present Agreement, subject to and in conformity with its constitutional procedures. 2. The Parties undertake not to apply existing obligations, enter into any obligations, or adopt laws or regulations in conflict with the present Agreement.

ARTICLE 10. 1. The present Agreement shall be ratified by both Parties in conformity with their respective constitutional procedures. It shall enter into force on the exchange of the instruments of ratification and shall supersede the previous agreements between Israel and Lebanon. 2. The Annex, the Appendix and the Map attached thereto, and the Agreed Minutes to the present Agreement shall be considered integral parts thereof. 3. The present Agreement may be modified, amended, or superseded by mutual agreement of the Parties.

ARTICLE 11. 1. Disputes between the Parties arising out of the interpretation or application of the present Agreement will be settled by negotiation in the Joint Liaison Committee. Any dispute of this character not so resolved shall be submitted to conciliation and, if unresolved, thereafter to an agreed procedure for a definitive resolution. 2. Notwithstanding the provisions of paragraph 1, disputes arising out of the interpretation or application of the Annex shall be resolved in the framework of the Security Arrangements Committee and, if unresolved, shall thereafter, at the request of either Party, be referred to the Joint Liaison Committee for resolution through negotiation.

ARTICLE 12. The present Agreement shall be communicated to the Secretariat of the United Nations for registration in conformity with the provisions of Article 102 of the Charter of the United Nations.

Done at Kiryat Shmona and Khaldeh this seventeenth day of May, 1983, in triplicate in four authentic texts in the Hebrew, Arabic, English and French languages. In case of any divergence of interpretation, the English and French texts will be equally authoritative.

ANNEX. SECURITY ARRANGEMENTS. Not reproduced.

SOVIET PROPOSALS FOR A MIDDLE EAST SETTLEMENT (JULY 29, 1984)

In July 1984, the Soviet Union put forward proposals for a settlement in the Middle East. This was during a period of intensified efforts for regional influence between the US and the USSR.

Concerned over the remaining explosive situation in the Middle East, the

Soviet Union is profoundly convinced that the vital interests of the peoples of that region, and likewise the interests of international security as a whole, urgently dictate the need for the speediest attainment of a comprehensive, just and lasting settlement of the Middle East conflict.

It is likewise firmly convinced that such a comprehensive, truly just and really lasting settlement can be drawn up and implemented only through collective efforts with the participation of all parties concerned.

Proceeding from this and wishing to contribute to establishing peace in the Middle East, it puts forward the following proposals on the principles of Middle East settlement and ways to reach it.

The principle of inadmissibility of seizure of foreign territories by aggression should be strictly observed. Consequently Arabs should be given back all the territories occupied by Israel since 1967 -- the Golan Heights, the West Bank, the Gaza Strip and the Lebanese lands. Settlements set up by Israel in Arab territories after 1967 should be dismantled. The borders between Israel and its Arab neighbors should be declared inviolable.

The inalienable right of the Palestinian people, with the Palestine Liberation Organization as its sole legitimate representative, to self-determination and creation of its own independent state on Palestinian soil liberated from Israeli occupation -- in the West Bank of the Jordan River and the Gaza Strip -- should be put into practice. As provided for by the resolution of the Arab summit conference at Fez and by Palestinians' consent, the West Bank and the Gaza Strip should be placed under UN supervision by Israel for a short transitional period not longer than several months. This sovereign independent Palestinian state would define its own relations with neighboring states including the possibility of establishing a confederation. Palestinian refugees should be granted the opportunity provided for by UN resolutions to return to their homes or to receive compensation for their property left behind.

East Jerusalem, occupied by Israel in 1967, is the location of major Muslim sacred sites and should be returned to the Arabs and become an integral part of the Palestinian state. Believers of all religions should be guaranteed free access to the holy sites of Jerusalem.

The right of all states in the region to a safe and independent existence and development should be realized on the basis of full reciprocity as it is impossible to ensure genuine security of one state while violating the security of others.

The cessation of the state of war should take place and peace should be established between Arab states and Israel. All parties to the conflict, including Israel and the Palestinian state, should commit themselves to mutually respecting each other's sovereignty, independence and territorial integrity, and to settling disputes by peaceful means through negotiation.

The permanent members of the UN Security Council or the Security Council as a whole could act to guarantee the peace agreement.

Ways of Settlement. Experience proves convincingly the futility and danger of efforts to solve the Middle East problem by imposing on the Arabs separate agreements with Israel.

The only true and effective way of a cardinal settlement of the Middle East problem is through a collective effort with the participation of all concerned parties within the framework of a specially convened international conference on the Middle East.

The Soviet Union believed that an international conference should be guided by the following concepts:

The Goals of the Conference. The conference should aim at finding a solution to all aspects of the Middle East conflict and should result in the signing of a treaty or treaties covering the following integral components of the settlement: withdrawal of Israeli forces from all Arab land occupied since 1967; implementation of lawful national rights of the Arab people of Palestine including their right to establish their own state; the establishment of peace which ensures the security and independent development of all the states which are party to the conflict. International guarantees for maintaining the terms of a settlement must be established. All agreements reached at the conference should be treated as a whole and be approved by all its participants.

Composition of the Conference. All the Arab countries having common borders with Israel: Syria, Jordan, Egypt, Lebanon and Israel itself should have the right to take part in the conference.

The Palestine Liberation Organization, as the sole legitimate representative of the Palestinian people, should be an equal participant. This is a matter of principle. A Middle East settlement is not possible without solving the Palestine problem and it cannot be resolved without the PLO participation.

The USSR and the USA having served as co-chairmen at the previous conference and having played an important role in the Middle East, should participate in the conference.

Other states of the Middle East and adjoining areas capable of making a positive contribution to the settlement in the Middle East could take part in the conference by common consent.

Procedure of the Conference. Like the preceding one, a new conference on the Middle East should be held under the aegis of the United Nations organization.

The conference's agenda could be carried out by working groups (commissions) created from among representatives of all the participants in the conference to examine key issues of settlement (withdrawal of Israeli troops and the border line; the Palestinian problem; the question of Jerusalem; an end to the state of war and establishment of peace; the problem of security of the states which participated in the conflict; and international guarantees for the observance of the agreements, etc.).

If necessary, bilateral groups could be set up to hammer out details of the agreements concerning only those two countries.

To examine the results of the activities of the working groups (commissions) and when necessary in other cases, plenary meetings should be held to endorse their decisions, with the common consent of all the participants in the conference.

At the initial stage of the conference's work, the states participating in it could be represented by foreign ministers, and subsequently by specially appointed representatives; when necessary, the ministers could periodically attend the conference at later stages.

HUSSEIN-ARAFAT ACCORD (FEBRUARY 11, 1985)

On February 11, 1985, in Amman, Jordan, Jordan's King Hussein and the Palestine Liberation Organization's Yasser Arafat joined in an agreement in an attempt to create momentum in resolving the Palestinian issue. They agreed to five main points as a framework for a comprehensive peace plan in the spirit of the 1982 Fez Plan and United Nations resolutions.

On February 19, 1986 King Hussein suspended his ties with the PLO citing a lack of progress toward peace talks and the PLO's refusal to accept Resolutions 242 and 338. The King noted: "Brothers and sisters, after two long attempts I and the Government of the Hashemite Kingdom of Jordan hereby announce that we are unable to continue to coordinate politically with the PLO leadership until such time as their word becomes their bond, characterized by commitment, credibility and constancy. On our part, we know of no other way of fostering confidence than by truthfulness or of strengthening it than by clarity. For confidence is paramount in constructive cooperation." In July, Hussein ordered all PLO offices closed and ordered Arafat's deputy, Khalil Wazir (Abu Jihad), to leave Jordan. The PLO formally renounced the 1985 agreement in April 1987.

The Government of the Hashemite Kingdom of Jordan and the Palestine Liberation Organization have agreed to march together towards the realization of a just and peaceful settlement of the Middle East problem and to put an end to the Israeli occupation of the Arab occupied territories, including Jerusalem, in accordance with the following principles: 1. Land in exchange for peace as cited in the UN resolutions, including the Security Council resolutions. 2. The Palestinian people's right to self-determination. The Palestinians will be able to exercise their inalienable right to self-determination when the Jordanians and Palestinians manage to achieve this within the framework of an Arab Confederation that it is intended to establish between the two states of Jordan and Palestine. 3. Solving the Palestinian refugee problem in accordance with the UN resolutions. 4. Solving all aspects of the Palestine question. 5. Based on this, peace negotiations should be held within the framework of an international conference to be attended by the five UN Security Council permanent member states and all parties to the conflict, including the PLO, which is the Palestinian people's sole legitimate representative, within a joint delegation -- a joint Jordan-Palestinian delegation.

HASSAN-PERES SUMMIT (JULY 23, 1986)

Israeli Prime Minister Shimon Peres visited King Hassan II in Morocco on July 22-23, 1986. Peres arrived in Fez on July 21 in an Israeli military plane from Tel Aviv, accompanied by three personal advisers, as well as Rafi Edri, a member of Israel's Knesset of Moroccan origin, who played an important role in organizing the meeting. The Israelis were met by an official delegation and were taken to Ifrane. Hassan and Peres met a number of times, both with and without advisers, during the visit. Although there had been numerous private and secret meetings, not only with Hassan, but with other Arab leaders by Israelis, Hassan thus became only the second Arab leader to publicly, officially, and openly meet with senior official Israelis. At the end of their meetings they issued a joint statement.

On July 22 and 23, 1986, His Majesty King Hassan II received Mr. Shimon Peres, Prime Minister of Israel, in his Ifrane Palace. During these talks, which were accomplished with frankness and devoted essentially to the study of the Fez Plan, the Moroccan King and the Israeli Prime Minister made an in-depth examination of the situation in the Middle East as well as of the conditions of form and substance capable of establishing an effective peace in that part of the world.

His Majesty King Hassan II presented and explained the value of each element of the Fez Plan which is two-folded: On one hand: because it is the only document objectively valid since it could be the basis of a just and durable peace and, on the other hand, to form the object of an Arab consensus, excluding any other plan or project of peace.

As for Mr. Peres, he presented his observations on this Fez Plan, and he put forward propositions as concerns the conditions which he deems necessary to the establishment of peace.

Since this meeting had a purely exploratory meaning and never for a moment aimed at the start of negotiations, His Majesty King Hassan II will inform the Arab leaders and Mr. Peres will inform his Government of the points of view which developed during the course of the discussions.

SHULTZ PLAN (MARCH 4, 1988)

On March 4, 1988, United States Secretary of State George Shultz, partly in response to the intifada, put forward a plan for resolving the Arab-Israeli conflict. Shultz delivered a letter to Israeli Prime Minister Yitzhak Shamir. Similar letters also were delivered to Jordanian King Hussein, Syrian President Hafez al-Assad, and Egyptian President Hosni Mubarak. In the case of the West Bank and Gaza, the proposal called for transitional arrangements negotiations interlocked in timing and sequence with final status talks, based on UN Security Council Resolutions 242 and 338. The initiative was designed to produce direct, bilateral Arab-Israeli negotiations to achieve comprehensive peace based on the provisions and principles of United Nations Security Council Resolution 242. The United States supported a properly structured international conference that would launch a series of bilateral negotiations. All attendees at the conference would be required to accept United Nations Security Council Resolutions 242 and 338 and to renounce violence and terrorism. The conference would be specifically enjoined from intruding in the negotiations, imposing solutions or vetoing what had been agreed bilaterally. The Shultz plan was similar to previous United States peace initiatives in that it sought to achieve a comprehensive peace through direct, bilateral Arab-Israeli negotiations.

Reaction to the plan was generally negative. Shamir opposed it as he was adamantly against the idea of an international conference and felt the central concept was contrary to Camp David. The Palestinian leaders were concerned that they were the junior partner to Jordan. King Hussein was ambivalent. The Soviet Union thought the international conference was only symbolic and that they didn't have a real role in the negotiating process. Syria also opposed the initiative. Only Egypt's President Hosni Mubarak endorsed the plan.

SHULTZ LETTER TO PRIME MINISTER SHAMIR, MARCH 4, 1988

I set forth below the statement of understanding which I am convinced is necessary to achieve the prompt opening of negotiations on a comprehensive peace. This statement of understandings emerges from discussions held with you and other regional leaders. I look forward to the letter of reply of the Government of Israel in confirmation of this statement.

The agreed objective is a comprehensive peace providing for the security of all the states in the region and for the legitimate rights of the Palestinian people.

Negotiations will start on an early date certain between Israel and each of its neighbors which is willing to do so. These negotiations could begin by May 1, 1988. Each of these negotiations will be based on United Nations Security Council Resolution 242 and 338, in all their parts. The parties to each bilateral negotiation will determine the procedure and agenda at their negotiation. All participants in the negotiations must state their willingness to negotiate with one another.

As concerns negotiations between the Israeli delegation and the Jordanian-Palestinian delegation, negotiations will begin on arrangements for a transitional period, with the objective of completing them within six months. Seven months after transitional negotiations begin, final status negotiations will begin, with the objective of completing them within one year. These negotiations will be based on all the provisions and principles of Untied Nations Security Council Resolution 242. Final status talks will start before the transitional period begins. The transitional period will begin three months after the conclusion of the transitional agreement and will last for three years. The United States will participate in both negotiations and will promote their rapid conclusion. In particular, the United States will submit a draft agreement for the parties' consideration at the outset of the negotiations on transitional arrangements.

Two weeks before the opening of negotiations, an international conference will be held. The Secretary General of the United Nations will be asked to issue invitations to the parties involved in the Arab-Israeli conflict and the five permanent members of the United Nations Security Council. All participants in the conference must accept United Nations Security Council resolution 242 and 338, and renounce violence and terrorism. The parties to each bilateral negotiation may refer reports on the status of their negotiations to the conference, in a manner to be agreed. The conference will not be able to impose solutions or veto agreements reached.

Palestinian representation will be within the Jordanian-Palestinian delegation. The Palestinian issue will be addressed in the negotiations between the Jordanian-Palestinian and Israeli delegations. Negotiations between the Israeli delegation will proceed independently of any other negotiations.

This statement of understandings is an integral whole. The United States understands that your acceptance is dependent on the implementation of each element in good faith.

SHULTZ DEPARTURE STATEMENT, ISRAEL, MARCH 4, 1988

It is always good to be back in Israel. I have again had productive meetings with Prime Minister Shamir and Foreign Minister Peres.

I have reviewed the ideas which we are convinced can point the way to a negotiating process between Israel and its Arab Neighbors -- and ultimately to a comprehensive peace in the region. I have reviewed the same ideas with King Hussein yesterday, and later today I will be seeing President Asad. I will also bring President Mubarak up to date before leaving the region.

I am confident that the ideas we have discussed meet Israel's fundamental needs, as they do those of Jordan. The road we are suggesting is not without risks, but we have always known that there is no risk-free road to peace. I can assure you, however, that the United States will not allow Israel's security to be undermined. We believe that the real risk for Israel lies not in a process of seeking a peaceful future but in a future without peace.

I will go home now, and the Government of Israel will consider its response to ideas we've discussed. The issues are weighty and complex. They are not new, but we all agree that now they are more urgent. An opportunity is available to the leaders of this region which may not come again for some time.

"THIS IS THE PLAN" *WASHINGTON POST*, MARCH 18, 1988

There are few fixed rules for resolving conflicts. Each conflict has a unique history and unique characteristics. Each party to a conflict has its own dreams, concerns, and fears. The task is to find the right inducements to draw the parties off the battlefield and into the negotiating room. The success of negotiations is attributable not to a particular procedure chosen but to the readiness of the parties to exploit opportunities, confront hard choices, and make fair and mutual concessions.

In the Arab-Israeli conflict, negotiations work. They provide the means for parties to learn to deal with each other. They produce durable and realistic agreements that meet the fundamental concerns of the parties. Experience shows that Arabs and Israelis can make agreements and keep them.

The United States has launched an initiative designed to produce negotiations -- direct, bilateral Arab-Israeli negotiations to achieve comprehensive peace. Our concept is based on all the provisions and principles of UN Security Council Resolution 242, which is the internationally accepted framework for negotiations. In the case of the West Bank and Gaza, the initiative involves a two-stage interlocked set of negotiations designed to produce rapid and fundamental change in the way Arabs and Israelis relate to each other.

The United States is a firm and consistent supporter of direct, bilateral negotiations between Israel and all of its neighbors as the means to achieve a comprehensive peace. At the same time, the United States has always been willing to consider any approach that could lead to direct negotiations, including an international conference.

In recent months, some parties have focused on a specific kind of international conference -- one that would have an authoritative role or plenipotentiary powers. In January of this year, the United States vetoed a resolution it the UN Security Council that called upon the Secretary General to convene such a conference. The United States made clear its belief that this kind of conference would make real negotiations impossible. It would be a vehicle for avoiding meaningful negotiations, not promoting them.

The issue confronting the parties in the Middle East, therefore, is not whether an international conference should or should not be convened. That misses the point. The Arabs require a conference to launch negotiations; without a properly structured conference, there will be no negotiations. But the wrong kind of conference should never be convened. The United States will not attend that kind of conference. No sovereign state would agree to attend the kind of conference that would presume to pass judgment on issues of national security.

The issue is whether the moment is here to negotiate an end to the Arab-Israeli conflict, whether each party is ready and able to confront hard choices and make difficult decisions, and whether the requirements of the parties are amenable to a procedural blend that satisfies minimal demands.

The strength of the American approach is its integrity: no individual aspect of it can be extracted, finessed, or ignored without sacrificing its balance. The conference we support launches a series of bilateral negotiations and, thereafter, may receive reports from the parties on the status of negotiation, in a manner to be agreed by the parties. All conference attendees will be required to accept Security Council Resolutions 242 and 338 and to renounce violence and terrorism. The conference will be specifically enjoined from intruding in the negotiations, imposing solutions, or vetoing what had been agreed bilaterally.

The United States is committed to this integral concept for beginning direct, bilateral negotiations. We will not permit any aspect of our proposal to be eroded, compromised, or expanded beyond its meaning. In particular, we will not permit a conference to become authoritative or plenipotentiary, or to pass judgments on the negotiations, or to exceed its jurisdiction as agreed by the parties.

The ingredients for a peace process are present. There is an unacceptable and untenable status quo. There are competing parties willing to shed illusions and temper dreams to the underlying realities. And there are realistic and achievable ideas on the table that meet the fundamental concerns of everyone.

Our task is also clear. We must act with integrity, resolve, and tenacity to bring Arabs and Israelis off the battlefield and into negotiations. The initiative put forward by the United States -- two interlocked stages of direct negotiations launched by a properly structured international conference -- is realistic and compelling.

This is the moment for a historic breakthrough, and this is the plan. The time for decisions is now.

HUSSEIN'S RENUNCIATION OF THE CLAIM TO THE WEST BANK (JULY 31, 1988)

On July 31, 1988, in a nationally televised speech "to the Arab nation," King Hussein of Jordan declared that he was renouncing Jordan's claim of sovereignty to the West Bank territory that was annexed by his grandfather, King Abdullah, after the first Arab-Israeli War.

Since Israel's occupation of the West Bank in 1967, Jordan had continued to provide the administrative and legal services initiated after Jordan annexed the West Bank in 1950. After 1967, most West Bank schools were Jordanian financed and managed, residents were issued Jordanian passports, Jordanian dinars were accepted as currency, births and deaths were Jordanian registered, and West Bank Palestinian representatives consisted of half of Jordan's 60-member lower house of parliament. Jordan paid partial or full salaries for 21,000 teachers, health workers, and civil servants.

The King reaffirmed Jordan's commitment to the peace process and mentioned its contributions toward an international peace conference, the purpose of which is to achieve a just and comprehensive peace settlement to the Arab-Israeli conflict "and the settlement of the Palestinian problem in all its aspects..." But, in declaring that Jordan is not Palestine and that an independent Palestinian state would be established on the occupied territory after its liberation, he challenged those who had advocated the policy that Jordan was Palestine so there was no point in discussing self-determination for the Palestinians as their homeland existed in Jordan.

The PLO declared the independence of the Israeli-occupied territories. The Palestinian declaration of independence was later read by Yasser Arafat at a special Palestine National Congress meeting on November 15, 1988.

In the name of God, the merciful, the compassionate, and peace be upon his faithful Arab messenger. Brother citizens: I send you greetings and am pleased to address you in your cities and villages, in your camps and dwellings, in your factories, institutions, offices, and establishments. I would like to address your hearts and minds in all parts of our beloved Jordanian land.

This is all the more important at this juncture, when we have initiated -- after seeking God's help and after thorough and extensive study -- a series of measures to enhance Palestinian national orientation and highlight Palestinian identity; our goal is the benefit of the Palestinian cause and the Arab Palestinian people. Our decision, as you know, comes after 38 years of the unity of the two banks and 14 years after the Rabat summit resolution designating the PLO as the sole legitimate representative of the Palestinian people. It also comes 6 years after the Fez summit resolution that agreed unanimously on the establishment of an independent Palestinian state in the occupied West Bank and the Gaza Strip as one of the bases and results of the peaceful settlement.

We are certain our decision to initiate these measures does not come as a surprise. Many of you have anticipated it, and some of you have been calling for it for some time. As for its contents, it has been a topic of discussion and consideration for everyone since the Rabat summit. Nevertheless, some may wonder: Why now? Why today and not after the Rabat or Fez summits, for instance? To answer this question, we need to recall certain facts that preceded the Rabat resolution. We also need to recall consideration that led to the debate over the slogan-objective which the PLO raised and worked to gain Arab and international support for, namely, the establishment of an independent Palestinian state. This meant, in addition to the PLO's ambition to embody the Palestinian identity on Palestinian national soil, the separation of the West Bank from the

Hashemite Kingdom of Jordan. ...

Among these facts there was our 1972 proposal regarding our concept of alternatives, on which the relationship between Jordan on one hand and the West Bank and Gaza on the other may be based after their liberation. Among these alternatives was the establishment of a relationship of brotherhood and cooperation between the Hashemite Kingdom of Jordan and the independent Palestinian state in case the Palestinian people opt for that. Simply, this means that we declared our clear-cut position regarding our adherence to the Palestinian people's right to self-determination on their national soil, including their right to establish their own independent state, more than 2 years before the Rabat summit resolution. This will be our position until the Palestinian people achieve their complete national goals, God willing.

The relationship of the West Bank with the Hashemite Kingdom of Jordan in light of the PLO's call for the establishment of an independent Palestinian state, can be confined to two considerations. First, the principled consideration pertaining to the issue of Arab unity as a pan-Arab aim, to which the hearts of the Arab peoples aspire and which they want to achieve. Second, the political consideration pertaining to the extent of the Palestinian struggle's gain from the continuation of the legal relationship of the Kingdom's two banks. Our answer to the question now stems from these two considerations and the background of the clear-cut and firm Jordanian position toward the Palestine question, as we have shown.

Regarding the principled consideration, Arab unity between any two or more countries is an option of any Arab people. This is what we believe. Accordingly, we responded to the wish of the Palestinian people's representatives for unity with Jordan in 1950. From this premise, we respect the wish of the PLO, the sole and legitimate representative of the Palestinian people, to secede from us as an independent Palestinian state. We say that while we fully understand the situation. Despite this, Jordan will continue to take pride in carrying the message of the Great Arab Revolt, adhering to its principles, believing in the one Arab destiny, and abiding by the joint Arab action. ...

Of late, it has become clear that there is a general Palestinian and Arab orientation which believes in the need to highlight the Palestinian identity in full in all efforts and activities that are related to the Palestine question and its developments. It has also become obvious that there is a general conviction that maintaining the legal and administrative relationship with the West Bank -- and the consequent special Jordanian treatment of the brother Palestinians living under occupation through Jordanian institutions in the occupied territories -- goes against this orientation. It would be an obstacle to the Palestinian struggle which seeks to win international support for the Palestine question, considering that it is a just national issue of a people struggling against foreign occupation.

In view of this orientation, which was bound to stem from a purely Palestinian desire and an unflinching Arab determination to support the Palestine question, we have a duty to favorably respond to its requirements. First and last, we are part of our nation and we are eager to support its causes, foremost among which is the Palestine question. Since there is unanimous conviction that the struggle for liberating the occupied Palestinian territory can be bolstered by disengaging the legal and administrative relationship between the two banks, then we must perform our duty and do what is required of us. ...

As we favorably responded to the appeals made to us by Arab leaders at the Rabat summit of 1974 which asked us to continue to deal with the occupied West Bank through Jordanian institutions to support the steadfastness of brethren there, we today favorably respond to the desire of the PLO, the sole legitimate representative of the Palestinian people, and also to the Arab orientation regarding consecrating the purely Palestinian identity in all of its elements in terms of form and content. We beseech God to make this step of ours a qualitative addition to the growing struggle being waged by the Palestinian people for the sake of attaining liberation and independence.

Brother citizens, these are the reasons, the considerations, and the convictions that prompted us to respond favorably to the PLO's desire and to the general Arab orientation which is in harmony with this desire, as we cannot continue to maintain this undecided situation which serves neither Jordan nor the Palestine question. We had to go out of the tunnel of fears and doubts to the atmosphere of tranquillity and clarity where mutual confidence flourishes and blossoms into understanding, cooperation, and affection in favor of the Palestine question and also in favor of Arab unity -- which will remain a cherished objective sought and demanded by all Arab peoples.

However, it should be clear that our measures regarding the West Bank are connected only with the Palestinian territory and its people, and not the Jordanian citizens of Palestinian origin in the Hashemite Kingdom of Jordan. All of them have citizenship rights and commitments just like any other citizen regardless of his origin.

They are an integral part of the Jordanian state to which they belong, on whose soil they live and in whose life and various activities they participate. Jordan is not Palestine and the independent Palestinian state will be established on the occupied Palestinian territory after its liberation, God willing. On this territory the Palestinian identity will be embodied and the Palestinian struggle will blossom as confirmed by the blessed uprising of the Palestinian people under occupation. ...

O citizens, brother Palestinians in the occupied Palestinian territory, in order to eliminate any doubts that would be cast on our measures, we would like to stress to you that these measures do not mean the relinquishment of our pan-Arab duty toward the Arab-Israeli conflict or the Palestine question. These measures also do not mean a relinquishment of our belief in Arab unity. We have basically taken these measures, as I said, in response to the wish of the PLO, the sole and legitimate representative of the Palestinian people, and in response to the prevailing Arab conviction that such measures would contribute to supporting the Palestinian people's struggle and their blessed uprising.

Jordan will continue to support the Palestinian people's steadfastness and their valiant uprising in the occupied Palestinian territory within the limits of its capabilities. I will not forget to say that when we decided to cancel the Jordanian development plan in the occupied Palestinian territory within the limits of its capabilities. I will not forget to say that when we decided to cancel the Jordanian development plan in the occupied territories, at the same time we managed to contact the various friendly governments and the international institutions that expressed their desire to contribute to the plan. We urged them to continue to finance development projects in the occupied Palestinian territory through the concerned Palestinian circles.

Brothers, Jordan has not relinquished and will not relinquish its support for the Palestinian people until they achieve their national objectives, God willing. No one outside Palestine has ever had or will ever have connection with Palestine or with its cause that is stronger than the connection of Jordan or my family with it. This is on the one hand. On the other hand, Jordan is a confrontation state, and its border with Israel is longer than that of any other Arab state.

In fact, Jordan's border with Israel is longer than the borders of the West Bank and the Gaza Strip together with it. Jordan also will not relinquish its commitment to participation in the peace process. We contributed to the efforts to achieve an international unanimity on holding an international conference for peace in the Middle East to reach a just and comprehensive peaceful settlement to the Arab-Israeli conflict, and to reach a settlement of all aspects of the Palestine question. We have defined our stands in this regard, as everyone knows, through the six principles that we previously announced to the public. Jordan, brethren, is a basic party to the Arab-Israeli conflict and the peace process. It shoulders its national and pan-Arab responsibilities accordingly.

I thank you and I repeat by heartfelt wishes to you, beseeching Almighty God to help us, guide us, make us please Him, and to grant our Palestinian brothers victory and success. He is the best of helpers.

HAMAS CHARTER (AUGUST 18, 1988)

The Islamic Resistance Movement (IRM), HAMAS (Harakat al-Muqawama al-Islamiyya -- literally meaning "enthusiasm" or "zeal" in Arabic) -- the Palestinian Islamist organization -- was founded, according to its own official history, on December 14, 1987. Its Charter was published in August 1988. The ultimate goal of this movement is to establish an Islamic state in lands with Muslim populations, including Israel. This movement is an off-shoot of the Muslim Brotherhood whose presence in the Gaza Strip can be traced to 1928. As a component of the Muslim Brotherhood, HAMAS considers itself the most recent link in the long chain of the jihad against Zionist occupation. HAMAS was formed by a group of Gazans led by the Muslim cleric Sheikh Ahmed Ismail Yassin, an Islamist activist, former chairman of the Islamic Congress and the most powerful Brotherhood leader in Gaza. This initial group also included Dr. Abd al Aziz Rantisi, who took over the leadership of HAMAS after Sheikh Yassin began serving a life sentence in prison.

The Covenant states that HAMAS derives its ideological origin, its fundamental precepts and world view from Islam. HAMAS believes that the Palestinian problem is an Islamic problem and can only be solved from the Islamic perspective. The struggle against the Jewish occupation requires that Islamic education guide the umma (Muslim community), scholars, journalists and teachers, in order to eliminate "the effects of the Ideological Invasion that was brought about at the hands of the Orientalists and Missionaries." HAMAS is opposed to peace initiatives or solutions and international peace conferences. It considers relinquishing any part of Palestine as giving up part of its religion, and it sees no solution to the Palestinian problem "except by Jihad." The initiatives, proposals and international conferences are "a waste of time." Since the signing of the Israel-PLO Declaration of Principles (1993) HAMAS's goal has been to undermine the peace process and to replace the PLO at the leadership of the Palestinians. HAMAS has been viewed as the Islamic alternative to the secular and leftist PLO. HAMAS opposes any compromise which would permit a continuation of what it views as non-Muslim occupation of Muslim lands.

HAMAS denotes Jihad "for the liberation of all of Palestine" as a personal religious duty incumbent upon every Muslim. At the same time, it rejects any political arrangement that would entail the relinquishment of any part of Palestine. The central goal of HAMAS is the establishment of an Islamic state in all of Palestine. The immediate means to achieve this goal is the escalation of the intifada, and ultimately all-out Jihad, with the participation not only of Palestinian Muslims but of the entire Islamic world.

In the Name of Allah, the Merciful, the Compassionate ...

"Israel will rise and will remain erect until Islam eliminates it as it had eliminated its predecessors."

INTRODUCTION ... This is the Charter of the Islamic Resistance Movement (HAMAS) which will reveal its face, unveil its identity, state its position, clarify its purpose, discuss its hopes, call for support to its cause and reinforcement, and for joining its ranks. For our struggle against the Jews is extremely wide-ranging and grave, so much so that it will need all the loyal efforts we can wield, to be followed by further steps and reinforced by successive battalions from the multifarious Arab and Islamic world, until the enemies are defeated and Allah's victory prevails.

PART I: KNOWING THE MOVEMENT ·

Article One. The Islamic Resistance Movement draws its guidelines from Islam; derives from it its thinking, interpretations and views about existence, life and humanity; refers back to it for its conduct; and is inspired by it in whatever step it takes.

Article Two. The Islamic Resistance Movement is one of the wings of the Muslim Brothers in Palestine. The Muslim Brotherhood Movement is a world organization, the largest Islamic Movement in the modern era. ...

Article Three. The basic structure of the Islamic Resistance Movement consists of Muslims who are devoted to Allah and worship Him ....

Article Four. The Movement welcomes all Muslims who share its beliefs and thinking, commit themselves to its course of action, keep its secrets and aspire to join its ranks in order to carry out their duty. Allah will reward them.

Article Five. As the Movement adopts Islam as its way of life, its time dimension extends back as far as the birth of the Islamic Message and of the Righteous Ancestor. Its ultimate goal is Islam, the Prophet its model, the Quran its Constitution. ...

Article Six. The Islamic Resistance Movement is a distinct Palestinian Movement which owes its loyalty to Allah, derives from Islam its way of life and strives to raise the banner of Allah over every inch of Palestine. Only under the shadow of Islam could the members of all regions coexist in safety and security for their lives, properties and rights. In the absence of Islam, conflict arises, oppression reigns, corruption is rampant and struggles and wars prevail....

Article Seven. By virtue of the distribution of Muslims, who pursue the cause of the HAMAS, all over the globe, and strive for its victory, for the reinforcement of its positions and for the encouragement of its Jihad, the Movement is a universal one. ... HAMAS is one of the links in the Chain of Jihad in the confrontation with the Zionist invasion. It links up with the setting out of the Martyr Izz a-din al-Qassam and his brothers in the Muslim Brotherhood who fought the Holy War in 1936; it further relates to another link of the Palestinian Jihad and the Jihad and efforts of the Muslim Brothers during the 1948 War, and to the Jihad operations of the Muslim Brothers in 1968 and thereafter.

But even if the links have become distant from each other, and even if the obstacles erected by those who revolve in the Zionist orbit, aiming at obstructing the road before the Jihad fighters, have rendered the pursuance of Jihad impossible; nevertheless, the HAMAS has been looking forward to implement Allah's promise whatever time it might take. ...

PART II: OBJECTIVES

Article Nine. HAMAS finds itself at a period of time when Islam has waned away from the reality of life. For this reason, the checks and balances have been upset, concepts have become confused, and values have been transformed; evil has prevailed, oppression and obscurity have reigned; cowards have turned tigers, homelands have been usurped, people have been uprooted and are wandering all over the globe. The state of truth has disappeared and was replaced by the state of evil. Nothing has remained in its right place, for when Islam is removed from the scene, everything changes. These are the motives.

As to the objectives: discarding evil, crushing it and defeating it, so that truth may prevail, homelands revert, calls for prayer be heard from their mosques, announcing the reinstitution of the Muslim state. Thus, people and things will revert to their true place. ...

Article Ten. The Islamic Resistance Movement, while breaking its own path, will do its utmost to constitute at the same time a support to the weak, a defense to all the oppressed. It will spare no effort to implement the truth and abolish evil, in speech and in fact, both here and in any other location where it can reach out and exert influence.

PART III: STRATEGIES AND METHODS

Article Eleven. The Islamic Resistance Movement believes that the land of Palestine has been an Islamic Waqf throughout the generations and until the Day of Resurrection, no one can renounce it or part of it, or abandon it or part of it. No Arab country nor the aggregate of all Arab countries, and no Arab King or President nor all of them in the aggregate, have that right, nor has that right any organization or the aggregate of all organizations, be they Palestinian or Arab, because Palestine is an Islamic Waqf throughout all generations and to the Day or Resurrection. ...

Article Twelve. HAMAS regards Nationalism (Wataniyya) as part and parcel of the religious faith. Nothing is loftier or deeper in Nationalism than waging Jihad against the enemy and confronting him when he sets foot on the land of the Muslims. And this becomes an individual duty binding on every Muslim man and woman; a woman must go out and fight the enemy even without her husband's authorization, and a slave without his masters' permission.

Article Thirteen. [Peace] initiatives, the so-called peaceful solutions, and the international conferences to resolve the Palestinian problem, are all contrary to the beliefs of the Islamic Resistance Movement. For renouncing any part of Palestine means renouncing part of the religion; the nationalism of the Islamic Resistance Movement is part of its faith, the movement educates its members to adhere to its principles and to raise the banner of Allah over their homeland as they fight their Jihad. ...

From time to time a clamouring is voiced, to hold an International Conference in search for a solution to the problem. Some accept the idea, others reject it, for one reason or another, demanding the implementation of this or that condition, as a prerequisite for agreeing to convene the Conference or for participating in it. But the Islamic Resistance Movement, which is aware of the parties to this conference, and of their past and present positions towards the problems of the Muslims, does not believe that those conferences are capable of responding to demands, or of restoring rights or doing justice to the oppressed. Those conferences are no more than a means to appoint the nonbelievers as arbitrators in the lands of Islam. ...

There is no solution to the Palestinian problem except by Jihad. The initiatives, proposals and International Conferences are but a waste of time, an exercise in futility. The Palestinian people are too noble to have their future, their right and their destiny submitted to a vain game. ...

Article Fourteen. The problem of the liberation of Palestine relates to three circles: the Palestinian, the Arab and the Islamic. Each one of these circles has a role to play in the struggle against Zionism and it has duties to fulfill. It would be an enormous mistake and an abysmal act of ignorance to disregard anyone of these circles. For Palestine is an Islamic land where the First Qibla and the third holiest site are located. That is also the place whence the Prophet, be Allah's prayer and peace upon him, ascended to Heavens. ... In consequence of this state of affairs, the liberation of that land is an individual duty binding on all Muslims everywhere. This is the base on which all Muslims have to regard the problem; this has to be understood by all Muslims. When the problem is dealt with on this basis, where the full potential of the three circles is mobilized, then the current circumstances will change and the day of liberation will come closer. ...

Article Fifteen. When our enemies usurp some Islamic lands, Jihad becomes a duty binding on all Muslims. In order to face the usurpation of Palestine by the Jews, we have no escape from raising the banner of Jihad. This would require the propagation of Islamic consciousness among the masses on all local, Arab and Islamic levels. We must spread the spirit of Jihad among the Umma, clash with the enemies and join the ranks of the Jihad fighters.

The 'ulama as well as educators and teachers, publicity and media men as well as the masses of the educated, and especially the youth and the elders of the Islamic Movements, must participate in this raising of consciousness. There is no escape from introducing fundamental changes in educational curricula in order to cleanse them from all vestiges of the ideological invasion which has been brought about by orientalists and missionaries. That invasion had begun overtaking this area following the defeat of the Crusader armies by Salah a-Din el Ayyubi. The Crusaders had understood that they had no way to vanquish the Muslims unless they prepared the grounds for that with an ideological invasion which would confuse the thinking of Muslims, revile their heritage, discredit their ideals to be followed by a military invasion. ... Imperialism has been instrumental in boosting the ideological invasion and deepening its roots, and it is still pursuing this goal. All this had paved the way to the loss of Palestine. We must imprint on the minds of generations of Muslims that the Palestinian problem is a religious one, to be dealt with on this premise. It includes Islamic holy sites such as the Aqsa Mosque, which is inexorably linked to the Holy Mosque as long as the Heaven and earth will exist, to the journey of the Messenger of Allah, be Allah's peace and blessing upon him, to it, and to his ascension from it. ...

Article Sixteen. We must accord the Islamic generations in our area an

Islamic education based on the implementation of religious precepts, on the conscientious study of the Book of Allah; on the Study of the Prophetic Tradition, on the study of Islamic history and heritage from its reliable sources, under the guidance of experts and scientists; and on singling out the paths which constitute for the Muslims sound concepts of thinking and faith. It is also necessary to study conscientiously the enemy and its material and human potential; to detect its weak and strong spots, and to recognize the powers that support it and stand by it. At the same time, we must be aware of current events, follow the news and study the analyses and commentaries on it, together with drawing plans for the present and the future and examining every phenomenon, so that every Muslim, fighting Jihad, could live out his era aware of his objective, his goals, his way and the things happening round him. ...

Article Seventeen. The Muslim women have a no lesser role than that of men in the war of liberation; they manufacture men and play a great role in guiding and educating the generation. ...

Article Eighteen. The women in the house and the family of Jihad fighters, whether they are mothers or sisters, carry out the most important duty of caring for the home and raising the children upon the moral concepts and values which derive from Islam; and of educating their sons to observe the religious injunctions in preparation for the duty of Jihad awaiting them. ...

Article Nineteen. Art has rules and criteria by which one can know whether it is Islamic or Jahiliyya art. The problems of Islamic liberation underlie the need for Islamic art which could lift the spirit, and instead of making one party triumph over the other, would lift up all parties in harmony and balance. ...

Article Twenty Two. The enemies have been scheming for a long time, and they have consolidated their schemes, in order to achieve what they have achieved. They took advantage of key-elements in unfolding events, and accumulated a huge and influential material wealth which they put to the service of implementing their dream. This wealth [permitted them to] take over control of the world media such as news agencies, the press, publication houses, broadcasting and the like. ... They also used the money to establish clandestine organizations which are spreading around the world, in order to destroy societies and carry out Zionist interests. Such organizations are: the Free Masons, Rotary Clubs, Lions Clubs, B'nai B'rith and the like. All of them are destructive spying organizations. They also used the money to take over control of the Imperialist states and made them colonize many countries in order to exploit the wealth of those countries and spread their corruption therein.

As regards local and world wars, it has come to pass and no one objects, that they stood behind World War I, so as to wipe out the Islamic Caliphate. They collected material gains and took control of many sources of wealth. They obtained the Balfour Declaration and established the League of Nations in order to rule the world by means of that organization. They also stood behind World War II, where they collected immense benefits from trading with war materials, and prepared for the establishment of their state. They inspired the establishment of the United Nations and the Security Council to replace the League of Nations, in order to rule the world by their intermediary. There was no war that broke out anywhere without their fingerprints on it. ...

Article Twenty Three. The HAMAS views the other Islamic movements with respect and appreciation. Even when it differs from them in one aspect or another or on one concept or another, it agrees with them in other aspects and concepts. It reads those movements as included in the framework of striving as long as they hold sound intentions and abide by their devotion to Allah, and as long as their conduct remains within the perimeter of the Islamic circle. All the fighters of Jihad have their reward. ...

Article Twenty Six. The HAMAS, while it views positively the Palestinian National Movements which do not owe their loyalty to the East or to the West, does not refrain from debating unfolding events regarding the Palestinian problem, on the local and international scenes. These debates are realistic and expose the extent to which [these developments] go along with, or contradict, national interests as viewed from the Islamic vantage point.

Article Twenty Seven. The PLO is among the closest to the HAMAS, for its constitutes a father, a brother, a relative, a friend. Can a Muslim turn away from his father, his brother, his relative or his friend? Our homeland is one, our calamity is one, our destiny is one and our enemy is common to both of us. Under the influence of the circumstances which surrounded the founding of the PLO, and the ideological confusion which prevails in the Arab world as a result of the ideological invasion which has swept the Arab world since the rout of the Crusades, and which has been reinforced by Orientalism and the Christian Mission, the PLO has adopted the idea of a Secular State, and so we think of it. Secular thought is diametrically opposed to religious thought. Thought is the basis for positions, for modes of conduct and for resolutions. Therefore, in spite of our appreciation for the PLO and its possible transformation in the future, and despite the fact that we do not denigrate its role in the Arab-Israeli conflict, we cannot substitute it for the Islamic nature of Palestine by adopting secular thought. For the Islamic nature of Palestine is part of our religion, and anyone who neglects his religion is bound to lose. ...

When the PLO adopts Islam as the guideline for life, then we shall become its soldiers, the fuel of its fire which will burn the enemies. And until that happens, and we pray to Allah that it will happen soon, the position of the HAMAS towards the PLO is one of a son towards his father, a brother towards his brother, and a relative towards his relative who suffers the other's pain when a thorn hits him, who supports the other in the Confrontation with the enemies and who wishes him divine guidance and integrity of conduct. ...

Article Twenty-Eight. The Zionist invasion is a mischievous one. It does not hesitate to take any road, or to pursue all despicable and repulsive means to fulfill its desires. It relies to a great extent, for its meddling and spying activities, on the clandestine organizations which it has established, such as the Free Masons, Rotary Clubs, Lions, and other spying associations. All those secret organizations, some which are overt, act for the interests of Zionism and under its directions, strive to demolish societies, to destroy values, to wreck answerableness, to totter virtues and to wipe out Islam. It stands behind the diffusion of drugs and toxics of all kinds in order to facilitate its control and expansion.

The Arab states surrounding Israel are required to open their borders to the Jihad fighters, the sons of the Arab and Islamic peoples, to enable them to play their role and to join their efforts to those of their brothers among the Muslim Brothers in Palestine.

The other Arab and Islamic states are required, at the very least, to facilitate the movement of the Jihad fighters from and to them. ...

Israel, by virtue of its being Jewish and of having a Jewish population, defies Islam and the Muslims. ...

Article Thirty. Men of letters, members of the intelligentsia, media people, preachers, teachers and educators and all different sectors in the Arab and Islamic world, are all called upon to play their role and to carry out their duty in view of the wickedness of Zionist invasion, of its penetration into many countries, and its control over material means and the media, with all the ramifications thereof in most countries of the world. Jihad means not only carrying arms and denigrating the enemies. Uttering positive words, writing good articles and useful books, and lending support and assistance, all that too is Jihad in the path of Allah, as long as intentions are sincere to make Allah's banner supreme. ...

Article Thirty One. HAMAS is a humane movement, which cares for human rights and is committed to the tolerance inherent in Islam as regards attitudes towards other religions. It is only hostile to those who are hostile towards it, or stand in its way in order to disturb its moves or to frustrate its efforts.

Under the shadow of Islam it is possible for the members of the three religions: Islam, Christianity and Judaism to coexist in safety and security. Safety and security can only prevail under the shadow of Islam, and recent and ancient history is the best witness to that effect. The members of other religions must desist from struggling against Islam over sovereignty in this region. For if they were to gain the upper hand, fighting, torture and uprooting would follow; they would be fed up with each other, to say nothing of members of other religions. The past and the present are full of evidence to that effect.

Islam accords his rights to everyone who has rights and averts aggression against the rights of others. The Nazi Zionist practices against our people will not last the lifetime of their invasion, for "States built upon oppression last only one hour, states based upon justice will last until the hour of Resurrection." ...

Article Thirty Two. World Zionism and Imperialist forces have been attempting, with smart moves and considered planning, to push the Arab countries, one after another, out of the circle of conflict with Zionism, in order, ultimately, to isolate the Palestinian People. Egypt has already been cast out of the conflict, to a very great extent through the treacherous Camp David Accords, and she has been trying to drag other countries into similar agreements in order to push them out of the circle of conflict.

HAMAS is calling upon the Arab and Islamic peoples to act seriously and tirelessly in order to frustrate that dreadful scheme and to make the masses aware of the danger of coping out of the circle of struggle with Zionism. Today it is Palestine and tomorrow it may be another country or other countries. For Zionist scheming has no end, and after Palestine they will covet expansion from the Nile to the Euphrates. Only when they have completed digesting the area on which they will have laid their hand, they will look forward to more expansion, etc. Their scheme has been laid out in the Protocols of the Elders of Zion, and their present [conduct] is the best proof of what is said there.

Leaving the circle of conflict with Israel is a major act of treason and it will bring curse on its perpetrators. ...

We have no escape from pooling together all the forces and energies to face this despicable Nazi-Tatar invasion. Otherwise we shall witness the loss of countries, the uprooting of their inhabitants, the spreading of corruption on earth and the destruction of all religious values. Let every person realize that he is accountable to Allah. ...

Within the circle of the conflict with world Zionism, the HAMAS regards itself the spearhead and the avant-garde. It joins its efforts to all those who are active on the Palestinian scene, but more steps need to be taken by the Arab and Islamic peoples and Islamic associations throughout the Arab and Islamic world in order to make possible the next round with the Jews, the merchants of war.

Article Thirty Three. The HAMAS sets out from these general concepts which are consistent and in accordance with the rules of the universe, and gushes forth in the river of Fate in its confrontation and Jihad waging against the enemies, in defense of the Muslim human being, of Islamic Civilization and of the Islamic Holy Places, primarily the Blessed Aqsa Mosque. This, for the purpose of calling upon the Arab and Islamic peoples as well as their governments, popular and official associations, to fear Allah in their attitude towards and dealings with HAMAS, and to be, in accordance with Allah's will, its supporters and partisans who extend assistance to it and provide it with reinforcement after reinforcement, until the Decree of Allah is fulfilled, the ranks are over-swollen, Jihad fighters join other Jihad fighters, and all this accumulation sets out from everywhere in the Islamic world, obeying the call of duty, and intoning "Come on, join Jihad!" ...

PART FIVE: THE TESTIMONY OF HISTORY

Article Thirty Four. Palestine is the navel of earth, the convergence of continents, the object of greed for the greedy, since the dawn of history. ...

The greedy have coveted Palestine more than once and they raided it with armies in order to fulfill their covetousness. Multitudes of Crusades descended on it, carrying their faith with them and waving their Cross. They were able to defeat the Muslims for a long time, and the Muslims were not able to redeem it until they sought the protection of their religious banner; then, they unified their forces, sang the praise of their God and set out for Jihad under the Command of Saladin al-Ayyubi, for the duration of nearly two decades, and then the obvious conquest took place when the Crusaders were defeated and Palestine was liberated. ...

This is the only way to liberation, there is no doubt in the testimony of history. That is one of the rules of the universe and one of the laws of existence. Only iron can blunt iron, only the true faith of Islam can vanquish their false and falsified faith. Faith can only be fought by faith. Ultimately victory is reserved to the truth, and truth is victorious. ...

Article Thirty Five. HAMAS takes a serious look at the defeat of the Crusades at the hand of Saladin al-Ayyubi and the rescue of Palestine from their domination; at the defeat of the Tatars at Ein Jalut where their spine was broken by Qutuz and Al-Dhahir Baibars, and the Arab world was rescued from the sweep of the Tatars which ruined all aspects of human civilization. HAMAS has learned from these lessons and examples, that the current Zionist invasion had been preceded by a Crusader invasion from the West; and another one, the Tatars, from the East. And exactly as the Muslims had faced those invasions and planned their removal and defeat, they are able to face the Zionist invasion and defeat it. This will not be difficult for Allah if our intentions are pure and our determination is sincere; if the Muslims draw useful lessons from the experiences of the past, and extricate themselves for the vestiges of the ideological onslaught; and if they follow the traditions of Islam.
EPILOGUE.

Article Thirty Six. The HAMAS, while breaking its path, reiterates time and again to all members of our people and the Arab and Islamic peoples, that it does not seek fame for itself nor material gains, or social status. Nor is it directed against any one member of our people in order to compete with him or replace him. There is nothing of that at all. It will never set out against any Muslims or against the non-Muslims who make peace with it, here or anywhere else. It will only be of help to all associations and organizations which act against the Zionist enemy and those who revolve in its orbit.

HAMAS posits Islam as a way of life, it is its faith and its yardstick for judging. Whoever posits Islam as a way of life, anywhere, and regardless of whether it is an organization, a state, or any other group, Hamas are its soldiers, nothing else.

We implore Allah to guide us, to guide through us and to decide between us and our folk with truth. ...

PALESTINE NATIONAL COUNCIL, ALGIERS (NOVEMBER 15, 1988)

On November 15, 1988, at the session of the Palestine National Council in Algiers, Algeria, PLO Chairman Yasser Arafat issued a formal "Declaration of Independence for the State of Palestine".

Arafat asserted that there existed an eternal bond between the land of Palestine, its people, and their history. That, despite being deprived of their political independence, Palestinian self-determination was rooted in their history as a nation as well as in United Nations General Assembly Resolution 181 (II), which partitioned Palestine into one Arab and one Jewish state. Arafat noted that "by virtue of natural, historical, and legal rights ... and relying on the authority bestowed by international legitimacy as embodied in the resolutions of the United Nations since 1947.... The Palestine National Council, in the name of God, and in the name of the Palestinian Arab people, hereby proclaims the establishment of the State of Palestine on our Palestinian territory with its capital Jerusalem."

In a political communique issued the same day the Palestine National Council formally committed the PLO to arrive at a comprehensive settlement with Israel that involved a two-state solution. The PNC affirmed its support for an international peace conference based on United Nations Security Council Resolutions 242 and 338; Israeli withdrawal from all Arab territories occupied since 1967, including Arab Jerusalem; the annulment of all measures instituted by the Israeli government during occupation; questions of Palestinian refugees to be settled in accordance with relevant United Nations resolutions; and Security Council guarantees for security and peace between all the states concerned, including that of Palestine.

The PNC meeting occurred as the intifada had thrust the Palestinian issue to the center of international attention. Then, on July 31, 1988, King Hussein renounced Jordan's claim to the West Bank, followed by an announcement that Jordan would no longer be party to future joint Palestinian-Jordanian delegations.

The Declaration received wide attention. Israel and the United States rejected it and the United States continued to refuse to open a direct dialogue with the PLO. It was not until after Arafat's December 13, 1988 address to the UN General Assembly and his subsequent press statement clarifying the PLO's position that the United States lifted its ban on dealing with the PLO.

In the name of God, the Compassionate, the Merciful.

Palestine, the land of the three monotheistic faiths, is where the Palestinian Arab people was born, on which it grew, developed, and excelled. The Palestinian people was never separated from or diminished in its integral bonds with Palestine. Thus the Palestinian Arab people ensured for itself an everlasting union between itself, its land, and its history.

Resolute throughout that history, the Palestinian Arab people forged its national identity, rising even to unimagined levels in its defense as invasion, the design of others, and the appeal special to Palestine's ancient and luminous place on that eminence where powers and civilizations are joined.... All this intervened thereby to deprive the people of its political independence. Yet the undying connection between Palestine and its people secured for the land its character and for the people its national genius.

Nourished by an unfolding series of civilizations and cultures, inspired by a heritage rich in variety and kind, the Palestinian Arab people added to its stature by consolidating a union between itself and its patrimonial land. The call went out from temple, church, and mosque to praise the Creator, to celebrate compassion, and peace was indeed the message of Palestine. And in generation after generation, the Palestinian Arab people gave of itself unsparingly in the valiant battle for liberation and homeland. For what has been the unbroken chain of our people's rebellions but the heroic embodiment of our will for national independence? And so the people were sustained in the struggle to stay and to prevail.

When in the course of modern times a new order of values was declared with norms and values fair for all, it was the Palestinian Arab people that had been excluded from the destiny of all other peoples by a hostile array of local and foreign powers. Yet again had unaided justice been revealed as insufficient to drive the world's history along its preferred course.

And it was the Palestinian people, already wounded in its body, that was submitted to yet another type of occupation over which floated the falsehood that "Palestine was a land without people." This notion was foisted upon some in the world, whereas in Article 22 of the Covenant of the League of Nations (1919) and in the Treaty of Lausanne (1923), the community of nations had recognized that all the Arab territories, including Palestine, of the formerly Ottoman provinces were to have granted to them their freedom as provisionally independent nations.

Despite the historical injustice inflicted on the Palestinian Arab people resulting in their dispersion and depriving them of their right to self-determination, following upon UN General Assembly Resolution 181 (1947), which partitioned Palestine into two states, one Arab, one Jewish, yet it is this resolution that still provides those conditions of international legitimacy that ensure the right of the Palestinian Arab people to sovereignty and national independence.

By stages, the occupation of Palestine and parts of other Arab territories by Israeli forces, the willed dispossession and expulsion from their ancestral homes of the majority of Palestine's civilian inhabitants was achieved by organized terror; those Palestinians who remained, as a vestige subjugated in its homeland, were persecuted and forced to endure the destruction of their national life.

Thus were principles of international legitimacy violated. Thus were the Charter of the United Nations and its resolutions disfigured, for they had recognized the Palestinian Arab people's national rights, including the Right of Return, the Right to Independence, the Right to Sovereignty over territory and homeland.

In Palestine and on its perimeters, in exile distant and near, the Palestinian Arab people never faltered and never abandoned its conviction in its rights of return and independence. Occupation, massacres, and dispersion achieved no gain in the unabated Palestinian consciousness of self and political identity, as Palestinians went forward with their destiny, undeterred and unbowed. And from out of the long years of trial in evermounting struggle, the Palestinian political identity emerged further consolidated and confirmed. And the collective Palestinian national will forged itself in a political embodiment, the Palestine Liberation Organization, its sole, legitimate representative, recognized by the world community as a whole, as well as by related regional and international institutions. Standing on the very rock of conviction in the Palestinian people's inalienable rights, and on the ground of Arab national consensus, and of international legitimacy, the PLO led the campaigns of its great people, molded into unity and powerful resolve, one and indivisible in the triumphs, even as it suffered massacres and confinement within and without its home. And so Palestinian resistance was clarified and raised into the forefront of Arab and world awareness, as the struggle of the Palestinian Arab people achieved unique prominence among the world's liberation movements in the modern era.

The massive national uprising, the *intifadah*, now intensifying in cumulative scope and power on occupied Palestinian territories, as well as the unflinching resistance of the refugee camps outside the homeland, have elevated consciousness of the Palestinian truth and right into still higher realms of comprehension and actuality. Now at last the curtain has been dropped around a whole epoch of prevarication and negation. The *Intifadah* has set siege to the mind of official Israel, which has for too long relied exclusively upon myth and terror to deny Palestinian existence altogether. Because of the Intifadah and its revolutionary irreversible impulse, the history of Palestine has therefore arrived at a decisive juncture.

Whereas the Palestinian people reaffirms most definitely its inalienable rights in the land of its patrimony:

Now by virtue of natural, historical, and legal rights and the sacrifices of successive generations who gave of themselves in defense of the freedom and independence of their homeland;

In pursuance of resolutions adopted by Arab summit conferences and relying on the authority bestowed by international legitimacy as embodied in the resolutions of the United Nations Organization since 1947;

And in exercise by the Palestinian Arab people of its rights to self-determination, political independence, and sovereignty over its territory;

The Palestine National Council, in the name of God, and in the name of the Palestinian Arab people, hereby proclaims the establishment of the State of

Palestine on our Palestinian territory with its capital Jerusalem (Al-Quds Ash-Sharif).

The State of Palestine is the state of Palestinians wherever they may be. the state is for them to enjoy in it their collective national and cultural identity, theirs to pursue in it a complete equality of rights. In it will be safeguarded their political and religious convictions and their human dignity by means of a parliamentary democratic system of governance, itself based on freedom of expression and the freedom to form parties. The rights of minorities will duly be respected by the majority, as minorities must abide by decisions of the majority. Governance will be based on principles of social justice, equality and nondiscrimination in public rights on grounds of race, religion, color, or sex under the aegis of a constitution which ensures the role of law and an independent judiciary. Thus shall these principles allow no departure from Palestine's age-old spiritual and civilizational heritage of tolerance and religious co-existence.

The State of Palestine is an Arab state, an integral and indivisible part of the Arab nation, at one with that nation in heritage and civilization, with it also in its aspiration for liberation, progress, democracy, and unity. The State of Palestine affirms its obligation to abide by the Charter of the League of Arab States, whereby the coordination of the Arab states with each other shall be strengthened. It calls upon Arab compatriots to consolidate and enhance the emergence in reality of our State, to mobilize potential, and to intensify efforts whose goal is to end Israeli occupation.

The State of Palestine proclaims its commitment to the principles and purposes of the United Nations, and to the Universal Declaration of Human Rights. It proclaims its commitment as well to the principles and policies of the Non-Aligned Movement.

It further announces itself to be a peace-loving state, in adherence to the principles of peaceful co-existence. It will join with all states and peoples in order to assure a permanent peace based upon justice and the respect of rights so that humanity's potential for well-being may be assured, an earnest competition for excellence be maintained, and in which confidence in the future will eliminate fear for those who are just and for whom justice is the only recourse.

In the context of its struggle for peace in the land of love and peace, the State of Palestine calls upon the United Nations to bear special responsibility for the Palestinian Arab people and its homeland. It calls upon all peace- and freedom-loving peoples and states to assist it in the attainment of its objectives, to provide it with security, to alleviate the tragedy of its people, and to help to terminate Israel's occupation of the Palestinian territories.

The State of Palestine herewith declares that it believes in the settlement of regional and international disputes by peaceful means, in accordance with the UN Charter and resolutions. Without prejudice to its natural right to defend its territorial integrity and independence, it therefore rejects the threat or use of force, violence, and terrorism against its territorial integrity, or political independence, as it also rejects their use against the territorial integrity of other states.

Therefore, on this day unlike all others, 15 November, 1988, as we stand at the threshold of a new dawn, in all honor and modesty we humbly bow to the sacred spirits of our fallen ones, Palestinian and Arab, by the purity of whose sacrifice for the homeland our sky has been illuminated and our land given life. Our hearts are lifted up and irradiated by the light emanating from the much blessed *intifadah*, from those who have endured and have fought the fight of the camps, of dispersion, of exile, from those who have borne the standard of freedom, our children, our aged, our youth, our prisoners, detainees, and wounded, all those whose ties to our sacred soil are confirmed in camp, village, and town. We render special tribute to that brave Palestinian woman, guardian of sustenance and life, keeper of our people's perennial flame. To the souls of our sainted martyrs, to the whole of our Palestinian Arab people, to all free and honorable peoples everywhere, we pledge that our struggle shall be continued until the occupation ends, and the foundation of our sovereignty and independence shall be fortified accordingly.

Therefore, we call upon our great people to rally to the banner of Palestine, to cherish and defend it, so that it may forever be the symbol of our freedom and dignity in that homeland, which is a homeland for the free, now and always.

In the name of God, the Compassionate, the Merciful.

"Say: 'O god, Master of the Kingdom, Thou givest the Kingdom to whom Thou wilt, and seizest the Kingdom from whom Thou wilt, and Thou abasest whom Thou wilt; in Thy hand is the good; Thou art powerful over everything."

Sadaqa Allahu al-'Azim

STOCKHOLM DECLARATION (DECEMBER 7, 1988)

In an attempt to initiate discussions between the Palestine Liberation Organization and American Jews, Swedish Foreign Minister Sten Anderson contacted the International Center for Peace in the Middle East in Tel Aviv and arranged for a group of five American Jews to meet with the Chairman of the PLO's foreign affairs committee, Khalid al-Hassan. The intent of the American Jewish group was to demonstrate to the American government that there was little reason not to enter into talks with the PLO. Yasser Arafat met with them in Stockholm and a statement was made public on December 7, 1988. The chairman of the Conference of Presidents of Major American Jewish Organizations, Morris Abram, accused the American Jews who signed the Stockholm Declaration of being "willing dupes" who were used by Arafat. United States Secretary of State George Shultz stated that his government still did not believe that the PLO had met the conditions necessary for discussions.

The Palestine National Council met in Algiers from 12 to 15 November 1988, and announced the Declaration of Independence which proclaimed the State of Palestine, and issued a political statement.

The following explanation was given by the representatives of the PLO of certain important points in the Palestinian Declaration of Independence and the political statement adopted by the PNC in Algiers.

Affirming the principle incorporated in those UN resolutions, which call for a two-state solution of Israel and Palestine, the PNC: 1. Agree to enter into peace negotiations at an international conference under the auspices of the U.N. with the participation of the permanent members of the Security Council and the PLO as the sole legitimate representative of the Palestinian people, on an equal footing with the other parties to the conflict; such an international conference to be held on the basis of UN Resolution 242 and 338 and the right of the Palestinian people to self-determination, without external interference as provided in the UN Charter, including the right to an independent state, which conference should resolve the Palestinian problem in all its aspects. 2. Established the independent State of Palestine and accepted the existence of Israel as a state in the region. 3. Declared its rejection and condemnation of terrorism in all its forms, including state terrorism. 4. Called for a solution to the Palestinian refugee problem in accordance with international law and practices and relevant UN resolutions (including right of return or compensation).

The American personalities strongly supported and applauded the Palestinian Declaration of Independence and the Political Statement adopted in Algiers and felt there was no further impediment to a direct dialogue between the United States Government and the PLO.

UNITED STATES DIALOGUE WITH THE PLO (DECEMBER 14, 1988)

As part of the Sinai II Accords process, a Memorandum of Agreement between the Governments of Israel and the United States, inter alia, spelled out the United States position concerning dealings with the PLO: "The United States will continue to adhere to its present policy with respect to the Palestine Liberation Organization, whereby it will not recognize or negotiate with the Palestine Liberation Organization so long as the Palestine Liberation Organization does not recognize Israel's right to exist and does not accept Security Council Resolutions 242 and 338." Later, in the Carter Administration, renunciation of terrorism was added to the requirements. In December 1988, Yasser Arafat, in a speech to the United Nations suggested that the PLO had decided to meet these requirements. But, the statement was not unambiguous. On December 14, Arafat, in a press conference in Geneva, Switzerland, clarified his position.

Let me highlight my views before you. Our desire for peace is a strategy and not an interim tactic. We are bent on peace come what may, come what may.

Our statehood provides salvation to the Palestinians and peace to both Palestinians and Israelis.

Self-determination means survival for the Palestinians and our survival does not destroy the survival of the Israelis as their rulers claim.

Yesterday in my speech I made reference to United Nations Resolution 181 as the basis for Palestinian independence. I also made reference to our acceptance of Resolution 242 and 338 as the basis for negotiations with Israel within the framework of the international conference. These three resolutions were endorsed by our Palestine National Council session in Algiers.

In my speech also yesterday, it was clear that we mean our people's rights to freedom and national independence, according to Resolution 181, and the right of all parties concerned in the Middle East conflict to exist in peace and security, and, as I have mentioned, including the state of Palestine, Israel and other neighbors, according to the Resolution 242 and 338.

As for terrorism, I renounced it yesterday in no uncertain terms, and yet, I repeat for the record. I repeat for the record that we totally and absolutely renounce all forms of terrorism, including individual, group and state terrorism.

Between Geneva and Algiers, we have made our position crystal clear. Any more talk such as "The Palestinians should give more" -- you remember this slogan? -- or "It is not enough" or "The Palestinians are engaging in propaganda games and public-relations exercises" will be damaging and counterproductive.

Enough is enough. Enough is enough. Enough is enough. All remaining matters should be discussed around the table and within the international conference.

Let it be absolutely clear that neither Arafat, nor any for that matter, can stop the intifada, the uprising. The intifada will come to an end only when practical and tangible steps have been taken towards the achievement of our national aims and establishment of our independent Palestinian state.

In this context, I expect the E.E.C. to play a more effective role in promoting peace in our region. They have a political responsibility, they have a moral responsibility, and they can deal with it.

Finally, I declare before you and I ask you to kindly quote me on that: We want peace. We want to live in our Palestinian state, and let live. Thank you.

In response, the United States announced that it was prepared to hold a substantive dialogue through U.S. Ambassador to Tunisia, Robert Pelletreau.

The Palestine Liberation Organization today issued a statement in which it accepted U.N. Security Council Resolutions 242 and 338, recognized Israel's right to exist in peace and security and renounced terrorism. As a result, the United States is prepared for a substantive dialogue with P.L.O. representatives.

I am designating our Ambassador to Tunisia as the only authorized channel for that dialogue. The objective of the United States remains as always, a comprehensive peace in the Middle East. In that light, I view this development as one more step toward the beginning of direct negotiations between the parties which alone can lead to such a peace.

Nothing here may be taken to imply an acceptance or recognition by the United States of an independent Palestinian state. The position of the U.S. is that the status of the West Bank and Gaza cannot be determined by unilateral acts of either side, but only through a process of negotiations. The United States does not recognize the declaration of an independent Palestinian state.

It is also important to emphasize that the United States commitment to the security of Israel remains unflinching.

GOVERNMENT OF ISRAEL PEACE INITIATIVE (MAY 14, 1989)

During a visit to Washington between April 12 and 16, 1989 Israeli Prime Minister Yitzhak Shamir, prodded by the Bush administration, offered a peace proposal containing several elements: Israel, Egypt, and the United States would renew their commitment to Camp David and peace; the United States and Egypt would ask the Arab states to end their hostility to Israel and accept negotiations; the United States would lead an international effort to solve the Palestine refugee problem; and Palestinians from the West Bank and Gaza Strip would be elected to form a delegation to negotiate an interim agreement and then a final settlement with Israel. The initiative was formulated by Shamir and Yitzhak Rabin and represented the consensus of Israel's national unity government. On May 14, 1989, the Israeli government formally approved the proposal to initiate negotiations between Israel and Palestinian representatives.

GENERAL: 1. This document presents the principles of a political initiative of the Government of Israel which deals with the continuation of the peace process; the termination of the state of war with the Arab states; a solution for the Arabs of Judea, Samaria and the Gaza district; peace with Jordan; and a resolution of the problem of the residents of the refugee camps in Judea, Samaria and the Gaza district. ...

BASIC PREMISES: 3. The initiative is founded upon the assumption that there is a national consensus for it on the basis of the basic guidelines of the Government of Israel, including the following points: a) Israel yearns for peace and the continuation of the political process by means of direct negotiations based on the principles of the Camp David Accords. b) Israel opposes the establishment of an additional Palestinian state in the Gaza district and in the area between Israel and Jordan. c) Israel will not conduct negotiations with the

PLO. d) There will be no change in the status of Judea, Samaria and Gaza other than in accordance with the basic guidelines of the Government.

SUBJECTS TO BE DEALT WITH IN THE PEACE PROCESS: 4. a) Israel views as important that the peace between Israel and Egypt, based on the Camp David Accords, will serve as a cornerstone for enlarging the circle of peace in the region, and calls for a common endeavor for the strengthening of the peace and its extension, through continued consultation. b) Israel calls for the establishment of peaceful relations between it and those Arab states which still maintain a state of war with it for the purpose of promoting a comprehensive settlement for the Arab-Israel conflict, including recognition, direct negotiation, ending the boycott, diplomatic relations, cessation of hostile activity in international institutions or forums and regional and bilateral cooperation. c) Israel calls for an international endeavour to resolve the problem of the residents of the Arab refugee camps in Judea. Samaria and the Gaza district in order to improve their living conditions and to rehabilitate them. Israel is prepared to be a partner in this endeavour. d) In order to advance the political negotiation process leading to peace, Israel proposes free and democratic elections among the Palestinian Arab inhabitants of Judea, Samaria and the Gaza district in an atmosphere devoid of violence, threats and terror. In these elections a representation will be chosen to conduct negotiations for a transitional period of self-rule. This period will constitute a test for co-existence and cooperation. At a later stage, negotiations will be conducted for a permanent solution during which all the proposed options for an agreed settlement will be examined, and peace between Israel and Jordan will be achieved. e) All the above-mentioned steps should be dealt with simultaneously. ...

THE PRINCIPLES CONSTITUTING THE INITIATIVE: STAGES: 5. The initiative is based on two stages. a) Stage A -- A transitional period for an interim agreement. b) Stage B -- Permanent Solution. 6. The interlock between the stages is a timetable on which the Plan is built: the peace process delineated by the initiative is based on Resolutions 242 and 338 upon which the Camp David Accords are founded. TIMETABLE: 7. The transitional period will continue for 5 years. 8. As soon as possible, but not later than the third year after the beginning of the transitional period, negotiations for achieving a permanent solution will begin.

PARTIES PARTICIPATING IN THE NEGOTIATIONS IN BOTH STAGES: 9. The parties participating in the negotiations for the First Stage (the interim agreement) shall include Israel and the elected representation of the Palestinian Arab inhabitants of Judea, Samaria and the Gaza district. Jordan and Egypt will be invited to participate in these negotiations if they so desire. 10. The parties participating in the negotiations for the Second Stage (Permanent Solution) shall include Israel and the elected representation of the Palestinian Arab inhabitants of Judea, Samaria and the Gaza district, as well as Jordan; furthermore, Egypt may participate in these negotiations. In negotiations between Israel and Jordan, in which the elected representation of the Palestinian Arab inhabitants of Judea, Samaria and the Gaza district will participate, the peace treaty between Israel and Jordan will be concluded.

SUBSTANCE OF TRANSITIONAL PERIOD: 11. During the transitional period the Palestinian Arab inhabitants of Judea, Samaria and the Gaza district will be accorded self-rule by means of which they will, themselves, conduct their affairs of daily life. Israel will continue to be responsible for security, foreign affairs and all matters concerning Israeli citizens in Judea, Samaria and the Gaza district. Topics involving the implementation of the plan for self-rule will be considered and decided within the framework of the negotiations for an interim agreement.

SUBSTANCE OF PERMANENT SOLUTION: 12. In the negotiations for a permanent solution every party shall be entitled to present for discussion all the subjects it may wish to raise. 13. The aim of the negotiations should be: a) The achievement of a permanent solution acceptable to the negotiating parties. b) The arrangements for peace and borders between Israel and Jordan.

DETAILS OF THE PROCESS FOR THE IMPLEMENTATION OF THE INITIATIVE: 14. First and foremost dialogue and basic agreement by the Palestinian Arab inhabitants of Judea, Samaria and the Gaza district, as well as Egypt and Jordan if they wish to take part, as above-mentioned, in the negotiations, on the principles constituting the initiative. 15. a) Immediately afterwards will follow the stage of preparations and implementation of the election process in which a representation of the Palestinian Arab inhabitants of Judea, Samaria and Gaza will be elected. This representation: I) Shall be a partner to the conduct of negotiations for the transitional period (interim agreement). II) Shall constitute the self-governing authority in the course of the transitional period. III) Shall be the central Palestinian component, subject to agreement after three years, in the negotiations for the permanent solution. b) In the period of the preparation and implementation there shall be a calming of the violence in Judea, Samaria and the Gaza district. 16. As to the substance of the elections, it is recommended that a proposal of regional elections be adopted, the details of which shall be determined in further discussions. 17. Every Palestinian Arab residing in Judea, Samaria, and the Gaza district, who shall be elected by the inhabitants to represent them -- after having submitted his candidacy in accordance with the detailed document which shall determine the subject of the elections -- may be a legitimate participant in the conduct of negotiations with Israel. 18. The elections shall be free, democratic and secret. 19. Immediately after the election of the Palestinian representation, negotiations shall be conducted with it on an interim agreement for a transitional period which shall continue for 5 years, as mentioned above. In these negotiations the parties shall determine all the subjects relating to the substance to the self-rule and the arrangements necessary for its implementation. 20. As soon as possible, but not later than the third year after the establishment of the self-rule, negotiations for a permanent solution shall begin. During the whole period of these negotiations until the signing of the agreement for a permanent solution, the self-rule shall continue in effect as determined in the negotiations for an interim agreement.

MADRID DECLARATION (JUNE 27, 1989)

The twelve heads of state of the European Community met in Madrid, Spain at their semi-annual European Community Summit on June 26 and 27, 1989. At the end of the summit they issued a formal statement on the Middle East.

The European Council has examined the situation in the Middle East conflict in the light of recent events and of contacts undertaken over several months by the Presidency and the Troika (the incumbent Presidency, its immediate predecessor and successor) with the parties concerned, and it has drawn the following conclusions:

1. The policy of the Twelve on the Middle East conflict is defined in the Venice Declaration of 13 June 1980 and other subsequent declarations. It consists in upholding the right to security of all States in the region, including Israel, that is to say, to live within secure, recognized and guaranteed frontiers, and in upholding justice for all the peoples of the region, which includes recognition of the legitimate rights of the Palestinian people, including their right to self-determination with all that this implies.

The Twelve consider that these objectives should be achieved by peaceful means in the framework of an international peace conference under the auspices of the United Nations, as the appropriate forum for the direct negotiations between the parties concerned, with a view to a comprehensive, just, and lasting settlement.

The European Council is also of the view that the Palestine Liberation Organization (PLO) should participate in this process. It expresses its support for every effort by the permanent members of the Security Council of the United Nations to bring the parties closer together, create a climate of confidence between them, and facilitate in this way the convening of the international peace conference.

2. The Community and its Member States have demonstrated their readiness to participate actively in the search for a negotiated solution to the conflict, and to cooperate fully in the economic and social development of the peoples of the region.

The European Council expressed its satisfaction regarding the policy of contacts with all the parties undertaken by the Presidency and the Troika, and has decided to pursue it.

3. The European Council welcomes the support given by the Extraordinary

Summit Meeting of the Arab League, held in Casablanca, to the decisions of the Palestinian National Council in Algiers, involving acceptance of Security Council Resolutions 242 and 338, which resulted in the recognition of Israel's right to exist, as well as the renunciation of terrorism.

It also welcomes the efforts undertaken by the United States in its contacts with the parties directly concerned and particularly the dialogue entered into with the PLO.

Advantage should be taken of these favorable circumstances to engender a spirit of tolerance and peace with a view to entering resolutely on the path of negotiations.

4. The European Council deplores the continuing deterioration of the situation in the Occupied Territories and the constant increase in the number of dead and wounded and the suffering of the population.

It appeals urgently to the Israeli authorities to put an end to repressive measures, to implement Resolutions 605, 607 and 608 of the Security Council and to respect the provisions of the Geneva Convention on the Protection of Civilian Populations in Times of War. They appeal in particular for the reopening of educational facilities in the West Bank.

5. On the basis of the positions of principle of the Twelve, the European Council welcomes the proposal for elections in the Occupied Territories as a contribution to the peace process, provided that; the elections are set in the context of a process towards a comprehensive, just, and lasting settlement of the conflict; the elections take place in the Occupied Territories including East Jerusalem, under adequate guarantees of freedom; no solution is excluded and the final negotiation takes place on the basis of Resolutions 242 and 338 of the Security Council of the United Nations, based on the principle of "land for peace."

6. The European Council launches a solemn appeal to the parties concerned to seize the opportunity to achieve peace. Respect by each of the parties for the legitimate rights of the other should facilitate the normalizing of relations between all the countries of the region. The European Council calls upon the Arab countries to establish normal relations of peace and cooperation with Israel and asks that country in turn to recognize the right of the Palestinian people to exercise self-determination.

MUBARAK TEN POINT PLAN (JULY 1989)

Despite the efforts of the Bush administration to promote Arab-Israeli negotiations on the basis of Israel's spring 1989 plan, progress was slow. In July 1989 Egyptian President Hosni Mubarak sought to facilitate the process with a ten point plan.

1. All Palestinians in the West Bank, the Gaza Strip and East Jerusalem should be allowed to vote and run for office. 2. Candidates should be free to campaign without interference from the Israeli authorities. 3. Israel should allow international supervision of the election process. 4. Construction or expansion of Jewish settlements would be frozen during this period. 5. The army would withdraw from the area of polling places on election day. 6. Only Israelis who live or work in the occupied territories would be permitted to enter them on election day. 7. Preparation for the elections should not take longer than two months; Egypt and the United States would help form the Israeli-Palestinian committee doing that work. 8. The Israeli Government should agree to negotiate the exchange of land for peace, while also protecting Israel's security. 9. The United States and Israel should publicly guarantee Israel's adherence to the plan. 10. Israel should publicly agree in advance to accept the outcome of the elections.

BAKER FIVE POINT PLAN (OCTOBER 1989)

In October 1989 (although formally released on December 6, 1989), United States Secretary of State James Baker announced a five point plan to clarify Egyptian President Hosni Mubarak's ten point proposal and thereby to advance the prospects for movement in the peace process.

1. The United States understands that because Egypt and Israel have been working hard on the peace process, there is agreement that an Israeli delegation should conduct a dialogue with a Palestinian delegation in Cairo. 2. The United States understands that Egypt cannot substitute itself for the Palestinians and Egypt will consult with Palestinians on all aspects of that dialogue. Egypt will also consult with Israel and the United States. 3. The United States understands that Israel will attend the dialogue only after a satisfactory list of Palestinians has been worked out. 4. The United States understands that the Government of Israel will come to the dialogue on the basis of the Israeli Government's May 14 initiative. The United States further understands that Palestinians will come to the dialogue prepared to discuss elections and the negotiating process in accordance with Israel's initiative. The U.S. understands, therefore, that Palestinians would be free to raise issues that relate to their opinion on how to make elections and the negotiating process succeed. 5. In order to facilitate this process, the U.S. proposes that the Foreign Minister of Israel, Egypt, and the U.S. meet in Washington within two weeks.

UNSC RESOLUTION 672 (OCTOBER 12, 1990)

On October 8, 1990, violence, in which Palestinians were shot and killed by Israeli border police, broke out at the Al Aksa Mosque in Jerusalem due to a combination of Palestinian provocation and police negligence. The situation became an international incident as the United Nations Security Council considered the matter. On October 12, 1990, the United Nations Security Council unanimously adopted Resolution 672.

The Security Council, Recalling its resolutions 476 (1980) and 478 (1980), *Reaffirming* that a just and lasting solution to the Arab-Israeli conflict must be based on its resolutions 242 (1967) and 338 (1973) through an active negotiating process which takes into account the right to security for all States in the region, including Israel, as well as the legitimate political rights of the Palestinian people, *Taking into consideration* the statement of the Secretary-General relative to the purpose of the mission he is sending to the region and conveyed to the Council by the President on 12 October 1990, 1. *Expresses alarm* at the violence which took place on 8 October at the Al Haram Al Sharif and other Holy Places of Jerusalem resulting in over twenty Palestinian deaths and the injury of more than one hundred and fifty people, including Palestinian civilians and innocent worshippers; 2. *Condemns* especially the acts of violence committed by the Israeli security forces resulting in injuries and loss of human life; 3. *Calls upon* Israel, the occupying Power, to abide scrupulously by its legal obligations and responsibilities under the Fourth Geneva Convention relative to the Protection of Civilian Persons in Time of War, of 12 August 1949, which is applicable to all the territories occupied by Israel since 1967; 4. *Requests,* in connection with the decision of the Secretary-General to send a mission to the region, which the Council welcomes, that he submit a report to it before the end of October 1990 containing his findings and conclusions and that he use as appropriate all of the resources of the United Nations in the region in carrying out the mission.

MADRID PEACE CONFERENCE LETTER OF INVITATION (OCTOBER 18, 1991)

The end of the Cold War and the Gulf War suggested new possibilities in the quest for an Arab-Israeli peace. United States President George Bush and Secretary of State James Baker noted that the new world order facilitated such an effort. Baker made eight trips to the region in the spring and summer of 1991 in an effort to convene a peace conference. In October, the United States and the Soviet Union issued invitations to Israel, Jordan, Lebanon, Syria and the Palestinians to an opening session in Madrid, Spain. The co-sponsors' letter laid out the framework for negotiations and provided details on the sessions and the approach to be followed. It reflected compromises by all sides developed in the course of Baker's shuttle diplomacy.

The Arab-Israeli peace conference convened in Madrid, Spain on October 30, 1991. It began ceremonially with a 3-day session where all parties were represented by official 14-member delegations. The Jordanian/Palestinian delegation had 14 representatives from each. The Palestinians also sent a six person advisory team that had no official standing but coordinated policy with the PLO. Presidents George Bush and Mikhail Gorbachev opened the conference. Bush called for peace based on security for Israel and fairness for the Palestinians. He said, "territorial compromise is essential for peace" and that only direct talks between Israelis and Arabs could bring peace about; the superpowers could not impose it. Israeli Prime Minister Yitzhak Shamir recounted the history of the Jews and argued that the cause of conflict is not territory but Arab refusal to recognize the legitimacy of Israel. He did not mention the occupied territories or Israeli settlements. Palestinian delegation head Haidar Abd al-Shafi asserted that the Palestinians were willing to live side by side with Israelis and accept a transitional stage, provided it led to sovereignty. He called on Israel to give Palestinian refugees displaced since 1967 the right to return and to stop settlements. Abd al-Shafi referred to the unnamed PLO as "our acknowledged leadership." Jordan Foreign Minister Kamal Abu Jaber, rebutting a common Israeli view, declared that Jordan has never been and will not be Palestine. Syrian Foreign Minister Farouk Al-Sharaa contended that Resolutions 242 and 338, or the "land for peace" formula, should be implemented. The opening session was followed by bilateral negotiations between Israel and each of the Arab delegations. The conference was an important step on the road to peace in that it involved direct, bilateral, public and official peace negotiations between Israel and its Arab neighbors.

After extensive consultations with Arab states, Israel and the Palestinians, the United States and the Soviet Union believe that an historic opportunity exists to advance the prospects for genuine peace throughout the region. The United States and the Soviet Union are prepared to assist the parties to achieve a just, lasting and comprehensive peace settlement, through direct negotiations along two tracks, between Israel and the Arab states, and between Israel and the Palestinians, based on United Nations Security Council Resolutions 242 and 338. The objective of this process is real peace.

Toward that end, the president of the U.S. and the president of the USSR invite you to a peace conference, which their countries will co-sponsor, followed immediately by direct negotiations. The conference will be convened in Madrid on October 30, 1991.

President Bush and President Gorbachev request your acceptance of this invitation no later than 6 P.M. Washington time, October 23, 1991, in order to ensure proper organization and preparation of the conference.

Direct bilateral negotiations will begin four days after the opening of the conference. Those parties who wish to attend multilateral negotiations will convene two weeks after the opening of the conference to organize those negotiations. The co-sponsors believe that those negotiations should focus on region-wide issues of water, refugee issues, environment, economic development, and other subjects of mutual interest.

The co-sponsors will chair the conference which will be held at ministerial level. Governments to be invited include Israel, Syria, Lebanon and Jordan. Palestinians will be invited and attend as part of a joint Jordanian-Palestinian delegation. Egypt will be invited to the conference as a participant. The European Community will be a participant in the conference, alongside the United States and the Soviet Union and will be represented by its presidency. The Gulf Cooperation Council will be invited to send its Secretary-general to the conference as an observer, and GCC member states will be invited to participate in organizing the negotiations on multilateral issues. The United Nations will be invited to send an observer, representing the secretary-general.

The conference will have no power to impose solutions on the parties or veto agreements reached by them. It will have no authority to make decisions for the parties and no ability to vote on issues of results. The conference can reconvene only with the consent of all the parties.

With respect to negotiations between Israel and Palestinians who are part of the joint Jordanian-Palestinian delegation, negotiations will be conducted in phases, beginning with talks on interim self-government arrangements. These talks will be conducted with the objective of reaching agreement within one year. Once agreed, the interim self-government arrangements will last for a period of five years; beginning the third year of the period of interim self-government arrangements, negotiations will take place on permanent status. These permanent status negotiations, and the negotiations between Israel and the Arab states, will take place on the basis of Resolutions 242 and 338.

It is understood that the co-sponsors are committed to making this process succeed. It is their intention to convene the conference and negotiations with those parties who agree to attend.

The co-sponsors believe that this process offers the promise of ending decades of confrontation and conflict and the hope of a lasting peace. Thus, the co-sponsors hope that the parties will approach these negotiations in a spirit of good will and mutual respect. In this way, the peace process can begin to break down the mutual suspicions and mistrust that perpetuate the conflict and allow the parties to begin to resolve their differences. Indeed, only through such a process can real peace and reconciliation among the Arab states, Israel and the Palestinians be achieved. And only through this process can the peoples of the Middle East attain the peace and security they richly deserve.

UNGA VOTE REPEALING RESOLUTION 3379 (XXX) (DECEMBER 16, 1991)

On November 10, 1975, the United Nations General Assembly, by a vote of 72 in favor to 35 against, with 32 abstentions, adopted resolution 3379 (XXX) in which it "Determines that zionism is a form of racism and racial discrimination." On December 16, 1991 the United Nations General Assembly repealed that resolution by a role call vote of 111 to 25 with 13 abstentions and 17 absent or not voting. The Arab states opposed the repeal, arguing that revocation would hinder the Middle East peace process. The Palestinian born, Saudi Arabian president of the General Assembly refused to chair the session. Some Arab states, including Egypt, Kuwait, Bahrain, Oman, Morocco, and Tunisia, decided not to vote on the issue.

United States Deputy Secretary of State Lawrence Eagleburger introduced the one-sentence resolution. The Soviet Union was among the 85 co-sponsors. Israel welcomed the decision and saw it as correcting a historic distortion.

The General Assembly Decides to revoke the determination contained in its resolution 3379 (XXX) of 10 November 1975.

ISRAEL-PLO RECOGNITION (SEPTEMBER 9, 1993)

Bilateral negotiations between Israel and the Arabs begun at Madrid continued in 1992 and 1993, albeit with interruptions. In early 1993 Israel and the Palestine Liberation Organization (PLO) conducted secret negotiations in Oslo which culminated in the signing of the Israel-PLO Declaration of Principles in Washington, D.C. on September 13, 1993. As part of the arrangement, Israel recognized the PLO as the representative of the Palestinian people. For its part, the PLO recognized Israel's right to exist in peace and security, accepted United Nations Security Council Resolutions 242 and 338, and renounced the use of terrorism and violence.

LETTER FROM ARAFAT TO RABIN:

The signing of the Declaration of Principles marks a new era in the history of the Middle East. In firm conviction thereof, I would like to confirm the following PLO commitments:

The PLO recognizes the right of the State of Israel to exist in peace and security.

The PLO accepts United Nations Security Council Resolutions 242 and 338.

The PLO commits itself to the Middle East peace process, and to a peaceful resolution of the conflict between the two sides and declares that all outstanding issues relating to permanent status will be resolved through negotiations.

The PLO considers that the signing of the Declaration of Principles constitutes a historic event, inaugurating a new epoch of peaceful coexistence, free from violence and all other acts which endanger peace and stability. Accordingly, the PLO renounces the use of terrorism and other acts of violence and will assume responsibility over all PLO elements and personnel in order to assure their compliance, prevent violations and discipline violators.

In view of the promise of a new era and the signing of the Declaration of Principles and based on Palestinian acceptance of Security Council Resolutions 242 and 338, the PLO affirms that those articles of the Palestinian Covenant which deny Israel's right to exist, and the provisions of the Covenant which are inconsistent with the commitments of this letter are now inoperative and no longer valid. Consequently, the PLO undertakes to submit to the Palestinian National Council for formal approval the necessary changes in regard to the Palestinian Covenant.

LETTER FROM ARAFAT TO NORWEGIAN FOREIGN MINISTER:

I would like top confirm to you that, upon the signing of the Declaration of Principles, the PLO encourages and calls upon the Palestinian people in the West Bank and Gaza Strip to take part in the steps leading to the normalization of life, rejecting violence and terrorism, contributing to peace and stability and participating actively in shaping reconstruction, economic development and cooperation.

LETTER FROM RABIN TO ARAFAT:

In response to your letter of September 9, 1993, I wish to confirm to you that, in light of the PLO commitments included in your letter, the Government of Israel has decided to recognize the PLO as the representative of the Palestinian people and commence negotiations with the PLO within the Middle East peace process.

ISRAEL-PLO DECLARATION OF PRINCIPLES (SEPTEMBER 13, 1993)

The Declaration of Principles (DOP) negotiated and agreed to by Israel and the PLO in Oslo, Norway in the spring and summer of 1993 was signed on the White House lawn in Washington, D.C. on September 13, 1993. Israeli Foreign Minister Shimon Peres and PLO Executive Committee member Mahmoud Abbas (Abu Mazin) signed the DOP in a ceremony on the White House lawn, witnessed by United States Secretary of State Warren Christopher and Russian Foreign Minister

Andrei Kozyrev, in the presence of United States President Bill Clinton, Israeli Prime Minister Yitzhak Rabin and PLO Chairman Yasser Arafat.

In addition to the main text, there were four annexes: Annes I: Protocol on the Mode and Conditions of Elections; Annex II: Protocol of Withdrawal of Israeli Forces from the Gaza Strip and Jericho Area; Annex III: Protocol on Israeli-Palestinian Cooperation in Economic and Development Programs; and Annex IV: Protocol on Israeli-Palestinian Cooperation Concerning Regional Development Programs. There were also agreed minutes providing more details and specifics concerning various articles of the declaration. The agreement entered into force on October 13, 1993 and negotiations on implementation began.

The Government of the State of Israel and the P.L.O. team (in the Jordanian-Palestinian delegation to the Middle East Peace Conference) (the "Palestinian Delegation"), representing the Palestinian people, agree that it is time to put an end to decades of confrontation and conflict, recognize their mutual legitimate and political rights, and strive to live in peaceful coexistence and mutual dignity and security and achieve a just, lasting and comprehensive peace settlement and historic reconciliation through the agreed political process. Accordingly, the two sides agree to the following principles:

Article I. AIM OF THE NEGOTIATIONS. The aim of the Israeli-Palestinian negotiations within the current Middle East peace process is, among other things, to establish a Palestinian Interim Self-Government Authority, the elected Council (the "Council"), for the Palestinian people in the West Bank and the Gaza Strip, for a transitional period not exceeding five years, leading to a permanent settlement based on Security Council Resolutions 242 and 338.

It is understood that the interim arrangements are an integral part of the whole peace process and that the negotiations on the permanent status will lead to the implementation of Security Council Resolutions 242 and 338.

Article II. FRAMEWORK FOR THE INTERIM PERIOD. The agreed framework for the interim period is set forth in this Declaration of Principles.

Article III. ELECTIONS. 1. In order that the Palestinian people in the West Bank and Gaza Strip may govern themselves according to democratic principles, direct, free and general political elections will be held for the Council under agreed supervision and international observation, while the Palestinian police will ensure public order. 2. An agreement will be concluded on the exact mode and conditions of the elections in accordance with the protocol attached as Annex I, with the goal of holding the elections not later than nine months after the entry into force of this Declaration of Principles. 3. These elections will constitute a significant interim preparatory step toward the realization of the legitimate rights of the Palestinian people and their just requirements.

Article IV. JURISDICTION. Jurisdiction of the Council will cover West Bank and Gaza Strip territory, except for issues that will be negotiated in the permanent status negotiations. The two sides view the West Bank and the Gaza

Strip as a single territorial unit, whose integrity will be preserved during the interim period.

Article V. TRANSITIONAL PERIOD AND PERMANENT STATUS NEGOTIATIONS. 1. The five-year transitional period will begin upon the withdrawal from the Gaza Strip and Jericho area. 2. Permanent status negotiations will commence as soon as possible, but not later than the beginning of the third year of the interim period, between the Government of Israel and the Palestinian people representatives. 3. It is understood that these negotiations shall cover remaining issues, including: Jerusalem, refugees, settlements, security arrangements, borders, relations and cooperation with other neighbors, and other issues of common interest. 4. The two parties agree that the outcome of the permanent status negotiations should not be prejudiced or preempted by agreements reached for the interim period.

Article VI. PREPARATORY TRANSFER OF POWERS AND RESPONSI-BILITIES. 1. Upon the entry into force of this Declaration of Principles and the withdrawal from the Gaza Strip and the Jericho area, a transfer of authority from the Israeli military government and its Civil Administration to the authorised Palestinians for this task, as detailed herein, will commence. This transfer of authority will be of a preparatory nature until the inauguration of the Council. 2. Immediately after the entry into force of this Declaration of Principles and the withdrawal from the Gaza Strip and Jericho area, with the view to promoting economic development in the West Bank and Gaza Strip, authority will be transferred to the Palestinians on the following spheres: education and culture, health, social welfare, direct taxation, and tourism. The Palestinian side will commence in building the Palestinian police force, as agreed upon. Pending the inauguration of the Council, the two parties may negotiate the transfer of additional powers and responsibilities, as agreed upon.

Article VII. INTERIM AGREEMENT. 1. The Israeli and Palestinian delegations will negotiate an agreement on the interim period (the "Interim Agreement"). 2. The Interim Agreement shall specify, among other things, the structure of the Council, the number of its members, and the transfer of powers and responsibilities from the Israeli military government and its Civil Administration to the Council. The Interim Agreement shall also specify the Council's executive authority, legislative authority in accordance with Article IX below, and the independent Palestinian judicial organs. 3. The Interim Agreement shall include arrangements, to be implemented upon the inauguration of the Council, for the assumption by the Council of all of the powers and responsibilities transferred previously in accordance with Article VI above. 4. In order to enable the Council to promote economic growth, upon its inauguration, the Council will establish, among other things, a Palestinian Electricity Authority, a Gaza Sea Port Authority, a Palestinian Development Bank, a Palestinian Export Promotion Board, a Palestinian Environmental Authority, a Palestinian Land Authority and a Palestinian Water Administration Authority, and any other Authorities agreed upon, in accordance with the Interim Agreement that will specify their powers and responsibilities. 5. After the inauguration of the Council, the Civil Administration will be dissolved, and the Israeli military government will be withdrawn.

Article VIII. PUBLIC ORDER AND SECURITY. In order to guarantee public order and internal security for the Palestinians of the West Bank and the Gaza Strip, the Council will establish a strong police force, while Israel will continue to carry the responsibility for defending against external threats, as well as the responsibility for overall security of Israelis for the purpose of safeguarding their internal security and public order.

Article IX. LAWS AND MILITARY ORDERS. 1. The Council will be empowered to legislate, in accordance with the Interim Agreement, within all authorities transferred to it. 2. Both parties will review jointly laws and military orders presently in force in remaining spheres.

Article X. JOINT ISRAELI-PALESTINIAN LIAISON COMMITTEE. In order to provide for a smooth implementation of this Declaration of Principles and any subsequent agreements pertaining to the interim period, upon the entry into force of this Declaration of Principles, a Joint Israeli-Palestinian Liaison Committee will be established in order to deal with issues requiring coordination, and other issues of common interest, and disputes.

Article XI. ISRAELI-PALESTINIAN COOPERATION IN ECONOMIC FIELDS. Recognizing the mutual benefit of cooperation in promoting the development of the West Bank, the Gaza Strip and Israel, upon the entry into force of this Declaration of Principles, an Israeli-Palestinian Economic Cooperation Committee will be established in order to develop and implement in a cooperative manner the programs identified in the protocols attached as Annex III and Annex IV.

Article XII. LIAISON AND COOPERATION WITH JORDAN AND EGYPT. The two parties will invite the Governments of Jordan and Egypt to participate in establishing further liaison and cooperation arrangements between the Government of Israel and the Palestinian representatives, on the one hand, and the Governments will include the constitution of a Continuing Committee that will decide by agreement on the modalities of admission of persons displaced from the West Bank and Gaza Strip in 1967, together with necessary measures to prevent disruption and disorder. Other matters of common concern will be dealt with by this Committee.

Article XIII. REDEPLOYMENT OF ISRAELI FORCES. 1. After the entry into force of this Declaration of Principles, and not later than the eve of elections for the Council, a redeployment of Israeli military forces in the West Bank and the Gaza Strip will take place, in addition to withdrawal of Israeli forces carried out in accordance with Article XIV. 2. In redeploying its military forces, Israel will be guided by the principle that its military forces should be redeployed outside populated areas. 3. Further redeployments to specified locations will be gradually implemented commensurate with the assumption of responsibility for public order and internal security by the Palestinian police force pursuant to Article VIII above.

Article XIV. ISRAELI WITHDRAWAL FROM THE GAZA STRIP AND JERICHO AREA. Israel will withdraw from the Gaza Strip and Jericho area, as detailed in the protocol attached as Annex II.

Article XV. RESOLUTION OF DISPUTES. 1. Disputes arising out of the application or interpretation of this Declaration of Principles, or any subsequent agreements pertaining to the interim period, shall be resolved by negotiations through the Joint Liaison Committee to be established pursuant to Article X above. 2. Disputes which cannot be settled by negotiations may be resolved by a mechanism of conciliation to be agreed upon by the parties. 3. The parties may agree to submit to arbitration disputes relating to the interim period, which cannot be settled through conciliation. To this end, upon the agreement of both parties, the parties will establish an Arbitration Committee.

Article XVI. ISRAELI-PALESTINIAN COOPERATION CONCERNING REGIONAL PROGRAMS. Both parties view the multilateral working groups as an appropriate instrument for promoting a "Marshall Plan," the regional programs and other programs, including special programs for the West Bank and Gaza Strip, as indicated in the protocol attached as Annex IV.

Article XVII. MISCELLANEOUS PROVISIONS. 1. This Declaration of Principles will enter into force one month after its signing. 2. All protocols annexed to this Declaration of Principles and Agreed Minutes pertaining thereto shall be regarded as an integral part hereof.

DONE at Washington, DC, this thirteenth day of September, 1993.

ISRAEL-JORDAN COMMON AGENDA (SEPTEMBER 14, 1993)

On September 14, 1993, Israel and Jordan signed a substantive common agenda providing their approach to achieving peace between them. On October 1, 1993, Jordanian Crown Prince Hassan and Israeli Foreign Minister Shimon Peres met at the White House with President Bill Clinton. They agreed to set up a bilateral economic committee and a US-Israeli-Jordanian trilateral economic committee. The first meeting of the trilateral committee was held on November 4, 1993 in Paris and a second was held in Washington on November 30, 1993.

A. Goal: The achievement of a just, lasting and comprehensive peace between the Arab States, the Palestinians and Israel as per the Madrid invitation.

B. Components of Israel-Jordan Peace Negotiations: 1. Searching for steps to arrive at a state of peace based on Security Council Resolutions 242 and 338 in all their aspects; 2. Security: a) Refraining from actions or activities by either side that may adversely affect the security of the other or may prejudge the final outcome of negotiations; b) Threats to security resulting from all kinds of terrorism; c) i. Mutual commitment not to threaten each other by any use of force and not to use weapons by one side against the other including conventional and non-conventional mass destruction weapons; ii. Mutual commitment, as a matter of priority and as soon as possible, to work towards a Middle East free from weapons of mass destruction, conventional and non-conventional weapons; this goal is to be achieved in the context of a comprehensive, lasting and stable peace characterized by the renunciation of the use of force, reconciliation and openness [Note: The above (item c-ii) may be revised in accordance with relevant agreements to be reached in the Multilateral Working Group on Arms Control and Regional Security]; d) Mutually agreed upon security arrangements and security confidence building measures; 3. a) Securing the rightful water shares of the two sides; b) Searching for ways to alleviate water shortage; 4. Refugees and Displaced Persons: Achieving an agreed just solution to the bilateral aspects of the problem of refugees and displaced persons in accordance with international law; 5. Borders and Territorial Matters: Settlement of territorial matters and agreed definitive delimitation and demarcation of the international boundary between Israel and Jordan with reference to the boundary definition under the Mandate, without prejudice to the status of any territories that came under Israeli Military Government control in 1967. Both parties will respect and comply with the above international boundary; 6. Exploring the potentials of future bilateral cooperation, within a regional context where appropriate, in the following: a) Natural Resources: Water, energy and environment; Rift Valley development; b) Human Resources: Demography; Labor; Health; Education; Drug Control; c) Infrastructure: Transportation: land and air; Communication; d) Economic areas including tourism; 7. Phasing the discussion, agreement and implementation of the items above including appropriate mechanisms for negotiations in specific fields; 8. Discussion on matters related to both tracks to be decided upon in common by the two tracks.

C. It is anticipated that the above endeavor will ultimately, following the attainment of mutually satisfactory solutions to the elements of this agenda, culminate in a peace treaty.

UNGA RESOLUTION 48/58 (DECEMBER 14, 1993)

On December 14, 1993, the United Nations General Assembly adopted a resolution endorsing the Israel-PLO Declaration of Principles and supporting the Middle East peace process, without the hitherto constant criticism of Israel. The vote was 155 in favor, 3 opposed, 1 abstention, and 25 absent.

The General Assembly, Stressing that the achievement of a comprehensive, just and lasting settlement of the Middle East conflict will constitute a significant contribution to strengthening international peace and security, *Recalling* the convening of the Peace Conference on the Middle East at Madrid on 30 October 1991, on the basis of Security Council resolutions 242 (1967) of 22 November 1967 and 338 (1973) of 22 October 1973, and the subsequent bilateral negotiations, as well as the meetings of the multilateral working groups, and noting with satisfaction the broad international support for the peace process, *Noting* the continuing positive participation of the United Nations as a full extraregional participant in the work of the multilateral working groups, *Bearing in mind* the Declaration of Principles on Interim Self-Government Arrangements, signed by Israel and the Palestine Liberation Organization in Washington, D.C., on 13 September 1993, *Also bearing in mind* the Agreement between Israel and Jordan on the Common Agenda, signed in Washington, D.C., on 14 September 1993, 1. *Welcomes* the peace process started at Madrid and supports the subsequent bilateral negotiations; 2. *Stresses* the importance of, and need for, achieving a comprehensive, just and lasting peace in the Middle East; 3. *Expresses its full support* for the achievements of the peace process thus far, in particular the Declaration of Principles on Interim Self-Government Arrangements signed by Israel and the Palestine Liberation Organization, and the Agreement between Israel and Jordan on the Common Agenda, which constitute an important initial step in achieving a comprehensive, just and lasting peace in the Middle East, and urges all parties to implement agreements reached; 4. *Stresses* the need for achieving rapid progress on the other tracks on the Arab-Israeli negotiations within the peace process; 5. *Welcomes* the results of the International Donors Conference to Support Middle East Peace, convened in Washington, D.C., on 1 October 1993, and the establishment of the high-level United Nations task force to support the economic and social development of the Palestinian people, and urges Member States to provide economic, financial and technical assistance to the Palestinian people during the interim period; 6. *Calls upon* all Member States also to extend economic, financial and technical assistance to States in the region, and to render support for the peace process; 7. *Considers* that an active United Nations role in the Middle East peace process and in assisting in the implementation of the Declaration of Principles can make a positive contribution; 8. *Encourages* regional development and cooperation in the areas where work has already begun within the framework of the Madrid Conference.

ISRAEL-PLO ECONOMIC AGREEMENT (APRIL 29, 1994)

Negotiations to implement the Israel-PLO Declaration of Principles led to an economic agreement on the relationship between the economies of Israel and the Palestinians signed on April 29, 1994, in Paris by Abu Ala (Ahmed Korei) of the PLO and Avraham Shohat, Israel's Finance Minister.

The agreement is long and deals with a variety of subjects including imports and import taxes, labor, monetary and fiscal policy, direct taxation, indirect taxation, agriculture, industry, energy, tourism, and insurance. The Palestinian Authority will establish a monetary authority whose main function will be to regulate and supervise banks operating in the autonomous areas, to manage foreign exchange reserves, and to supervise foreign exchange transactions. A Palestinian Tax Administration will conduct its own direct tax policy, including income tax on individuals and corporations. A Value Added Tax (VAT) system similar to that operating in Israel will be instituted by the Palestinian Authority. Palestinians will continue to work in Israel. Agricultural and manufactured goods will be allowed to enter Israel freely, with some quotas on certain agricultural products. A Palestinian Tourist Administration will be established to control matters relating to tourism in the areas under control of the Palestinian Authority. Israeli businesses will be able to invest in Jericho and Gaza and Palestinians in the autonomous regions will be able to invest in Israel.

PREAMBLE

The two parties view the economic domain as one of the cornerstones in their mutual relations with a view to enhance their interest in the achievement of a just, lasting and comprehensive peace. Both parties shall cooperate in this field in order to establish a sound economic base for these relations, which will be governed in various economic spheres by the principles of mutual respect of each other's economic interests, reciprocity, equity and fairness.

This protocol lays the groundwork for strengthening the economic base of the Palestinian side and for exercising its right of economic decision making in accordance with its own development plan and priorities. The two parties recognise each other's economic ties with other markets and the need to create a better economic environment for their peoples and individuals.

Article I: FRAMEWORK AND SCOPE OF THIS PROTOCOL. 1. This Protocol establishes the contractual agreement that will govern the economic relations between the two sides and will cover the West Bank and the Gaza Strip during the interim period. The implementation will be according to the stages envisaged in the Declaration of Principles on Interim Self Government Arrangements signed in Washington D.C. on September 13, 1993 and the Agreed Minutes thereto. It will therefore begin in the Gaza Strip and the Jericho Area and at a later stage will also apply to the rest of the West Bank, according to the provisions of the Interim Agreement and to any other agreed arrangements between the two sides. 2. This Protocol, including its Appendixes, will be incorporated into the Agreement on the Gaza Strip and the Jericho Area (in this Protocol - the Agreement), will be an integral part thereof and interpreted accordingly. This paragraph refers solely to the Gaza Strip and the Jericho Area. 3. This Protocol will come into force upon the signing of the Agreement. 4. For the purpose of this Protocol, the term "Areas" means the areas under the jurisdiction of the Palestinian Authority, according to the provisions of the Agreement regarding territorial jurisdiction. The Palestinian jurisdiction in the subsequent agreements could cover areas, spheres or functions according to the Interim Agreement. Therefore, for the purpose of this Protocol, whenever applied, the term "Areas" shall be interpreted to mean functions and spheres also, as the case may be, with the necessary adjustments.

Article II: THE JOINT ECONOMIC COMMITTEE. 1. Both parties will establish a Palestinian-Israeli Joint Economic Committee (hereinafter - the JEC) to follow up the implementation of this Protocol and to decide on problems related to it that may arise from time to time. Each side may request the review of any issue related to this Agreement by the JEC. 2. The JEC will serve as the continuing committee for economic cooperation envisaged in Annex III of the Declaration of Principles. 3. The JEC will consist of an equal number of members from each side and may establish sub-committees specified in this Protocol. A sub-committee may include experts as necessary. 4. The JEC and its sub-committees shall reach their decisions by agreement and shall determine their rules of procedure and operation, including the frequency and place or places of their meetings.

Article III: IMPORT TAXES AND IMPORT POLICY. 1. The import and customs policies of both sides will be according to the principles and arrangements detailed in this Article. ...

Article IV: MONETARY AND FINANCIAL ISSUES. 1. The Palestinian Authority will establish a Monetary Authority (PMA) in the Areas. The PMA will have the powers and responsibilities for the regulation and implementation of the monetary policies within the functions described in this Article. 2. The PMA will act as the Palestinian Authority's official economic and financial advisor. 3. The PMA will act as the Palestinian Authority's and the public sector entities' sole financial agent, locally and internationally. 4. The foreign currency reserves (including gold) of the Palestinian Authority and all Palestinian public sector entities will be deposited solely with the PMA and managed by it. 5. The PMA will act as the lender of last resort for the banking system in the Areas. 6. The PMA will authorize foreign exchange dealers in the Areas and will exercise control (regulation and supervision) over foreign exchange transactions within the Areas and with the rest of the world. 7. a. The PMA will have a banking supervision department that will be responsible for the proper functioning, stability, solvency and liquidity of the banks operating in the Areas. ...

Article V: DIRECT TAXATION. 1. Israel and the Palestinian Authority will each determine and regulate independently its own tax policy in matters of direct taxation, including income tax on individuals and corporations, property taxes, municipal taxes and fees. ...

Article VI: INDIRECT TAXES ON LOCAL PRODUCTION. 1. The Israel and the Palestinian tax administrations will levy and collect VAT and purchase taxes on local production, as well as any other indirect taxes, in their respective areas. ...

Article VII: LABOR. 1. Both sides will attempt to maintain the normality of movement of labor between them, subject to each side's right to determine from time to time the extent and conditions of the labor movement into its area. If the normal movement is suspended temporarily by either side, it will give the other side immediate notification, and the other side may request that the matter be discussed in the Joint Economic Committee. The placement and employment of workers from one side in the area of the other side will be through the employment service of the other side and in accordance with the other sides' legislation. The Palestinian side has the right to regulate the employment of Palestinian labor in Israel through the Palestinian employment service, and the Israeli Employment Service will cooperate and coordinate in this regard. ...

Article VIII: AGRICULTURE. 1. There will be free movement of agricultural produce, free of customs and import taxes, between the two sides, subject to the following exceptions and arrangements. ...

Article IX: INDUSTRY. 1. There will be free movement of industrial goods free of any restrictions including customs and import taxes between the two sides, subject to each side's legislation. 2. a. The Palestinian side has the right to employ various methods in encouraging and promoting the development of the Palestinian industry by way of providing grants, loans, research and development assistance and direct-tax benefits. The Palestinian side has also the right to employ other methods of encouraging industry resorted to in Israel. b. Both sides will exchange information about the methods employed by them in the encouragement of their respective industries. c. Indirect tax rebates or benefits and other subsidies to sales shall not be allowed in trade between the two sides. 3. Each side will do its best to avoid damage to the industry of the other side and will take into consideration the concerns of the other side in its industrial policy. 4. Both sides will cooperate in the prevention of deceptive practices, trade in goods which may endanger health, safety and the environment and in goods of expired validity. 5. Each side will take the necessary measures in the area under its jurisdiction to prevent damage which may be caused by its industry to the environment of the other side. 6. The Palestinians will have the right to export their industrial produce to external markets without restrictions, on the basis of certificates of origin issued by the Palestinian Authority. 7. The JEC will meet and review issues pertaining to this Article.

Article X: TOURISM. 1. The Palestinian Authority will establish a

Palestinian Tourism Authority which will exercise, inter alia, the following powers in the Areas. a. Regulating, licensing, classifying and supervising tourist services, sites and industries. b. Promoting foreign and domestic tourism and developing the Palestinian tourist resources and sites. c. Supervising the marketing, promotion and information activities related to foreign and domestic tourism. 2. Each side shall, under its respective jurisdiction, protect, guard and ensure the maintenance and good upkeep of historical, archaeological, cultural and religious sites and all other tourist sites, to fit their status as well as their purpose as a destination for visitors. ...

Article XI: INSURANCE ISSUES. 1. The authorities, powers and responsibilities in the insurance sphere in the Areas, including inter alia the licensing of insurers, insurance agents and the supervision of their activities, will be transferred to the Palestinian Authority. ...

CAIRO AGREEMENT (MAY 4, 1994)

Yasser Arafat and Yitzhak Rabin signed an agreement in Cairo on May 4, 1994 that contained accords reached on elements of the Israel-PLO Declaration of Principles. The agreement formally began Israel's withdrawal from the Gaza Strip and the Jericho area and granted Palestinians a measure of self-rule.

The Government of the State of Israel and the Palestine Liberation Organization (hereinafter "the PLO"), the representative of the Palestinian people;

PREAMBLE. WITHIN the framework of the Middle East peace process initiated at Madrid in October 1991; REAFFIRMING their determination to live in peaceful coexistence, mutual dignity and security, while recognizing their mutual legitimate and political rights; REAFFIRMING their desire to achieve a just, lasting and comprehensive peace settlement through the agreed political process; REAFFIRMING their adherence to the mutual recognition and commitments expressed in the letters dated September 9, 1993, signed by and exchanged between the Prime Minister of Israel and the Chairman of the PLO; REAFFIRMING their understanding that the interim self-government arrangements, including the arrangements to apply in the Gaza Strip and the Jericho Area contained in this Agreement, are an integral part of the whole peace process and that the negotiations on the permanent status will lead to the implementation of Security Council Resolutions 242 and 338; DESIROUS of putting into effect the Declaration of Principles on Interim Self-Government Arrangements signed at Washington, D.C. on September 13, 1993, and the Agreed Minutes thereto hereinafter "the Declaration of Principles"), and in particular the Protocol on withdrawal of Israeli forces from the Gaza Strip and the Jericho Area; HEREBY AGREE to the following arrangements regarding the Gaza Strip and the Jericho

Area:

Article I. Definitions For the purpose of this Agreement. a. the Gaza Strip and the Jericho Area are delineated on map Nos. 1 and 2 attached to this Agreement; b. "the Settlements" means the Gush Katif and Erez settlement areas, as well as the other settlements in the Gaza Strip, as shown on attached map No. 1; c. "the Military Installation Area" means the Israeli military installation area along the Egyptian border in the Gaza Strip, as shown on map No. 1; and d. the term "Israelis" shall also include Israeli statutory agencies and corporations registered in Israel.

Article II. Scheduled Withdrawal of Israeli Military Forces. 1. Israel shall implement an accelerated and scheduled withdrawal of Israeli military forces from the Gaza Strip and from the Jericho Area to begin immediately with the signing of this Agreement. Israel shall complete such withdrawal within three weeks from this date. 2. Subject to the arrangements included in the Protocol Concerning Withdrawal of Israeli Military Forces and Security Arrangements attached as Annex I, the Israeli withdrawal shall include evacuating all military bases and other fixed installations to be handed over to the Palestinian Police, to be established pursuant to Article IX below (hereinafter "the Palestinian Police"). 3. In order to carry out Israel's responsibility for external security and for internal security and public order of Settlements and Israelis, Israel shall, concurrently with the withdrawal, redeploy its remaining military forces to the Settlements and the Military Installation Area, in accordance with the provisions of this Agreement. Subject to the provisions of this Agreement, this redeployment shall constitute full implementation of Article XIII of the Declaration of Principles with regard to the Gaza Strip and the Jericho Area only. 4. For the purposes of this Agreement, "Israeli military forces" may include Israel police and other Israeli security forces. 5. Israelis, including Israeli military forces, may continue to use roads freely within the Gaza Strip and the Jericho Area. Palestinians may use public roads crossing the Settlements freely, as provided for in Annex I. 6. The Palestinian Police shall be deployed and shall assume responsibility for public order and internal security of Palestinians in accordance with this Agreement and Annex I.

Article III. Transfer of Authority. 1. Israel shall transfer authority as specified in this Agreement from the Israeli military government and its Civil Administration to the Palestinian Authority, hereby established, in accordance with Article V of this Agreement, except for the authority that Israel shall continue to exercise as specified in this Agreement. 2. As regards the transfer and assumption of authority in civil spheres, powers and responsibilities shall be transferred and assumed as set out in the Protocol Concerning Civil Affairs attached as Annex II. 3. Arrangements for a smooth and peaceful transfer of the agreed powers and responsibilities are set out in Annex II. 4. Upon the completion of the Israeli withdrawal and the transfer of powers and responsibilities as detailed in paragraphs 1 and 2 above and in Annex II, the Civil Administration in the Gaza Strip and the Jericho Area will be dissolved and the Israeli military government will be withdrawn. The withdrawal of the military government shall not prevent it from continuing to exercise the powers and responsibilities specified in this Agreement. 5. A Joint Civil Affairs Coordination and Cooperation Committee (hereinafter "the CAC") and two Joint Regional Civil Affairs Subcommittees for the Gaza Strip and the Jericho Area respectively shall be established in order to provide for coordination and cooperation in civil affairs between the Palestinian Authority and Israel, as detailed in Annex II. 6. The offices of the Palestinian Authority shall be located in the Gaza Strip and the Jericho Area pending the inauguration of the Council to be elected pursuant to the Declaration of Principles.

Article IV. Structure and Composition of the Palestinian Authority. 1. The Palestinian Authority will consist of one body of 24 members which shall carry out and be responsible for all the legislative and executive powers and responsibilities transferred to it under this Agreement, in accordance with this Article, and shall be responsible for the exercise of judicial functions in accordance with Article VI, subparagraph 1.b. of this Agreement. 2. The Palestinian Authority shall administer the departments transferred to it and may establish, within its jurisdiction, other departments and subordinate administrative units as necessary for the fulfillment of its responsibilities. It shall determine its own internal procedures. 3. The PLO shall inform the Government of Israel of the names of the members of the Palestinian Authority and any change of members. Changes in the membership of the Palestinian Authority will take effect upon an exchange of letters between the PLO and the Government of Israel. 4. Each member of the Palestinian Authority shall enter into office upon undertaking to act in accordance with this Agreement.

Article V. Jurisdiction. 1. The authority of the Palestinian Authority encompasses all matters that fall within its territorial, functional and personal jurisdiction, as follows: a. The territorial jurisdiction covers the Gaza Strip and the Jericho Area territory, as defined in Article I, except for Settlements and the Military Installation Area. Territorial jurisdiction shall include land, subsoil and territorial waters, in accordance with the provisions of this Agreement. b. The functional jurisdiction encompasses all powers and responsibilities as specified in this Agreement. This jurisdiction does not include foreign relations, internal security and public order of Settlements and the Military Installation Area and Israelis, and external security. c. The personal jurisdiction extends to all persons within the territorial jurisdiction referred to above, except for Israelis, unless otherwise provided in this Agreement. 2. The Palestinian Authority has, within its authority, legislative, executive and judicial powers and responsibilities, as provided for in this Agreement. 3. a. Israel has authority over the Settlements, the Military Installation Area, Israelis, external security, internal security and public order of Settlements, the Military Installation Area and Israelis, and those agreed powers and responsibilities specified in this Agreement. b. Israel shall exercise its authority through its military government, which, for that end, shall continue to have the necessary legislative, judicial and executive powers and responsibilities, in accordance with international law. This provision shall not derogate from Israel's applicable legislation over Israelis in personam. 4. The exercise of authority with regard to the electromagnetic sphere and airspace shall be in accordance with the provisions of this Agreement. 5. The provisions of this Article are subject to the specific legal arrangements detailed in the Protocol Concerning Legal Matters attached as Annex III. Israel and the Palestinian Authority may negotiate further legal arrangements. 6. Israel and the Palestinian Authority shall cooperate on matters of legal assistance in criminal and civil matters through the legal subcommittee of the CAC.

Article VI. Powers and Responsibilities of the Palestinian Authority. 1. Subject to the provisions of this Agreement, the Palestinian Authority, within its jurisdiction: a. has legislative powers as set out in Article VII of this Agreement, as well as executive powers; b. will administer justice through an independent judiciary; c. will have, inter alia, power to formulate policies, supervise their implementation, employ staff, establish departments, authorities and institutions, sue and be sued and conclude contracts; and d. will have, inter alia, the power to keep and administer registers and records of the population, and issue certificates, licenses and documents. 2. a. In accordance with the Declaration of Principles, the Palestinian Authority will not have powers and responsibilities in the sphere of foreign relations, which sphere includes the establishment abroad of embassies, consulates or other types of foreign missions and posts or permitting their establishment in the Gaza Strip or the Jericho Area, the appointment of or admission of diplomatic and consular staff, and the exercise of diplomatic functions. b. Notwithstanding the provisions of this paragraph, the PLO may conduct negotiations and sign agreements with states or international organizations for the benefit of the Palestinian Authority in the following cases only: (1) economic agreements, as specifically provided in Annex IV of this Agreement; (2) agreements with donor countries for the purpose of implementing arrangements for the provision of assistance to the Palestinian Authority; (3) agreements for the purpose of implementing the regional development plans detailed in Annex IV of the Declaration of Principles or in agreements entered into in the framework of the multilateral negotiations; and (4) cultural, scientific and educational agreements. c. Dealings between the Palestinian Authority and representatives of foreign states and international organizations, as well as the establishment in the Gaza Strip and the Jericho Area of representative offices other than those described in subparagraph 2.a. above, for the purpose of implementing the agreements referred to in subparagraph 2.b. above, shall not be considered foreign relations.

Article VII. Legislative Powers of the Palestinian Authority. 1. The Palestinian Authority will have the power, within its jurisdiction, to promulgate legislation, including basic laws, laws, regulations, and other legislative acts.

2. Legislation promulgated by the Palestinian Authority shall be consistent with the provisions of this Agreement. 3. Legislation promulgated by the Palestinian Authority shall be communicated to a legislation subcommittee to be established by the CAC (hereinafter "the Legislation Subcommittee"). During a period of 30 days from the communication of the legislation, Israel may request that the Legislation Subcommittee decide whether such legislation exceeds the jurisdiction of the Palestinian Authority or is otherwise inconsistent with the provisions of this Agreement. 4. Upon receipt of the Israeli request, the Legislation Subcommittee shall decide, as an initial matter, on the entry into force of the legislation pending its decision on the merits of the matter. 5. If the Legislation Subcommittee is unable to reach a decision with regard to the entry into force of the legislation within 15 days, this issue will be referred to a board of review. This board of review shall be comprised of two judges, retired judges or senior jurists (hereinafter "Judges"), one from each side, to be appointed from a compiled list of three Judges proposed by each. In order to expedite the proceedings before this board of review, the two most senior Judges, one from each side, shall develop written informal rules of procedure. 6. Legislation referred to the board of review shall enter into force only if the board of review decides that it does not deal with a security issue which falls under Israel's responsibility, that it does not seriously threaten other significant Israeli interests protected by this Agreement and that the entry into force of the legislation could not cause irreparable damage or harm. 7. The Legislation Subcommittee shall attempt to reach a decision on the merits of the matter within 30 days from the date of the Israeli request. If this Subcommittee is unable to reach such a decision within this period of 30 days, the matter shall be referred to the Joint Israeli-Palestinian Liaison Committee referred to in Article XV below (hereinafter "the Liaison Committee"). This Liaison Committee will deal with the matter immediately and will attempt to settle it within 30 days. 8. Where the legislation has not entered into force pursuant to paragraphs 5 or 7 above, this situation shall be maintained pending the decision of the Liaison Committee on the merits of the matter, unless it has decided otherwise. 9. Laws and military orders in effect in the Gaza Strip or the Jericho Area prior to the signing of this Agreement shall remain in force, unless amended or abrogated in accordance with this Agreement.

Article VIII. Arrangements for Security and Public Order. 1. In order to guarantee public order and internal security for the Palestinians of the Gaza Strip and the Jericho Area, the Palestinian Authority shall establish a strong police force, as set out in Article IX below. Israel shall continue to carry the responsibility for defense against external threats, including the responsibility for protecting the Egyptian border and the Jordanian line, and for defense against external threats from the sea and from the air, as well as the responsibility for overall security of Israelis and Settlements, for the purpose of safeguarding their internal security and public order, and will have all the powers to take the steps necessary to meet this responsibility. 2. Agreed security arrangements and coordination mechanisms are specified in Annex I. 3. A joint Coordination and Cooperation Committee for mutual security purposes (hereinafter "the JSC"), as well as three joint District Coordination and Cooperation Offices for the Gaza district, the Khan Yunis district and the Jericho district respectively (hereinafter "the DCOs") are hereby established as provided for in Annex I. 4. The security arrangements provided for in this Agreement and in Annex I may be reviewed at the request of either Party and may be amended by mutual agreement of the Parties. Specific review arrangements are included in Annex I.

Article IX. The Palestinian Directorate of Police Force. 1. The Palestinian Authority shall establish a strong police force, the Palestinian Directorate of Police Force (hereinafter "the Palestinian Police"). The duties, functions, structure, deployment and composition of the Palestinian Police, together with provisions regarding its equipment and operation, are set out in Annex I, Article III. Rules of conduct governing the activities of the Palestinian Police are set out in Annex I, Article VIII. 2. Except for the Palestinian Police referred to in this Article and the Israeli military forces, no other armed forces shall be established or operate in the Gaza Strip or the Jericho Area. 3. Except for the arms, ammunition and equipment of the Palestinian Police described in Annex I, Article III, and those of the Israeli military forces, no organization or individual in the Gaza Strip and the Jericho Area shall manufacture, sell, acquire, possess, import or otherwise introduce into the Gaza Strip or the Jericho Area any firearms, ammunition, weapons, explosives, gunpowder or any related equipment, unless otherwise provided for in Annex I.

Article X. Passages. Arrangements for coordination between Israel and the Palestinian Authority regarding the Gaza-Egypt and Jericho-Jordan passages, as well as any other agreed international crossings, are set out in Annex I, Article X.

Article XI. Safe Passage between the Gaza Strip and the Jericho Area. Arrangements for safe passage of persons and transportation between the Gaza Strip and the Jericho Area are set out in Annex I, Article IX.

Article XII. Relations Between Israel and the Palestinian Authority. 1. Israel and the Palestinian Authority shall seek to foster mutual understanding and tolerance and shall accordingly abstain from incitement, including hostile propaganda, against each other and, without derogating from the principle of freedom of expression, shall take legal measures to prevent such incitement by any organizations, groups or individuals within their jurisdiction. 2. Without derogating from the other provisions of this Agreement, Israel and the Palestinian Authority shall cooperate in combatting criminal activity which may affect both sides, including offenses related to trafficking in illegal drugs and psychotropic substances, smuggling, and offenses against property, including offenses related to vehicles.

Article XIII. Economic Relations. The economic relations between the two sides are set out in the Protocol on Economic Relations signed in Paris on April

29, 1994 and the Appendices thereto, certified copies of which are attached as Annex IV, and will be governed by the relevant provisions of this Agreement and its Annexes.

Article XIV. Human Rights and the Rule of Law. Israel and the Palestinian Authority shall exercise their powers and responsibilities pursuant to this Agreement with due regard to internationally-accepted norms and principles of human rights and the rule of law.

Article XV. The Joint Israeli-Palestinian Liaison Committee. 1. The Liaison Committee established pursuant to Article X of the Declaration of Principles shall ensure the smooth implementation of this Agreement. It shall deal with issues requiring coordination, other issues of common interest and disputes. 2. The Liaison Committee shall be composed of an equal number of members from each Party. It may add other technicians and experts as necessary. 3. The Liaison Committee shall adopt its rules of procedure, including the frequency and place or places of its meetings. 4. The Liaison Committee shall reach its decisions by Agreement.

Article XVI. Liaison and Cooperation with Jordan and Egypt. 1. Pursuant to Article XII of the Declaration of Principles, the two Parties shall invite the Governments of Jordan and Egypt to participate in establishing further liaison and cooperation arrangements between the Government of Israel and the Palestinian representatives on the one hand, and the Governments of Jordan and Egypt on the other hand, to promote cooperation between them. These arrangements shall include the constitution of a Continuing Committee. 2. The Continuing Committee shall decide by agreement on the modalities of admission of persons displaced from the West Bank and the Gaza Strip in 1967, together with necessary measures to prevent disruption and disorder. 3. The Continuing Committee shall deal with other matters of common concern.

Article XVII. Settlement of Differences and Disputes. Any difference relating to the application of this Agreement shall be referred to the appropriate coordination and cooperation mechanism established under this Agreement. The provisions of Article XV of the Declaration of Principles shall apply to any such difference which is not settled through the appropriate coordination and cooperation mechanism, namely: 1. Disputes arising out of the application or interpretation of this Agreement or any subsequent agreements pertaining to the interim period shall be settled by negotiations through the Liaison Committee. 2. Disputes which cannot be settled by negotiations may be settled by a mechanism of conciliation to be agreed between the Parties. 3. The Parties may agree to submit to arbitration disputes relating to the interim period, which cannot be settled through conciliation. To this end, upon the agreement of both Parties, the Parties will establish an Arbitration Committee.

Article XVIII. Prevention of Hostile Acts. Both sides shall take all measures necessary in order to prevent acts of terrorism, crime and hostilities directed against each other, against individuals falling under the other's authority and against their property, and shall take legal measures against offenders. In addition, the Palestinian side shall take all measures necessary to prevent such hostile acts directed against the Settlements, the infrastructure serving them and the Military Installation Area, and the Israeli side shall take all measures necessary to prevent such hostile acts emanating from the Settlements and directed against Palestinians.

Article XIX. Missing Persons. The Palestinian Authority shall cooperate with Israel by providing all necessary assistance in the conduct of searches by Israel within the Gaza Strip and the Jericho Area for missing Israelis, as well as by providing information about missing Israelis. Israel shall cooperate with the Palestinian Authority in searching for, and providing necessary information about, missing Palestinians.

Article XX. Confidence Building Measures. With a view to creating a positive and supportive public atmosphere to accompany the implementation of this Agreement, and to establish a solid basis of mutual trust and good faith, both Parties agree to carry out confidence building measures as detailed herewith: 1. Upon the signing of this Agreement, Israel will release, or turn over, to the Palestinian Authority within a period of 5 weeks, about 5,000 Palestinian detainees and prisoners, residents of the West Bank and the Gaza Strip. Those released will be free to return to their homes anywhere in the West Bank or the Gaza Strip. Prisoners turned over to the Palestinian Authority shall be obliged to remain in the Gaza Strip or the Jericho Area for the remainder of their sentence. 2. After the signing of this Agreement, the two Parties shall continue to negotiate the release of additional Palestinian prisoners and detainees, building on agreed principles. 3. The implementation of the above measures will be subject to the fulfillment of the procedures determined by Israeli law for the release and transfer of detainees and prisoners. 4. With the assumption of Palestinian authority, the Palestinian side commits itself to solving the problem of those Palestinians who were in contact with the Israeli authorities. Until an agreed solution is found, the Palestinian side undertakes not to prosecute these Palestinians or to harm them in any way. 5. Palestinians from abroad whose entry into the Gaza Strip and the Jericho Area is approved pursuant to this Agreement, and to whom the provisions of this Article are applicable, will not be prosecuted for offenses committed prior to September 13, 1993.

Article XXI. Temporary International Presence 1. The Parties agree to a temporary international or foreign presence in the Gaza Strip and the Jericho Area (hereinafter "the TIP"), in accordance with the provisions of this Article. 2. The TIP shall consist of 400 qualified personnel, including observers, instructors and other experts, from 5 or 6 of the donor countries. 3. The two Parties shall request the donor countries to establish a special fund to provide finance for the TIP. 4. The TIP will function for a period of 6 months. The TIP may extend this period, or change the scope of its operation, with the agreement of the two Parties. 5. The TIP shall be stationed and operate within the following cities and villages: Gaza, Khan Yunis, Rafah, Deir El Ballah, Jabaliya, Absan, Beit Hanun and Jericho. 6. Israel and the Palestinian Authority shall agree on a special Protocol to implement this Article, with the goal of concluding negotiations with the donor countries contributing personnel within two months.

Article XXII. Rights, Liabilities and Obligations. 1. a. The transfer of all powers and responsibilities to the Palestinian Authority, as detailed in Annex II, includes all related rights, liabilities and obligations arising with regard to acts or omissions which occurred prior to the transfer. Israel will cease to bear any financial responsibility regarding such acts or omissions and the Palestinian Authority will bear all financial responsibility for these and for its own functioning. b. Any financial claim made in this regard against Israel will be referred to the Palestinian Authority. c. Israel shall provide the Palestinian Authority with the information it has regarding pending and anticipated claims brought before any court or tribunal against Israel in this regard. d. Where legal proceedings are brought in respect of such a claim, Israel will notify the Palestinian Authority and enable it to participate in defending the claim and raise any arguments on its behalf. e. In the event that an award is made against Israel by any court or tribunal in respect of such a claim, the Palestinian Authority shall reimburse Israel the full amount of the award. f. Without prejudice to the above, where a court or tribunal hearing such a claim finds that liability rests solely with an employee or agent who acted beyond the scope of the powers assigned to him or her, unlawfully or with willful malfeasance, the Palestinian Authority shall not bear financial responsibility. 2. The transfer of authority in itself shall not affect rights, liabilities and obligations of any person or legal entity, in existence at the date of signing of this Agreement.

Article XXIII. Final Clauses. 1. This Agreement shall enter into force on the date of its signing. 2. The arrangements established by this Agreement shall remain in force until and to the extent superseded by the Interim Agreement referred to in the Declaration of Principles or any other agreement between the Parties. 3. The five-year interim period referred to in the Declaration of Principles commences on the date of the signing of this Agreement. 4. The Parties agree that, as long as this Agreement is in force, the security fence erected by Israel around the Gaza Strip shall remain in place and that the line demarcated by the fence, as shown on attached map No. 1, shall be authoritative only for the purpose of this Agreement. 5. Nothing in this Agreement shall prejudice or preempt the outcome of the negotiations on the interim agreement or on the permanent status to be conducted pursuant to the Declaration of Principles. Neither Party shall be deemed, by virtue of having entered into this Agreement, to have renounced or waived any of its existing rights, claims or positions. 6. The two Parties view the West Bank and the Gaza Strip as a single territorial unit, the integrity of which will be preserved during the interim period. 7. The Gaza Strip and the Jericho Area shall continue to be an integral part of the West Bank and the Gaza Strip, and their status shall not be changed for the period of this Agreement. Nothing in this Agreement shall be considered to change this status. 8. The Preamble to this Agreement, and all Annexes, Appendices and maps attached hereto, shall constitute an integral part hereof. Done in Cairo this fourth day of May, 1994.

The document was signed by Israel and the PLO and was witnessed by The United States of America, The Russian Federation, and The Arab Republic of Egypt.

UNSC RESOLUTION 904 (MARCH 18, 1994)

The continued negotiations between Israel and the PLO were punctuated by a series of violent acts designed to disrupt progress toward implementation of the DOP. Among these acts, the Hebron massacre in the Tomb of the Patriarchs on February 25, 1994 proved to be particularly disruptive. On March 18, 1994, the United Nations Security Council adopted resolution 904 in response to the massacre and its effects on the Arab-Israeli peace process.

The Security Council, *Shocked* by the appalling massacre committed against Palestinian worshippers in the Mosque of Ibrahim in Hebron, on 25 February 1994, during the holy month of Ramadan, *Gravely concerned* by the consequent Palestinian casualties in the occupied Palestinian territory as a result of the massacre, which underlines the need to provide protection and security for the Palestinian people, *Determined* to overcome the adverse impact of the massacre on the peace process currently under way, *Noting with satisfaction* the efforts undertaken to guarantee the smooth proceeding of the peace process and calling upon all concerned to continue their efforts to this end, *Noting* the condemnation of this massacre by the entire international community, *Reaffirming* its relevant resolutions, which affirmed the applicability of the Fourth Geneva Convention of 12 August 1949 to the territories occupied by Israel in June 1967, including Jerusalem, and the Israeli responsibilities thereunder, 1. *Strongly condemns* the massacre in Hebron and its aftermath which took the lives of more than 50 Palestinian civilians and injured several hundred others; 2. *Calls upon* Israel, the occupying Power, to continue to take and implement measures, including, inter alia, confiscation of arms, with the aim of preventing illegal acts of violence by Israeli settlers; 3. *Calls for* measures to be taken to guarantee the safety and protection of the Palestinian civilians throughout the occupied territory, including, inter alia, a temporary international or foreign presence, which was provided for in the declaration of principles, within the context of the ongoing peace process; 4. *Requests* the co-sponsors of the peace process, the United States of America and the Russian Federation, to continue their efforts to invigorate the peace process, and to undertake the necessary support for the implementation of the above-mentioned measures; 5. *Reaffirms* its support for the peace process currently under way, and calls for the implementation of the declaration of principles, signed by the Government of Israel and the Palestine Liberation Organization on 13 September 1993 in Washington D.C. without delay.

SHAMGAR COMMISSION REPORT (JUNE 26, 1994)

Following the Hebron massacre, the Government of Israel decided, on February 27, 1994, to appoint a Commission of Inquiry (later it was decided it would be composed of five members) to look into the event. On February 28, the President of the Supreme Court, Justice Meir Shamgar, decided that he would serve as Chairman of the Commission and that the other members would be Justice Eliezer Goldberg, Judge Abd el-Rahman Zoubai, Professor Menachem Yaari and Lieutenant General (res.) Moshe Levy. Investigators were appointed to collect information, and the Commission heard most of the testimony in public sessions. The Commission held 31 sessions and heard evidence from 106 witnesses. It also engaged in a thorough and detailed examination of the Tomb of the Patriarchs and the surrounding area.

The Shamgar Commission issued its report on June 26, 1994. It referred to the killings as a "base and murderous act" and said that "the massacre was one of the harshest expressions of the Jewish-Arab conflict." It concluded that Dr. Baruch Goldstein had acted alone and was the only person to blame for the killings. "The evidence presented to us indicates that he acted alone. We were not presented with credible proof that he was helped, while carrying out the killing or prior to that time, by another individual acting as an accomplice. Nor was it proved to us that he had secret partners." The commission assigned no blame to either military or political officials but criticized Israeli army and border police procedures suggesting that they needed to be tightened in Hebron, especially at the Cave of Machpela. The commission also suggested that Jewish and Muslim worshipers must be separated at the Cave of the Patriarchs.

Chapter 1. Introduction. Following the massacre in the Tomb of the Patriarchs in Hebron which occurred on 14 Adar, 5754 -- 2.25.94, the government decided on 16 Adar, 5754 -- 2.27.94 to appoint a Commission of Inquiry. On 17 Adar, 5754 -- 2.28.94, after consultation with the President of the Supreme Court, it was decided that the Commission would consist of five members. On 17 Adar, 5754 -- 2.28.94, the President of the Supreme Court, Justice Meir Shamgar, decided that he would serve as Chairman of the Commission, and that its other members would be: Justice Eliezer Goldberg, Judge Abed el-Rahman Zouabi, Professor Menachem Ya'ari and Lieutenant

General (res.) Moshe Levy. ...

Chapter 8. Conclusions. ... 2. Responsibility for the Killing and Whether the Assailant Had an Accomplice. (a) Dr. Baruch Goldstein bears direct responsibility for the massacre because the evidence unequivocally indicates that he carried it out. Furthermore, all stages of the event ... indicate that his actions were premeditated. The evidence presented to us indicates that he acted alone. ...

Chapter 9. Recommendations. 1. Arrangements for Prayer and for Security at the Tomb of the Patriarchs. In accordance with the fundamental principles which lie at the heart of the prayer arrangements at the Tomb of the Patriarchs, both Moslems and Jews may pray at the Tomb. We accept these principles. Nevertheless, in light of the lessons to be drawn from the massacre, it is necessary to cancel or to change some of the practical arrangements which were in force in the past. In our recommendations, we were guided by the following principles: first, it would be wise to prevent friction between Jews and Moslems, arising among other reasons, from the fact that prayers are held alternately in the same places, and Jewish and Moslem worshipers come into contact with each other, due to a tight prayer schedule, the result of the fact that worshipers share the same prayer halls at short intervals. This at times has resulted in power struggles which should be prevented; second, the possibility of an attack by Jews against Moslem worshipers must also be taken into account, and not only the contrary, which is as it was in the past. Perhaps the danger of such attacks has even increased; third, sophisticated electronic security devices should be installed; fourth, it will be necessary to station a permanent force on security duty, trained to handle the sensitive and unusual circumstances which arise at a place of worship, which is sacred to the two religions.

Based on these premises, we recommend, first and foremost, that arrangements intended to create complete separation between the Moslem and Jewish worshipers be adopted, in order to ensure the safety of all worshipers, and to prevent friction, disputes and acts of violence. ...

Chapter 10. Epilogue. The massacre at the Tomb of the Patriarchs in Hebron was a base and murderous act, in which innocent people bending in prayer to their maker were killed. It is an unforgivable act, which caused inconsolable grief to the families of the fallen and injured victims, several of whom were permanently disabled.

The massacre was one of the harshest expressions of the Jewish-Arab conflict.

We were asked to investigate the massacre and to determine findings and draw conclusions regarding the circumstances related to it. Thus, in our investigations, we covered the circumstances surrounding the massacre and its results, and we also dealt with certain general issues which, while not directly related to the massacre, were part of the circumstances indirectly related to the event. We discussed these issues in an effort to remove every obstacle and impediment to, and to assist in the maintenance of, the just administration of government.

We presented the lessons which must be learnt from this tragic incident so that, as far as possible, the repetition of criminal acts such as these can be prevented. We made a series of recommendations meant to assist in returning things to normal both in the Tomb of the Patriarchs in particular, and generally in Hebron.

Let us hope that our inquiry and our Report will indeed contribute to that end. ...

WASHINGTON DECLARATION (JULY 25, 1994)

As Israel and the PLO continued their efforts to implement the Declaration of Principles, Israel and Jordan conducted negotiations to achieve peace along the lines of their 1993 Agreed Common Agenda. On July 25, 1994, King Hussein of Jordan and Prime Minister Yitzhak Rabin of Israel signed the Washington Declaration in Washington, D.C.

A. After generations of hostility, blood and tears and in the wake of years of pain and wars, His Majesty King Hussein and Prime Minister Yitzhak Rabin are determined to bring an end to bloodshed and sorrow. It is in this spirit that His Majesty King Hussein of the Hashemite Kingdom of Jordan and Prime Minister and Minister of Defense, Mr. Yitzhak Rabin of Israel, met in Washington today at the invitation of President William J. Clinton of the United States of America. This initiative of President William J. Clinton constitutes an historic landmark in the United States' untiring efforts in promoting peace and stability in the Middle East. The personal involvement of the President has made it possible to realize agreement on the content of this historic declaration.

The signing of this declaration bears testimony to the President's vision and devotion to the cause of peace.

B. In their meeting, His Majesty King Hussein and Prime Minister Yitzhak Rabin have jointly reaffirmed the five underlying principles of their understanding on an Agreed Common Agenda designed to reach the goal of a just, lasting and comprehensive peace between the Arab States and the Palestinians, with Israel.

1. Jordan and Israel aim at the achievement of just, lasting and comprehensive peace between Israel and its neighbors and at the conclusion of a Treaty of Peace between both countries.

2. The two countries will vigorously continue their negotiations to arrive at a state of peace, based on Security Council Resolutions 242 and 338 in all their aspects, and founded on freedom, equality and justice.

3. Israel respects the present special role of the Hashemite Kingdom of Jordan in Muslim Holy shrines in Jerusalem. When negotiations on the permanent status will take place, Israel will give high priority to the Jordanian historic role in these shrines. In addition the two sides have agreed to act together to promote interfaith relations among the three monotheistic religions.

4. The two countries recognize their right and obligation to live in peace with each other as well as with all states within secure and recognized boundaries. The two states affirmed their respect for and acknowledgment of the sovereignty, territorial integrity and political independence of every state in the area.

5. The two countries desire to develop good neighborly relations of cooperation between them to ensure lasting security and to avoid threats and the use of force between them.

C. The long conflict between the two states is now coming to an end. In this spirit the state of belligerency between Jordan and Israel has been terminated.

D. Following this declaration and in keeping with the Agreed Common Agenda, both countries will refrain from actions or activities by either side that may adversely affect the security of the other or may prejudice the final outcome of negotiations. Neither side will threaten the other by use of force, weapons, or any other means, against each other and both sides will thwart threats to security resulting from all kinds of terrorism.

E. His Majesty King Hussein and Prime Minister Yitzhak Rabin took note of the progress made in the bilateral negotiations within the Jordan-Israel track last week on the steps decided to implement the sub-agendas on borders, territorial matters, security, water, energy, environment and the Jordan Rift Valley.

In this framework, mindful of items of the Agreed Common Agenda (borders and territorial matters) they noted that the boundary sub-commission has reached agreement in July 1994 in fulfillment of part of the role entrusted to it in the sub-agenda. They also noted that the sub-commission for water, environment and energy agreed to mutually recognize, as the role of their negotiations, the rightful allocations of the two sides in Jordan River and Yarmouk River waters and to fully respect and comply with the negotiated rightful allocations, in accordance with agreed acceptable principles with mutually acceptable quality. Similarly, His Majesty King Hussein and Prime Minister Yitzhak Rabin expressed their deep satisfaction and pride in the work of the trilateral commission in its meeting held in Jordan on Wednesday, July 20th 1994, hosted by the Jordanian Prime Minister, Dr. Abdessalam al-Majali, and attended by Secretary of State Warren Christopher and Foreign Minister Shimon Peres. They voiced their pleasure at the association and commitment of the United States in this endeavor.

F. His Majesty King Hussein and Prime Minister Yitzhak Rabin believe that steps must be taken both to overcome psychological barriers and to break with the legacy of war. By working with optimism towards the dividends of peace for all the people in the region, Jordan and Israel are determined to shoulder their responsibilities towards the human dimension of peace making. They recognize imbalances and disparities are a root cause of extremism which thrives on poverty and unemployment and the degradation of human dignity. In this spirit His Majesty King Hussein and Prime Minister Yitzhak Rabin have today approved a series of steps to symbolize the new era which is now at hand:

1. Direct telephone links will be opened between Jordan and Israel.

2. The electricity grids of Jordan and Israel will be linked as part of a regional concept.

3. Two new border crossings will be opened between Jordan and Israel -- one at the southern tip of Aqaba-Eilat and the other at the a mutually agreed point in the north.

4. In principle free access will be given to third country tourists traveling between Jordan and Israel.

5. Negotiations will be accelerated on opening an international air corridor between both countries.

6. The police forces of Jordan and Israel will cooperate in combating crime with emphasis on smuggling and particularly drug smuggling. The United States will be invited to participate in this joint endeavor.

7. Negotiations on economic matters will continue in order to prepare for future bilateral cooperation including the abolition of all economic boycotts.

All these steps are being implemented within the framework of regional infrastructural development plans and in conjunction with the Jordan-Israel bilaterals on boundaries, security, water and related issues and without prejudice to the final outcome of the negotiations on the items included in the Agreed Common Agenda between Jordan and Israel.

G. His Majesty King Hussein and Prime Minister Yitzhak Rabin have agreed to meet periodically or whenever they feel necessary to review the progress of the negotiations and express their firm intention to shepherd and direct the process in its entirety.

H. In conclusion, His Majesty King Hussein and Prime Minister Yitzhak Rabin wish to express once again their profound thanks and appreciation to President William J. Clinton and his Administration for their untiring efforts in furthering the cause of peace, justice and prosperity for all the peoples of the region. They wish to thank the President personally for his warm welcome and hospitality. In recognition of their appreciation to the President, His Majesty King Hussein and Prime Minister Yitzhak Rabin have asked President William J. Clinton to sign this document as a witness and as a host to their meeting.

The declaration was signed by His Majesty King Hussein, Prime Minister Yitzhak Rabin, and by President William J. Clinton.

EARLY EMPOWERMENT AGREEMENT (AUGUST 29, 1994)

On August 24, 1994 an agreement on the early transfer of certain civil responsibilities in the West Bank from Israel to the Palestinian Authority was initialed in Cairo. This early empowerment agreement was a provision of the Israel-Palestinian Declaration of Principles and was signed by Major General Danny Rothchild of the Israel Defense Forces (IDF) and Palestinian Authority member Nabil Shaath in a ceremony at the Erez crossing between Israel and the Gaza Strip on August 29, 1994.

The Agreement on Preparatory Transfer of Powers and Responsibilities provides for the transfer of powers to the Palestinian Authority in five spheres: (1) Education and culture: responsibility over higher education, special education, cultural and educational training activities, institutions and programs, and private, public non-governmental or other educational or cultural activities or institutions. (2) Health: authority over all health institutions. (3) Social welfare: authority over governmental and non-governmental organizations and institutions, including charitable societies and institutions and voluntary and non-profit organizations. (4) Tourism: regulating, licensing, grading, supervising and developing the tourist industry. (5) Direct taxation and indirect taxation: Authority for the income tax and for Value Added Tax.

The educational system was transferred to the Palestinian Authority on August 28, 1994. On November 15, 1994, Israel transferred authority in the fields of welfare and tourism to the Palestinians. On December 1, 1994 Israel transferred responsibility for health and taxation to the Palestinian Authority. This completed the implementation of the early empowerment agreement.

The Government of the State of Israel and the Palestine Liberation Organization (hereinafter "the PLO"), the representative of the Palestinian people;

PREAMBLE

WITHIN the framework of the Middle East peace process initiated at Madrid in October 1991; REAFFIRMING their determination to live in peaceful coexistence, mutual dignity and security, while recognizing their mutual legitimate and political rights; REAFFIRMING their desire to achieve a just, lasting and comprehensive peace settlement through the agreed political process; REAFFIRMING their adherence to the mutual recognition and commitments expressed in the letters dated September 9, 1993, signed by and exchanged between the Prime Minister of Israel and the Chairman of the PLO; REAFFIRMING their understanding that the interim self-government arrangements, including the preparatory arrangements to apply in the West Bank contained in this Agreement, are an integral part of the whole peace process and that the negotiations on the permanent status will lead to the implementation of Security Council Resolutions 242 and 338; FOLLOWING the Agreement on the Gaza

Strip and the Jericho Area as signed at Cairo on May 4, 1994 (hereinafter "the Gaza-Jericho Agreement"); DESIROUS of putting into effect the Declaration of Principles on Interim Self-Government Arrangements as signed at Washington, D.C. on September 13, 1993 (hereinafter "the Declaration of Principles"), and in particular Article VI regarding preparatory transfer of powers and responsibilities and the Agreed Minutes thereto; HEREBY AGREE to the following arrangements regarding the preparatory transfer of powers and responsibilities in the West Bank:

Article I. Definitions. For the purpose of this Agreement, unless otherwise indicated in the attached Protocols: a. the term "the Palestinian Authority" means the Palestinian Authority established in accordance with the Gaza-Jericho Agreement; b. the term "Joint Liaison Committee" means the Joint Israeli-Palestinian Liaison Committee established pursuant to Article X of the Declaration of Principles; c. the term "Interim Agreement" means the interim agreement referred to in Article VII of the Declaration of Principles; and d. the term "Israelis" also includes Israeli statutory agencies and corporations registered in Israel.

Article II. Preparatory Transfer of Powers and Responsibilities. 1. Israel shall transfer and the Palestinian Authority shall assume powers and responsibilities from the Israeli military government and its Civil Administration in the West Bank in the following spheres: education and culture, health, social welfare, tourism, direct taxation and Value Added Tax on local production (hereinafter "VAT"), as specified in this Agreement (hereinafter "the Spheres"). 2. For the purposes of this Agreement, the Palestinian Authority shall constitute the authorized Palestinians referred to in Article VI of the Declaration of Principles. 3. The Parties will explore the possible expansion of the transfer of powers and responsibilities to additional spheres.

Article III. Scope of the Transferred Powers and Responsibilities. 1. The scope of the powers and responsibilities transferred in each Sphere, as well as specific arrangements regarding the exercise of such powers and responsibilities, are set out in the Protocols attached as Annexes I through VI. 2. In accordance with the Declaration of Principles, the jurisdiction of the Palestinian Authority with regard to the powers and responsibilities transferred by this Agreement will not apply to Jerusalem, settlements, military locations and, unless otherwise provided in this Agreement, Israelis. 3. The transfer of powers and responsibilities under this Agreement does not include powers and responsibilities in the sphere of foreign relations, except as indicated in Article VI(2)(b) of the Gaza-Jericho Agreement.

Article IV. Modalities of Transfer. 1. The transfer of powers and responsibilities in the sphere of education and culture pursuant to this Agreement will be implemented on August 29, 1994. The transfer of powers and responsibilities in the remaining Spheres will be implemented in accordance with Article XI below. 2. The transfer of powers and responsibilities shall be coordinated through the Civil Affairs Coordination and Cooperation Committee referred to in Article X below and shall be implemented in accordance with the arrangements set out in this Agreement in a smooth, peaceful and orderly manner. 3. Upon the signing of this Agreement, the Israeli side shall provide the Palestinian side with, or enable free access to, all information that is necessary for an effective and smooth transfer. 4. On the date of the transfer of powers and responsibilities, Israel shall also transfer all movable and immovable property which exclusively serves the offices of the Civil Administration in the Spheres, including premises, whether government-owned or rented, equipment, registers, files and computer programs. The treatment of property which serves the offices transferred to the Palestinian Authority as well as offices which are not so transferred will be as mutually agreed between the two sides, such as on the basis of sharing or exchange. 5. The coordination of the transfer of powers and responsibilities pursuant to this Article shall also include a joint review of the Civil Administration contracts the duration of which extends beyond the date of the transfer with a view to deciding which contracts will remain in force and which will be terminated.

Article V. Administration of the Transferred Offices. 1. The Palestinian Authority shall be fully responsible for the proper functioning of the offices included in the Spheres and for the management of their personnel in all aspects, including employment and placement of employees, payment of their salaries and pensions and ensuring other employee rights. 2. The Palestinian Authority will continue to employ Palestinian Civil Administration employees currently employed in the offices included in each Sphere and shall maintain their rights. 3. The main office of each of the Spheres will be situated in the Jericho Area or in the Gaza Strip. The Palestinian Authority will operate the existing subordinate offices in the West Bank. The two sides may agree on the establishment of additional subordinate offices in the West Bank, if necessary, in such locations as mutually agreed. 4. The Palestinian Authority has the right to coordinate its activities in each of the Spheres with other Spheres in which it is empowered.

Article VI. Relations Between the Two Sides. 1. With regard to each Sphere, the Palestinian Authority shall coordinate with the Civil Administration on issues relating to other spheres in which the Palestinian Authority is not empowered. 2. The military government and its Civil Administration shall assist and support the Palestinian Authority in promoting the effective exercise of its powers and responsibilities. In addition, the military government and its Civil Administration shall, in exercising their own powers and responsibilities, take into account the interests of the Palestinian Authority and do their utmost to remove obstacles to the effective exercise of powers and responsibilities by the Palestinian Authority. 3. The Palestinian Authority shall prevent any activities with a military orientation within each of the Spheres and will do its utmost to maintain decorum and discipline and to avoid disruption in the institutions under its responsibility. 4. The Palestinian Authority will notify the military government and its Civil Administration and will coordinate with them regarding any planned public large-scale events and mass gatherings within the Spheres. 5. Nothing in this Agreement shall affect the continued authority of the military government and its Civil Administration to exercise their powers and responsibilities with regard to security and public order, as well as with regard to other spheres not transferred.

Article VII. Legislative Powers of the Palestinian Authority. 1. The Palestinian Authority may promulgate secondary legislation regarding the powers and responsibilities transferred to it. Such legislation includes amendments and changes to the existing laws, regulations and military orders specified in Appendix A to each Annex. 2. Legislation promulgated by the Palestinian Authority shall be consistent with the provisions of this Agreement. ...

Article VIII. Law Enforcement. 1. The Palestinian Authority may bring disciplinary proceedings concerning persons it employs in the West Bank before disciplinary tribunals operating in the Gaza Strip or the Jericho Area. 2. The Palestinian Authority may, within each of the Spheres, authorize employees to act as civilian inspectors to monitor compliance with laws and regulations in that Sphere, within the powers and responsibilities transferred to the Palestinian Authority. ... 4. Except as specifically provided in this Agreement, all powers and responsibilities regarding law enforcement, including investigation, judicial proceedings and imprisonment, will continue to be under the responsibility of the existing authorities in the West Bank.

Article IX. Rights, Liabilities and Obligations. 1. a. The transfer of powers and responsibilities to the Palestinian Authority under this Agreement will include all related rights, liabilities and obligations arising with regard to acts or omissions which occurred prior to the transfer. Israel and the Civil Administration will cease to bear any financial responsibility regarding such acts or omissions and the Palestinian Authority will bear all financial responsibility for these and for its own functioning. ...

Article X. Liaison and Coordination. 1. The Joint Civil Affairs Coordination and Cooperation Committee established in accordance with the Gaza-Jericho Agreement, (hereinafter "the CAC"), will deal with all issues of mutual concern regarding this Agreement. 2. The operation of the CAC shall not impede daily contacts between representatives of the Civil Administration and the Palestinian Authority in all matters of mutual concern.

Article XI. Budgetary Issues. 1. The military government and its Civil Administration shall provide the Palestinian Authority with full information concerning the budget of each Sphere. 2. The Palestinian Authority shall immediately employ personnel who will promptly begin the process of becoming acquainted with the current budget issues. On the date of the transfer of powers and responsibilities in each of the Spheres, these personnel will assume responsibility for all accounts, assets and records on behalf of the Palestinian Authority. 3. Israel shall continue to provide the services of Israeli experts currently employed in the fields of income tax and VAT to ensure a smooth transition and efficient establishment of the taxation system of the Palestinian Authority. The terms of their employment shall be agreed upon by the two sides. 4. The Palestinian Authority will do its utmost to establish its revenue collection system immediately with the intent of collecting direct taxes and VAT. 5. The two sides will jointly approach the donor countries during the upcoming meetings of the Consultative Group and of the Ad Hoc Liaison Committee, scheduled for September 8 through 10, 1994 in Paris, with a request to finance the shortfall that may be created in the collection of the direct taxes and the VAT during the initial period while the Palestinian Authority establishes its own revenue collection system. 6. The two sides will meet no later than three days after the conclusion of these meetings in order to decide on the date of transfer of powers and responsibilities in the remaining Spheres, based, among other things, on the response of the donor countries to the joint request. 7. The CAC will provide the donor countries, when necessary, with information to help adjust the allocation of contributions as a result of variations in tax collection. 8. The Palestinian Authority shall also assume full responsibility for any additional expenditures beyond the agreed budget which is attached as Schedule 1, as well as for any shortfall in tax collection that is not actually covered by the donor countries. 9. If actual revenues from the Spheres, including the donor contributions, exceed the budgeted revenues, the excess shall be applied to development of the Spheres. 10. The inclusion of the sphere of VAT in the spheres to be transferred to the Palestinian Authority shall constitute the adjustment referred to in paragraph (3) of the Agreed Minute to Article VI(2) of the Declaration of Principles, and no further adjustment shall be required.

Article XII. Mutual Contribution to Peace and Reconciliation. With regard to each of the Spheres, Israel and the Palestinian Authority will ensure that their respective systems contribute to the peace between the Israeli and Palestinian peoples and to peace in the entire region, and will refrain from the introduction of any motifs that could adversely affect the process of reconciliation.

Article XIII. Final Clauses. 1. This Agreement shall enter into force on the date of its signing. 2. The arrangements established by this Agreement are preparatory measures and shall remain in force until and to the extent superseded by the Interim Agreement or by any other agreement between the Parties. 3. Nothing in this Agreement shall prejudice or preempt the outcome of the negotiations on the Interim Agreement or on the permanent status to be conducted pursuant to the Declaration of Principles. Neither Party shall be deemed, by virtue of having entered into this Agreement, to have renounced or waived any of its existing rights, claims or positions. 4. The two Parties view the West Bank and the Gaza Strip as a single territorial unit, the integrity of which will be preserved during the interim period. 5. The Gaza Strip and the Jericho Area shall continue to be an integral part of the West Bank and the Gaza Strip. The status of the West Bank shall not be changed for the period of this

Agreement. Nothing in this Agreement shall be considered to change this status. 6. The Preamble to this Agreement and the Annexes, Appendices and Schedules attached hereto, shall constitute an integral part hereof.

Done at Erez this twenty-ninth day of August 1994.

Annex I

Protocol Concerning Preparatory Transfer of Powers and Responsibilities in the Sphere of Education and Culture. 1. The powers and responsibilities of the military government and its Civil Administration in the sphere of education and culture will be transferred to and will be assumed by the Palestinian Authority. 2. The sphere of education and culture shall include all matters dealt with in the laws, regulations and military orders listed in Appendix A, as well as the responsibility over higher education, special education, cultural and educational training activities, cultural and educational institutions and programs, and private, public, non-governmental or other educational or cultural activities or institutions.

Appendix A

Laws, Regulations and Military Orders in the Sphere of Education and Culture. [Not reproduced here]

Annex II

Protocol Concerning Preparatory Transfer of Powers and Responsibilities in the Sphere of Health. 1. The powers and responsibilities of the military government and its Civil Administration in the sphere of health will be transferred to and will be assumed by the Palestinian Authority. 2. The sphere of health shall include all matters dealt with in the laws, regulations and military orders listed in Appendix A, including the responsibility over all health institutions, whether private, public, non-governmental or other. ...

Appendix A

Laws, Regulations and Military Orders in the Sphere of Health. [Not reproduced here]

Annex III

Protocol Concerning Preparatory Transfer of Powers and Responsibilities in the Sphere of Social Welfare. 1. The powers and responsibilities of the military government and its Civil Administration in the sphere of social welfare will be transferred to and will be assumed by the Palestinian Authority. 2. The sphere of social welfare shall include all matters dealt with in the laws, regulations and military orders listed in Appendix A, as well as responsibility over governmental and non-governmental organizations and institutions, including charitable societies and institutions and voluntary and non-profit organizations. ...

Appendix A

Laws, Regulations and Military Orders in the Sphere of Social Welfare. [Not reproduced here]

Annex IV

Protocol Concerning Preparatory Transfer of Powers and Responsibilities in the Sphere of Tourism. 1. The powers and responsibilities of the military government and its Civil Administration in the sphere of tourism will be transferred to and will be assumed by the Palestinian Authority. 2. The sphere of tourism shall include all matters dealt with in the laws, regulations and military orders listed in Appendix A. This includes the responsibility for regulating, licensing, grading, supervising and developing the tourist industry and its services within the scope of such terms in the laws, regulations and military orders listed in Appendix A, as well as maintaining and promoting foreign and domestic tourism, developing visitors' interest in tourist sites and encouraging the development of tourist services around them in coordination with the Civil Administration, or if the site is under the responsibility of another authority - in coordination with that other authority. It also includes organizing exhibitions, popular and cultural festivals and events and tourism conferences. This sphere shall cover tourism activities conducted by private, public, non-governmental and foreign bodies. ...

Appendix A

Laws, Regulations and Military Orders in the Sphere of Tourism [Not reproduced here]

Annex V

Protocol Concerning Preparatory Transfer of Powers and Responsibilities in the Sphere of Direct Taxation. 1. The powers and responsibilities of the Civil Administration in the sphere of direct taxation regarding income tax on income accrued or derived in the West Bank will be transferred to and will be assumed by the Palestinian Authority. Powers and responsibilities regarding property tax will continue to be exercised by the Civil Administration, though the income from this tax will be transferred to the Palestinian Authority, after deducting the sums due to the municipalities. ...

Appendix A

Laws, Regulations and Military Orders in the Sphere of Direct Taxation. [Not reproduced here]

Appendix B

Tax Enforcement. [Not reproduced here]

Annex VI

Protocol Concerning Preparatory Transfer of Powers and Responsibilities in the Sphere of VAT on Local Production.

1. The powers and responsibilities of the Civil Administration in the sphere of VAT on local production in the West Bank will be transferred to and will be assumed by the Palestinian Authority. ...

OSLO DECLARATION (SEPTEMBER 13, 1994)

On the first anniversary of the signing of the Israel-PLO Declaration of Principles, Yasser Arafat and Shimon Peres met in Oslo and issued the Oslo Declaration.

1. On the occasion of meeting in Oslo on September 13 for the first anniversary of the signing of the Declaration of Principles, Foreign Minister Bjoern Tore Godal, Chairman Yasser Arafat and Foreign Minister Shimon Peres declared their appreciation for the gradual implementation of the Declaration of Principles in Gaza and Jericho first and the beginning of the implementation of the agreement regarding early empowerment in the West Bank.

Mr. Arafat and Mr. Peres expressed their appreciation to the people and the Government of Norway for their unique role in the historic breakthrough between the Israeli people and the Palestinian people.

Representatives of the United States, the Federal Republic of Germany in her capacity as President of the European Union, Japan, the EU Commission and the United Nations were present at an unofficial meeting between the parties and the donor community.

2. The two sides declared their commitment to fully implement the Declaration of Principles and to continue the process between them based on the Declaration of Principles and on subsequent agreements.

3. The two sides declared that they see the role of the ongoing political process between them as contributing to the security of both sides and are committed to taking the necessary measures to put an end to acts of violence, moving to implement outstanding and mutual confidence building measures, promoting their economic relationship, and developing the economy of the Palestinian Authority.

4. In this context, the two sides have agreed to ask the Government of Norway, as chair of the Ad Hoc Liaison committee, to convene an unofficial emergency meeting as soon as possible in Paris to be guided by the following principles and needs:

a. The two sides call on the donor community to make an immediate effort to meet the recurrent costs of the Palestinian Authority and the early empowerment.

b. Both sides accept the request by the AHLC chairman that they shall not bring before the donor community (the AHLC or the Consultative Group) those political issues that are of disagreement between them. They will deal with such issues between themselves, based on the Declaration of Principles and subsequent agreements.

c. The PLO reaffirms its commitment to develop the tax collection system of the Palestinian Authority in order to limit the timetable for foreign assistance to cover recurrent costs. Donor contributions to finance recurrent costs will gradually decrease with the increase of Palestinian revenues.

d. The emergency financial needs, including existing arrears, of the Palestinian Police should be financed by the donor community preferably until the end of 1994 only (and not exceeding the end of March 1995).

Mr. Arafat and Mr. Peres will together approach the Secretary-General of the United Nations to request that the United Nations Development Programme should serve as the mechanism for immediately channeling existing funds to the Palestinian Police.

e. The parties have decided that, based on donor contributions, they will sign an understanding setting out the responsibilities of the donors, Israel and the Palestinian Authority at next week's meeting of the AHLC, concerning financing of the early empowerment based on Palestinian-Israeli cooperative efforts to establish a fully-functioning Palestinian tax collection mechanism. A draft understanding will be distributed among the donors prior to the meeting.

f. Subsequently, regarding the operation of the Holst Fund, the United States, Norway, the United Nations and others will commence a high level and intensive effort to generate funds and to reallocate existing funds. The United States has informed the parties that it will dispatch envoys to various capitals, including those in the region. Donors have advised that they will make a great effort to contribute to the Holst Fund and other recurrent cost instruments.

g. A special effort will be made to seek support for transitional projects and short-term job creation projects which donors can implement quickly.

h. The successful implementation of the above efforts to cover the urgent needs of the Palestinian Authority, the Palestinian Police and early empowerment will enable the donor community to focus on the longer-term development needs of Gaza and the West Bank.

i. In order to encourage fast implementation of Palestinian project development in the West Bank, the Civil Administration and PECDAR will discuss their means of cooperation under the existing system and procedures until full empowerment in the West Bank is reached.

5. Mr. Arafat and Mr. Peres expressed their satisfaction with the recent positive developments in the peace process, including the recent developments between Jordan and Israel, the recent statements by Syria and by Israel, the recent statements by Syria and by Israel and the upcoming Casablanca conference.

ISRAEL-JORDAN PEACE TREATY (OCTOBER 26, 1994)

On October 17, 1994, Israel and Jordan initialled a peace agreement in Amman, Jordan. The signing ceremony took place on October 26, 1994 in the Jordan Valley. Prime Minister Abdul-Salam Majali of Jordan and Prime Minister Yitzhak

Rabin of Israel signed the treaty while United States President Bill Clinton served as a witness. The peace treaty comprises thirty articles, and includes five annexes which deal with boundary demarcations, water issues, police cooperation, environmental issues and mutual border crossings. The treaty resolved the major outstanding issues between the two parties in the areas of security, border demarcation, water, and the establishment of normalized relations. The border was to be based on maps drawn up by the British Mandate. Jordan agreed to lease back to Israel (for 25 years with an option to renew) cultivated agricultural lands which Israel agreed to return to Jordan. Israel agreed to transfer water to Jordan from existing sources and they will jointly operate new water purification plants. Both parties agreed not to join, aid or cooperate with a party whose goal is to attack the other side and neither will allow any military force or equipment which may harm the other side to enter their territory. They pledged to cooperate in combatting terrorism and to solve the refugee problem. They will establish peace, full diplomatic and normalized relations. Israel will also recognize Jordan's special role with respect to the Muslim holy places in Jerusalem. They will seek economic cooperation as a pillar of peace as noted various areas of potential effort, especially tourism.

TREATY OF PEACE BETWEEN THE STATE OF ISRAEL AND THE HASHEMITE KINGDOM OF JORDAN.

Preamble. The Government of the State of Israel and the Government of the Hashemite Kingdom of Jordan: Bearing in mind the Washington Declaration, signed by them on 25th July, 1994, and which they are both committed to honour; Aiming at the achievement of a just, lasting and comprehensive peace in the Middle East based an Security Council resolutions 242 and 338 in all their aspects; Bearing in mind the importance of maintaining and strengthening peace based on freedom, equality, justice and respect for fundamental human rights, thereby overcoming psychological barriers and promoting human dignity; Reaffirming their faith in the purposes and principles of the Charter of the United Nations and recognising their right and obligation to live in peace with each other as well as with all states, within secure and recognised boundaries; Desiring to develop friendly relations and co-operation between them in accordance with the principles of international law governing international relations in time of peace; Desiring as well to ensure lasting security for both their States and in particular to avoid threats and the use of force between them; Bearing in mind that in their Washington Declaration of 25th July, 1994, they declared the termination of the state of belligerency between them; Deciding to establish peace between them in accordance with this Treaty of Peace; Have agreed as follows:

Article 1. Establishment of Peace. Peace is hereby established between the State of Israel and the Hashemite Kingdom of Jordan (the "Parties") effective from the exchange of the instruments of ratification of this Treaty.

Article 2. General Principles. The Parties will apply between them the provisions of the Charter of the United Nations and the principles of international law governing relations among states in times of peace. In particular: 1. They recognise and will respect each other's sovereignty, territorial integrity and political independence; 2. They recognise and will respect each other's right to live in peace within secure and recognised boundaries; 3. They will develop good neighbourly relations of co-operation between them to ensure lasting security, will refrain from the threat or use of force against each other and will settle all disputes between them by peaceful means; 4. They respect and recognise the sovereignty, territorial integrity and political independence of every state in the region; 5. They respect and recognise the pivotal role of human development and dignity in regional and bilateral relationships; 6. They further believe that within their control, involuntary movements of persons in such a way as to adversely prejudice the security of either Party should not be permitted.

Article 3. International Boundary. 1. The international boundary between Israel and Jordan is delimited with reference to the boundary definition under the Mandate as is shown in Annex I (a), on the mapping materials attached thereto and co-ordinates specified therein. 2. The boundary, as set out in Annex I (a), is the permanent, secure and recognised international boundary between Israel and Jordan, without prejudice to the status of any territories that came under Israeli military government control in 1967. 3. The Parties recognise the international boundary, as well as each other's territory, territorial waters and airspace, as inviolable, and will respect and comply with them. 4. The demarcation of the boundary will take place as set forth in Appendix (I) to Annex I and will be concluded not later than nine months after the signing of the Treaty. 5. It is agreed that where the boundary follows a river, in the event of natural changes in the course of the flow of the river as described in Annex I (a), the boundary shall follow the new course of the flow. In the event of any other changes the boundary shall not be affected unless otherwise agreed. 6. Immediately upon the exchange of the instruments of ratification of this Treaty, each Party will deploy on its side of the international boundary as defined in Annex I (a). 7. The Parties shall, upon the signature of the Treaty, enter into negotiations to conclude, within 9 months, an agreement on the delimitation of their maritime boundary in the Gulf of Aqaba. 8. Taking into account the special circumstances of the Naharayim/Baqura area, which is under Jordanian sovereignty, with Israeli private ownership rights, the Parties agreed to apply the provisions set out in Annex I (b). 9. With respect to the Zofar/Al-Ghamr area, the provisions set out in Annex I (c) will apply.

Article 4. Security. 1. a. Both Parties, acknowledging that mutual understanding and co-operation in security-related matters will form a significant part of their relations and will further enhance the security of the region, take upon themselves to base their security relations on mutual trust, advancement of joint interests and co-operation, and to aim towards a regional framework of partnership in peace. b. Towards that goal the Parties recognise the achievements of the European Community and European Union in the development of the Conference on Security and Co-operation in Europe (CSCE) and commit themselves to the creation, in the Middle East, of a CSCME (Conference on Security and Co-operation in the Middle East). This commitment entails the adoption of regional models of security successfully implemented in the post World War era (along the lines of the Helsinki process) culminating in a regional zone of security and stability. 2. The obligations referred to in this Article are without prejudice to the inherent right of self-defence in accordance with the United Nations Charter. 3. The Parties undertake, in accordance with the provisions of this Article, the following: a. to refrain from the threat or use of force or weapons, conventional, non-conventional or of any other kind, against each other, or of other actions or activities that adversely affect the security of the other Party; b. to refrain from organising, instigating, inciting, assisting or participating in acts or threats of belligerency, hostility, subversion or violence against the other Party; c. to take necessary and effective measures to ensure that acts or threats of belligerency, hostility, subversion or violence against the other Party do not originate from, and are not committed within, through or over their territory (hereinafter the term "territory" includes the airspace and territorial waters). 4. Consistent with the era of peace and with the efforts to build regional security and to avoid and prevent aggression and violence, the Parties further agree to refrain from the following: a. joining or in any way assisting, promoting or co-operating with any coalition, organisation or alliance with a military or security character with a third party, the objectives or activities of which include launching aggression or other acts of military hostility against the other Party, in contravention of the provisions of the present Treaty. b. allowing the entry, stationing and operating on their territory, or through it, of military forces, personnel or materiel of a third party, in circumstances which may adversely prejudice the security of the other Party. 5. Both Parties will take necessary and effective measures, and will co-operate in combating terrorism of all kinds. The Parties undertake: a. to take necessary and effective measures to prevent acts of terrorism, subversion or violence from being carried out from their territory or through it and to take necessary and effective measures to combat such activities and all their perpetrators. b. without prejudice to the basic rights of freedom of expression and association, to take necessary and effective measures to prevent the entry, presence and co-operation in their territory of any group or organisation, and their infrastructure, which threatens the security of the other Party by the use of or incitement to the use of, violent means. c. to co-operate in preventing and combating cross-boundary infiltrations. 6. Any question as to the implementation of this Article will be dealt with through a mechanism of consultations which will include a liaison system, verification, supervision, and where necessary, other mechanisms, and higher level consultation. The details of the mechanism of consultations will be contained in an agreement to be concluded by the Parties within 3 months of the exchange of the instruments of ratification of this Treaty. 7. The Parties undertake to work as a matter of priority, and as soon as possible in the context of the Multilateral Working Group on Arms Control and Regional Security, and jointly, towards the following: a. the creation in the Middle East of a region free from hostile alliances and coalitions; b. the creation of a Middle East free from weapons of mass destruction, both conventional and non-conventional, in the context of a comprehensive, lasting and stable peace, characterized by the renunciation of the use of force, reconciliation and goodwill.

Article 5. Diplomatic and Other Bilateral Relations. 1. The Parties agree to establish full diplomatic and consular relations and to exchange resident ambassadors within one month of the exchange of the instruments of ratification of this Treaty. 2. The Parties agree that the normal relationship between them will further include economic and cultural relations.

Article 6. Water. With the view to achieving a comprehensive and lasting settlement of all the water problems between them: 1. The Parties agree mutually to recognise the rightful allocations of both of them in Jordan River and Yarmouk River waters and Araba/Arava ground water in accordance with the agreed acceptable principles, quantities and quality as set out in Annex II, which shall be fully respected and complied with. 2. The Parties, recognising the necessity to find a practical, just and agreed solution to their water problems and with the view that the subject of water can form the basis for the advancement of co-operation between them, jointly undertake to ensure that the management and development of their water resources do not, in any way, harm the water resources of the other Party. 3. The Parties recognise that their water resources are not sufficient to meet their needs. More water should be supplied for their use through various methods, including projects of regional and international co-operation. 4. In light of paragraph 3 of this Article, with the understanding that co-operation in water-related subjects would be to the benefit of both Parties, and will help alleviate their water shortages, and that water issues along their entire boundary must be dealt with in their totality, including the possibility of trans-boundary water transfers, the Parties agree to search for ways to alleviate water shortage and to co-operate in the following fields: a. development of existing and new water resources, increasing the water availability including co-operation on a regional basis as appropriate, and minimising wastage of water resources through the chain of their uses; b. prevention of contamination of water resources; c. mutual assistance in the alleviation of water shortages; d. transfer of information and joint research and development in water-related subjects, and review of the potentials for enhancement of water resources development and use. 5. The implementation of both Parties' undertakings under this Article is detailed in Annex II.

Article 7. Economic Relations. 1. Viewing economic development and prosperity as pillars of peace, security and harmonious relations between states, peoples and individual human beings, the Parties, taking note of understandings reached between them, affirm their mutual desire to promote economic co-operation between them, as well as within the framework of wider regional economic co-operation. 2. In order to accomplish this goal, the Parties agree to the following: a. to remove all discriminatory barriers to normal economic relations, to terminate economic boycotts directed at each other, and to co-operate in terminating boycotts against either Party by third parties; b. recognising that the principle of free and unimpeded flow of goods and services should guide their relations, the Parties will enter into negotiations with a view to concluding agreements on economic co-operation, including trade and the establishment of a free trade area, investment, banking, industrial co-operation and labour, for the purpose of promoting beneficial economic relations, based on principles to be agreed upon, as well as on human development considerations on a regional basis. These negotiations will be concluded no later than 6 months from the exchange the instruments of ratification of this Treaty; c. to co-operate bilaterally, as well as in multilateral forums, towards the promotion of their respective economies and of their neighbourly economic relations with other regional parties.

Article 8. Refugees and Displaced Persons. 1. Recognising the massive human problems caused to both Parties by the conflict in the Middle East, as well as the contribution made by them towards the alleviation of human suffering, the Parties will seek to further alleviate those problems arising on a bilateral level. 2. Recognising that the above human problems caused by the conflict in the Middle East cannot be fully resolved on the bilateral level, the Parties will seek to resolve them in appropriate forums, in accordance with international law, including the following: (a) in the case of displaced persons, in a quadripartite committee together with Egypt and the Palestinians: (b) in the case of refugees, (i) in the framework of the Multilateral Working Group on Refugees; (ii) in negotiations, in a framework to be agreed, bilateral or otherwise, in conjunction with and at the same time as the permanent status negotiations pertaining to the territories referred to in Article 3 of this Treaty; 3. through the implementation of agreed United Nations programmes and other agreed international economic programmes concerning refugees and displaced persons, including assistance to their settlement.

Article 9. Places of Historical and Religious Significance. 1. Each party will provide freedom of access to places of religious and historical significance. 2. In this regard, in accordance with the Washington Declaration, Israel respects the present special role of the Hashemite Kingdom of Jordan in Muslim Holy shrines in Jerusalem. When negotiations on the permanent status will take place, Israel will give high priority to the Jordanian historic role in these shrines. 3. The Parties will act together to promote interfaith relations among the three monotheistic religions, with the aim of working towards religious understanding, moral commitment, freedom of religious worship, and tolerance and peace.

Article 10. Cultural and Scientific Exchanges. The Parties, wishing to remove biases developed through periods of conflict, recognise the desirability of cultural and scientific exchanges in all fields, and agree to establish normal cultural relations between them. Thus, they shall, as soon as possible and not later than 9 months from the exchange of the instruments of ratification of this Treaty, conclude the negotiations on cultural and scientific agreements.

Article 11. Mutual Understanding and Good Neighbourly Relations. 1. The Parties will seek to foster mutual understanding and tolerance based on shared historic values, and accordingly undertake: a. to abstain from hostile or discriminatory propaganda against each other, and to take all possible legal and administrative measures to prevent the dissemination of such propaganda by any organisation or individual present in the territory of either Party; b. as soon as possible, and not later than 3 months from the exchange of the instruments of ratification of this Treaty, to repeal all adverse or discriminatory references and expressions of hostility in their respective legislation; c. to refrain in all government publications from any such references or expressions; d. to ensure mutual enjoyment by each other's citizens of due process of law within their respective legal systems and before their courts. 2. Paragraph 1 (a) of this Article is without prejudice to the right to freedom of expression as contained in the International Covenant on Civil and Political Rights. 3. A joint committee shall be formed to examine incidents where one Party claims there has been a violation of this Article.

Article 12. Combating Crime and Drugs. The Parties will co-operate in combating crime, with an emphasis on smuggling, and will take all necessary measures to combat and prevent such activities as the production of, as well as the trafficking in illicit drugs, and will bring to trial perpetrators of such acts. In this regard, they take note of the understandings reached between them in the above spheres, in accordance with Annex III and undertake to conclude all relevant agreements not later than 9 months from the date of the exchange of the instruments of ratification of this Treaty.

Article 13. Transportation and Roads. Taking note of the progress already made in the area of transportation, the Parties recognise the mutuality of interest in good neighbourly relations in the area of transportation and agree to the following means to promote relations between them in this sphere: 1. Each party will permit the free movement of nationals and vehicles of the other into and within its territory according to the general rules applicable to nationals and vehicles of other states. Neither party will impose discriminatory taxes or restrictions on the free movement of persons and vehicles from its territory to the territory of the other. 2. The Parties will open and maintain roads and border--crossings between their countries and will consider further road and rail links between them. 3. The Parties will continue their negotiations concerning mutual transportation agreements in the above and other areas, such as joint projects, traffic safety, transport standards and norms, licensing of vehicles, land passages, shipment of goods and cargo, and meteorology, to be concluded not later than 6 months from the exchange of the instruments of ratification of this Treaty. 4. The Parties agree to continue their negotiations for a highway to be constructed and maintained between Egypt, Israel and Jordan near Eilat.

Article 14. Freedom of Navigation and Access to Ports. 1. Without prejudice to the provisions of paragraph 3, each Party recognises the right of the vessels of the other Party to innocent passage through its territorial waters in accordance with the rules of international law. 2. Each Party will grant normal access to its ports for vessels and cargoes of the other, as well as vessels and cargoes destined for or coming from the other Party. Such access will be granted on the same conditions as generally applicable to vessels and cargoes of other nations. 3. The Parties consider the Strait of Tiran and the Gulf of Aqaba to be international waterways open to all nations for unimpeded and non-suspendable freedom of navigation and overflight. The Parties will respect each other's right to navigation and overflight for access to either Party through the Strait of Tiran and the Gulf of Aqaba.

Article 15. Civil Aviation. 1. The Parties recognise as applicable to each other the rights, privileges and obligations provided for by the multilateral aviation agreements to which they are both party, particularly by the 1944 Convention on International Civil Aviation (The Chicago Convention) and the 1944 International Air Services Transit Agreement. 2. Any declaration of national emergency by a Party under Article 89 of the Chicago Convention will not be applied to the other Party on a discriminatory basis. 3. The Parties take note of the negotiations on the international air corridor to be opened between them in accordance with the Washington Declaration. In addition, the Parties shall, upon ratification of this Treaty, enter into negotiations for the purpose of concluding a Civil Aviation Agreement. All the above negotiations are to be concluded not later than 6 months from the exchange of the instruments of ratification of this Treaty.

Article 16. Posts and Telecommunications. The Parties take note of the opening between them, in accordance with the Washington Declaration, of direct telephone and facsimile lines. Postal links, the negotiations on which having been concluded, will be activated upon the signature of this Treaty. The Parties further agree that normal wireless and cable communications and television relay services by cable, radio and satellite, will be established between them, in accordance with all relevant international conventions and regulations. The negotiations on these subjects will be concluded not later than 9 months from the exchange of the instruments of ratification of this Treaty.

Article 17. Tourism. The Parties affirm their mutual desire to promote co-operation between them in the field of tourism. In order to accomplish this goal, the Parties -- taking note of the understandings reached between them concerning tourism -- agree to negotiate, as soon as possible, and to conclude not later than three months from the exchange of the instruments of ratification of this Treaty, an agreement to facilitate and encourage mutual tourism and tourism from third countries.

Article 18. Environment. The Parties will co-operate in matters relating to the environment, a sphere to which they attach great importance, including conservation of nature and prevention of pollution, as set forth in Annex IV. They will negotiate an agreement on the above, to be concluded not later than 6 months from the exchange of the instruments of ratification of this Treaty.

Article 19. Energy. 1. The Parties will co-operate in the development of energy resources, including the development of energy-related projects such as the utilisation of solar energy. 2. The Parties, having concluded their negotiations on the interconnecting of their electric grids in the Eilat-Aqaba area, will implement the interconnecting upon the signature of this Treaty. The Parties view this step as a part of a wider binational and regional concept. They agree to continue their negotiations as soon as possible to widen the scope of their interconnected grids. 3. The Parties will conclude the relevant agreements in the field of energy within 6 months from the date of exchange of the instruments of ratification of this Treaty.

Article 20. Rift Valley Development. The Parties attach great importance to the integrated development of the Jordan Rift Valley area, including joint projects in the economic, environmental, energy-related and tourism fields. Taking note of the Terms of Reference developed in the framework of the Trilateral Israel-Jordan-US Economic Committee towards the Jordan Rift Valley Development Master Plan, they will vigorously continue their efforts towards the completion of planning and towards implementation.

Article 21. Health. The Parties will co-operate in the area of health and shall negotiate with a view to the conclusion of an agreement within 9 months of the exchange of instruments of ratification of this Treaty.

Article 22. Agriculture. The Parties will co-operate in the areas of agriculture, including veterinary services, plant protection, biotechnology and marketing, and shall negotiate with a view to the conclusion of an agreement within 6 months from the date of the exchange of instruments of ratification of this Treaty.

Article 23. Aqaba and Eilat. The Parties agree to enter into negotiations, as soon as possible, and not later than one month from the exchange of the instruments of ratification of this Treaty, on arrangements that would enable the joint development of the towns of Aqaba and Eilat with regard to such matters, inter alia, as joint tourism development, joint customs, free trade zone, co-operation in aviation, prevention of pollution, maritime matters, police, customs and health co-operation. The Parties will conclude all relevant agreements within 9 months from the exchange of instruments of ratification of the Treaty.

Article 24. Claims. The Parties agree to establish a claims commission for the mutual settlement of all financial claims.

Article 25. Rights and Obligations. 1. This Treaty does not affect and shall not be interpreted as affecting, in any way, the rights and obligations of the Parties under the Charter of the United Nations. 2. The Parties undertake to fulfil in good faith their obligations under this Treaty, without regard to action or inaction of any other party and independently of any instrument inconsistent with this Treaty. For the purposes of this paragraph each Party represents to the other that in its opinion and interpretation there is no inconsistency between their existing treaty obligations and this Treaty. 3. They further undertake to take all the necessary measures for the application in their relations of the provisions of the multilateral conventions to which they are parties, including the submission of appropriate notification to the Secretary General of the United Nations and other depositories of such conventions. 4. Both Parties will also take all the necessary steps to abolish all pejorative references to the other Party, in multilateral conventions to which they are parties, to the extent that such references exist. 5. The Parties undertake not to enter into any obligation in conflict with this Treaty. 6. Subject to Article 103 of the United Nations Charter, in the event of a conflict between the obligations of the Parties under the present Treaty and any of their other obligations, the obligations under this Treaty will be binding and implemented.

Article 26. Legislation. Within 3 months of the exchange of ratifications of this Treaty the Parties undertake to enact any legislation necessary in order to implement the Treaty, and to terminate any international commitments and to repeal any legislation that is inconsistent with the Treaty.

Article 27. Ratification. 1. This Treaty shall be ratified by both Parties in conformity with their respective national procedures. It shall enter into force on the exchange of instruments of ratification. 2. The Annexes, Appendices, and other attachments to this Treaty shall be considered integral parts thereof.

Article 28. Interim Measures. The Parties will apply, in certain spheres, to be agreed upon, interim measures pending the conclusion of the relevant agreements in accordance with this Treaty, as stipulated in Annex V.

Article 29. Settlement of Disputes. 1. Disputes arising out of the application or interpretation of this Treaty shall be resolved by negotiations. 2. Any such disputes which cannot be settled by negotiations shall be resolved by conciliation or submitted to arbitration.

Article 30. Registration. This Treaty shall be transmitted to the Secretary General of the United Nations for registration in accordance with the provisions of Article 102 of the Charter of the United Nations.

Done at the Arava/Araba Crossing Point this day Heshvan 21st, 5775, Jumada Al-Ula 21st, 1415 which corresponds to 26th October, 1994 in the Hebrew, English and Arabic languages, all texts being equally authentic. In case of divergence of interpretation the English text shall prevail.

The Treaty was signed for the State of Israel by Prime Minister Yitzhak Rabin and for the Hashemite Kingdom of Jordan by Prime Minister Abdul Salam

Majali and was witnessed by William J. Clinton, President of the United States of America.

List of Annexes, Appendices and Other Attachments.

Annex I: (a) International Boundary. (b) Naharayim/Baqura Area. (c) Zofar Area. Appendices (27 sheets): I. Emeq Ha'arava (10 sheets), 1:20,000 orthophoto maps; II. Dead Sea (2 sheets), 1:50,000 orthoimages; III. Jordan and Yarmouk Rivers (12 sheets), 1:10,000 orthophoto maps; IV. Naharayim Area (1 sheet), 1:10,000 orthophoto map; V. Zofar Area (1 sheet), 1:20,000 orthophoto map; VI. Gulf of Eilat (1 sheet), 1:50,000 orthoimage.

Annex II: Water.

Annex III: Crime and Drugs.

Annex IV: Environment.

Annex V: Interim Measures.

CASABLANCA DECLARATION (NOVEMBER 1, 1994)

As the peace process continued, hundreds of Arabs and Israelis, corporate executives and government officials, met in Casablanca, Morocco from October 30 to November 1, 1994 to explore the idea of creating new economic cooperation in the Middle East and North Africa. At the conclusion of the conference they issued the Casablanca Declaration which outlined a plan to link Arab-Israeli peace with regional economic growth.

1. At the invitation of His Majesty King Hassan II of Morocco and with the support and endorsement of Presidents Bill Clinton of the United States and Boris Yeltsin of the Russian Federation, the representatives of 61 countries and 1114 business leaders from all regions of the world, gathered for a Middle East/North Africa Economic Summit in Casablanca from October 30 to November 1, 1994. The participants paid tribute to His Majesty, King Hassan II, in his capacity as President and Host of the Conference and praised His role in promoting dialogue and understanding between the parties in the Middle East conflict. They also expressed their appreciation to the Government and people of Morocco for their hospitality and efforts to ensure the success of the Summit.

2. The Summit leaders feel united behind the vision that brought them to Casablanca, that of a comprehensive peace and a new partnership of business and government dedicated to furthering peace between Arabs and Israelis.

3. Government and business leaders entered into this new partnership with a deeper understanding of their mutual dependence and common goals. Business leaders recognized that governments should continue to forge peace Agreements and create foundations and incentives for trade and investment. They further

recognize the responsibility of the private sector to apply its new international influence to advance the diplomacy of peace in the Middle East and beyond. Governments affirmed the indispensability of the private sector in marshalling, quickly, adequate resources to demonstrate the tangible benefits of peace. Together, they pledged to show that business can do business and contribute to peace as well; indeed, to prove that profitability contributes mightily to the economic scaffolding for a durable peace.

4. The Summit commended the historic political transformation of the Region as a consequence of significant steps towards a just, lasting and comprehensive peace, based on U.N. Security Council Resolutions 242 and 338, a process that began with the 1979 Treaty of Peace between Egypt and Israel and enlarged dramatically by the Madrid Peace Conference, three years ago. That process has born fruit in Israel-Palestine Liberation Organization Declaration of Principles. The recent signing of the Treaty of Peace between Israel and Jordan gave a new dimension to the process. The decisions of Morocco and Tunisia to establish, respectively, liaison offices and liaison channels with Israel constituted another new positive development. These accomplishments and the next stages of rapid movement toward a comprehensive peace in the region, including Syria and Lebanon, need to be powerfully reinforced by solid economic growth and palpable improvement of the life and security of the peoples of this region. The Summit stressed that Syria and Lebanon have an important role to play in the development of the region. The Summit expressed a strong hope that they will soon be able to join the regional economic effort.

5. In this connection, the participants noted that the urgent need for economic development of the West Bank and Gaza Strip requires special attention from the international community, both public and private, in order to support the Israel-Palestine Liberation Organization Declaration of Principles and subsequent implementing agreements to enable the Palestinian people to participate on equal bases in the regional development and cooperation. They stressed the equal importance of moving ahead on Jordanian-Israeli projects as well as on cooperative projects between Israel and Jordan in order to advance the Jordanian-Israeli Treaty of Peace.

6. The participants recognized the economic potential of the Middle East and North Africa and explored how best to accelerate the development of the Region and overcome, as soon as possible, obstacles, including boycotts and all barriers to trade and investment. All agreed that there is a need to promote increased investment from inside and outside the Region. They noted that such investment requires free movement of goods, capital and labor across borders in accordance with market forces, technical cooperation based on mutual interest, openness to the international economy and appropriate institutions to promote economic interaction. They also noted that the free flow of ideas and increased dialogue, especially among the business communities in the Region, will strengthen economic activity. In this context, the participants noted favorably the decision

of the Council for Cooperation of the Gulf States regarding the lifting of the secondary and the tertiary aspects of the boycott of Israel.

7. Based on the agreements between Israel and the PLO, it is important that the borders of the Palestinian Territories be kept open for labor, tourism and trade to allow the Palestinian Authority, in partnership with is neighbors, the opportunity to build a viable economy in peace.

8. The participants paid tribute to the multilateral negotiations initiated in Moscow in 1992 which have significantly advanced the objectives of the peace process. The governments represented at Casablanca will examine ways to enhance the role and activities of the multilateral negotiations, including examining regional institutions which address economic, humanitarian and security issues. The participants noted that the progresses made in the peace process should go along with a serious consideration of the socio-economic disparities in the Region and require to address the idea of security in the Region in all its dimensions: social, economic and political. In this context, they agreed that these issues need to be addressed within the framework of a global approach encompassing socio-economic dimensions, safety and welfare of Individuals and Nations of the Region.

9. The participants recognized that there must be an ongoing process to translate the deliberations of Casablanca into concrete steps to advance the twin goals of peace and economic development and to institutionalize the new partnership between governments and the business community. To this end:

a) The governments represented at Casablanca and private sector representatives stated their intention to take the following steps:

-- Build the foundations for a Middle East and North Africa Economic Community which involves, at a determined stage, the free flow of goods, capital and labor throughout the Region.

-- Taking into account the recommendations of the regional parties during the meeting of the sub-committee on finances of the REDWG monitoring committee, the Casablanca Summit calls for a group of experts to examine the different options for funding mechanisms including the creation of a Middle East and North Africa Development Bank. This group of experts will report on its progress and conclusions within six months in the light of the follow on Summit to the Casablanca Conference.

-- The funding mechanism would include appropriate bodies to promote dialogue on economic reform, regional cooperation, technical assistance and long-term development planning.

-- Establish a regional Tourist Board to facilitate tourism and promote the Middle East and North Africa as a unique and attractive tourist destination.

-- Encourage the establishment of a private sector Regional Chamber of Commerce and Business Council to facilitate intra-regional trade relations. Such organizations will be instrumental in solidifying ties between the private and public sectors of the various economies.

b) The participants also intend to create the following mechanisms to implement these understandings and embody the new public-private collaboration:

-- A Steering Committee, comprised of government representatives, including those represented in the Steering Committee of the multilateral group of the peace process, will be entrusted with the task of following up all issues arising out of the Summit and coordinating with existing multilateral structures such as the REDWG and other multilateral working groups. The Steering Committee will meet within one month following the Casablanca Summit to consider follow on mechanisms. The Committee will consult widely and regularly with the private sector.

-- An executive Secretariat to assist the Steering Committee, located in Morocco, will work for the enhancement of the new economic development pattern, thus, contributing to the consolidation of the global security in the Region. The Secretariat will assist in the organization of a Regional Chamber of Commerce and a Business Council. It will work to advance the public-private partnership by promoting projects, sharing data, promoting contacts and fostering private sector investment in the Region. The Secretariat will assist in the implementation of the various bodies referred to in the present Declaration. The Steering Committee will be responsible for the funding arrangements, with the support of the private sector.

10. The participants welcomed the establishment of a Middle East/North Africa Economic Strategy Group by the Council on Foreign Relations. This private sector group will recommend strategies for regional economic cooperation and ways to overcome obstacles to trade and private investment. It will operate in close association with the Secretariat and submit its recommendations to the Steering Committee.

11. The participants also welcomed the intention of the World Economic Forum to form a business interaction group that will foster increased contacts and exchanges among business communities and submit its recommendations to the Steering Committee.

12. The participants in the Casablanca Summit pledged to transform this event into lasting institutional and individual ties that will provide a better life for the peoples of the Middle East and North Africa. They resolved that the collaboration of the public and private sectors that constituted the singularity of the Casablanca Summit will serve as a milestone in the historic destiny that is now playing itself out in the Middle East/North Africa Region.

13. The participants expressed their appreciation to the Council on Foreign Relations and to the World Economic Forum for their substantive contribution to the organization of the Casablanca Summit.

14. The participants expressed their intention to meet again in Amman, Jordan, in the first half of 1995 for a second Middle East/North Africa Economic Summit, to be hosted by His Majesty King Hussein.

CAIRO SUMMIT STATEMENT (FEBRUARY 2, 1995)

The peace process was marked, over time, by numerous meetings of the parties often designed to endorse and facilitate the process. Meeting in Cairo in early 1995, Egypt, Jordan, Israel and the Palestinian Authority issued a summit statement in this vein.

1. The leaders of Egypt, Jordan, Israel and the Palestinian Authority, meeting in Cairo on February 2, 1995 reaffirmed their determination to continue the Middle East peace process towards the fulfillment of a just, lasting and comprehensive peace in the region.

2. The parties are committed to fully honor and implement, in letter and spirit, the historic accords reached between them. They reaffirmed their commitment to implement all the outstanding parts of those agreements and their intention to pursue their efforts towards a comprehensive peace in the Middle East. The parties also reaffirmed the necessity of moving promptly to conclude the negotiations on the Interim Agreement between Israel and the Palestinian Authority in all its aspects. The parties emphasized the urgency of taking the necessary measures to enhance the Palestinian-Israeli peace process and to improve the climate and build confidence between the parties.

3. The parties expressed their appreciation for the swift implementation of the peace treaty between Jordan and Israel. They expressed the hope that the near future would witness the achievement of peace accords between Israel and Syria and Lebanon.

4. The leaders reiterated their appreciation for Egypt's leading role for peace in the Middle East which is essential for the success of the peace process.

5. The peace process in the Middle East is an historic necessity serving the interest of all its peoples and individuals. Therefore it will prevail against all the forces that attempt to undermine it. The four parties condemned all the outbreaks of bloodshed, terror and violence in the region, and reaffirmed their intention to stand staunchly against and put an end to all such acts.

6. Within the framework of peace and reconciliation in the region, with enhanced security, economic prosperity and a higher standard of living for their peoples, the leaders reaffirmed their intention to:

-- Achieve equal security and mutual confidence at lower levels of armaments, appreciating President Mubarak's disarmament proposal on weapons of mass destruction. The parties shall pursue a mutually verifiable Middle East zone free of weapons of mass destruction, nuclear, chemical and biological, and their delivery systems.

-- Enhance economic cooperation and encourage joint projects, and attract the international private sector, particularly in preparation for the Amman summit (October 30, 1995). As part of this process, the parties are committed to support the establishment of a regional development bank.

-- Give special attention to strengthening the educational capabilities of the region, with special emphasis on science, technology and computerization. In this regard, the parties will seriously consider and explore with the European Union the convening of a special education conference devoted to this aim.

In pursuit of the implementation of this declaration, the representatives of the four parties, at Foreign Ministers level, will conduct consultations to facilitate their cooperation. The first meeting at this level will take place next week in Washington.

Following the Cairo Meeting Chairman Arafat and Prime Minister Rabin have agreed to meet next Thursday in Erez to continue negotiations on the bilateral issues.

President Mubarak, King Hussein, Prime Minister Rabin and Chairman Arafat, will meet again if necessary to pursue their joint efforts aimed at reinforcing the process of comprehensive peace in the Middle East.

BIBLIOGRAPHY

The Arab-Israeli conflict has been the subject of a voluminous literature. The purpose here is to call attention to a selected group of especially useful volumes, primarily reference works, that supplement the materials in this volume. Numerous works, many of high quality, that focus on specific and narrow aspects of the conflict are not listed here, although references to them will be found in the works cited below.

The interested reader is referred to Bernard Reich, Editor-in-Chief, *An Historical Encyclopedia of the Arab-Israeli Conflict* (Westport, Connecticut and London: Greenwood Press, 1995) which discusses the various events, elements personalities, documents, etc., of the conflict and provides bibliographies specific to each of the items. Martin Gilbert, *Atlas of the Arab-Israeli Conflict*, Sixth edition (New York: Oxford University Press, 1993) is an historical atlas tracing the evolution of the conflict in maps and text.

General histories that provide an introduction to the development of the conflict and the efforts to resolve it include: Ian J. Bickerton and Carla L. Klausner, *A Concise History of the Arab-Israeli Conflict*, Second Edition (Englewood Cliffs, NJ: Prentice Hall, 1995); Charles D. Smith, *Palestine and the Arab-Israeli Conflict*, 2nd ed. (New York: St. Martin's Press, 1992); and Mark Tessler, *A History of the Israeli-Palestinian Conflict* (Bloomington and Indianapolis: Indiana University Press, 1994). J.C. Hurewitz, *The Struggle for Palestine* (New York: W.W. Norton, 1950) provides an overview of the mandate period.

Several bibliographical collections will facilitate identification of much of the relevant literature. Ronald M. De Vore, Editor, *The Arab-Israeli Conflict: A Historical, Political, Social and Military Bibliography* (Santa Barbara, California and Oxford, England: CLIO Books, 1976); Walid Khalidi and Jill Khadduri, Editors, *Palestine and the Arab-Israeli Conflict: An Annotated Bibliography*

(Beirut: Institute for Palestine Studies; Kuwait: University of Kuwait, 1974).

The Arab-Israeli conflict has generated thousands of documents, both official and unofficial. Some of the more useful, albeit outdated, collections include: Charles L. Geddes, Editor, *A Documentary History of the Arab-Israeli Conflict* (New York, Westport, Connecticut, and London: Praeger, 1991); Walter Laqueur and Barry Rubin, Editors, *The Israel-Arab Reader: A Documentary History of the Middle East Conflict*, Revised and updated edition (New York: Penguin Books, 1984); Yehuda Lukacs, Editor, *The Israeli-Palestinian Conflict: A Documentary Record, 1967-1990* (Cambridge, New York, Port Chester, Melbourne, Sydney: Cambridge University Press, 1992); and John Norton Moore, Editor, *The Arab-Israeli Conflict, Volume III: Documents* (Princeton, N.J.: Princeton University Press, 1974). Sponsored by the American Society of International Law.

The United States government has published several documentary collections that often have the added benefit of useful chronologies and commentaries. *The Quest For Peace* (Washington, D.C.: Department of State, 1984) [Department of State Publication 9373] incorporates the principal United States public statements and related documents on the Arab-Israeli peace process between 1967 and 1983. Among the Congressional publications are: United States Senate, Committee on Foreign Relations, *A Select Chronology and Background Documents Relating to the Middle East* (Washington, D.C.: U.S. Government Printing Office, 1967); United States Senate, Committee on Foreign Relations, *A Select Chronology and Background Documents Relating to the Middle East*, First Revised Edition (Washington, D.C.: U.S. Government Printing Office, 1969); United States Senate, Committee on Foreign Relations, *A Select Chronology and Background Documents Relating to the Middle East*, Second Revised Edition (Washington, D.C.: U.S. Government Printing Office, 1975); United States House of Representatives, Committee on Foreign Affairs, *The Search for Peace in the Middle East: Documents and Statements, 1967-79* (Washington, D.C.: U.S. Government Printing Office, 1979); United States House of Representatives, Committee on Foreign Affairs, *Documents and Statements on Middle East Peace, 1979-82* (Washington, D.C.: U.S. Government Printing Office, 1982); United States House of Representatives, Committee on Foreign Affairs, *Documents on Middle East Peace, 1982-88* (Washington, D.C.: U.S. Government Printing Office, 1989).

The Journal of Palestine Studies (a quarterly on Palestinian Affairs and the Arab-Israeli Conflict), published by The University of California Press for the Institute for Palestine Studies and Kuwait University, is an invaluable source for the study of the conflict despite its strong bias toward the Palestinian position.

INDEX

This index does not include individuals, places, events, and other items that are peripheral to the central themes of the conflict and are mentioned only minimally in the book. Also, terms such as Israel, Palestine, Arab, Jordan, Egypt, Syria, Lebanon, PLO, etc. (and variations of them) appear with such frequency that they would have to be listed on virtually every page and are similarly excluded from this index. Bold numbers indicate the text of the document.

About the Editor

BERNARD REICH, Professor of Political Science and International Affairs, George Washington University, has served as a consultant to various U.S. government agencies and an adjunct faculty member of several defense and armed forces schools and institutes and of the Department of State's Foreign Service Institute. He has visited various Middle Eastern countries at governmental invitation and has lived there on Fulbright and National Science Foundational fellowships. He is a member of the Board of Advisory Editors of the *Middle East Journal* and has published widely on the Middle East. His recent books for Greenwood Press include *An Historical Encyclopedia of the Arab-Israeli Conflict* (forthcoming January 1996); *Securing the Covenant: United States–Israel Relations after the Cold War* (1995); *Israeli Politics in the 1990s: Key Domestic and Foreign Policy Factors* (1991); and *Political Leaders of the Contemporary Middle East and North Africa: A Biographical Dictionary* (1990), among others.